OCEAN

NORTHWEST AMERINDS

ALASKA

CHUKCHI

ARCTIC OCEAN

1

2

5

3

4

21

C A N A D A

HUDSON
BAY

33
34
36
35

37
38

GREENLAND

TIC OCEAN

NO STONE UNTURNED

Also by Louis A. Brennan

THESE ITEMS OF DESIRE

MASQUE OF VIRTUE

MORE THAN FLESH

DEATH AT FLOOD TIDE

Louis A. Brennan

NO STONE
UNTURNED

AN ALMANAC
OF NORTH AMERICAN PREHISTORY

Drawings by Ingrid Fetz

 RANDOM HOUSE · *New York*

For My Mother and Father

ACKNOWLEDGMENTS

Since this book is almost wholly dependent on points of view, reports, insights and authoritative opinions of others, it is with a particularly keen sense of indebtedness and gratitude that I acknowledge permission to quote, as follows:

From *American Antiquity*, published by the Society for American Archaeology, University of Utah Press, Salt Lake City; Raymond H. Thompson, editor; and from *Memoirs of the Society for American Archaeology*, these authors and source materials:

Theodore P. Bank II, "Cultural Succession in the Aleutians." Vol. 19, No. 1, 1953.

Gordon Ekholm, "A Possible Focus of Asiatic Influence in the Late Classic Cultures of Meso-America," Memoir No. 9, *Asia and North America: Transpacific Contacts*, 1953.

Agnes McClain Howard, "Ancestor of Pottery?" Vol. XX, No. 2, 1954.

Wesley I. Hurt, Jr., "A Comparative Study of the Preceramic Occupations of North America." Vol. XVIII, No. 3, 1953.

Jesse D. Jennings, *Danger Cave*, Memoir No. 14, 1957; and *Seminars in Archaeology: 1955*, Memoir No. 11, 1957.

Y. V. Knorozov, translated by Sophie D. Coe, "The Problem of the Study of Maya Hieroglyphic Writing." Vol. XXIII, No. 3, 1958.

Alex D. Krieger, "Early Man," in "Notes and News." Vol. XIX, No. 4, 1954.

Paul C. Mangelsdorf, "New Evidence on the Origin and Ancestry of Maize." Vol. XIX, No. 4, 1954.

George I. Quimby, "Cultural and Natural Areas Before Kroeber." Vol. XIX, No. 4, 1954.

Froelich Rainey, "The Significance of Recent Archaeological Discoveries in Inland Alaska," Memoir No. 9, *Asia and North America: Transpacific Contacts*, 1953.

T. D. Stewart, review of *The Problem of the Early Peopling of the Americas as Viewed from Asia*, by Joseph B. Birdsell. Vol. XVIII, No. 1, 1952.

Paul Tolstoy, "Some Amerasian Pottery Traits in North Asian

Prehistory," Vol. XIX, No. 1; "The Archaeology of the Lena Basin and Its New World Relationships, Part II," Vol. XXIV, No. 1, 1958.

From *The Testimony of the Spade,* Geoffrey Bibby. Alfred A. Knopf, Inc., New York, 1957.

From *Physical Anthropology of the American Indian,* William S. Laughlin, ed., "The Dentition of the American Indian," Albert A. Dahlberg. The Viking Fund, Inc., New York, 1951.

From *Hopewellian Communities in Illinois,* Thorne Deuel, ed.; *The Hopewellian Community,* Thorne Deuel. Illinois State Museum, Springfield, 1952.

From *Scientific American,* June, 1954, "Early Man in the Arctic," J. L. Giddings, Jr.

From *Archaeology of Eastern United States,* James B. Griffin, ed., "Culture Periods in Eastern United States Archaeology," James B. Griffin. The University of Chicago Press, Chicago. Copyright, 1952, by the University of Chicago.

From *Early Man in the New World,* Kenneth MacGowan. Macmillan Company, New York, 1950.

From *The Ancient Civilizations of Peru,* J. Alden Mason. Pelican Books, Penguin Books, Inc., Baltimore, 1957.

From *Man: His First Million Years* (including translation of Papago song), Ashley Montagu. World Publishing Company, New York, 1957.

From *Prehistoric Settlement Patterns in the New World,* Gordon R. Willey, ed., "Prehistoric Settlement Patterns in Northeastern North America," William A. Ritchie. Viking Fund Publications in Anthropology, No. 23, New York, 1956.

From *Man and the Vertebrates,* Vol. II, A. S. Romer. Pelican Books, Penguin Books, Inc., Baltimore, 1954.

From *Anthropology Today,* A. L. Kroeber, chairman of preparation, "Archaeological Theories and Interpretations: New World," Gordon R. Willey. University of Chicago Press, Chicago. Copyright, 1953, by the University of Chicago.

My acknowledgment of indebtedness to the foregoing and to others mentioned less lengthily or quoted indirectly in the text is not to be construed as endorsement by them of the view of American prehistory developed herein. I have freely used the ideas and observations and investigations of others for reworking into ideas for which I alone take responsibility.

LOUIS A. BRENNAN

CONTENTS

ILLUSTRATIONS

Drawings

NO STONE UNTURNED

1

 *Thirty Thousand Years, Plus*

Between October 12, 1492, when Christopher Columbus, navigator, set Spanish boot on an island that may or may not have been San Salvador but certainly was an outpost of the Western Hemisphere, and Saturday, October 12, 1957, when the United States Military Academy at West Point played the University of Notre Dame in Philadelphia—sixty minutes of football that almost had a bearing on what is called the mythical National Championship—465 years had elapsed. This less than five centuries, this not quite half a millennium, is the full span of American history.

Perhaps a boatload of Scottish knights on their way to the Crusades were blown by overmastering winds to these coasts in the twelfth century, if certain gravings on a rock in Massachusetts mean what they seem to mean; maybe Nova Scotia was Leif Ericson's Vinland of 1000 A.D.; could be that Irish monks in search of infidels made a landfall here in the eighth century; certainly they had the beautiful faith and the Gaelic perversity to sail westward when their contemporaries sailed only north, south and east, if at all. But even if these incidents are propped up to look like milestones in the record, this is a chronology of only twelve centuries. What happened, then, along the Ohio River and along the Missouri, in Oregon and in Florida, among the Smokies and among the Rockies *during the 30,000 years before that?* Those 300 centuries are, at a minimum, the span of prehistory of America, the New World.

Prehistory being, by definition, that period of man's existence prior to the intentional recording for posterity of the succession of human events according to a calendar or time system, American prehistory might very well have to begin and end with the statement that it had to have happened.

On the one hand it was an extensively populated hemisphere that Columbus mistook for India, from glaciated Greenland, near whose utmost cape lies the North Magnetic Pole, to dismal Tierra del Fuego, some 10,000 miles south, where the continent of South America reaches within 500 miles of Palmer Peninsula, on the antipodal continent of Antarctica. But on the other hand none of these aborigines had anything to offer, beyond the most ambiguous oral traditions, about how they had got to America, how long they had been here, or what they had been doing since their arrival. So, no records, no data; no data, no incidents; no incidents, no story.

But we are not quite so badly off. There is in plain and public sight the entire text of American prehistory, and we have, over the past decade in particular, made an encouraging beginning at its decipherment. This unwritten and haphazard, yet prodigally informative, thesaurus is no less than the ground we walk on, and there is scarcely a field, or even a back yard, on this continent which cannot add a paragraph to it, or at the very least an adverbial phrase.

I make this statement as a witness to its literal truth, having found artifacts of some antiquity not only in the back yards of two different homes of mine in Ossining, New York, but in the front yard of one of them. Nor were the front-yard artifacts in any way concomitants of the back-yard ones, for they had arrived, an arrowhead and a potsherd, in a load of dirt brought in by the Street Department from two miles away to back-fill a new curb. And it is not that I, an avocational archaeologist, was either fortunate or deliberate in my choice of home sites. With relatives scattered from Princeton, New Jersey, to Portsmouth, Ohio, I have had in no instance to walk farther than the field or lot next door to their residences to come upon the telltale flint chips, the fire-cracked pebbles, the shell, the potsherds, or the whole implements of the stone-age occupation of those parts. For more than a decade I have been following plows and bulldozers, scrutinizing erosion gullies and stream banks, test pitting in likely and unlikely places; and the turning up everywhere of one bit of evidence or another of American prehistory has been mainly a matter of persistence in the search. The amount of archaeological material still latent in our ripped and riven topsoil astonishes me more each spring, even as I am appalled at the amount of it that must have been already looted away in the past century of construction and cultivation, and at the page after page of this tome of prehistory which has been forever defaced.

How much more of this stone and earthen almanac of the past will be expunged by new housing developments and new factory construction, by fill diggers and gravel-pit operators, in the coming year alone can induce scholar's trauma if brooded on too long. In the eastern third of the United States it may be that the context of a whole archaeological era, that of the paleo-Indian hunter of mammoths and other big game, has disappeared; evidences of the existence of these people have turned up in desultory and tantalizing handfuls, but the habitation sites where their activities would be summarized in the debris they left behind are still buried as deeply and privily as Captain Kidd's treasure, or are no longer extant.

In the eastern United States almost any consideration of public policy or individual convenience takes precedence over archaeology and prehistory, but in the west things are beginning to be done differently. There it is rapidly becoming the enlightened custom to write into contracts for major construction projects, such as power and pipe lines and new highways, financial provisions for archaeological surveys, excavations when indicated, and even publication of the results. During the driving of one such archaeology-careful pipe line across southern Arizona, in 275 miles of right-of-way inspection and open-trench checking, 46 sites of prehistoric significance were exposed, almost 1 for every 6 linear miles. This will amount to considerable prehistory—and museum display material—when it has all been dug up and studied. But the most important yield of this engagingly prudent procedure was the skull of a 10,000- to 20,000-year-old paleo-Indian hunter, the oldest human cranium found under validated archaeologic and geologic conditions on the continent.

Yet there are certainly many reasons, other than the zeal of its archaeologists and the substantial co-operation they are beginning to evoke, for the relative frequency of discoveries of important prehistoric outcrops in the west, because it is be-

coming apparent that most of the authenticated data on really
early Americans comes from there. Richard D. Daugherty, in
his 1956 monograph *Early Man in the Columbia Intermontane
Province*, lists a hundred and ninety-three sites or occurrences
of materials over 6000 years old between Texas and Alaska.
And some of the earliest material, the evidence which gives
sanction to the statement that men have made their living on
this hemisphere for 30,000 years, comes from the very far west,
from the island of Santa Rosa, 30 miles off Santa Barbara, California.

Since 1947 this moderate-sized island, one of a group of
three, has been under investigation by the Santa Barbara
Museum of Natural History because of the incidence there of
fossil bones of a unique and somewhat anomalously named
beast, the dwarf mammoth. Whereas a full-sized specimen of
the mammoth, which inhabited the mainland and gave its
present meaning to the name, stood from 10 to 14 feet high at
the shoulder, depending on the species (Jumbo, J. P. Barnum's
outsized exhibition elephant, stood 10 feet), the dwarf mammoth ranged between 4 and 6 feet. His analogue among
modern animals is the pygmy elephant, and his size was probably a reductive adaptation to the cramped habitat and restricted pasturage after Santa Rosa was disconnected from the
continent. This kind of thing seems to have happened over
and over in biology, even in the instance of man, as a saving
adjustment to a shrinking in environment; a species is either
reduced in size to perdure in the newly circumscribed range,
or is reduced in numbers to the point of extinction.

The geologic event that separated Santa Rosa Island and its
neighbors from the mainland—they are now some 30 miles
out at sea—must have taken place well over 1,000,000 years
ago, according to present geologic doctrine. The maximum
depth of water between the islands and Santa Barbara is over
700 feet today, and even during the periods of heaviest glaciation during the Pleistocene, or ice age, when so much water
was locked up in continental ice sheets that the ocean was
400 feet lower (by the generally accepted estimate) than it is
now, the Santa Rosa group (which was probably then one
island) was isolated by 2 miles of water, in some places 300
feet deep.

Having successfully adjusted to his reduced circumstances (and he was able to do this because there were no predatory animals marooned with him), the dwarf mammoth did very well for himself for eon after eon—and the only thing that affected his comfort was man.

Why man came to Santa Rosa is a question not likely to be answered offhand, for he does not seem to have been a specifically hunting type looking for mammoths. Nowhere in or about the fire pits on Santa Rosa where he cooked his feasts, or in or about the strewn bones and cracked skulls of the dwarf mammoth that provided the barbecue, has any weapon turned up. As of the latest reported excavations, the only "artifacts" left behind by Santa Rosa man were simple flint chips and abalone shell, useful for cutting up the meat, but of no special help in hunting it. It is true that spears of sharpened wood, long since decayed, may have been used, but it is also true that hunting the dwarf mammoth may not have required a weapon at all. This was very likely not a formidable beast, and, having lived an undisturbed life for so long, he may have lost all instinct for attack and defense. Santa Rosa man may have, quite actually, scared him to death over cliffs or run him to death by exhaustion, the way wolves once nagged the buffalo on the prairie, until they dropped.

Now it has been a habit of man, the singular habit by which we have been able to chart his career a half-million years into the past, to shape weapons and tools of imperishable stone, and whether he made them or chose them from among the natural pebbles of beach and bank, he seems to have used them almost from the moment he was thinking man. For, and make no mistake about it, stone is simply premetallurgical metal, and without its prior use there would never have been a metallurgy. From the first cerebral itch of a tool idea, the pebble chopper which is illustrated on page 49—whose haft or handle was simply the human arm and which was adaptable to a hundred jobs, including root digging, marrowbone splitting and mating combat—to trimly fashioned knives and points for tipping javelins, spears, darts or arrows, made well into the Bronze Age, man's development has been not only traceable by but perhaps was partly attributable to the efficiency and durability with which stone has served him. Even when he favored wood or bone for tool stuff, man had, perforce, to size and shape this stock with the cutting edge of flint.

From the beginning man seems to have made two types of tools, and even before he designedly shaped stone to them, he seems to have selected natural stones for the same purposes: the pointed tool for penetration, and the long-edged tool for scraping and cutting. Taken together—and they were not always mutually exclusive—these two types have been the associates of man to a degree that makes them personal fossils, as intimately his as his own bones, as in fact they were his fang and claw, in his competition with the fauna of his daily experience.

Yet Santa Rosa man, as far as the evidence goes, made neither of these characteristically human artifacts. The few, though convincing, evidences of his occupation of the island are his fire pits, the disarticulation of the skeletons of the dwarf mammoths in such a way as to show that the carcasses were butchered, and the unshaped chips he used like table knives to cut away his mouthfuls. What kind of man was this? For over 200,000 years before this invasion of Santa Rosa, men had elsewhere been chipping flint and quartzite into both utilitarian and adroitly crafted implements. Were these Santa Rosans only backward members of our own species, Homo sapiens sapiens (by Carleton Coon's sensible new classification of men), or were they of another, cousinly but nonprogressive, species, like the half-man Australopithecines or Southern Apes of South Africa? The lack of formalized stone tools on Santa Rosa might be understandable if the period of its occupation had been very brief or if it had not been so isolated that seasonal visiting was unlikely; but by the Carbon-14 method of dating the charcoal in the fire pits (a method that Willard Libby developed out of researches into nuclear fission during the war), man was cozily cohabiting Santa Rosa with the dwarf mammoth for 13,000 years.

For 650 generations, then, at 20 years to the generation (though this primitive human being probably produced a new generation in from 12 to 15 years), men lived here in this paradise free of an economic necessity that would have compelled them to make serviceable tools, and without their imaginations' being creatively nagged to do so. If ever there was an original site of the Garden of Eden, this island of Santa Rosa was it. An unfailing larder of dietetically sufficient meat rich in proteins, vitamins, calories and the trace minerals was as available as the packages in a super market, and bland fruits, nuts and berries must have fallen from their branches and opened to the touch of the famished, for that other artifact of specialized food-gathering man, the grinding stone or mano, with which he macerates the harsher foods to a digestible consistency, is also absent. The failure to find even scraper-like tools can lead to only one conclusion—that hides did not need to be dressed to provide shelter tents and were not dressed for clothing. Under these conditions Santa Rosa alone, and certainly when the ocean had subsided enough to enlarge it by joining it with its neighboring islands for a relatively short epoch, should have been able to support a self-generating population. When, in the trammels of time, have so many had it so good for so long?

But what initiative had taken this unaspiring kind of man in the first place across the deep channel between the coast and Santa Rosa, never any less than two miles wide and usually much more, as must have been the case if the geology of this coast was as orthodox geologists now view it?

It is not likely that the first immigrant was tempted to Santa Rosa by the sight of the dwarf mammoths, assuming that they had preceded him across; even when the strait was only two miles wide, it would have taken a good long-glass to make out the nature of the beast, and whether he was kill or killer. Nor could this first immigrant have known beforehand about the easy living the dwarf mammoth herds had to offer, for there were no dwarf mammoths on the mainland. Nor would the sheer love of hunting have been the motivation, for this first immigrant was not a specialized hunter, as we know from his lack of game-taking equipment. He was not a specialized food gatherer either, being without the specialized equipment of the grinding stone; hence he would not have braved drowning in search of a particular vegetable staple growing scarce in his immediate vicinity.

All things considered, since we find him dwelling along the shore, this first immigrant must have been a tidewater gatherer, a beachcomber, a strandlooper who lived on the easy getting of shellfish, on what the surf washed up, and on what

was trapped in tidal pools. But, granting such a trade and
appetite, had the waters of the mainland shore become suddenly unproductive, he would simply have moved up or down
the coast; there would have been no cause for him to believe
that the same infertile water wrought richer on the opposite
beach, across the strait.

We can be sure that this first immigrant did not jaunt to
Santa Rosa for the sheer love of exploring. There was a whole
continent to the east of him that could have been explored dry-
shod. Nor was he a sea adventurer, since he hadn't the notion
of a tool with which to make a canoe, nor even a hand ax with
which to hack down a tree to make a raft.

In short, it does not seem likely that the kind of man Santa
Rosa man has shown himself to be would take off for Santa
Rosa of his own volition. Did he, then, beset by enemies, have
to make his escape aquatically? Here again it seems that he
might have been more inclined to keep to the land, where
flight could be swifter and there were more places to hide.

One conclusion, though it is not inescapable, has a certain
fascination: that the first migrant to Santa Rosa went there because he was forced to go—by his own people. In short, he was
driven there in exile, as to a sort of Devil's Island, or was con-
signed to death by drowning at sea but managed to struggle to
a landfall on Santa Rosa still breathing. One thing we can be
sure of—that whenever there has been any sort of human society there have been laws and offenders against the laws, and
for some reason or other there have always been crimes
deemed capitally punishable. The only reason, it seems to me,
that phlegmatic Santa Rosa man would have crossed the
water to his island in the first place was that it was an alternative to death.

What heinous transgression could this malefactor have committed? In so primitive a tribe it could well have been nothing
more than a forward adolescent's tampering with one of the
females of the chief's harem, rather like the situation in the
stage and movie versions of *The King and I*. For in so primitive
a tribe the chief was likely to claim that all nubile girls belonged to him. If this were so then the girl betrayed must
have been condemned with her seducer and set adrift with
him; for a tribe, or mayhap even a race, was founded on Santa

Rosa, and a viable one at that, propagating itself into 650 generations. Perhaps its genetic viability was, from time to time, quickened by the arrival of new miscreants from the mainland. And then again it may have stunted itself with inbreeding, and if the scientists of the Santa Barbara Museum are lucky enough to happen on the skeleton of a later Santa Rosa man, it would not be surprising if, like the mammoths, he were a pygmy.

But what must not be overlooked is that there is one final way to explain the presence of dwarf-mammoth gnawers on Santa Rosa, though it is quite radical in its simplicity. If these human migrants had no water craft to transport them to Santa Rosa, and the geology posits that the strait was too wide for voluntary swimming, it takes no more than the courage of reasonableness to contradict the posited geology and to argue that they, along with the mammoths, must have walked. The geologic premise in this problem is that the Santa Rosa archipelago was separated from the mainland 1,000,000 years ago. Thus if we see man as walking there overland and not on water, we have a choice of assuming that man was an inhabitant of California 1,000,000 years ago, or that it has been considerably less than 1,000,000 years since Santa Rosa was not an island but a peninsula.

Of these two assumptions the first is scientifically insupportable; the only fire-using human being of this order of antiquity that I ever heard of was Victor Mature in a movie called *1,000,-000 B.C.*, wherein dinosaurs, which had been extinct since 70,-000,000 B.C., played featured roles. The second assumption is merely, at present, universally and unanimously unpalatable. But if there is one geologic region about which our ignorance is nearly total, it is that three-quarters of the planet's surface beneath oceanic depths, and what data we have now about the California littoral or tidewater zone stops at the water's edge.

Or at least it did, until the period during which this book was written, which was the International Geophysical Year, dedicated to a massive attack by every branch of physical science on all that is unknown about our terrestrial environment. Among the projects of IGY was an examination of the Pacific Ocean floor by the Scripps Institution of Oceanography, of La Jolla, California, and by reason of information made public in

preliminary reports on this work, it is by no means fatuous now
to think that man was marooned on Santa Rosa at about the
same time as the mammoth genetically inclined toward dimin-
utiveness, by a not too remote subsidence of the Pacific coast
of the Americas so vast as to have been previously invisible to
science. Since the effects of this subsidence bear more directly
and importantly on a later period of American prehistory, that
of the Mayas and Aztecs, their full description can wait until
that period is arrived at in the course of our narration; but the
mere fact of it has a significance that has to be noted in a beginning chapter on American prehistory.

Thor Heyerdahl, who led the Kon-Tiki expedition, which
floated by raft on the principal propulsion of a weak oceanic
current from Peru to the South Sea Polynesian islands, may
be as wrong as most anthropologists think him in believing that
his voyage proved that the Polynesian islands were settled by a
South American people. But he put his finger on one weakness
of American archaeology, its overconfident reliance on a hemispheric geography as now mapped by Rand McNally, and on
weather, oceanic current and other geophysical conditions as
known for the scant two centuries these have been sketchily
recorded. Archaeologists are nowadays trained to incorporate
into their hypotheses the effects of the fluctuations of glaciers
on man's ancient environments, but they have slighted the mu-
tations that must have been wrought in and by the world ocean
as though it were unprofessional to get their feet wet. The Pacific Ocean in modern outline is an insuperable barrier to the
kind of over-water transportation known to primitive man, but
we are predicating not fact but an insufficiency of it if we insist
on an ancient Pacific as impassable as it is now, or if we cannot
tolerate the possibility that Santa Rosa was a California coastal
headland 30,000 to 40,000 years ago.

The world in which we live is nowhere stable and in no wise
fixed; the forces that have shaped it are not quiescent; the na-
ïvely egocentric notion that these forces, having shaped the
earth for the habitation of man, lapsed into a state of rest, their
work accomplished, is one with the primitive notion that the
sun was put into the sky to give mankind heat and comfort.
The only certainty we can know about yesterday's world is that
it differed, somewhere, significantly from today's. We know a

great deal about many regions of yesterday's world; we have presumed a state of ignorance to be a state of knowledge in vast areas, like the Pacific, and have said that we know this or that much without the fair and honest acknowledgment that so much is next to nothing. Among the facts that have long been known is the existence of the west-flowing South Equatorial Current, the current which bore the Heyerdahl expedition from Peru to Polynesia. What was not known, until the project vessels of the Scripps Institution and the United States Fish and Wildlife Service returned and reported in June, 1958, was that this was a weak countercurrent, a sort of backwash, of a much mightier and faster current that flows eastward beneath it, 250 miles wide, with the force of a thousand Mississippis. It extends from a depth of one hundred to eight hundred feet below the sea surface and is at least 3500 miles long. What this current must have meant to the Pacific when the world ocean was 400, or 200, or 100 feet lower than it is now, and all Pacific islands were consequently enlarged, we cannot yet say, but surely we must be excited enough to dream hypotheses.

This is the very sparkle of the exhilaration of prehistory, that its most complacent theories can be embarrassed at any minute by an impudent fact, and that within the last decade (Carbon-14 dating is only 10 years old) science has itself contrived several ingenious ways of engendering impudent fact where only smugness flourished before. On the face of it, the presence of man on Santa Rosa Island with an obviously long-isolated breed of mammoth seems only a slightly awkward situation which might be explained in any number of incidental and unpedestrian ways. But it may very easily prove to be, and we can look forward with relish to its being, the first hint of the way puzzling, not to say mysterious, elements in Mayan and pre-Aztecan cultures are to be elucidated.

Because he is very nearly the earliest of the earliest Americans, Santa Rosa man is but the first case in the casebook that is American prehistory, nor is it loose analogy to call these situations "cases" in the popular or Ellery Queen sense of the word. Each site of prehistoric man's abiding presents itself exactly as though it were the scene of a crime—physical clues are scattered about in circumstantial confusion and from them must be deduced what happened here, and when, and who was involved. But archaeology is detective work without being criminology. Its patient Holmeses investigate, with microscope and reasoned surmise, the deaths of tribes and races whom time has slain and tried to conceal forever in geologic graves. The killer cannot, of course, ever be collared and jailed, but justice can nevertheless be done the victims. Their humanity is recovered from the dust and honored again, as it should be, by the interest we pay it, for it is our humanity too. These mortals of prehistory are all too plainly but our younger, simpler selves, and it is an overweening man who can study their artifices and stratagems for survival in a world never made for their comfort and content and honestly claim he could have performed any better—or as well, given the odds. It is not to belittle that the unenterprise of Santa Rosa man has been noted; there are not too many beings of this or any age who are unwilling to live out their lives as effortlessly as they can within the world as they find it. And Santa Rosa man may have had the virtues of his failings; he may have been kind to his children and without malice for his neighbors, monogamous in social outlook and democratic-conservative in politics, a bird watcher by avocation and such a lover of nature in conviction that he had no ambition to subjugate it to his will lest he destroy it for his pleasure.

But whatever else the Santa Rosa breed of man was, he was biologically sturdy enough to multiply and spread. Somebody very like him in habit once lived, we find, at Tule Springs, in the desert part of Nevada, but it was not desert then, since this Tule Springs man camped on the banks of a stream and this camp site was soon after (geologically soon, that is) covered over by a lake. Here are the same accumulations of ash beds and charcoal; the same strewing of animal bones, though these are the bones of extinct camel, extinct American horse, extinct deer and the true or great mammoth; and finally the same simple chips used as knives.

The Tule Springs tool inventory is more complete than Santa Rosa's but hardly more inspiring. The tools are, to quote the excavators, "crudely made." There were two camp sites; one is about 625 feet long by 200 feet wide, the other somewhat smaller. From these two locations several archaeological parties have taken only two biface (worked on both sides) discoidal forms (use indeterminate), a biface chopper, two scrapers, chips and pointed tools of roughly worked or splintered bone. This is a very minimum number of the very minimum of types of tools. Here are no distinctive spear points or shaped knives

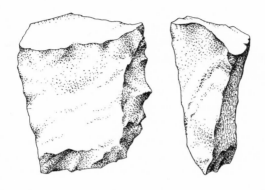

STONE CHOPPER

    The chopper, simply a broad-edged hand stone, is very likely the first formalized tool of stone made by man. Certainly it seems to have been the tool made by the earliest Amerinds, of circa 40,000 B.P., before they made anything else of stone recognizable as a tool for use and reuse. This chopper is relatively advanced, in that it has been made of the center split of a 6-inch quartzite pebble and has two cutting edges. Found on the shore of the Hudson River with pottery of an early Point Peninsula phase people, it is perhaps 3000 years old. Choppers were being made by some Amerinds practically into historic times.

of the specialized hunter; here are no manos of the specialized food gatherer, such as the Oak Grove people of later date in California, who harvested acorns, ground them into a meal and, after leaching out the noxious tannin, made, presumably, hoecakes of them. Even the bone splinters recovered may not have been used for awls, without which hides cannot be pierced for drawstrings or thongs to fasten them together, for the two scrapers found are not typical hide-working scrapers and no other hint of hide dressing has turned up.

    Like Santa Rosa man, Tule Springs man lived in the open,

at a time when weather was not at an optimum, or even as temperate as it is in those regions now. Santa Rosa man preyed on the probably defenseless dwarf mammoth; at Tule Springs the bones of the kills are of very young animals and of old ones— that is, the easiest killed and the least likely to be dangerous. But in both cases it was big-meat game that seems to have been sought for primary sustenance. The correspondence of Santa Rosa man and Tule Springs man amounts to corroboration— though it could all be changed by the discovery of a single projectile point or a well-used grinding stone. But on present evidence everything checks, even to the order of their dating. Three Carbon-14 dates for the oldest Santa Rosa charcoal give an average of 29,650 years B.P. (Before Present),* plus or mi-

---

* This footnote, the only one in the book, seems necessary to explain a system of dating that may be unfamiliar to some readers. The letters B.P. after a date mean Before Present, "present" being considered to be for our purposes the year 2000 A.D. Though it is now the favored practice among professional archaeologists to translate Carbon-14 ages into dates B.C. or A.D., the intent in this volume is to convey the total age of sites, cultures, artifacts, and whatever else is dated, for instant contemporary understanding. An archaeologist writing in a professional journal would date a 2500-year-old site as (approximately) 450 B.C., whereas the same date would be given here as 2500 B.P. By using the A.D.–B.C., or historical, chronology, the archaeologist fixes his prehistoric materials in relation to the year when the C14 tests on them were run. Since the charcoal, wood, shell, bone, fiber or other datable material recovered from an excavation may have been sufficient for only one test, and the site from which it was taken may never be datable again by other means, the reason for this exactitude stands out plainly.

But it is not an exactitude of any importance to us who want to know how old the dated material is relative to our present without recalculation. When a C14 date is released by a laboratory, it is given with a plus-or-minus ($\pm$) range of variation, since this is the result the C14 method yields: e.g., the average of Santa Rosa dates is 29,650 $\pm$ 2500 years. What this means is that the mathematical probability is high that the age of Santa Rosa charcoal falls between 29,650 years plus 2500 years (32,-150), and 29,650 years minus 2500 years (27,150). This variation, which is the margin of computing and/or counting error, is rather larger for the Santa Rosa material than in most tests, where it averages perhaps 5 percent or less of the mean age; it can be reduced somewhat by longer counting periods, which increase the expense without, in most cases, adding any significant refinement to the result. But in few cases of concern to archaeology will the combined plus-minus variation be less than two hundred years. In short, C14 dates are far more accurate than guesses, but they are, by a matter of two centuries or more, less than precise.

Hence, where a date has been given in the archaeological literature as 6030 $\pm$ 600 B.C., for example, we have added 2000 years and given the total age as about 8030 B.P. Obviously this places our "present" some four

nus 2500. Tule Springs charcoal was dated at *more than* 23,800
B.P.; how much more was not determinable by the technicians
because the sample was too small. But it may well date at 30,-
000, and so Tule Springs man may not be Santa Rosa man's
collateral descendant, but a distant cousin.

The time difference is of no importance, however. These two
peoples were of like antiquity of culture, and the culture is primordial. It is a triviality that the combined margin of error for
Santa Rosa man is 5000 years, and 5000 years is the total of
recorded history, during the elapse of which all the cities of the
world were built and some were destroyed and rebuilt only to
fall again; and all the books were written to preserve all the
truth and all the error man has achieved or devised; and civilization itself, that slow flower, has bloomed once, been cut back
to the root, recovered its vitality and could even now, for all we
know, be desperately stricken again. Santa Rosa man may be
28,000 years old or 33,000, and Tule Springs man more than
23,800 but less than 40,000, yet when we say that he is 30,000
years old the dating is as accurate, in the relative sequence of
human events, as when we say Columbus discovered America
in 1492.

Though it is but a tenth of the long career of the fire- and
tool- and word-using human race, perhaps as little as a twen-

---

decades in the future, in the year 2000 A.D. But as we approach 2000 A.D.,
our deliberately chosen "present" becomes more nearly the exact present.
And after 2000 A.D. it will be another 40 years before our 2000 A.D.
present deviates from the exact present by as much as it does now. What
we have assumed is a present of 2000 A.D. ± 40 years. The likelihood that
any archaeological information or doctrine will remain unchanged for 40
years, let alone 80 years, is not high.

This 40 ± variation of ours is no more than that which is inherent in
C14 itself. This radioactive isotope of the element carbon is present in the
air and is absorbed into the bone and fiber of all organic matter, animal or
vegetable. All radioactive materials are designated by what is called a
"half-life"; that is, one-half of any given quantity of a radioactive material
will break up or decay within the period specified, and the rate can be
neither increased nor decreased by any agency known to this earth. The
half-life of C14 is now accepted as being 5568 ± 40 years. Essentially
the C14 method of dating consists of Geiger-counting the scintillations as
the C14 atoms absorbed by the once-living matter being tested decay
into nitrogen atoms.

It should be remembered, in reading C14 dates, that any "contamination" of a sample of archaeological material by nonarchaeological material
(such as tree roots) will lessen the total age.

tieth, 30,000 years is still five times the era of history. Thirty
thousand years ago in western Europe, whence came the forefathers of most modern North Americans and many South
Americans, the Neanderthals—those short-legged, hang-jawed,
bent-necked creatures who looked superficially like experimental or working models of modern man but were in fact his
rivals for the job of representing the human race on the earth,
those anthropoidal but genuinely soulful men who may be said
to have had the first intimations of immortality since they buried their dead with care and respect, those half-brothers of our
Homo sapiens sapiens selves who may have made tools and
controlled fire as soon in the course of evolution as our own
progenitors—those men we call cave men were the French-
men, and Germans, the Spanish and Portuguese of the day.
They vanished from the archaeological scene soon after, at
about the time the tall, stalwart and striking-looking Cro-Mag-
nons of the species of modern man appeared, as most subsequent land-grabbers appeared, from the East.

Perhaps the Neanderthals were exterminated by conquest,
or simply petered out from a kind of racial senility, having
flourished for 200,000 years, but almost certainly some of them
vanished no farther than into the genes of our own ancestors.
Skeletons of a suitable antiquity have been discovered in Palestine which can be explained in no other way than that Homo
sapiens sapiens mated successfully with homo sapiens nean-
derthalensis, producing a hybrid on whose vigor we may still
be drawing. At stud, Homo sapiens sapiens seems always to
have been a prepotent sire, and he owes his dominance of the
world today, in all probability, more to genetic élan and the
aggressiveness that usually accompanies a strong biological
urge than to any absolute superiority of brain power over other,
now vanished, human types.

Whether this extinguishment of Neanderthal is dated at 30,-
000 years ago, as some estimate, or at 20,000, which can be as
easily argued—like the loose tolerance in the dating of Santa
Rosa and Tule Springs man, this is of academic interest only.
It is the event that counts. After it the conclusion was foregone
that all Europe would be populated by Neoanthropus—that is,
modern man, our thousand-times-great-grandfathers—and the
world would belong to one species of human being, rather than

being divided between two, as it might have been; for Neanderthal was certainly not ineducable and there is no inherent reason why, since he had achieved humanity, he could not in the fullness of his own development have produced civilization.

The appearance of man 30,000 years ago on Santa Rosa and at Tule Springs was an event of similar character. Man (and all evidence points to his being Neoanthropus), having crossed from Asia into Alaska, as he had to, and having somehow come through the last great glacier, the Wisconsin, or over it, or around it, or having even preceded it, and having gained the ice-free, climatically compatible regions of the American continents, was inevitably going to thrive and increase there. The populating of the Western Hemisphere was adventitious; it need not have happened, and Columbus might have found an empty land that day. No species of human being has been shown, by any acceptable evidence, to have originated in either America. That man found these continents as soon as he did and entered them through the remote polar-zone corridor open to his intrusion is a wonder that to some suggests predestination or divine guidance. There is a less high-minded explanation, however; man is only one genus of the many genera of animals who lived during the geologic era called the Pleistocene, which was the climax period of mammalian life, and when the Pleistocene fauna with which he was associated, mammoths and bison and Alaskan lions, drifted into America from Asia, he drifted with them. Very likely he was encouraged in this urge to migrate by other, stronger men, who usurped his hunting grounds and drove him thence, for man has no enemy more to be feared than man.

Beginning with the decisive occurrences of circa 30,000 B.P., the course of events in western Europe and in our hemisphere runs, for many millennia, in parallel. Each area was on the outskirts of the birthplace of races, which by the paleontology was southern Asia, or northern Africa, or both. Each was a frontier to which tribes burgeoning into races pushed out in their prolific exuberance or economic necessity. Western Europe never ceased, for the next 1500 generations, to be periodically overrun by peoples from the East, not until the Goths and Visigoths and Huns had finally brought down the first western pagan

Graeco-Roman civilization, not until the Mohammedans had, almost a century before Columbus sailed for America, nearly brought down the civilization reviving under Christianity. It was not too long before this, about 1200 A.D., that Genghis Khan whipped up a storm in China that spread disturbance in all directions. This Tartar explosion not only coincides in time with one of the many influxes into America, it may have actually caused the last major one, by the Athapascans, whose representatives best known to the public are the Navahos and the Apaches. (I always feel that it somehow places me in the great stream of prehistory and history that I was born in 1911, the year of the last Apache uprising in Arizona.)

When Columbus arrived that day at an outpost of the New World, he had not yet fully demonstrated that the world was round—it was left for Magellan to do that; he had done something immeasurably greater—he had *made* it round. He had lapped together the two far-flung margins of the earth and by this jointure had unified it into one world, its geography everywhere contiguous, its peoples everywhere related.

Nothing could have posed more keenly than this meeting of the two frontiers in the persons of the genius navigator, Columbus, and the chief of the primitive Tainos the question of why Spain at the western edge of the known world had so outstripped this Caribbean islet at the eastern edge. It is a question that does not quite answer itself. Europe had been enriched by inundation after inundation of peoples in the fullness of their vigor and aspiration. Through the tiny, hidden, highwater leak of Bering Strait and/or isthmus, only a trickle of migrants, only the offshoots, possibly only the disgruntled, the failing, the wayward, the backward, came, or were forced, into America. If the individual genius—the daring and original mind which leads people in the mass on the path it marks out through its own intuitions—occurs only at a constant percentage in that mass, as heavy water occurs only at a constant percentage in the immensity of the sea, or if genius is a function of the yeasty ebullience of mass, then the Americans have always been at a mathematical disadvantage. At the time of the American Revolution, 150 years after the first serious colonization of the present United States, there were more white inhabitants in the thirteen colonies than there were aborigines in the rest

of the incipient United States put together, and this after 30,-
000 years of procreation under these skies.

But all this is an explanation, without being an answer.

Thirty years ago America did not have a prehistory of 30,-
000 years. Authority in the field of American archaeology and
physical anthropology, on what it then believed to be the best
available evidence, granted only 3000 years and defended
this estimate with intimidating zeal.

But in 1927 that dogma died and was buried in the back dirt
of the exhumation of the bones of a vanished form of bison,
within whose rib cage were found the spear points, of novel
pattern, of hunters who have since come to be known as Folsom man (after the site of discovery near Folsom, New Mexico), and whose existence, from the geology of the site, was
incontestably ancient. He was generally accorded an age, of
geologic rather than chronological order, of 10,000 to 20,000
years (his actual age turns out to be 10,000), and American
archaeology began to take on vintage flavor. The new doctrine
of at least 30,000 years, and very possibly much more, is no
older than 1955 and is an outright gift of the C14 method of
dating, for the Tule Springs site had been known since 1933
without causing any great stir until M. R. Harrington, of the
Southwest Museum of Los Angeles, re-examined it and sub-
mitted a sample of its campfire charcoal to Willard Libby's laboratory.

Carbon-14 dating is a theoretically simple process—once
Dr. Libby (then of the University of Chicago Institute of Nuclear Studies and later a member of the Atomic Energy Com-
mission) had thought of it—though it is tedious in its laboratory
procedure; and it gives dates of a chronological order, whereas
before there were only geologic estimations, with a different
answer to each dating problem by each examining geologist, to
rely on in establishing dates in prehistory. The statistical percentage margin of error can be considerable, as the Santa Rosa
charcoal results show, and there are certain other errors to
which it is subject, including possible adjustment of its basic
assumptions, but now that it has been in use nearly a decade
and has yielded datings which are not only consistent within
its own methodology but which cross-check with known dates

and datings by other methods, its validity is universally ac-
knowledged. In its early stages its scope was not beyond 25,-
000 years because of the minute quantity of C14 present in
datable matter and the nature of C14 itself, but later refinements have pushed this to 40,000. The only serious fault that
can be found with it is its cost.

Its invention, or discovery (the first list of C14-determined
dates was released, with a nice sense of appropriateness, on
January 1, 1950), was to prehistory what the invention of the
microscope was to bacteriology, with the additional features of
Cinemascope and Technicolor, for it was a breath-taking prehistoric world that came suddenly into focus. Man had lived
here in America, in the midst of an uncaged zoo of the mightiest and most active animals ever to roam the earth—the mammoth and the mastodon, the saber-tooth cat, the Alaskan lion
(*Felis atrox*, or the terrible cat, bigger by a quarter than any
existing lion), the gigantic short-faced bear, the twenty-foot-
tall ground sloth, the camel, the enormous *Bison antiquus*, the
American horse, the dire wolf. He had not only outlived these,
but had survived the vicissitudes of climate to which the great
Pleistocene fauna apparently succumbed. He had seen the
Wisconsin glacier, at least, wax and wane; he had seen the huge
lakes, Bonneville, and Lahontan, in the now arid west, and the
deserts of New Mexico, Arizona, Nevada and Utah lush with
grass in one vast pasture; he had seen volcanoes erupt and the
very sea retreat and advance; he had set up his camps, or buried his dead, or killed his game, or fought his skirmishes or
scouted or set his foot in the hunt for game and vegetals on
every achievable square foot of the hemisphere; he had adjusted himself to every living condition between the midnight
sun of the Arctic and the ceaseless storms of the Straits of Magellan, from jungle to desert, from Death Valley to the slopes of
Aconcagua; and he had come so near to achieving what even
we might admit was civilization that it is certain that had he
been let alone another 500 years, the Columbus who then discovered America would no more have thought of claiming
these two continents for his king than he would have thought
of annexing China.

American prehistory is a story not often retold. Until the discovery of C14, and the stimuli and clarifications it brought to

archaeologists—and the vindication it brought to the intuitions of many of them—the story could not be told at all with any sense of beginning and of wholeness. Periodically, for archaeologists work diligently and mainly, to judge by the salaries, for the little trove they recover, it will have to be told again. But now the outline has emerged; there is a story to tell.

2

 *It Is Earlier Than You Think*

Though it is a risky business, as will be soon manifest, to designate any racial specimen as the earliest American, we must regard Tule Springs and Santa Rosa man as primal because it is hard to conceive of a more primitive kind of human culture than theirs. The distinction of being the earliest representative of these earliest Americans belongs, as of this date, to Lewisville (Texas) man, who will receive his credits later since he serves to introduce another geologic factor in the shaping of man's environment—the glaciers—even as Santa Rosa man served to alert us to the vast Pacific floor subsidence. What requires remark here is that American prehistory seems to begin with man at a cultural level that human beings had reached elsewhere in the world 300,000 years before.

It begins with man still at the suckling age, culturally speaking, still feeding at the breast of Mother Nature; he adapts stone to a rudimentary purpose rather than fashioning it into a tool to do a job of work; he controls fire but conceivably does not know how to make it; he is shelterless except for the walls of hot air a campfire throws up against the slash of the wind (Australian aborigines actually do make a kind of fire shelter by building two or three fires and sleeping among them); he is a hunter, but closer to the scavenging coyote than the predatory wolf, able to maintain an ecological place for himself only because he is neither too competitive nor too conspicuous, and neither too horizontally rigid to reach for fruited bough and overhanging berry nor too vertically rigid to stoop and prehensilly scrabble for roots and ground nuts, snakes and toads, beetles and limpets. It is still a question whether he will ever be any more than an environment-adjusted animal and it is unthinkable that he has any ambition to develop himself because he cannot have any notion that he has development in him.

How American prehistory happened to begin so late has already been hinted at. It is usually the nonprogressive peoples, the peoples who are not trying very hard, the peoples who find it easier to change their abiding places than themselves, who drift or are pushed into geographically peripheral precincts. This is not by any means a difficult conclusion to draw. The hinterlands of the present world are still the haunts of Tierra del Fuegans and Eskimos, of Laplanders and Australian bushmen, and America was just such an ultima Thule in bygone millennia.

As it now appears, America was entered comparatively late and possessed by people who had little to bring with them, and if the prehistory of America could be explained in a breath, albeit a long one, it would be vocalized thus: This hemisphere was not (until Europeans came) settled and colonized by immigrants loaded down with cultural baggage from the centers of the highest civilization of the time; it was merely seeded, by exiles stripped to the portable essentials; it was only impregnated by humankind who had nothing more to endow it with than their humanity. But the period of parturition of a race is long indeed, and the wonder is that Pizarro and Cortez found ripe for rape and looting civilizations materially the equal of their own, except in the matter of gunpowder and ships, and morally not inferior if ritual human sacrifice is compared with blood punishment for heresy, and state serfdom with feudal peonage. In a way it is sad that America was not left unmolested for another few hundred years. By and large, our America is now but another Europe. Had it been given leave to progress and develop in its own way—ah, would the New World and the Old now be so fratricidally close?

To return to our point, it is satisfying to know that the prehistory of America begins where a good biography ought to begin, with man, its subject, in his racial infancy and a long, full life ahead of him. But this was not a licit thought in the doctrine of American prehistory of a generation ago, and more than one scholar suffered the total or partial eclipse of his good name for indulging in it.

A Mongol strain of men, to whom was popularly given the localized and unscientific name of American Indian when they were discovered to be resident in America, had come surging across Bering Strait no longer than 3000 to 3500 years ago and had spread themselves throughout a literally New World that had never before felt the tread of primate or human foot—this was the doctrine that was not only held but strictly enforced by a clique of scientific bureaucrats during the quarter-century preceding the discovery of Folsom man; and it was still influential, in several modifications and guises, until after 1950, when C14 dating stripped away its last claim even to plausibility. Actually, not until 1953 did the pall of half a century of anthropological thought control begin to lift appreciably. Of a symposium held in Los Angeles which concerned itself with the possibility of primordial American cultures, Alex Krieger, who was then the editor of the Early Man Department of *American Antiquity*, official publication of the Society for American Archaeology, wrote with amazement: "A *novel* aspect [of the symposium] was the fact that a discussion of mid-Wisconsin [early man] and even interglacial man [even earlier man] was receiving a hearing from such an interested audience."

In order to be spared the suspicion that I am overestimating the weight of this anthropological opinion, I take the following from Kenneth MacGowan's *Early Man in the New World*.

"Holmes and Hrdlicka [renowned anthropologists] routed their opponents [the advocates of man earlier than 3000 years ago] completely. How completely may be judged from the fact that when it became proper to issue the Putnam [F. W. Putnam of the Peabody Museum at Harvard] Anniversary Volume at Putnam's seventieth birthday [in 1909], not one of the twenty-five essays in anthropology dedicated to him dealt with the thesis of which he had been one of the chief champions—early man in America.

"Men discovered new sites, but, if they had the temerity to announce their finds, their work was ignored or scouted. For twenty-five or thirty years, as Frank H. H. Roberts, Jr. [now of the Smithsonian Institution], writes, the subject of early man in the New World became virtually taboo, and no scientist desirous of a successful career dared intimate that 'he had discovered indications of a respectable antiquity for the Indian.' Opponents of early man had definitely retarded progress in this field."

And MacGowan is speaking of a period that was at its height from about 1890 until the late 1920's.

This Mongol-Indian immigrant, whom Ales Hrdlicka and W. H. Holmes, Henry C. Mercer and Herbert J. Spinden cried up as the first American, was the bearer, they said, of a full neolithic (new, or latest, stone age) cultural equipment, including pottery and horticulture, mound building and the shaman's tube that was to become the tobacco pipe. That he had invented anything after his arrival here was absurd; he had, obviously, adapted indigenously American plants such as corn and potatoes to a horticultural tradition he was already familiar with, and he had done rather singular things in architectural stone in the Aztec and Mayan areas, but either he had brought the know-how of all this with him, or a later immigrant had introduced it.

When in 1926–27 the projectile points of Folsom man turned up in New Mexico in a stratum that the geologists said had to be at least thrice 3000 years old, there was among most archaeologists a certain degree of acquiescence to the new data (though Spinden never did give in, and was still insisting, when he retired from the Smithsonian, that Folsom man was only 3500 years old)—or the archaeologists would have had the geologists, a hardy and hard-headed crew, on their necks. But the acquiescence was chronological only. The new line became that Folsom man—the paleo-Indian hunter—had bumbled into America 10,000 years ago, right enough, but in a mesolithic (middle stone age) state of development—that is, without pottery, horticulture, mounds, etc. Hence, in order to explain the pottery, mounds, etc., that were existent in America, authorities still had to fall back on a Mongol-Indian flow of immigrants at about 3000 to 4000 years ago. Folsom man was interesting, of course, but solely because of his antiquity, not because of any permanent consequences he effected either on the land or in its population.

It can safely be predicted that Santa Rosa–Tule Springs–
Lewisville man will not cure Americanists of this habit of yielding on the age of an early, paleolithic (old stone age) American
while repudiating everything else about him, including the
biological likelihood that he begot offspring who, in order to
survive and multiply themselves, passed through a succession
of cultural phases of their own origination.

Again, in order that I may not seem to exaggerate, I have
recourse to a quotation, this time from Gordon R. Willey, an
archaeologist of note and authority who will be referred to
later more approvingly. This statement was made in a contribution to *Anthropology Today,* a symposium volume summa-
rizing the way things stood in anthropology-archaeology-pre-
history in 1953, when the volume was published. It was written
in 1952, apparently, which was after the introduction of C14
dating but before the dating of Santa Rosa, Tule Springs and
Lewisville man. As of today Willey may accept these early man
dates and their implications, for all I know, but this quotation
is recent enough to illustrate my point, of the cant and slant
warped into American archaeology as a whole by the Hrdickla
bias.

Willey is considering the dilemma posed by the fact that
Folsom-like projectile points, known to be 10,000 years old in
America, are found in Siberia at a later, neolithic age level, the
dilemma being that if the Folsom point makers were of Asiatic
origin the timing ought to be the other way around—earlier in
Siberia, later in New Mexico. Willey writes:

"Just how far back these eastern Siberian neolithic points
and scrapers can be dated is the crux of the argument, but
both Ward and Movius are of the opinion that 4000 B.C. would
be the outside limit. If this is true, there is a glaring chronological discrepancy between these Siberian complexes and the
early American lithic. There are three possible interpretations
of this dilemma: (1) the American dating of Folsom-Yuma is
too early; (2) the Siberian dating of the preceramic neolithic
is too late; (3) the American Folsom-Yuma complexes were independently invented and bear no historical relationship to the
Siberian neolithic. *I believe that we can rule the third explanation out as an extreme 'isolationist' point of view.*" (Italics
mine.)

Willey could never have hoped to "rule the third explanation out" on the limp and offhand pretext that it was an "extreme 'isolationist' point of view" had he been addressing himself to a society of dialecticians or even to ordinarily skeptical and argumentative scientists. But, being himself indoctrinated, he had no hesitance about assuming that the opprobrious words "extreme 'isolationist'" would pass with the similarly indoctrinated in lieu of the refutation he lacked and the logic he felt free to snub.

Now this "extreme isolationist" point of view, which holds that Folsom projectile points were independently invented in America, is precisely the outlook this volume will unabashedly take; most of what is early American and much of what is later American is truly American, invented, created or developed by an American race whose integrality of character is deep enough in time that its differentiation from other races should be recognized by its own racial name, for which Amerind seems as good a coinage as any. To veer from this, it seems to me, would be the equivalent of saying that there never had been a Santa Rosa–Tule Springs–Lewisville man, and that his discoverers were charlatans.

Incredible as it may seem, after Willey's dismissal of this view as extreme isolationism, there is an extremer one—that the Amerind did not migrate into America in paleolithic times, and in a paleolithic cultural mood, because he originated here. I know of no one to quote in evidence that there is such a view because it is an utterly disreputable one. It has been repeated for half a century at least, in every textbook in half a dozen sciences, that no primates were included in the fauna of the Americas, and without primate lines there was nothing for a human line to evolve from. But how long the extremest of all possible isolationist views will remain disreputable it is not safe to predict. It was reported in the *New York Times* during August of 1958, without too much elaboration, that a Smithsonian Institution party had recovered several genera and species of primates from fossil beds in Wyoming. How these might fit into an evolutionary line tending toward a human form remains to be analyzed and published. But who knows where all these vagrant little facts may lead?

American primates notwithstanding, the utter failure of a

diligent American paleontology to uncover fossil hominids—
manlike forms—leaves us no alternative but to conceive of the
Amerind as an immigrant from the putative birthplace of humanity, now believed to be Africa. We can guess something
about the time of immigration if we can determine the kind of
lithic technology the first Amerind brought with him, and we
have a collection, scant but sufficient, of the stone tools of an
early man, the chopper and chips and discs of Tule Springs,
ready for our analysis. It will be the task of the next chapter to
find a likely spot in the universal paleolithic taxonomy for the
Tule Springs implements, and a likely ancestry for Tule Springs
man.

3

Long-Heads and Round-Heads

The case against an occupation of this hemisphere by a genuine paleolithic man has always rested on the absence from our soils and gravels of two kinds of remains: evolutionarily early skulls and admittedly paleolithic artifacts. Since these two categories comprise the only kinds of human vestige likely to have survived the effacement of the ages, the case would seem to be closed. And it was, as long as there was no change in the understanding of what was primeval in tools and primogenitive in skulls.

That it knew what was primogenitive in skull type, science had for decades no serious cause to doubt, not after Eugène Dubois, a Dutch army physician, convinced by the evolutionary logic of the 1880's that there was a "missing link" between man and apelike ancestors, took passage to Java, of all places, to search for it with an egoist's faith in its existence and his own destiny as its discoverer, and in no time at all, considering the kind of errand it was, dug out of a river bank the skullcap and other bones of a hominid he immediately called *Pithecanthropus erectus*—upright ape man—for the good reason that this was a fair and honest description of both a "missing link" and what he found.

The proponents of human evolution were twice rejoiced; not only had they now in their hands the proof positive that man had evolved from an apelike line, they had both ends of this line within their cognizance. Pithecanthropus was the beginning, the first rough draft of what in time had been refined into modern man, they believed, and it now became the simple task of archaeologists to search out all the skeletal forms and gradations between Pithecanthropus and modern man, and of the paleontologists to establish what was the proper precedence of each form.

The archaeologists performed well enough, bringing in from various startling places—nearly everywhere except America—the ridge-browed or otherwise apelike skulls of Sinanthropus or Peking man, Rhodesian man, Solo man, Gigantopithecus, a whole family of Australopithecines, even the half-fraudulent Piltdown man. Of course Heidelberg man had been around in somebody's attic for some time, and he fit comfortably into the taxonomy, as did Neanderthal, the veritable cave man of popular caricature and comic strip, who is the most abundant of fossil hominids. It might have been overlooked that the Americas had produced nothing like the singular Pithecanthropus or the big-jawed Rhodesian man, but when no skeleton of the ubiquitous Neanderthal, who had died out only during the last glaciation, could be reported, it was in time assumed that America had nothing to contribute to human paleontology.

Paleo-anthropology was equally set in its mind about what was meant by a paleolithic industry. It admitted the necessity of eoliths or dawn stones—battered pebbles and edged spalls or chips—and it admitted in fact man's most rudimentary tool, the pebble chopper, as first steps in man's effort to achieve a technology in stone, but what it meant by paleolithic, at a minimum, was hand axes. And certainly it was within its rights at the time in demanding that minimum. At Olduvai Gorge, in Tanganyika, East Africa, where geology has kept a 400,000-year record of man's exercises in stone, almost as though on shelves for alphabetical reference, Lewis Leakey, the excavator, found that hand axes had been made for probably a quarter of a million years. And they are far from peculiarly African artifacts; they occur from Tanganyika to London, and all across Europe and the Middle East to India. As a matter of fact, in the history of prehistory the entire doctrine that man existed on this earth before Bishop Ussher's piously calculated date for the biblical Creation of 4004 B.C. was founded on the hand ax.

This was the artifact that Boucher de Perthes, a French customs official but no organization man, began noticing in and collecting from the glacial gravels of the Somme River, first as curiosities and then as exemplars of an idea. Being but an amateur at natural sciences (this was a mere century ago and there were academicians even then in geology and anatomy and the like), when he presented to the councils of the professionals a portfolio of these battered stones and the infidel theory that they were the tools of men who lived before the biblical Flood,

ACHEULEAN HAND AX

The hand ax differs from the chopper most apparently in that it is pointed, rather like a great, heavy spearhead. Experts can distinguish many styles in what seems, at a glance, to be a relatively simple tool form. The above specimen, found in France, is designated Acheulean in style, and its like is found from southern Africa to England. Tools resembling this one have been found in America, but they are not called Acheulean because the Acheulean, of 150,000 years ago, is a tool-making tradition which cannot be demonstrated to have spread to America.

Boucher de Perthes was for twenty years spurned like a pack peddler. But in 1859—that is, only as lately ago as the eve of the Civil War (and of Darwin's *Origin of Species*)—the great English geologist Charles Lyell placed his international reputation on Boucher's side; the wax of incredulity melted in the ears of the scholarly, and Boucher walked away from sessions of the British Association and the Royal Society with a victory more decisive than Copernicus' for an idea every whit as revolutionary. For Copernicus had merely said that the sun, not the earth, was the center of our universe. The day was no shorter nor the year any longer by reason of this contribution. But if man had once had to make his living with the likes of a hand ax, was he a fallen angel? Or an upstart beast?

It is the most remarkable tool man ever made, this hand ax; once it existed, Sputnik was inevitable. It was made by at least two kinds of anthropoids, Paleoanthropus (old-type man, to which the Neanderthals belong) and Neoanthropus (new-type man, to which modern man belongs), and the making of it, the development of the craft of making it generation after generation, was, it is easy to believe, the very process by which men taught themselves to become men.

There is a pretty fashion among writers of calling the hand ax pear-shaped or almond-shaped; it has always looked to me like a cross between a beet and a radish—a flattened beet-radish, with a knobby top to fit the palm and a pointed end for penetration on impact. The French designation *coup de poing* —roughly, a striking stone—says neatly what it is, while the English "hand ax" tries more ambitiously to say how it works and what it does, without, it seems, satisfying archaeologists, who never mention it without grumbling that they don't know what it was used for.

This seems unnecessarily finicky. From the beginning it was obviously a tool and used for whatever came to hand. Regardless of what it became thereafter, it must have always had some tool-like utility. It is so generalized, it has features of so many tools, it is rather like a lithic Boy Scout knife, and it must have been the source of all man's later tool ideas, for it would certainly cut, pound, gouge, gash, score, scrape, rout, dig, chop —not well, but well enough for a beginning. Even so, any tool looks unhandy to the man not primed to its use, and it is outright presumption to suppose that a deft twist of the paleolithic wrist couldn't have accomplished with these thingamajigs tricks of the trade quite beyond us.

As man went on making hand axes century after century after century, his lapidary craftsmanship grew surer and his eye for symmetry quickened but he did not trifle with the hand ax's basic form. That persisted into a time when the hand ax may no longer have been made as a tool at all, but as a ritual object, and specimens appear of such proportions and so beautifully fashioned that it is evident their makers had in mind for them purposes transcending the daily chores. It is Carleton Coon's insight that these pieces are of sacred implication. They may have been, in this sense, sacramentals as the Catholic Church uses that term; that is, objects which direct the mind to right thinking and right behavior. Or it is possible that they were even more than this; man had made them for so long he could not imagine himself without them, as though they were intrinsic to his nature and yet apart from him, a gift from and therefore the symbol of a mystic and unseen power, a divinity. For instance, what is the meaning of the profusion of whole and seemingly unused hand axes at Olorgesailie, near Nairobi, in Africa, where tens of thousands of them lie on the ground apparently as they were finished and laid aside 200,000 years ago. What was this place? A Lourdes? A Mecca? Or was it only a Detroit?

Thousands of hand axes in Europe, in the Middle East and India, tens of thousands in Africa—and nothing in America that would pass the simple tests of these simple tools: that was the apparent situation. Nor was it because they hadn't been looked for. There was a spell of high optimism from 1870 to perhaps 1890, when the discovery of paleolithic man in America was believed imminent and every student of the antiquarian looked up the nearest cave and began to burrow—because in western Europe every rock shelter and bluff overhang yielded relics of paleolithic man as potato patches yield potatoes—for the pot of fame at the American end of the paleolithic rainbow. Something always turned up in these prospectings—and many an archaeologist wishes he had those caves at his mercy now—but the excavators considered it a loot of brummagem. The skulls were no different in general form from the digger's own and there were only pottery and basketry and projectile points to take home to the museum's lumber room. Very shortly, in consequence, these vain efforts to find an early American begat skepticism about his existence, which soon developed into a habit of rejecting data, rather than interpreting it, on the grounds that no amount of data could prove what, *a priori*, didn't exist.

There was one attempt to gather together specimens of an American hand-ax culture that ought not, perhaps, to go unmentioned here, less because of its unique manner of assembling the collection—by a sort of popular subscription—than because it produced no impeccable hand axes, while inspiring the improvisation of a deadly tactic against them which came in time to be a standard coup against all presentations of early-man evidence.

Late in the 1880's, Thomas Wilson, of the National Museum, in Washington, who was then at work on a classification system of stone artifacts, became convinced that he had a separable category of upwards of 900 items that ought to be classified as hand axes. To strengthen quantitatively the evidence in hand he sent out solicitations to the antiquity-minded all over the nation and within a matter of a year or two was in receipt of another 700 hand-ax-like objects, with descriptions of some 800 more. This totaled as many hand axes as there were in all the museums of Europe at the time.

Now it is obvious, when you think about it a moment, that the first stage of work in the reduction of a pebble or nodule of stone from its original lumpiness will often produce something like a hand ax, if the pebble is chipped all over. This primary, pointed ovate form is, quite clearly, all that the hand-ax makers were interested in or capable of conceiving, and they stopped with it, devoting their efforts thereafter to trimming and slimming it down.

Later traditions went beyond this primary or core shape, sculpting out tools the hand-ax makers hadn't invented, either by further work on the core itself, or by working on the spalls and splits knocked off the main core, which fractives thus became secondary cores or were used as tools themselves. At sites of lithic industry of any intensity there will almost always be found some of these primary or secondary cores, lost or left behind for contingent or technical reasons, or simply abandoned because of revealed flaws in the stone. Still other primary cores, some thick and rough, some thinned and symmetrical, fall into a class now called quarry blanks; that is, a nodule or pebble was dressed down for convenience and lightness in transport, just as timber is limbed and cut into sized logs for hauling out of the woods. Hoards of these cores are frequently found buried like miser's gold about Indian camps and settlements, from which adventitious circumstance they have frequently been called cache blades. Mathematical probability itself dictates that many examples of abandoned cores or quarry blanks will resemble hand axes.

When, therefore, quarry blanks, cache blades, rejects and cores appeared frequently in Wilson's collection, it was necessary only to point out that such things were certainly being made even as Lewis and Clark poled up the Missouri, and Wilson's archeology-by-mail project looked as naïve as the correspondence of schoolboy pen pals. Perhaps it was, but had Wilson been a little less premature he might have succeeded in marshaling the evidence of paleolithic man for the courts of archaeology by mere subpoena. All he needed was that a single contributor package off to him a numerically impressive collection of plausible hand axes gathered from sites that seemed to have some geological or geographical relation to one another, and he would have brought off a trick as cleverly simple as Columbus' egg.

In time such a collection did appear. It was gathered by E. B. Renaud, a pupil of Abbé Breuil, the foremost authority on European paleolithic industry, in Black's Fork Valley in Wyoming. But the time was in the 1930's and early 1940's, fifty years too late for Wilson's purposes. From some hundred and five sites Renaud had by 1940 picked up about 2000 worked-stone pieces, many of them of a form similar to, and considered by some specialists to be, hand axes. Generally speaking, however, Renaud now regards his Black's Fork Valley material, which has since been increased by pieces from a total of 493 sites in four western states, as Clactonian in character, the Clactonian being a very widespread, very early Eurasian industry perhaps 300,000 years old. Renaud never claimed an equivalent age for his American Clactonian. What he did, and still does (1957) claim is that, "It seems, therefore, much more reasonable to consider the Clactonian merely as an early and relatively simple technique of manufacturing flakes and flake implements by the hand-hammer method." In short, the Clactonian is a paleolithic technique, and because it produces spalls as a principal product and these spalls resemble recent spalls, then Renaud's Clactonian was recent; this is the Hrdlickan ploy.

Well tested in many such encounters, this ploy was used in a much more serious affair, with amazing effect, by Ales Hrdlicka of the National Museum, a physical anthropologist by profession, who made himself *arbiter elegantiarum* among the archaeologists by little more than the lifelong use of it. A physical anthropologist stands in a peculiarly responsible and judicial relationship to the archaeologist, because it is to him that the excavator must take for analysis—and verdict—the skulls and skeletal bits and pieces he unearths. To Hrdlicka, then, with an established reputation in Old World paleoanthropology, came the cranial trove of aboriginal America for over two decades. He was a man of great energy, and what was not presented for his review he made it his business to look into nevertheless. So strong were his opinions that by his polemic use of them he made them statutory. And Hrdlicka was never able to find what he called primitive features in any of the American skulls that came under his evaluation. Some, of undeniably nontypical aspect, he dubbed "variant"—but primitive in the sense that they had belonged to a man dead for hoary millennia? Never.

He did not attack the archaeology or the geology of the finds —he let like-minded men in those disciplines, taking their cue from him, carry that share of the load. What he did was much more dramatic, and for some reason much more devastating to aspirations to antiquity. He availed himself of the ploy of the hand axes and, having at his beck the resources of a museum, brought forth from its vaults skulls of Hopewell Mound Builders (he thought them recent) which duplicated measurement for measurement and feature for feature the skulls for which their finders claimed some considerable remoteness from the present. The Mound Builders were relatively recent, he argued, wherefore their skulls were modern in form; if another skull resembled these, it was obviously modern in form and hence, semantically, recent in age. This was not science; it was more fascinating than that; it was Houdiniism.

It is not now to the point that C14 dating has since shown that the Mound Builders are not as recent by a thousand years as Hrdlicka thought them. When the first C14 dates for the Mound Builders were published in 1950, placing those remarkable people from 2000 to 2500 years in the past, there was hardly an archaeologist in the American field who was not nonplused, and some veterans refuse to believe it yet. But what Hrdlicka bungled, in his *a priori* zeal, and what might have established his reputation for all time had he noted it, was that both groups of skulls—those claimed to be old and the Mound Builder skulls he compared them with—were long-headed, and long-headedness is a primeval cranial characteristic.

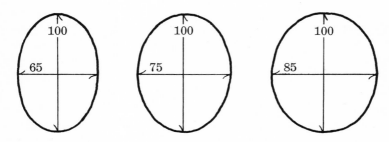

CRANIAL VARIATION

A skull that has the proportions of the oval at the left is long-headed, or dolichocephalic; the right-hand outline is round-headed, or brachycephalic. Neither is at the extreme of the cranial range. The center figure is in the mesocephalic range. Round-headedness is a progressive trait in most modern races; long-headedness seems to be disappearing. Wives who are exasperated at the persistence with which their husbands cling to old hats would do well to recognize that heads have not only sizes but shapes, and it takes time to break in the correct size until it is in correct and comfortable shape.

What long-headedness is will require but a moment's digression. When the axis of breadth of a skull is 75 percent or less of its axis of length, that skull is said to be dolichocephalic or dolichocranic, or long-headed. When this ratio (called the cranial index) increases to between 75 and 80, the skull is mesocephalic, or in the middle range. Beyond 80 the skull becomes brachycephalic, that is, broad-headed or round-headed.

The text for the significance of long-headedness comes from A. S. Romer's recent, authoritative *Man and the Vertebrates*, Volume Two. "Extinct human types," Romer says, "were almost all dolichocephalic; very probably brachycephaly is a

comparatively late human development. In Europe broad-
heads were rare until quite late prehistoric times; in America
there is much evidence that long-headed folk preceded the
more typical brachycephalic Indians. Among existing Old
World races we find that dolichocephaly is prevalent in Africa
and Australia and the fringes of Europe and Asia; brachycephalic skulls are dominant in all the more central portions of
Eurasia, suggesting a newer development."

In short, what Hrdlicka might have done, with profit to American prehistory, was to have looked at his data through the
other end of the argument. When the skulls of allegedly early
men were discovered to resemble those of men then thought
to be recent, all the facts were there in plain sight to relate
them to each other as early ancestor and modern descendant.
It took casuistry to relate them physically and temporally as
contemporary kinfolk.

But this was what Hrdlicka had to do; he was trapped and
he had trapped himself. He had made his reputation supporting the thesis that man had come to this hemisphere in a very
well-developed neolithic cultural stage and at most 3000 to
4000 years ago. But in Asia at the time of this emigration there
were only Mongoloids, and Mongoloids are nothing if not
racially round-headed. To have derived long-headed men from
Asia, Hrdlicka would have had to reach far back in time, much
farther than he was prepared to go in the absence of "primitive" skulls. So long-headedness had to be irrelevant to any
consideration of prehistoric chronology by Ales Hrdlicka.

Apparently Hrdlicka never committed to record what he
actually meant by primitive skulls. But a glance at his career
and his preoccupation with Old World paleontology makes
surmise simple. He meant a Solo man, or a Rhodesian man
(the provenience of which he managed to becloud when he
investigated it, just as he muddied the waters of Aleutian
archaeology when he plunged into them); he meant something like Neanderthal, about which he had the reputation of
being an expert; he meant something apelike, low-browed,
chinless and big-toothed. He meant something that he could,
almost by his subjective judgment alone, exclude from America.

Perhaps it ought to be interjected here that what is being

subjected to close review is not Ales Hrdlicka in either his personal or his scientific deportment. Every man has a right to his opinions, and the fact that they seem to be myopic should not prejudice his right to hold them. It is as morally repugnant in science as it is in politics to pursue a man to his grave and beyond with recriminations over his advocacy of what seemed tenable views in his time. In the first place it is corollary to, as it is a logical necessity of, a few being right now and then that most of us are wrong most of the time; in the trial-and-error method of finding truth most of us are assigned to the plying of error. What Hrdlicka did was what any good poker player would do—he assumed he held the winning hand until somebody called him with a better one. But nobody did. The scholarly reconstruction of the prehistory of America has suffered less from what Hrdlicka said, probably, than from what his contemporaries didn't speak up to say. He summarized and gave voice not only to what they thought but, more depressingly, to how they thought, and if he had not performed the office so ably someone else would have had it thrust upon him.

For almost four decades, Hrdlicka, with the enthusiastic support of men in his own field, and of colleagues in geology and anthropology and archaeology, held the line against seditious claims of discovery of early Americans. One wing was firmly anchored in the premise that in America there was no evidence of primitive skull types, and the other was as firmly staked down by the contention that there was no paleolithic industry here either; and the line was never breached. Nor was it ever overthrown by frontal refutation; that is, by the discovery of an American Olduvai Gorge with thousands of generations of hand axes stacked away for quick consultation, nor by a gold strike of Neanderthaloid skulls in the moraine gravels of Ohio. It was simply outflanked, when with the marshaling of new evidence it began to be plain that skulls did not have to be apelike to be ancient, and tools did not have to be hand axes to be paleolithic.

As long as it was admissible to think that Homo sapiens sapiens had evolved through gradations from more to less apelike, it was admissible to demand apelike features in the skulls of primitive men. But the new gospel is, bluntly, that modern man is not of the genealogy of Pithecanthropus-Neanderthal.

His lineage is his own. Smooth-browed, bechinned, he is descended only from himself, and his ancestors were as long
upon the earth as Neanderthal's, for the oldest fossil skull fragment ever recovered is that of Kanam man, a Homo sapiens
sapiens Adam 500,000 years old. There is no record that I know
of that Hrdlicka ever took Kanam man under advisement,
though the partial jawbone which is all there is of Kanam
man was discovered by Leakey in 1932, during Hrdlicka's heyday.

Even in quite late publications, it is still the fashion among
archaeologists and anthropologists to call the Pithecanthropus
breed of hominids by the name of Paleoanthropus—old-type
man—and modern man Neoanthropus—new-type man—but
these designations are easily seen now to be misnomers; neither type is, on certain evidence, older than the other. There is
a sense, however, though it was not included in the intent of
the nomenclature, in which these designations will do. Neo-
man is of a breed that remains pedomorphic throughout the
life of the individual; that is, the adult is childlike in appearance, and his features are those of his infancy, uniformly developed. But Paleoanthropus—paleo-man—is gerontomorphic;
the adult displays an exaggeration of features which were not
prominent in infancy. Thus the gorilla baby is almost as
smooth-browed as a human baby, and if it retained this
characteristic as it grew would look very much less fearsome
full grown than a gorilla does, and very much more human.
Cats are pedomorphic; collie dogs are gerontomorphic, their
puppy noses specializing into long, Pinocchio-like muzzles.
Thus neo-man continues relatively youthful-looking all his life,
while paleo-man grows more and more old-fashioned in mien.
Nor is this true of the individual paleo-man alone. Racially he
is gerontomorphic, too; the last Neanderthals, for instance, were
the most Neanderthal, or apelike in appearance, of the line.

The perception by science of pedo- and gerontomorphism
caused paleontologists to take another look for the progenitors
of Homo sapiens sapiens, with the result that a line of monkey-
apes, of a species called Proconsul, who scampered the earth
more than 10,000,000 years ago, began to receive a great deal
of attention. Pedomorphic, smooth-browed, with incipient

chins and teeth potentially developable into human dentition, pedestrian rather than arboreal travelers, the Proconsuls provide a most conformable derivation for neo-man. An exaggeration of but one feature, the brain, and the accommodation of the rest of the features to this exaggeration, seem all that is needed to give Proconsul a passably human countenance.

Very clearly in this line of evidence is an anthropoid ape whose complete skeleton was daintily dissected from a block of coal in the coal measures near Grosseto, Italy, in August, 1958, by a team of excavators headed by Dr. Johannes Hürzeler of Basel University, Switzerland, and Dr. Helmut de Terra, now of Columbia University, under the sponsorship of the benevolent and indispensable Wenner-Gren Foundation for Anthropological Research. The skeleton exhumed under these circumstances, after more than two years of search, was that of Oreopithecus (Mountain Ape), a creature a little over four feet tall which walked more or less erect and fits the description of the ideal forebear of neo-man even better than Proconsul, as he well might. Also of the order of 10,000,000 years old—according to Loren G. Eiseley, in his *The Immense Journey*, published in 1957, when Oreopithecus was known only from scattered fragments of bone—Oreopithecus is placed by Dr. Hürzeler in the direct line of ascent to neo-man, after Proconsul and prior to the Australopithecines, which Oreopithecus resembles strongly and which now seem to have been users of clubs of antelope thigh bone to kill for food and were possibly users of fire.

The difference between gerontomorphism and pedomorphism sounds tenuous and genetically subtle, but the difference between paleo-man and neo-man is anything but that. Paleo-man is prognathous; that is, his muzzle, the region of mouth and nose, is outthrust, as is true of most animals which use their mouths for many manipulative tasks, since they must accomplish with their jaws what they have no hands for doing. The forwardness of the muzzle is further enhanced by a receding chin and a back-sloping forehead, the chin recessiveness being caused by the lack of chin bone, and the sloping forehead by the set of the brain far back in the cranium. Interrupting this backward slope is the supraorbital ridge or torus, the famous "beetle-brow"—bony projections over the eyes fused together in a single bar of outstanding bone.

The advantages of this supraorbital ridge to an animal that fights with its teeth and pushes face first into all encounters are plain enough, but its importance is profounder than this. For this ridge is the anchor for the very heavy jaw muscles required to operate a masticatory apparatus that had to deal with the rawest and roughest of diets. In neo-man the jaw muscles are anchored by a chin projection on the mandible and a general heaviness of the cranial bone, and the result of this difference is a face in more or less vertical plane, especially since the brain of neo-man is set farther forward in the skull than that of paleo-man, and when it developed, it swelled frontally, pushing out the forehead.

The rivalry between paleo-man and neo-man seems to have been given a genetic trial by nature. Of one rather unexpected circumstance the paleontologists are fairly sure: Neanderthal and his neo-man contemporary were interfertile, and the result of at least one actual cross, it is believed by Carleton Coon and others, is the big-brained, very handsome Cro-Magnon man. Neanderthal had a great deal to bring to this union—a powerful physique, a brain-case capacity in the male of 1550 centimeters, and a certain ruggedness of facial bone structure to bolster the "childishness" of neo-man. But it was the pedomorphism and the vertical face of neo-man that prevailed, and paleo-man disappeared from the earth.

The primitive features of archaic neo-man skulls are therefore nothing like what Hrdlicka was looking for. They are: smooth brow, with brain set rather forward in the skull; long-headedness—as in all early man representatives, but of a different configuration, the head being flat-sided; very heavy bone structure and large teeth—as in all early men, and for the same dietary reason; a positive chin, and hence no pronounced prognathism. It takes an expert to detect the differences between the skulls of long-headed modern and archaic neo-men.

There is, of course, an exception to this incisive dichotomy— what would classification be without one, to save the natural world from the regimentation "orderly" minds would love to impose on it? This anomaly is the Australoid, who survives to-

day in the persons of some 60,000 or less pure-blooded Australian bushmen or blackfellows, and who, everybody limply
agrees, is Homo sapiens sapiens though he is brow-ridged,
weak-chinned, small-brained, prognathous, long-headed and
culturally nonprogressive. Romer says that his brow ridges are
reminiscent of Neanderthal, and it is tempting to think that he
is a Neanderthal-Neoanthropus cross in which Neanderthal
genes proved the stronger and the resultant hybrid was no improvement on either parent. But if the skull found in Rhodesia,
South Africa, and already referred to as paleoanthropic Rhodesian man, is the ancestor of the Australoid, as some think, it is
odd that he comes from a part of Africa where there isn't the
trace of a Neanderthal. In that locale, of course, are the Australopithecines, the family of primates lovingly gathered together by Raymond Dart of Witwatersrand University and
Robert Broom and proposed by them as inclusive in the genus
of humanity, as well as other, puzzling hominid specimens with
big jaws, rough-hewn skulls and apish aspects who may hold
the cardinal secret of man's evolution, or who may be out of
the race entirely. J. B. Birdsell, who has done considerable
work in physical anthropology in Australia, claims that there
really is no Australoid, and that the Australian blackfellow is a
comparatively recent cross with no more pertinence to human
origins than Abie's Irish Rose.

The Australoid is injected here, not only to keep the record
straight about a human species that may be neo-man, paleo-
man, a bit of both or neither, but because some Americanists
have thought he, or people of his stock, were among the early
emigrants from Asia to America. Many European authorities
have found what they judge to be Australoid features in the
skulls of Amerinds, a view Hrdlicka would have no more of
than that they were Neanderthaloid. It is quite possible that
Hrdlicka was right, but only as a by-product of being wrong.
By denying Australoid and/or Neanderthal details to Amerinds he thought he was excluding primitive man from America,
when all he was excluding was paleo-man, a different proposition altogether, and one about which the skeletal evidence—
or lack of it—still works in Hrdlicka's favor. But so savage was
Hrdlicka's attack on skulls claimed to be primitive that scientists seem to be loath to re-examine them even today; appar-

ently the incubi of past controversy still trouble their minds. Suffice to say, however, that if the Australoid did send off-shoots to America, he was not paleo-man enough to have provided the primitive features that might (or might not) have swung Hrdlicka to an acceptance of early Americans.

By using the pedomorphic approach to the evolutionary development of neo-man, there has been created, we hope, a disposition to believe that there must be fossils of neo-man as old as those of Neanderthal, or 300,000-year-old Sinanthropus or Dubois' original Pithecanthropus. If, as we believe, it was principally neo-man who populated America, then we cannot avoid the responsibility of examining his earliest fossils and any artifacts that may have been associated with him, for what insights they afford us about the earliest American technology and culture. But where are these early fossils?

The earliest finds (earliest in both senses, the remains themselves being earliest, and these finds preceding other such finds) were come upon in 1932, by the oft-mentioned Lewis Leakey, in East Africa, which owes the exposition of its importance in world prehistory primarily to him.

From a geologic context which Leakey knew to be about 500,000 years old, he took the partial mandible now known as Kanam man, and from a context dated at 300,000 years and within a few miles of the Kanam site, he took fragments of four different skulls which are now grouped as Kanjera man; both finds being in association with the fossil bones of extinct beasts appropriate to the context. But the Kanam jaw had a rudimentary chin and the Kanjera skulls, on reconstruction, proved to be fully human in size and form, and in 1932 it was unthinkable that neo-man had been alive with the now extinct dinotherium (thunder beast) and such fauna. Three years after the Kanam and Kanjera finds, a British geologist of wide repute visited the sites, which Leakey had warned were undergoing severe erosion, and found that the precise loci were no longer to be ascertained. He might have said so fully and let the case rest on Leakey's testimony. But apparently you don't make the trip to Africa and return without reporting something more substantial than that you have nothing to report, and the geologist's curt statement on what he hadn't found was quickly interpreted as meaning there probably hadn't been anything of note in the first place. Kanam and Kanjera went to archaeological limbo, to await resurrection.

Meanwhile, in 1935, the year of the geological report on Kanam and Kanjera, an English dentist and amateur archaeologist, A. T. Marston, came across the central and rear portions of a skullcap in gravels of the second interglacial period at Swanscombe, on the Thames River. This time the geologic context was carefully authenticated by competent geologists, and the skull, under intensive study, was found to be that of a young woman whose brain, as Coon nicely puts it, was "of modern size and form, providing the same capacities for behavior and learning as the brains of modern women." Anatomically her forehead was of modern shape—no torus—but the bone was extraordinarily thick-walled, to withstand the stresses of the heavy temporal muscles which operated a powerful jaw. Not only do these details match the details of the Kanjera skulls, but the Thames second-interglacial gravels are of the order of 300,000 years old. This age was corroborated by fluorine tests completed after the war, which do not give absolute dates like C14, but do give relative ones, and they showed the Swanscombe skull to be coeval with the second-interglacial fossils strewn about in the same stratum.

With Swanscombe man, distaff side, having passed its tests successfully, there was no longer any *a priori* argument against Kanjera; and if Kanjera man was thinkable, so was a thousand-times-great-grandfather in the same neighborhood thinkable too. For Kanam and Kanjera are in a part of Africa that was never glaciated. Glacier periods elsewhere were pluvials—times of heavy rainfall—there, and heavy rainfall and a warm or temperate climate make for lush vegetation, teeming animal life, and a generally desirable environment in which to live.

As superstition has it, meaningful events often come in threes, and the third find of indubitable Homo sapiens sapiens with archaeological seniority was made in 1947 at Fontéchevade, in the Charente Department in western France. Here Mme. G. Henri-Martin (another amateur), continuing excavation in a cave from which Neanderthal remains had previously been taken, dug beneath the Neanderthal layer into the lower depths and found the skullcap of a woman (query, do women

outlast men even as fossils, as they survive them, according to
insurance tables, in the flesh?) and the poor fragment of her
companion's forehead. Had Fontéchevade been the first cave
ever excavated for paleolithic remains, as it might easily have
been, Fontéchevade being in a very archaeologically popular
region, the position of Neanderthal above neo-man evidence
might well have saved prehistorians decades of misunder-
standing. Thus theory is always at the mercy of casual circumstance. On analysis Mrs. Fontéchevade proved to be of the
same family and physical attributes as Miss Swanscombe,
though 100,000 to 150,000 years less aged, with a brain modern
in size and form, enclosed in an archaically heavy brain case.
The doctrine of pithecanthropic ancestry of neo-man now becomes dead letter and all assumptions based on it may be ex-
cised from the literature.

Even as the book of evolutionary knowledge was being re-
written, so was its companion volume on paleolithic technology.
For almost as long as paleolithic tools have been studied, two
kinds have been recognized: those made by dressing down
the nodule or core to satisfactory shape—technically called
core industry; and those made by knocking off a spall and re-
touching this as desired—called flake industry. It is now being
said that whether an industry is classified as core or as flake is
largely a matter of the ratio of one to the other, and of
whether a staple tool like a hand ax is habitually made out of
core or out of flake. In core industries the by-product flake with
its ready-made cutting edge was undoubtedly utilized, as in
predominantly flake industries the cores were not discarded if
they could be usefully employed. These core and flake traditions have led some archaeologists, Jacquetta Hawkes in particular (in her and Christopher Hawkes' *Prehistoric Britain*
and elsewhere), to see an identification of neo-man with core-
tool makers and paleo-man with flake-tool makers. This may
have some validity in England and western Europe, within
certain time boundaries, but whether it holds true all over the
world in just this way is open to question.

The point has been made that hand axes occur from mid-
Africa to mid-England—specimens were found with both the
Swanscombe and Kanjera skulls—and as far east as India; but

they have not been found in the region east and north of India, which is exactly the region out of which man had to emigrate to reach the Western Hemisphere. Here occurs, in the place of hand axes, a tradition of pebble tools centered on what is called a chopper—a cruder, broader-bladed implement that had approximately the same utility as the hand ax.

Now you have only to refer to the inventory at Tule Springs to reassure yourself that choppers are found in America; but at

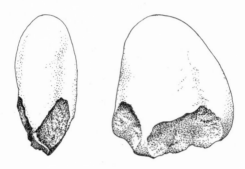

PEBBLE CHOPPER

This pebble chopper can be and probably was made in 30 seconds or less, by striking off four flakes, two on each side but not opposite each other, so that the cutting edge is scalloped. In the right hands, it will decapitate a fish, disjoint a deer leg or size up a cudgel as neatly as an ax. Its one fault is that it won't hold an edge. Pebble choppers appear at the very bottom of stone industry at Olduvai, and are the principal tool through most of the paleolithic in areas east of India.

Tule Springs the type is called "chopper or hand ax." This is not necessarily equivocation on the part of the taxonomist. When European specialists speak of hand axes they mean those types associated with a succession of technological traditions: the Chellean, Acheulean (found with Swanscombe man) or Mousterian (found with Neanderthal). But these are standardized implements, and they have to have been refinements on an earlier, cruder thing which must have resembled a chopper. What can be done to a chunk of stone in the primary stages of turning it into a useful tool is severely restricted. Three to five bold, well-struck-off flakes will turn a fist-sized river pebble into a pebble chopper. Perhaps ten or fifteen will make it a hand ax. Michelangelo, chisel in hand, had to begin very much as paleolithic man did when he wanted a chopper; he had to begin by taking nicks out of shapeless stones. The principal difference is that Michelangelo had a somewhat more advanced objective in mind.

What may some day become a key anthropological question is why man west of India concentrated so fervidly on the hand ax, which is really only an advanced stage in the dressing of stone and not an advanced tool type. If I understand Coon aright, he suggests that the hand ax became a cult object, which means that it was embedded in a body of myth and superstition amounting to a religion; and religion is always conservative. East of the dividing line in India, lithic technology, minus a cultism that would exalt the advanced chopper, or hand ax, followed more practical lines of development. For the uses it served, the chopper was good enough, and not improved by being prettied up, so its makers went on making it without the extras—in America until as late as 1000 years ago, or perhaps later.

The point to be remembered is that the chopper is a paleolithic tool; it is America's hand ax, and the only ambiguity about the Tule Springs specimen has to be in nomenclature. It was a tool made to do what hand-ax users did with hand axes and chopper users did with choppers. But there is nothing about it as a tool to demand that it be thought of as deriving from any place in particular. It is still the simplest of tool ideas, if you except the flake, and it may precede even that, for the flake, as a tool, is a by-product of stone dressing.

Nothing can be more obvious than that, if man is going to make tools at all, he must sooner or later begin to shape stone; he may prefer tools of wood and/or bone, but he cannot make them until he has found a material that will provide him with an incisive edge to hew or hack or sever. Man would have learned that chips have a natural cutting edge from some such accident as drawing his own blood with one. But chips do not occur frequently enough in most places to supply the needs of constant users. Therefore, when our first genius registered the laboratory observation that the impact of stone on stone occasioned chips he had the brilliant idea of making his own

chips. Once he had done this it was inevitable, though uncon-
scionably slow in coming, that he learn to knock off the approximate size and shape of chips that he wanted. It is only at
this point that flake or chip technology is properly differentiated from core technology—when cores are so prepared beforehand, with a plane surface for striking, that a controlled
and craftsmanlike blow will produce a chip that is already a
tool or near-tool.

My belief is that the makers of predominately chip tools
came by their tradition as a result of desiring to work wood
and perhaps bone, making cudgels, stabbing sticks or wooden
spears and the like, the shaping of which requires a knifelike
edge. It follows, hence, that the earliest chip-tool makers must
have dwelt where wood was abundant.

But the predominantly core-making tool fashioners must
have dwelt on grassy plains where there was little incidence of
wood, or at least of workable wood. Having acquired the use of
pebbles to smash bone for the extraction of marrow—a rich
food which would usually have been available to them, in
their adaptation to scavenging upon the big kills of the big killers—these grasslanders would have learned about spalling
from the breakdown under impact of the weak or schistose
rock they used in the smashing. Their interest, however, would
not have been in the smaller chips, the cutting characteristic of
which was of no particular use to them, but in the increased
efficiency of the larger core after it had been thinned to an
edge or point. When they came to shape a pebble purposively,
then, they would have shaped it according to previous experience; that is, they already knew what they wanted from having
made it accidentally. As uses for chips became evident, for
scraping and more precise cutting than their core tools were
capable of, the core-tool makers undoubtedly put them to
these uses, but incidentally and not emphatically, so that when
they moved on, as they seem to have, from African grasslands
to European woodlands in the wake of the melting of glaciers,
they took their core tools with them into the new environment.
If they here encountered, as they must have, chip-tool makers, some sort of intermingling of techniques would be likely to
have taken place, with each tool tradition stimulating the other
where it was lax.

If this is true, both Hallam Movius, who believes there is no association of one tradition with Paleoanthropus discrete from another with Neoanthropus, and Jacquetta Hawkes, who believes there is, would be right, but at different epochs. The way man would turn stone into tools must have been determined by the environment where he lived when he first made stone tools. The earliest man would certainly just as soon have used sticks instead of stones, if sticks were to be had for the choosing; if they were not he had to make a stone tool that would do the work directly; if they were, he had to think about a stone tool that would turn wood into a tool, as well as one that did the work directly.

Fortunately for this view, the sequence of tools at Olduvai Gorge, incomparably the finest index of paleolithic technology in the world, supports it; as a matter of honest fact, gives rise to it. Olduvai Gorge, which is in a desert now, like Tule Springs, was in grass country during man's habitation of the region, and a lake swelled and shrank there, even as at Tule Springs. Those hand axes at Olduvai, layer on layer in cultural pagination, are underlaid by some 80 feet of deposits from pebble tool–chopper cultures. The tools found with Kanam man were pebble tools of an even earlier type. Pebble tools are technically core tools, a pebble or chunk of stone being minimally chipped to effect an edge or point—in the early stages, on one face only. In time among the Olduvai pebble tools there appears the chopper, just where it should be, a rough hand ax with a broad cutting blade like a conventional ax or a kitchen salad chopper, a form apparently and in fact precedent to the true hand ax. Exactly how Tule Springs man, dweller on grassy plains, came by his chopper-making habit is by no means a closed question.

So, as man may be early in America without being paleoanthropic, a tool assemblage may be paleolithic without hand axes; it may be in a pebble tool–chopper tradition. The chopper has been recognized in the Western Hemisphere ever since William Ritchie first set up in 1932 a category of choppers in his Lamoka Lake material of central New York State. Chopper tools have now been recognized in cultures all over America at sites early, middle (Lamoka Lake dates at about 5500 B.P.) and late, and though we have had to come by a long and devious route, we are now ready to take a further look at the scant technology of Tule Springs.

When M. R. Harrington, of the Southwest Museum at Los Angeles, heard in 1933 about the discovery of the Tule Springs site by Fenley Hunter, of the American Museum of Natural History, Harrington, a veteran of the fight for early man in America, the following year dispatched a party to test it. On this expedition the artifacts recovered were "a large uniface scraper, a biface chopper, and a disc-shaped biface implement."

Harrington's purpose had been paleontological; he was after the bones of mammoth, camel, ancient horse, etc.; but he recovered an obsidian flake used for cutting and "also several crudely chipped stone scrapers and choppers or hand axes," and put them away for future reference.

In 1955 a larger party from Harrington's Southwest Museum, now aware that Tule Springs charcoal was more than 23,800 years old, began to dig again. This time they discovered "another *biface, disc-shaped, chipped artifact* of stone—and what appears to be a crude side \scraper—an elongated pebble chipped along one side," which would fall by definition into the pebble-tool series.

Let us now, just for the fun of it, revert to Fontéchevade Cave, where a tool industry was found with the 150,000-year-old Mr. and Mrs. Fontéchevade. It included, according to the summary appearing in Geoffrey Bibby's *The Testimony of the Spade*, "large flakes with minimal secondary fashioning and *disk-shaped* cores with a zigzag edge." (All italics mine.)

These disc- or disk-shaped bifaces appearing coincidentally with early men half a world apart have no other name than that used in the above descriptions because nobody has been able to suggest a purpose or a meaning for them, either in America or in France.

4

Whence, Why and How

It might be charged by the careful reader that the ending of the previous chapter, with its suggestive bracketing of the biface discs of Fontéchevade and Tule Springs, is itself a flagrant instance of the Hrdlicka ploy, of which the chapter made such a point of disapproving. It seemed to say that Tule Springs biface discs and flakes resemble—semantically—Fontéchevade biface discs and flakes, and that therefore Fontéchevade dates Tule Springs.

If that is the suspicion, it will not be allowed to fester. All that has been done is to hold up for comparison two assemblages of paleolithic tools, neither of which includes projectile points or milling stones, both of which include an enigmatic biface disc, and each of which was manufactured by neo-man; the Fontéchevade assemblage certainly, the Tule Springs assemblage probably. By the Hrdlicka ploy, of course, this would make Fontéchevade nearly as recent as Tule Springs, rather than vice versa, but we are in no hurry to draw extraneous conclusions; all we seek from the resemblance is a clue or two.

Very pertinent thereto, then, is a piece by J. E. Weckler in the December, 1957, issue of *Scientific American,* in which Weckler frames this thought, which seems already to have occurred to other minds: Neo-man is a species of African fauna which "summered" racially in Europe between glacial periods; Miss Swanscombe, as noted, was found with second-interglacial fossils, and Mrs. Fontéchevade with kitchen bones of third-interglacial beasts. But eastern Asia, the point of departure for America, was the birth and rearing place of paleo-man, Weckler thinks. When these two races did finally commingle socially and biologically it was in the Near East (Skhul is the site of one such get-together) and on the initiative of the paleo-man species Neanderthal, pushing west from his oriental homeland under some stimulus or pressure only to be guessed at. But Neanderthal gave even more to neo-man than the good genetic traits we have already supposed; he taught neo-man to live in caves and otherwise protect himself against incle-ment weather, Weckler says, and neo-man was able to live in

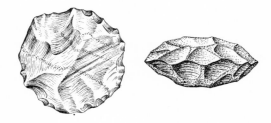

DISCOIDALS
     The chipped stone disc on the left is from a Desert Culture site, where it is believed to have been used as a scraper, or scraper-plane, since it has a more or less flat ventral surface. The disc on the right is of the Tayacian culture of Fontéchevade man and no certain use is sug-gested by its shape, though it has a sinuous cutting edge all around. Round, sinuous cutting-edge tools are char-acteristic of the early but undated Topanga Canyon cul-ture in California and, according to Douglas Byers, of the earliest but undated lithic culture in New England.

proximity to European ice only after he had learned these les-sons.
     The insight we wish to appropriate for immediate use from Weckler's piece is not that Neanderthal alone lived in eastern Asia (no fossil evidence yet supports this view, as Weckler ad-mits), but that neo-man was a warm-climate denizen exclu-sively, and that he followed that climate wherever it—and the fauna dependent on it—led him.
     Thus Africa-acclimated Homo sapiens sapiens came to Eu-rope only when the weather was at least subtropical, and re-

tired south like the birds when there began to be frost on the punkin. The second interglacial, the period of the Swanscombe fossils, was a very long, warm period indeed, generally accorded a duration of a hundred and ninety thousand years. What are now thought of as equatorial fauna, elephants and the hippopotamus and such, browsed in the jungle around the Swanscombe camp, and a semitropical floral and faunal environment encircled the globe at similar latitudes across Asia and Canada. The Arctic Circle was certainly deiced and probably very temperate. On the face of it sun-loving Neoanthropus had as much reason to wander into farthest Asia, following the warm zones, as into England. The way is much longer, certainly, and more arduous to travel, but 190,000 years is a very long stretch of travel time. It therefore seems an excellent working hypothesis that neo-man, following the herds of ruminants on which he was, with other carnivores, at least partially dependent, went wherever they went, which took them, among other places, to Siberia and thence America.

When, as all prosperity must, the second interglacial period ended, the descendants of the Swanscombe stock were pushed by the slow advance of the third great glaciation—and without knowing it—back to Africa. But the strays who were caught in Siberia, what of them? Even if it were thinkable that they knew where Africa was, and knew that 10,000 generations ago they had come from there, the way back was blocked by glacier mountains, if by nothing else. Before the advance of ice, then, there was only one way to retreat—to the east, which is toward the sea in most places, but toward America in at least one.

This view will seem much too radical to some, who will contend that neo-man was simply not numerous enough at this stage of the game, not a successful enough animal, to have spread himself over so much territory. But after the third glacier comes the third interglacial period, which returned warm climates to northern latitudes. It was only a third as long as the second interglacial, but 60,000 years is more than enough time for a band of neo-men and their descendants and offshoots to divagate from Africa to Bering Strait even if they shifted their hunting grounds only a mile a year. The earth is, after all, only 25,000 miles around at the equator.

But there is not now, and there has not been within recorded time, as everybody knows, any conjunction by land of eastern-most Asia, which is the Chukchi Peninsula, and westernmost America, which is the Alaska Peninsula. For years, then, pre-historians had made quite a puzzle of this fact: How was the 20-mile passage across the stormy waters of Bering Strait, which lies between Chukchi and Alaska, to have been man-aged by a culturally simple people, with craft no more sea-worthy than canoes or bullboats, if they had even these? Hrdlicka had no trouble with the problem; his neolithic immi-grants were simply defined as a people who did not cross to America until they had the technology to make the craft to do it. But Folsom man, hunter of the now extinct *Bison taylori*, was certainly no neolithic man, and he positively could not be accounted for as a boatman. Then the prehistorians locked themselves into a dialectic refrigerator precisely like the one they are now in on Santa Rosa Island: How could men without water transport have got from the place where they obviously originated to the place where they obviously were?

As has been pointed out, you don't have to linger in this merely casuistical imprisonment any longer than you want to. There are several ways out. One is, by the laws of argument at least, to take the fact that man is in America, and would have found it difficult to get here from any other place, as evidence that the Amerind is a development of uniquely American fauna; and if the aforementioned discovery of Western Hemi-sphere primates becomes significant, this may be the liberating way out. But at present it is most unpopular, and is regarded as simple-minded.

With the compounding of evidence that man was in Amer-ica at a very early condition of culture, and predicating that as a species he originated elsewhere, most prehistorians now as-sume that the crossing between Chukchi and Alaska was no crossing at all but one continuous dry-land perambulation. This can be done even more simply than at Santa Rosa, where we have to depend on a subsidence of the Pacific littoral as a means of breaking Santa Rosa from the mainland. This subsid-ence, the nub of which seems to have been south of the equator, may prove in time to have had effects as far north as

Alaska, but strictly local conditions can be shown to have been responsible for the parting of the bond between the continents of Asia and North America.

When glaciers were the principal topographical feature of

THE ALASKA-CHUKCHI PROVINCE

When the waters of the world ocean were about 200 feet lower than they are now, about 15,000 years ago, a dry-land province estimated to be of the size and shape of the above provided a livable Amerasian milieu for man and beast. If the ocean was ever lower than this, the province was obviously larger, and it was gradually erased from topography as the ocean refilled with glacial melting. This province was probably unglaciated, but its climate must have been comparatively severe during its long winters, and both the cultures of its human inhabitants and the habits of its fauna must have been Arctic-adapted. David Hopkins of the United States Geological Survey has lately (1959) estimated this province to have been 1000 miles wide, north to south, at about 35,000 B.P.

continental landscapes, so much water was locked up in them, as previously noted, that the level of the world ocean was as much as 400 feet lower than at present. But a course can now be charted across the narrowest part of Bering Strait, which is nowhere more than a hundred and twenty feet undersea. The simple subtraction of 120 from 400 gives us some idea of the height, extension and even duration of an isthmus that linked Asia and America as North and South America are linked now. This linkage would have been meaningless in glacial times if Alaska had been, like the territory to north, east and south, heavily glaciated. But it was not; throughout the Wisconsin period, when the icecap reached as far south as Long Island, the Alaska-Chukchi province remained a habitable environment for mammoth and bison and their associated carnivores, and hence for man.

And to this already sufficient explanation may be added a further circumstance. With the burden of ice lying on midcontinent, the continental edges uprose, as the sides of a mattress do when you lie in the middle, and the Bering isthmus may very well have been further elevated by such an effect. This combination of upthrust land and lowered seas does a great deal more than merely give passage between Siberia and Alaska; it raises from beneath the sea an entire province which, if it, too, were unglaciated, like Alaska—as it almost certainly was—must be of radical importance to the anthropology of primitive man.

We have already supposed that the hospitable climate of either the second or third interglacial would have provided an attractive asylum for early man in Siberia and that the reicing of the land would have cut off any retreat by the southwesterly route along which neo-man had come deviously out of Africa. This glaciation was not continental, however, like that on the American side of the Pacific. The Siberian plains at the latitude of glaciated Canada seem not to have supported an icecap because snow, the material of which icecaps are made, did not fall in glacial abundance there. But glaciers did form in the mountains, clogging the high valleys and passes, with the result that the fauna of the region, and man with it, was herded toward the sea, where it probably would have gone in the event of nothing more than a colder climate anyway, temperatures being higher and more equable at sea level. Being the omnivore that he is, man would have found the food resources of the littoral quickly enough, and so we have no difficulty imagining him strandlooping his way along the rim of the Pacific from Siberia to Santa Rosa. But shore dinners were

probably not forced on most of the population. In the vast
Siberio-Alaskan province just described, of which much is now
submarine, we know from the bewildering plenitude of fossil
bones in Pleistocene (the Pleistocene includes the four great
glaciations and the three interglacial periods) geological deposits that there was no lack of animal life. And a good many
of the species represented were of animals which arrived there
only during the Pleistocene—among which, it seems from
W. B. Scott's *A History of Land Mammals of the Western
Hemisphere,* are the bison group, probably the musk ox, the
true bears, the Rocky Mountain bighorn, the Alaskan lion and
the lynx.

It begins to appear now that to call the Amerind an emigrant
from Asia to America is to stretch the connotation of the word
beyond all candor. Man was obviously an inhabitant of this
Siberio-Alaskan province when it was cut in two by the co-
ordinate subsidence of continental margins and the swelling of
the sea from the return to it of glacial melt-water. Thus he became an American by geophysical decree, not really by migration, not really by crossing Bering Strait.

That such a separation of Asia and America occurred at the
end of the Wisconsin glacier does not imply that there was
such a separation during each interglacial, with its concomitant
high sea level. What does seem probable is that during these intervals erosional assaults could be carried on against the Bering
isthmus which accomplished its demolition only during the
last one. A glance at the map of our new state will confirm that
Bering Strait is actually the channel through which the northern Pacific—or that embayment of it called the Bering Sea—
pours into the Arctic Ocean. When there was an isthmus across
this channel, massive oceanic assaults were made on it from
both sides, and each low-land, high-water interglacial afforded
more exploitation of this weak spot in the wall that separated
the two great basins of water. After some final cliff was under-
mined and a breach was made and the Pacific and Arctic were
free to get at each other, the communicating currents must
have accelerated the razing of this intercontinental bridge.
How much of the 20 fathoms that Bering Strait lacks of being
Bering isthmus is due to land subsidence, how much to high
water and how much to sheer erosional destruction—which

may still be going on as the currents flow north—may never be known; but this is no reason for discounting any one of them.

The conclusion to be drawn is that it is no more astonishing to find early man in America, which is now separated from his point of departure by 20 miles of water, than to find early man in England, now separated from Europe by a similar strait. England became an island about 8000 B.P. It does not seem incumbent on us to believe that the Asiatic-American umbilical was cut in times much remoter than that.

But if Weckler is right, the principal inhabitant of eastern Asia paleolithically was the paleo-man stock of Neanderthal, as known in the putative related form of Sinanthropus, or Peking man. Why do we insist, then, on reaching all the way into Africa, or interglacial Europe, for the Amerind's ancestors?

It has not gone unrecorded here that Hrdlicka's demand for primitive cranial features has pointed up, as nothing else could, the salient lack of them in American skulls. This negative evidence is supported by the rather more positive evidence of the Tule Springs, Santa Rosa and Lewisville man finds, which, while they produced no skulls, gave testimony as to how these early Americans lived. And it is not the Neanderthal way.

Neanderthal is the best known of fossil species of men because of his habit of living in caves and of burying his dead underfoot under fairly preservative conditions. Not so the Fontéchevade neo-man type, albeit she and her man were living—for all we know had taken refuge—in a cave. Perhaps, truant from her true husband or his true wife, they had set up a clandestine ménage for safety's sake, for the Fontéchevade stone tools identify these temporary troglodytes as belonging to a culture called Tayacian, and Tayacians did not live in caves. The main Tayacian camp seems to have been on the plateau above the Fontéchevade cavern, under the open sky.

Perhaps they were claustrophobic by nature, these Tayacians of neo-man breed; perhaps there were superstitions about hobgoblins among them, originating in misadventures with cave-dwelling bears, lions, serpents and spiders, or with pneumonia, or even falling roofs, since the roof did fall at Fontéchevade, and perhaps on the Fontéchevade lovers themselves for their sins. Or they may simply have been heaven

worshipers. At any rate, the skulls of all other neo-men—Swanscombe, Kanam, Kanjera—have been found in open country,
and that has to be one reason there are so few of them.

Tule Springs was an open-sky camp site.

So were Santa Rosa and Lewisville; so were the camps of
Renaud's Clactonians; so were those of the depositors of the
tools of paleolithic design that Ruth D. Simpson of the Southwest Museum has been assembling for years from the shores of
southwestern lakes that have long since ceased to exist; so were
the locations where tarried the hackers out of the extremely
crude tools Thomas Clements, of the University of Southern
California Department of Geology, has picked up in Death
Valley, the like of which have also been picked up in Lower
California, by Brigham A. Arnold, of the Department of Geography, University of California at Berkeley; so must have
been the stopovers of the makers of tools found along Imlay
Channel in Michigan, where Carmen Baggerly has picked up
thousands of worked pebbles which he relates in form to those
imputed to the paleolithic in southeastern Asia. Small wonder
the first seekers of an early American found nothing when they
dug in caves. The earliest Americans were not cave men.

5

Importers and Inventors

Fontéchevade does help us understand Tule Springs, then; the discongruities of time and space will prevent us from carrying an analogy too far, but, to be fair, it makes more vivid what analogy exists. The cultural and technological phase that the European Tayacians were passing through a hundred and fifty thousand years ago, Tule Springs man was passing through *more than* (the more than must be emphasized) 24,-000 years ago. Now it would be a pleasant change of pace to leave Tule Springs man and his Lewisville and Santa Rosa compeers and get on with the next 30,000 years of American prehistory. But, as we have indicated, American prehistory can be written from two contrary biases, the Hrdlicka one and the one Willey calls "extreme isolationism"—the one here espoused. It is necessary, by reason of this espousal, not only to profess the existence of an early paleolithic American, but to argue that he had consequences. For if he simply existed, and then vanished, he is worth a footnote only, not the several chapters that have been devoted to him. Most archaeologists will not now be too captious about his mere existence; but the proposition that this must have resulted in progeny who eventually became the Amerinds of, say, 1000 years ago, and the further proposition that this progeny must have passed through several cultural stages, the implements and methods of which they thought up out of their own heads—these challenge vested interests in physical and cultural anthropology and the challenge must be met.

Choosing, by the eeny-meeny-miney-mo system, to face the cultural anthropologists first, we are compelled to begin by

saying that our extreme isolationism is known among them as
the view of "independent invention," or more often, "the fal-
lacy of independent invention." The orthodox view, that what
appears in America as culturally new or progressive was an
Asiatic import, is called the "diffusion-by-migration" theory.

To the minds of the orthodox, the Amerind not only did not
invent—or even precipitate the innovation of—agriculture,
pottery, the bow and other projectile weapons, basket weaving,
shelter building, canoe construction, and other useful arts and
artifacts, he was not even capable of conceiving them. The
sanction for this derives, I am afraid, from the wholly unjusti-
fied presumption that these arts and artifacts could, by divine
plan, be invented only once, at a single point in time and
space, and the rest of mankind had to wait for knowledge of
them and their manufacture to be bruited to them by conquest
or trade. It is my impression that this attitude is a translation
into cultural anthropology of the story of the Garden of Eden,
and is self-evident principally to those who hold that the doctrine of original sin has historic validity. Certainly a great deal
of archaeological time and money has been spent in searches
for the place where agriculture or some other cultural innovation began. There would be no objection to this if, when such a
place is discovered, it is simply designated *a* place, and not,
with premature self-importance, *the* place.

Those American prehistorians who submit themselves to
baptism into diffusion-by-migration, under whatever modification, by their college instructors have given their loyalties into
the hands of Ales Hrdlicka in naïveté and innocence; thereafter,
though they may accept the excavated, C14-validated existence of a Lewisville man, it is heresy to take him seriously.
For it is equally a matter of excavated, C14-validated fact that
horticulture and pottery and mound building do not appear
on the American scene until many thousands of years later.
And since these are innovations, and innovations must have
been brought here from the Garden of Eden, where they were
invented, then the Hrdlicka theory of late migrations is substantially vindicated, and Lewisville and Tule Springs man
might just as well not have been found.

Such an innocent was the last person you would have expected to be, the late, great Earnest Hooton of Harvard, who

flouted Hrdlicka's physical-anthropological tenet of an American Indian of pure Mongoloid extraction without a flinch. But he was a diffusion-by-migration-ist nevertheless, and the most cogent and entertaining of polemicists for his side.

"I have no use at all," he said in 1947, "for the anthropological isolationists who are determined to maintain the incredible dogma that there was no diffusion of inventions and ideas from the old world to the new, but only of naked human animals."

Overlook the fact that there is inherent in this the possibility that Amerinds might have invented some of their own artifacts. A diffusionist may admit as much in logic, but never when asked for an opinion *ad hoc*. If he were to admit that a single major advance—the independent invention of the projectile point, for instance—had been made by the Amerind on his own, then he would have admitted in principle the inventive capability of the Amerind—and once that cat is out of the bag there is no telling where it will drop its kittens. If projectile points, then why not pottery?

Regard, instead, the wonderful rolling thunder of "incredible dogma," delivered as from a Calvinist pulpit, and the scornful lightning lash of "naked human animals." For this is elenchus at its best, and by style alone Hooton has concealed from the casual reader, and from himself, two homely inconsistencies: (1) that the excavated record does not list a succession of visitations of Asiatics bearing cultural gifts like the Magi; such visitations are simply predicated on the grounds that innovations prove they must have happened; and (2) that man did come to America, as we have been at some pains to show, as a naked, or nearly naked, human animal.

Had Hooton been aware of the Santa Rosa, Lewisville and Tule Springs finds he would probably have been one of the first to acknowledge their significance, for he was not a man who feared to change his opinion in the middle of his reputation. But what must be noted is that his pronouncement assumed that these naked human animals would not be found, and that the beaten paths of Asiatic culture bearers would be.

Those readers who find themselves so stimulated by American prehistory that they want to read more about it should be here apprised that they will find these two assumptions em-

bedded in almost every report or treatment of American archaeology written before, to pick a presidential year, 1956. In
the December, 1955, issue of the *National Geographic Magazine* there is a long—21-page—specially illustrated piece on
the subject of the Folsom fluted-point maker and his predeces-
sor the Clovis fluted-point maker, and it is entitled "Ice Age
Man, the First American." Prepared with the assistance of
Frank H. H. Roberts, the Smithsonian authority on early Americans, it presents very circumstantially, with maps of migration
routes as though these had been traced by surveyor's rod and
theodolite, the description of these hunters beating their way
through Arctic tempests, across Bering Strait and south to
Colorado, New Mexico and Texas. So elaborate and assured is
the presentation that it takes considerable effort of the will not
to succumb to its gospel.

But no rumor could be more ill founded. As long ago as 1952
Alex Krieger was pointing out the dangers of bringing the
Clovis-Folsom point makers out of Siberia, where no such projectile-point complex had been found, in the same symposium
volume in which Gordon Willey was trying to explain away
the awkward fact that the traces of such a complex that had
been found in Siberia were younger than in America. Comes
now, in 1957, Paul Tolstoy, who has taken as his field of special
interest the archaeology of that Siberio-Alaskan province we
have surmised to have been cut in two by the trench of Bering
Strait. In his definitive "The Archaeology of the Lena Basin
and Its New World Relationships," published in *American
Antiquity* for July, 1957, Tolstoy writes:

"As for paleo-Indian [Clovis-Folsom-Yuma] point forms, it
can only be repeated here that the negative evidence from
Siberia is by now obtrusive enough to raise serious doubts as to
their derivation from Asian prototypes."

A fuller case for the invention of the Clovis-Folsom fluted
complex, as well as other projectile-point forms, in America, by
Amerinds, will be expounded later; it is adverted to here only
as an instance in which one of the diffusionist assumptions—
that culture bearers from Asia could be taken for granted—
has become the dubious seed from which has sprung a rank
growth of anthropological error—in this case, charted in a
magazine which is particularly careful about avoiding it. But

this is only an instance, not the whole story; Amerind cultures, trait by trait, and Amerind peoples, tribe by tribe, have all in their time been pulled out of the Asiatic grab bag on the sole and explicit grounds that the Amerind had not a potentiality for bettering himself, nor the talent to invent the means.

It now becomes proper and possible to set the task of this book exactly: it is to follow the sequence of Amerind cultures as though that sequence began with, or at a stage approximating, Lewisville–Tule Springs, and proceeded developmentally hence to the days when the Amerind *was* visited by culture bearers—from Europe.

It is not by any means established that Tule Springs man, with his chopper–hand axes and discoidal bifaces, is representative of the earliest American cultural stage. The finds already mentioned, by Renaud, Simpson, Clements, Arnold and Baggerly, and others by George Carter of Johns Hopkins University, resemble the rudimentary lithic complex at the base of the Olduvai Gorge column, the out-and-out pebble-tool, large-flake tradition. They are mainly surface recoveries, except for one not very helpful site of Carter's, and hence cannot solve geologically any problems of priority. But what is to be noted about them is that typologically they seem to be precedent to the Tule Springs phase, and that in 1956, when Miss Freddie Curtiss, in the name of the Archaeological Survey Association, took to Europe some forty-seven selected ones (including some Black's Fork specimens) for examination by experts in the European paleolithic, the experts promptly rejected the odd-ball pieces, but found some that were not in the least odd-ball, that conformed nicely to standardized European types of the earliest lithic horizons—Clactonian-Abbevillean.

We will claim, then, that what happened between the manufacture of these crude and eolithic tools and the Tule Springs inventory was the first step in an Amerind industrial advance. The next step is predicated on much the same kind of evidence. After Tule Springs, as was previously mentioned, a wet era set in, and the Tule Springs site became lake bottom. This era was succeeded in the climatic cycle by an arid period throughout the entire west—from the Rockies to the coastal Cascade Range—when all lakes began to dry up. By tracing

along the beach lines of these ancient lakes as they receded,
Simpson, Clements, Arnold, *et al.*, have been able to discern a
succession of cultures in the artifacts they find strewn along
the strand lines. These cultures we know to be subsequent
to Tule Springs, not only by the chronology of geologic events
but by the new types of tools that make their appearance—
projectile points and grinding stones (they occur on a succession of fossil beaches of playas, or dried-up ancient lakes, and
are here called the Playa Sequence). This hard-to-define cultural horizon is the critical period of the Amerind's inventiveness, when he first made the specialized tool for hunting, the
spear point, and that tool for the preparation of vegetable
foods, the mano. It is only stressing the obvious to remind
ourselves that most Amerinds were still living by the stone
projectile point or the mano or both in 1492; and the mano
has not gone out of general use in Mexico and in Central and
South America even today.

After Tule Springs we do not come upon a documented and
dated site, then, until the time of the lowest levels of the Wendover Caves, in Utah, which were excavated under the direction
of Jesse D. Jennings and reported on by him in *Danger Cave,*
the fourteenth in the series of Memoirs of the Society for American Archaeology and one of the two or three most important
treatises ever issued in American prehistory. There are three
of these caves, Danger, Raven and Juke Box (so help me; it
got its name from the fact that during the Second World War,
G.I.'s in training nearby poured a concrete floor there, installed
a juke box and instituted a self-morale-building program), and
the materials from the oldest levels gave a C14 date of 11,-
000 B.P. These oldest levels are pivotal to our belief in a sequential development from Tule Springs, which is not only in the
same Great Basin area but relatively near the caves, for not
only do they contain an amazing inventory of artifacts, including the spear thrower or throwing stick (atlatl) and baskets
and fiber sandals and netting and matting of cordage, but in
their lithic technology, to quote Jennings, "Percussion techniques predominate; preferential use of large flakes, cores and
spalls." This is the old, the Tule Springs tradition, over 12,000
years later.

Once inside Danger Cave, the most important of the three,

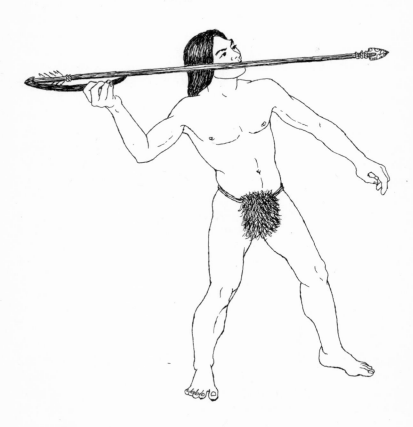

SPEAR CASTING WITH AN ATLATL

The atlatl (an Aztec word) has been used for spear casting by Amerinds for at least 10,000 years. There are several forms. In one form the spear shaft lies in a groove or channel and the butt of the spear rests against an up-crook pocket. The usefulness of the curve in the above model is that the finger hold does not interfere with the lie of the shaft. In another form the spear butt is engaged by a distal bone hook and the spear shaft is held away from the atlatl by the fingers. These forms, and probably others, were used in America. The atlatl makes possible a harder cast with a flatter trajectory.

we are nearly home. The occupation levels here ascend from 11,000 B.P. to the third century after Christ. Other sites in the vicinity pick up the chronology from there and bring it to the day you read this, for the Gosiute Indians still wander that neighborhood, around Great Salt Lake, which is the bleak fossil of the once great fresh-water inland sea of Lake Bonneville, like unlaid ghosts mourning over a ruin. And their desert-adapted culture has not appreciably changed since the first human entry into Danger Cave just as it was released from the shrinking waters of Bonneville.

This quick run-through of the continuity of cultures from Tule Springs to contemporary Gosiute illustrates by what right and on what grounds the diffusionist-migrationist attitude is opposed. Jennings' absorbing reconstruction of the Danger Cave sequence can hardly be read without partisanship being roused: what Jennings discovers these people, whom he designates the Desert Culture, to have accomplished, in adapting successfully to one of the most treacherous environments in the world, ought not to be taken away from them and assigned to others by academic willfulness. But sentiment would be a trivial excuse were it not encouraged by homely reason. Unless Tule Springs man killed himself off by sudden conversion to a cult of celibacy, either he was exterminated in the Great Basin area by the pitiless caprices of the climate, or he coped with them, and survived. When we find the projectile points and manos of the Playa Sequence we surmise that he had learned to make up for the scarcity of game on the droughted grasslands by devising a weapon that insured him of getting what there was, and he had learned to make a tool (or to use a natural one, for any hand-size pebble is a mano) which would render the grain of these grasslands directly edible, when there was no game to do it for him. These tools certify survival. But when we come to Danger Cave we know we have found in detail what the Playa Sequence only sketched. This Desert Culture could not have been an import; it is too precisely adjusted to the environment in which it was found, with a tool or a method for exploiting intensively every resource that could give aid and comfort to man, to have any relevance to any other set of conditions; these tools and methods were too bone-instinctively and blood-intuitively reactive to every exigency, every vagary of this milieu not to have racially grown up with it.

Now it has crossed my mind that the point at which many archaeologists stick, in this matter of isolationism versus cultural injections, is at the verb "to invent." It immediately and directly denotes the construction of a heretofore unthought-of implement employing a heretofore unthought-of principle to perform a specific task. In just this sense I doubt that the spear

OLDEST DATED POINT

These are the two faces of the oldest dated (about 11,000 years) projectile point in America at this time. (The dating of the Clovis fluted point found with Lewisville man is questionable, as explained elsewhere.) It comes from the lowest level at Danger Cave, and though it is incipiently stemmed and unfluted, its overall lanceolate form seems to relate it to either the Clovis or the one-shouldered Sandia, both of which are certainly as old or older but neither of which has been C14 fixed as to earliest provenience.

was ever invented, in America or anywhere else. But when you throw your imagination into low gear, and adjust its speed to the problems of primitive people, you can see many ways in which spears, tipped with stone projectile points, might come about without, in the strictest sense, being invented.

Later it will be proposed that the basic Tule Springs scavenger-hunters split into two living traditions, the herd hunters of the Clovis-Folsom stock, and the food gatherers of the Desert Culture. Both of these traditions developed stone projectile points, and after some reflection we can suppose a natural and simple way for each to have fallen into the habit.

It is my fancy that the first spearlike implement used by the Desert Culture was a poke stick or probe. Food gatherers would be particularly likely to have used staves or poles or long sticks to poke into animal burrows, into rock crevices, and even to reach with; and when they attached a flake to the end of this poker it would not have been so much to make it lethal—a pointed end would have served this purpose—as to make a snag or hook by which the reluctant prey could be dragged forth when transfixed. But this chip would need to be pointed or sharpened in order to enter the carcass in the first place. When, by reason of the toughness of the prey, or the necessity of getting at the bottom of things, the poker user pushed it hard, releasing it from his hand, he made a cast. How long it would be before a man throwing a poke stick at an animal in a hole would think of throwing it at an animal out of a hole, I can't pretend to know enough about primitive minds to guess. But in any case the spear was probably put together for another use before it became a spear by somebody's learning to cast accurately with it.

In the case of the spear used by the herd hunters, I imagine it to have also been a conversion through several steps from a stick, in this case a kind of fending stick or shepherd's staff. When these herd hunters caught a stray, usually a weakling or a young one away from the herd, their maneuver was to drive it toward a swamp, where it would bog down, or toward a cliff, over which it would topple to its death. A stick or cudgel was certainly a natural implement for this kind of job, being brandished as the animal was herded toward destruction, used as a goad when the hunter got close enough, and used as a fending rod on those occasions when the hunted beast turned and charged. When the prey became mired finally, but was still alive and kicking, these shepherd's staves, sharpened to a point, were used, we may say unequivocally, to lance him to death—and so were, but for the matter of being cast from a distance away, already spears. (From the close observation afforded by this kind of kill, the pattern of an ani-

mal's mortal zones would have been learned long before it
became a matter of hunting technique to hit them on the run.)
Obviously the only problem here is to get a stone point on what
is already a spear. This came about, I feel sure, not with the
intent of making the spear itself more efficient, but of combining the functions of spear and knife in one simple, easy-
to-carry hunting implement. The stone point added nothing
appreciable, at least in the beginning, to the penetrating effec-
tiveness of a wooden spear with its own fire-hardened point,
but the hunter did have available then the cutting edge of
stone, which no reshaping or improvement of the wooden shaft
would have given him. This reconstruction gains something if
you consider that the hunter, at least when he went hunting,
had no place to carry his implements except in his hands because he was a "naked human animal."

The stone-tipped spear was not "invented," we must conclude; it is the sum total of several phases of opportunism in
food-getting experience, and it could plainly have been arrived at from several different directions. The two routes outlined above are particularly applicable to the Amerinds of
Tule Springs provenience, because they did split into two different traditions of getting their living, I believe, and it was not
so much their success in inventing the game-taking spear that
confirmed them in their ways of life, as the separate experience
series by which they arrived at it.

Let us imagine, for the moment, that two small bands of
Tule Springs–type Amerinds come together by chance at a water hole in the postpluvial period, when their country is beginning to become arid. Their only hunting tool or weapon is
a sharpened staff which they use in a dozen different ways.
Having shared the last of their food at a meager evening feast,
the two chiefs face the task of leading their followers to the
source of the next meal.

Chief Straight Stick, having only stripling and inexperienced
youths in his band, or having surveyed the grasslands without
finding any sign of big game, elects to go upstream, in the hope
that something will turn up. Eventually he comes to a hillside
swarming with rattlesnakes (those who have read the Lewis
and Clark expedition accounts will know what I mean; there
were places where rattlesnakes swarmed by the thousands),

and for this kind of game his stripling huntsmen, with their poke sticks, are ideally adapted. The band lives mainly on rattlesnake fillets, and now, feeling some confidence in its ability to take care of itself by exploiting rock crevices and animal burrows, seeks out those places where such food can be found. And after that day they never seriously return to herd following again. Eventually they will develop a javelin-spear, perhaps five or six feet long, from their poke stick, as we have outlined. But it will not be the same kind of spear the herd followers develop.

But Chief Hard Head, on the other hand, can count on three or four full-grown hunters, and he leads them across the prairie in a hunt for a stray mammoth or bison that cannot keep up with the herds, which are growing fewer as the grass thins out. Now Chief Hard Head, in his last encounter with game, had had the misfortune to lose his stone knife somewhere, which caused him considerable delay in feeding himself. This has always been an annoyance to Hard Head, and this time, when he chips out a new knife, he simply thongs it to his weapon stick for safekeeping. The band is lucky; it falls in with a crippled bison yearling which has broken a leg by stepping into a hole, and Hard Head's knife is at hand, when he needs it, to cut up the kill. Because this band is skilled and hardy, it continues to find big game and consequently is more confirmed than ever in this way of life. Eventually the whole band takes up Hard Head's practice of lashing knife to weapon stick, until one day a lazy oaf decides it is too much trouble to be forever tying the knife on the shaft and untying it, so he ties his knife to the end of the shaft, where it can be used without being untied. Very soon he is not only cutting with this knife, but stabbing and thrusting with it, oafishly unmindful that when he launches it in a distance cast he has, by this arm movement, invented the stone-tipped spear—again.

It may be seriously doubted that the plot was quite as neat as this, with the generalized Tule Springs scavengers differentiating into the specialized herd hunters and the versatile Desert Culture all in one morning, yet the circumstances must have been as simple. When climatic and ecological conditions continue unchanged, decisions do not have to be made daily; routine dictates them. But as a drought or other blight begins

MANO AND METATE

This Desert Culture homemaker is grinding seeds
into flour or meal with two grinding stones, a pebble mano
(Spanish for hand) stone, and a free-stone slab metate.
Such a combination of implements was portable and in
stoneless environments had to be carried from camp to
camp; the wear on many of these artifacts attests to generations of use. But often enough, an exposure of bedrock
with a relatively flat surface was used as the metate, and
any hand-sized river pebble became a mano.

to affect normal food supplies, then alterations have to be made
in the pattern of living, so that new food sources can be acquired, and these alterations must begin with as simple, but as
momentous a decision as Chief Straight Stick and his under-

manned tribe taking to the hills. So many millions of times
must such problems have presented themselves to the human
race that the factor of probability alone would so operate that
some of the solutions led out of the labyrinth of savagery.

It is not hard to believe that the stone-tipped spear—as
well as grinding stones and many another implement of basic
stone-age usage—was invented again and again in the fashion
just suggested. Were it not that we can imagine such a plausible and impersonal mechanism of "invention," we might be
somewhat more tentative about the succession of cultures between Tule Springs and Danger Cave being a growth of related cultures. But the suspicion persists that had Tule Springs
stock not carried on "invention" and advancement, it would
have petered out into extinguishment.

What ought, perhaps, to be emphasized is that in taking issue with the migrationists, we do not suggest that the Amerind
was too proud or independent or mulish to borrow. Certainly
he threw away his robes and tomahawks, bows and pottery,
quickly enough when he encountered the white man's wool
blankets and steel axes, muskets and iron kettles. What it is
plainly up to the migrationists to show is not only that there
were gift-laden migrations from Asia, but that they brought
something the Amerind did not already have.

6

 *March of the Mongols*

 Having had our tilt at the cultural anthropologists and their diffusion-by-migration theory of Amerind prehistory, we must now confront the much more formidable position held by the physical anthropologists. For it is inseparable from our argument that the Amerind contrived his own culture that he is *sui generis,* of a race distinct and self-contained, with blood lines not too often crossed, and never obliterated, by neo-Asiatic hybridization.

This argument forces us into direct contradiction of universal anthropological authority, which without exception repeats and repeats and repeats that the American Indian is Mongoloid, through and through, from cranial index to hair follicles. But if the logic of our "isolationism" demands this contradiction, then we will undertake the task of supporting it; this is the logical imperative.

Almost the first discovery in our research on the thesis of an American Indian race is that such a thesis has never been seriously advanced before. It is implicit in MacGowan's neat briefing of the evidence on early Americans, but he does not state it nor, I believe, quite intend it. Yet it is a thesis that, by the very nature of inductive logic, demands to be posed and examined full dress. For a physical anthropologist to rest at all secure in a conclusion that the American Indian is racially Mongoloid, he must also have tried the available data in other arrangements to be sure it is not equally susceptible to the opposite conclusion. But beyond the sheer neglect to do this, which is due, I believe, to overconfidence by physical anthropologists in the incontrovertibility of their observations—which as often as not appear quite subjective—is another untested possibility—that what is descriptively Mongoloid in the Amerind is not, by any logical compulsion, congenitally Mongoloid.

The multi-migrationists are not entirely without differences within their own ranks. At one pole is Ales Hrdlicka, who maintained the Mongoloid racial purity of the American Indian with an emotional fervor that was more literary than scientific. Exactly opposed to this severely monoracist-origin view was the hospitable view of Hooton—whose migrationist bias we know well from previous quotation—who saw in the American Indian a little of everybody. In a day when his reputation was probably not as puissant as Hrdlicka's, he spoke out loud the results of his craniometric study of a series of skulls at Pecos Pueblo, New Mexico—of a respectable age of 1500 to 1800 years—wherein he saw traits suggesting to him: a remote Mediterranean ancestry (this would be Caucasoid, or "white"); a somewhat brow-ridged, "primitive" strain, probably Australoid; a dark-colored strain, Negroid but not Negro; finally a Mongoloid strain, both pure and diluted by Armenoid (round-headed) and proto-Nordic genes.

This was quite a package, but Hooton's observations had considerable influence with other anthropologists, who began to see the Amerind as of polyracist origin also, with only the difference that each found traces of different strains in different proportions. In a critique of these polyracists, J. B. Birdsell in 1949 icily dismissed all this polyracist-origin nonsense with the comment that it was founded on cultural, not skeletal argument. A one-time pupil of Hooton's, but certainly no disciple, Birdsell, after a stint of anthropology in Asia, threw the weight of his conclusions strongly in Hrdlicka's favor. In his paper, "The Problem of the Early Peopling of the Americas As Viewed from Asia," delivered before the Fourth Viking Fund Seminar in Physical Anthropology, Birdsell expounded this opinion:

"I have developed the hypothesis that these aborigines are of dihybrid racial origin, that the *universally admitted Mongoloid element* [italics mine] has been adulterated only by an archaic Caucasoid contribution from the Amurians, a group considered to have been ancestral to the living Ainus and to the Murrayians." Though this is, verbally, a middle position between Hrdlicka's mono- and Hooton's polyracist-origin theses, it is actually almost identical with Hrdlicka's, for it sees the hybridization as repressive of the Caucasoid contribution in favor of almost complete Mongolization. And the position of the very influential A. L. Kroeber, of the University of California, fits tidily in the tight interstice between Hrdlicka and Birdsell.

When, therefore, A. S. Romer, in his 1954 edition of *Man and the Vertebrates*, came, in the course of a general discussion of racial origins, to the American Indian, he could only sum up anthropological judgment thus: "It was suggested earlier that Mediterraneans may have been early invaders of the Americas. [Romer is quite aware that something is off-key in this paean to Mongoloidism, but it is not his problem.] However that may be, the great majority of the American [Indian] population is of Mongoloid descent."

There it is, the latest, the ultimate word: The American Indian is Mongoloid, and any racial strains and cultural traditions earlier than Mongoloid incursions in force were trivial and superficial.

And the Mongol was late on the prehistoric scene. Hear Birdsell:

"First, the available evidence suggests that the Mongoloid race has reached its present geographic limits by a very rapid, possibly an explosive, expansion. Anthropologists seem to be in general agreement upon this point. Second, the advent of the essential elements of neolithic culture seriously disturbed the pattern of the hunting and collecting economy. Agriculturists potentially can attain a much higher population density than peoples limited to a hunting and collecting economy. This factor has important repercussions in terms of population genetics. It seems probable that the appearance of agriculture and the expansion of the Mongoloids are not separate factors but rather appeared conjointly in Asia."

Let us accept this as meant: Mongols became ascendant as a population element simultaneously with the expansion of agriculture into Asia from Asia Minor, where it is thought to have originated. The excavations of Robert J. Braidwood for the Oriental Institute of the University of Chicago in the Jarmo area of Iraq, specifically seeking for the rootlets of agricultural beginnings in a place where they seemed to run deepest, found the first traces at about 8000 B.P. When there is subtracted from these eight millennia an interval for the spread of agriculture to eastern Asia (the early agricultural Chinese Yangshao site is guess-dated at about 5000 years ago), plus an interim while agriculture was giving impetus to the "explosive" expansion of Mongoloids and building up the internal population pressures which compelled emigration to America, and, finally, the travel time to highland Peru, any expert in third-grade mathematics can snap out the arithmetic remainder: the Mongol American Indian had to be as late a comer as Hrdlicka grimly insisted.

How can this encirclement be escaped: the Mongoloidism of the Indian proves his recency; his recency proves his Mongoloidism? The chapter just preceding was devoted to a précis of Amerind culture from Tule Springs to Gosiute Indians; must we now admit that this culture prevailed only in the Great Basin and did not spread over all America; and that the rest of America was substantially and effectively settled by Mongol-Indians much later in prehistory?

We do not have to, if we say what the situation starkly requires that we say—that the American Indian is not Mongoloid; that he is racially Amerind. So let us say it, then, and see where it gets us.

Exactly what a Mongoloid is, descriptively, is rather generally agreed on. He is round-headed; he is wide-faced, with prominent cheekbones or malars; he has brown eyes over which droop the epicanthic folds that give him his slanty-eyed oriental look; he has a smallish, fleshy nose; he has shovel-shaped incisor teeth; he is not inclined to hairiness; he is stocky of build.

Does the American Indian resemble the Mongoloid exactly? Hooton's study of the Pecos skulls led him to answer no, and to suggest all sorts of admixtures; and he was generally supported by European physical-anthropological and American cultural-anthropological opinion. Romer frankly discusses some of the long-headed (in contradistinction to Mongoloids as round-heads) groups found now and in the past in this hemisphere, and Birdsell writes, in the piece already quoted, "In any case,

the living peoples of mainland Asia today do not provide the
full evidence needed to solve aboriginal American racial origins."

Amerind variance from the Mongoloid norm or genotype
we will leave to Romer to detail. He says, "There are, however, some differences from the Mongoloid pattern; the skin
has more of a brownish or reddish tint; the nose, in sharp contrast to the typical Mongoloid, is frequently high-bridged and
convex, and there is seldom any marked trace of the Mongoloid fold of the eyelid." Add to this that the malars are not
as prominent as in full Mongols, and that chin development
varies, and the argument for an American Indian race—for
the Amerinds—has won itself a vantage.

Now these differences do not seem to mean so much to
Birdsell. "Surveys of living Indian populations have in every
case revealed evidence of Mongoloid elements. In many
groups a Caucasoid strain also appears to be present. In a few
areas it is suggestive of an Amurian [east Asian] origin."

Hooton derived this Caucasoid strain—now generally con-
ceded to be present in the Amerind, though in various degrees
—from a multiplicity of sources, among them the Australoid,
considered by him to be an ancient Caucasoid-Negroid cross.
Hrdlicka fairly screamed at this suggestion of Australoid cross
in his pure Mongol-Indians, and Birdsell seems to have found
the way to get the Caucasoid strain in while screening the
Australoid out.

Having worked from direct, in-the-field observation of modern aborigines, Birdsell holds that the Australian is a comparatively recent type, a trihybrid cross which has stabilized,
in its present homeland, out of Carpenterians, a tall, dark people; Negritos, a small, dark people; and Caucasoid Amurians.

These Amurians had to be, in Birdsell's accounting, of a roving and fraternizing disposition. Not all of them got to Australia, to submerge their genetic personalities in the trihybrid
blackfellows. Some of them turned north and there interbred
with Mongols. The result, Birdsell says, is *offspring who look
like American Indians.*

How could anybody, with such evidence staring him in the
face, believe, then, that American Indians were anything other
than Mongols slightly bastardized by a skylarking delegation of

Amurians passing through on their way to nowhere? This is
Birdsell's proposition and it is one of the latest and most serious attempts to establish a Mongol lineage for Amerinds; it
was received with straight-faced gravity by reviewers in scholarly journals, among them a reviewer in *American Antiquity*,
who remarked: "Out of Birdsell's work in Australia has grown
a plausible explanation of the peopling of America that should
make it embarrassing for anyone to find Australoids and Mela-
nesoids among the remains of our early Americans."

Embarrassing? Why? With this look-alike procedure—and
the convenient ignoring of cultural and geographical factors—
you could prove the American Indian to be the descendant of
almost anybody, because it depends on what he subjectively
looks like to me and to you. That he looks like Amurian-Mongoloid crosses of today may not be to the point at all, for if
he has any antiquity at all, he may have looked like somebody
else on arriving here. The reader will, of course, recognize
the old Hrdlicka bread-and-butter ploy, used quite recklessly,
but appropriately, in support of a favorite Hrdlicka concept. Hrdlicka, in relating Ohio Mound Builder skulls to California Indian skulls, after all only leaped a continent for his
comparison. Birdsell, in relating Amurians to California Indians, has blithely vaulted the world's largest body of water at
its widest point.

For the American Indians that Birdsell's Amurian Mongols
looked like were not the Sioux nor the Mayas nor the Iroquois
nor the Lamokans nor the Incas nor the Mound Builders, but
Cahuilla tribesmen from inland Southern California. By cited
reference Birdsell extends the resemblance somewhat, but the
effort of extension only serves to draw attention to the egre-
giousness of the project. If there is a way to make Mongoloid-
Indian co-genesis plausible this is not it. Birdsell's scholarship
seems to a layman serious enough, and his evidence meth-
odologically sound enough, but it stops so far short of his conclusion, the Amurian-Mongol parentage of the American Indian, that his leap across the chasm can be taken to indicate
only that he wanted at all costs to get there.

I will not go into Birdsell's swipes at the hawklike Indian
nose, that very markedly non-Mongoloid trait, since they seem

to mean that he wishes people wouldn't mention it so often or at least would give some attention to other explanations of its flagrant mockery of Mongoloidism, and their only effect is to display Birdsell's antagonism for what is being silently thumbed at him.

There can be only one possible reaction to the Birdsell thesis, treated here not for itself alone but because it represents the pro-Mongoloid school: It is really a very difficult task to prove the Mongoloidism of the American Indian when you get down where the rubber meets the road, and when the genesis of the Amerind is cleared up it will not be by the physical anthropologists, but by a careful correlation of the archaeological-cultural evidence Birdsell thinks so little of.

But some progress has been made. How do Amerinds now diverge from Mongoloids? The color is not quite the same; the nose is sharply variant; the eye fold seldom occurs; the malars are reduced; the chin is not predictable. But there still remain in common the shovel-shaped incisor, the round-headedness and the straight black hair. Or do these remain?

The shovel-shaped incisor might be indicative if it were found only in Mongoloid heads but it is as old as Sinanthropus, in whose 350,000-year-old fossils it has been found. And when you stop talking about incisors only and listen on the subject of the Amerind's total dentition (to Albert Dahlberg, of the University of Chicago), you learn: "Indian teeth are less specialized in most respects than other racial groups. Carabelli's cusp is very infrequently seen in Asiatics. . . . On the other hand the Indian population to the south [of the Eskimos] all seem to have a degree of this trait." I am not expert on dentition but I am dubious of comparisons in which but one tooth and not the mouthful has to carry the argument.

Nor is the Indian so all-out round-headed as a glib plying of the term insinuates. Of the eight population varieties into which Georg K. Neumann classifies Indians in his "Archeology and Race in the American Indian" (in a symposium volume, *Archeology of Eastern United States*), two have cranial indices of 71, which is quite long-headed; two are just at the border of long-headedness, at 75; one is 76, one 77 and one 78; only the Deneids, from the Pacific Northwest, where the one indisputable Mongoloid invasion of the Athapascans left its mark, are safely broad-headed, at 81. The simple and unweighted average of Neumann's classifications is 75.5; the median is 76.

If Birdsell had been frankly scouting out look-alikes, Hrdlicka had already given him one. (Yes, Hrdlicka did soften somewhat on mono-Mongoloidism, and on early man, too, in the evening of his career.) And it was a better one than Birdsell's Amurian-Mongoloid crosses. It was Magdalenian man, a western European whose bones are found apparently synchronous with a style of ancient cave paintings of fifteen to twelve thousand years ago. Coon thus describes him: "Those [skulls] of the Magdalenian show an increase in facial flatness comparable to that of Mongoloids, *except for the nose, which remained prominent.*" (Italics mine, and for obvious reason.)

The Magdalenians were hunters of reindeer, that is, dwellers in a normally cold climate, like the Eskimo, with whom they have been compared; and Coon has explained this kind of broad face, under the skin of which there are specialized layers of fat the better to head into icy blasts, as an adaptation to a cold, dry climate. The Mongoloid face is not, then, something that has happened only once in the career of mankind, as a result of an inimitable mixture of genetic strains; it can occur wherever an arid Arctic climate has had to be endured long enough to have induced the adaptation. And that climate is not something that existed only in Asia; Amerinds faced it for perhaps twenty thousand years in glacial and postglacial America. What, then, distinguishes one race of cold-climate hunters from another? The nose, and the Amerind nose is Magdalenian, not Mongoloid.

So the Mongol argument hangs, it would seem, by the hair.

In the preceding recital of Amerind-Mongol pseudo similarities, the occurrence of round-headedness in our Amerinds was passed over much too facilely for the kind of problem we have already posed it to be.

Of the round-headedness of the final Amerind population, the peoples swept into oblivion by white conquerors, MacGowan has this to say: "To be sure, we have now—and have had—Indians with long skulls, particularly in the eastern part of the United States, and to some extent on the Great Plains.

But their number is not large, and can never have been large, compared with the great bulk of round-headed Indians of the two Americas."

This overstates the case for round-headedness in two ways: It does not expressly say when round-headedness was dominant, and by using the blanket term round-headed it conceals the fact that whereas two of Neumann's eight population varieties are round-headed, two are also long-headed; and the other four are in the middle range where those who see them as long-headed have as good a claim to them as those who see them as round-headed. The truth is that all Amerinds, taken together, are not as round-headed as all Mongols taken together, and Amerind round-headedness is not decisive either for or against a Mongol heritage.

Nevertheless, Amerind round-headedness cannot be disposed of by verbal maneuver and its incidence imposes on us the obligation of explaining how it came about, if it is not to be explained by Mongol bequest. We have already made it quite clear that long-headedness is an invariable characteristic of both neo- and paleo-man primitive skulls; and not only have we taken the position that primal Amerinds came early enough to America to have carried their brains in dolichocephalic brain cases, but we now urge that this long-headed lineage was never seriously interrupted over most of America. Do we hold, then, that long-head ancestors begat round-head descendants? The answer, of course, is yes.

If a primal feature of all human and hominid skulls was dolichocephaly, then the present-day predominance of round-headedness can be the result only of a progressive tendency toward round-headedness, expedited by dietary and other factors, and there is no inherent reason why this same tendency should not have been as operative in an Amerind population as elsewhere. In this light the middle groups of Neumann's series should now be viewed as belonging to the upper limits of long-headed classification, since the direction of change is from long-headed to round-headed.

What MacGowan meant is that the number of Amerind individuals, as distinguished from the number of types, who were round-headed considerably exceeded the number of individuals who were long-headed. But this is what we would expect.

The tendency to round-headedness is encouraged and accelerated by a change from dietary reliance on rough foods to a reliance on soft, mainly carbohydrate vegetable staples, since soft foods do not require as heavy a development of the muscles of mastication. And this is exactly the change brought about by the introduction of the corn-beans-pumpkin horticultural complex among the Amerinds. Among some the introduction was comparatively late; among others it merely replaced or supplemented an already bland fare of vegetable foods obtained by harvest of wild plants and shellfish; among still others advanced tendencies toward round-headedness were certainly speeded up by interbreeding. All in all, then, the rates at which groups of Amerinds progressed toward round-headedness would have been uneven, and we would expect to find Amerind skull types distributed along the cranial-measurement scale just about as Neumann has classified them. But we would expect most individuals to be round-headed, as MacGowan reports, because the soft diets which encouraged round-headedness were derived from abundant and constant sources of shellfish or vegetable harvest which provided a stable basis for population and hence contributed to its increase in the areas of plenty.

But archaeology cannot simply be argued; it must be dug up. And what is dug up is what is indispensable in our thesis of transformation: Underlying later, round-headed populations in every important area of American prehistory are long-headed peoples of non-Mongoloid pattern. A quick roundup of instances can well begin with the long-headed Basket Makers of the southwestern United States, and at the opposite end of a cross-country diagonal are the Lamokans in the Finger Lakes region of New York, of an age of 5500 years, and succeeded in the New York region by a long line of peoples Ritchie has named Point Peninsula. In the middle sector of this axis are the dolichocephalic shell-midden people of Pickwick Basin in Alabama, other archaic-age peoples of Ohio, Illinois, Kentucky, Indiana, etc., and the important Hopewellians. In Florida the skull of 6000-year-old Melbourne man is long-headed; in the Pacific Northwest, Philip Drucker points out that under the round-headed Deneids lies the culture of earlier long-heads. At the land's end of Tierra del Fuego the

Yahgans are long-headed; at the Arctic verge of North America the Eskimos, for all the anomaly of their Mongoloid, cold-adapted visages, are likewise.

What happened to all these long-heads, if the contact-period Indians were round-headed by the testimony of archaeology?

In the first place the excavated evidence for the immigrations of Mongoloid round-heads rushing in to replace long-heads just does not exist. Froelich Rainey (who may be the only archaeologist-anthropologist with a TV following, through the program he moderated some years ago called *What in the World*), a specialist in the Arctic, after mentioning that Alaska is poor pickings archaeologically, observed in a symposium in 1952, ". . . we have no evidence for those migrations across the [Bering] Strait which we have all assumed took place during the neolithic period." And he concludes his paper, on Siberio-Alaskan contacts, thus: "It is also a fair guess that there was a very long period after the present climatic conditions developed when neolithic men found this region of the world too tough to handle." What the archaeology still suggests, in 1958, is, at best, according to the previously mentioned study by Paul Tolstoy, contact between Alaskan Amerinds and Asiatics in this Amerasian province. Tolstoy sees diffusion of traits by this contact, diffusion in both directions, diffusion but no migrations.

Nor does the spade uncover the scenes of carnage that would attend a decimation of long-heads by mighty round-head warriors. Indeed, in the Pickwick Basin shell middens, where a habitation span of perhaps 4000 years is heaped together, the transition from long-heads to round-heads is accomplished without any breaks in the cultural continuity. If there was an intrusion of round-heads into the long-headed population, it was by a people without anything very exotic to offer; why one set of people would want to dispossess another set from one of these shell heaps, when he could start his own shell heap almost anywhere he chose, is no less a good archaeological question for being slightly derisive.

But it is in the record that real intrusions did take place. The long-heads in the drama were Ritchie's Lamokans, long-headed and of "gracile build," who were residing peaceably at Lamoka Lake, New York, some 5500 years ago. At about

4500 years ago there entered this neighborhood a robust, round-headed people whom Ritchie calls Laurentians, who made, aptly enough, large, broad projectile points, whereas the Lamokans made small, narrow, slender ones. There were other differences in cultural inventory, and when Ritchie found Lamokan skeletons with Laurentian projectile points in their backs and then no further trace of Lamokans, he suspected ambushes, internecine warfare, and eventual Lamokan extermination. The suspicion was short-lived. Continuing his investigations, Ritchie finally came upon a site on Frontenac Isle in Cayuga Lake where the signs of acculturation were unmistakable—Lamokan and Laurentian tools domestically commingled and skeletal material that could only be interpreted as hybridizations of Lamokan gracile long-headedness and Laurentian robust round-headedness. What strife there had been between Lamokans and Laurentians had evidently been domestic.

At the time of discovery this incursion of round-headed Laurentians had the look of being the Mongol immigration nearly every archaeologist then accepted as an article of faith, and the view was unchanged by evidence that showed the Laurentians to have come from the West, probably along the southern shore of the Great Lakes, and very likely out of Wisconsin. But Wisconsin is only a way point on the route, if you veer northwest from there, to Bering Strait.

It all seemed very clear; the Laurentians brought one tool with them, the so-called semilunar knife, which is like a salad chopper and was usually made of rubbed slate; such a knife is still used among the Eskimos of today, and is called the ulu, or woman's knife. There seemed to be a Laurentian-Arctic relationship. Yet the longer these two cultures were stared at, the more it became evident that, despite the difference in tool inventories, both Lamokans and Laurentians were adapted to essentially the same kind of habitat and means of livelihood; they coalesced with the greatest of ease because there were no differences to be ironed out, and the Frontenac culture was only a continuation of both.

The Laurentians were traced westward because of their possession of certain tools of copper, and in Wisconsin and the copper district of Michigan there were known to have lived people who were given the name of the Old Copper culture because of their work in the pure copper that occurs in nuggets and easily mined outcrops thereabouts. This was all very interesting, but not especially hair-raising until quite recently, when a C14 test gave the Old Copper culture an age

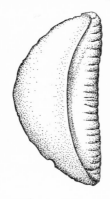

SEMILUNAR KNIFE

The derivation of the semilunar knife from the chopper, especially a two-edged chopper like that shown in Chapter I, seems a reasonable deduction. But the semilunar knife has no such wide distribution nor early appearance as the chopper and seems to have been used by "Eskimo"-related cultures. Here are shown both chipped (right) and rubbed or ground (left) forms, the rubbed form being distinctly Eskimoid, though found in New Jersey and New York.

of about 7500 years; which means, simply, that Old Copper folk had been living in this area a couple of thousand years before a group of them, out of pique or sheer exuberance, decided to move eastward and become Laurentians. No Asian immigrants, these Laurentians, then, but as home-grown as pawpaws, and a second look at their projectile-point inventory confirmed this: there were forms here that had counterparts or prototypes all over the United States.

But we are interested, at this stage of discussion, in cranial indices. The Old Copper people were long-headed, as befitted Amerinds 7500 years old, but not too long-headed, as befitted the progenitors of the Laurentians. The cranial index of the observable skeletal material is 74.

We may conclude that this Laurentian case of brachycephaly evolved in America, then, but this is not quite the same thing as seeing it evolve. For such an observation we will have to return to the Pickwick Basin shell heaps, now under the waters of TVA-created lakes, but excavated before flooding, under the direction of William S. Webb and David L. DeJarnette, by WPA, in its time the greatest of all contributors to work in American prehistory. Many of these middens are tremendous, stacking as high as 30 to 35 feet of interlarded shell and high-water silt deposits. The excavation was done before C14, but charcoal from the 4-foot level of a midden 10 feet deep was dated, when that technique could be applied to it, at 4700 B.P. And in case the charcoal had become contaminated in the meantime, it must be remembered that the adulterant will always induce a more recent rather than a more remote age. Because the dated charcoal was less than half the depth of the midden it is not to be deduced that the age of the bottom level was twice 4700 years, but perhaps 6000 B.P. is not too wild an estimate for this midden's beginning.

The study of and reporting on the skeletal material found scattered throughout these middens (shell, by counteracting acidity, makes a good preserving matrix) was done by Marshall T. Newman and Charles E. Snow. They found that the early shell was deposited by distinctly long-headed people and the top levels by distinctly round-headed people, and they summed up their findings thus: "It seems a reasonable guess that in at least part of this area an earlier dolichocranic population was later displaced, *probably after considerable admixture*, by a brachycephalic people."

The italics are mine, for this *considerable admixture* is the focus of our interest. There was no break in the cultural column, no clues to violence and nothing apparent in either the shell heaps or their dwellers to excite cupidity to conquest. We have every right to believe that the population was homogeneous and of a related, uninterrupted lineage. For if there ever were perfect laboratory conditions for turning long-heads into round-heads these shell heaps afforded them. What diet could be softer than one of which a staple was the flesh of river mussels, and other staples consisted of boiled roots, berries, fish, ground seeds and nut meats? When, during the course of midden habitation, pottery appears, nothing more need be said.

It has been pointed out by Coon, and others, that the "article of diet" which probably started man on the road to thinner skulls, brachycephaly and smaller teeth, was fire. By roasting meat, man softened its fibers so that jaws and teeth were spared some of the work of making it assimilable, and they responded to lighter duty by reducing in accordance with the task. The skull, no longer having to sustain the pull of muscles and jaws strong enough to crack nuts, became thinner-walled, rounding out with nothing to constrict it externally, and with the brain doing a little broadening of its own. But roasting is only the beginning of ways to use fire to soften food; there are parching and baking and boiling and stewing. Stews and soups practically do not have to be chewed at all. Though Amerinds could make stews and soups in baskets by stone boiling, clay pots eliminated this cumbersome method, and we can be sure that after pottery appeared in the Pickwick Basin middens, soups and stews were unfailingly on the menu.

The Pickwick Basin river-bank dwellers—who lived this mussel-eating life for perhaps three to five thousand years, a period as long as the recorded history of human beings—can be summarized thus: The only certifiable agent which can account for the "admixture" of long-heads and round-heads, and the replacement of primal long-headedness by developmentally later round-headedness, is hereditary change, with each generation of crania advancing it by an imperceptible degree.

If it were possible to recover nearly all the skulls of every generation that contributed to the accumulation of the Pickwick Basin shell heaps and to place them in proper genealogical order, this gradual curve of change—or change of curve— would be justified by illustration—or perhaps it would be invalidated. But when we must conclude that we have but a fraction of the total population, we must also consider it likely that whole generations are either missing or insufficiently represented. In this case we may not treat the data assemblage as though it were a whole; we must assume that what is missing had meaning and information to contribute.

When physical anthropologists take the skulls placed in their hands by the archaeologists and begin to dichotomize them

into long-heads and round-heads, their assumption is that they
already know what meaning and information these missing
clues will contribute: they are to contribute more long-heads,
and they will increase the statistics but not alter the meaning.
A mild protest has already been registered against this lumping
practice; a skull with an index of 65 and one with an index
of 74.5 are both lumped as long-headed, but the round-headed
skull indexed at 75.5 is hardly less long-headed or more round-
headed than the 74.5 skull. To classify a skull as long-headed
is a half-truth if it is a member of a series not likewise long-
headed within a narrow range, for it implies that this is a
static cranial characteristic which the owner transmitted unchanged, despite or because of the food he ate and how he
lived, when what the owner actually did transmit was a weak-
ening in his long-headedness and a yielding to round-headedness, to which he added some slight impetus by the way he
lived his personal span of years.

The foregoing is by no means intended as a critique of the
work done on the Pickwick Basin skeletal remains by Newman and Snow, a task I am not in the least prepared to
attempt. When the analysis was made, all physical anthropology and archaeology was under the influence of the Hrdlickan dictum of round-headed Mongol invasion and nobody
was asking how it came about that round-heads always replaced long-heads whenever the period of habitation was pro-
longed. The truth is that the Pickwick study is the first in which
conclusions were reached that were later—in the hands of
Snow—to precipitate the view taken here, that long-headedness was dynamically changing into round-headedness, under
the obvious environmental influences.

Within the periphery of the entire Pickwick shell midden
series, Newman and Snow were able to isolate groups of
skulls with a kind of tribal or clan identity. Taking these into
consideration, they wrote this summarization:

"The shell mound series, separately and collectively, appear
to be somewhat more variable than the rather homogeneous
Basket-Maker series from Grand Gulch, Utah. They show about
the same order of variability as the northeastern Algonkin series which is made up of crania from five states, but if anything
are a little more homogeneous. In short, while the shell mound

series appear to be fairly homogeneous, they are by no means
so much so as is possible in American Indians."

But "fairly homogeneous" is sufficient to cover the fact of
their continuity, their innocence of wholesale replacement,
while the qualification "by no means so much so as is possible"
leaves tolerance enough for the change we have boldly supported.

There are other such situations of earlier long-heads and
later round-heads in what can reasonably be assumed to have
been a closed-habitation situation, and Hrdlicka was involved
in one of these, to the edification of neither himself nor any of
the disciplines over which he had influence.

The Aleutian Islands, streaming from the chin of Alaska almost all the way across the Pacific like the beard of Rip van
Winkle in a following wind, would have an irresistible attraction to a man of Hrdlicka's views. Almost any archaeologist
would consider himself blessed among men to be given a
chance to investigate there, but as the stoutest champion of
late Asiatic migrations Hrdlicka had a particular stake in what
their archaeology had to disclose. It certainly was thinkable
at that time that a maritime-skilled neolithic man had short-
hopped his way into America by boat with the Aleutians as
ports of call, whether or not other men had come by the less
aquatic route of Bering Strait, far to the north. Almost any
scientist would have approached the Aleutians with the antici-
pation of opening a surprise package. But not Hrdlicka. The
Aleutians were no surprise to him. Before he dirtied a spade
he knew what he was going to find.

Theodore P. Bank II, who has done recent work in the Aleutians, very soberly reports (in a paper called "Cultural Succession in the Aleutians," published in 1953) of Hrdlicka's work
there in the 1930's, ". . . he collected from many sites ranging
across the entire Aleutian chain and succeeded in assembling
a large body of skeletal material, which he proceeded to sort
into two groups based upon morphological differences. One
group had distinctly broad heads and the other comparatively
long heads. . . . From this he inferred that there had been
two migrations of physically distinct people into the Aleutians,
the first composed of 'Pre-Aleuts' who were followed a thousand

years or so later by the 'Aleuts.' He failed, however, to find an accompanying abrupt change in culture upon the arrival of the later people. *Unfortunately, Hrdlicka kept inadequate field records and his large skeletal series must be viewed with considerable reservation because he pooled the skeletons without any regard for excavated depth or cultural association."* (Italics mine.)

No more damning bill of particulars against an archaeologist could be written; it is the more damning because it is not an intentional indictment at all but a necessary explanation of why Hrdlicka's material is not amenable to re-evaluation and hence is of no possible use to present-day Arctic specialists. Nor is Bank's report circumstantial; one of its sources is the eyewitness account of W. S. Laughlin, who accompanied Hrdlicka and saw it all happen.

This, of course, seems more reprehensible to us than it did to Hrdlicka. He was a man of enormous ability, which was at the service of an ineffable self-confidence. It did not occur to him that he was perpetrating an outrageous scientific swindle. As soon as he found round-heads and long-heads, he knew, he knew beyond any possibility of method or technique proving him wrong, that his views of round-head Mongoloid immigrants were vindicated and that he was right.

The actual situation in the Aleutians, viewed by a reliable specialist of a later generation, George I. Quimby, is thus summed up in Bank's piece:

"A recent examination of Aleutian artifacts by Quimby [1946, 1948] has led him to return to the concept of three periods, which, however, are not generalized culture periods but rather stages in the development of artifactual types. *His view is that both culture and physical type changed gradually* during the occupational span, which, as will be pointed out later, is a view that can be supported by archaeological evidence at hand." (Italics mine.)

"Both culture and physical type changed gradually"—how simply it reads and how succinctly it totals up the presentation of this section of our argument. If this modulation of the long-head into the round-head occurred in one place in American prehistory it cannot be eliminated as an occurrence in other places where the conditions were right, except on positive evidence that something else did occur to produce an apparently similar effect. Yes, round-headedness was distributed throughout America by migration—internal migrations of Amerinds who had acquired it in the course of their long and environmentally adjusted occupancy of this hemisphere.

The hardest leg of the course has been run; round-headedness does come about in response to what are almost certainly natural environmental constraints. There are also other, artificial, much more direct and immediate constraints—deliberate deformation by head binding, and the use of the cradle board for infants. Snow and Newman noted that where they found round-headedness in Pickwick Basin they also began to find evidences of head deformation. And J. Franklin Ewing, S.J., has summed up evidence from all over the world to the effect that ultrabrachycephaly correlates with head binding and with head shaping by the cradle board. Snow, studying the skulls of the round-headed Adena folk, who lived not only synchronously with the long-head Hopewellian Mound Builders, whom Hrdlicka found so handy, but among them, noted that, acting on some theory of beauty or mechano-psychology, they practiced both cradle boarding and head binding. These are but instances; the papoose strapped to a squaw's back, his head being shaped by a hard cradle board, is one of the few impressions most of us hold about Indians in general that is generally accurate. But this seems all too absurdly simplistic, after the panting and the strain of the Pickwick Basin propounding. Could so peremptory a means have been sufficient to impose a significant change on a whole body of people?

There seems no longer to be any doubt that it did. As early as 1936, Carl C. Seltzer formulated the thesis that the long-headed Basket Makers of the southwest had become, about 700 A.D., the round-headed Pueblos after adopting the hard cradle board. Seltzer reiterated this proposition in 1944 and it has been confirmed by all subsequent archaeological work in the southwest. The cultural continuity, hence the physical consanguinity, of Basket Makers and Pueblos is now accepted as axiomatic, and they are called by one name, the Anasazi.

Nor can the Mongols be credited with a cultural assist to physical round-headedness by having contributed head binding or cradle boarding as customs to Amerinds. Mongols are conspicuously not head deformers.

Rainey's conclusion that there is no evidence in Alaskan archaeology to support migrationist theories may now be extended to the entire Western Hemisphere. No migratory infusions are required to explain anything in American human physical prehistory, though this must be stated with the caution that an uncompromising attitude about migrations does not exclude diffusion of some cultural traits through contact of stable, resident Asiatic and American peoples, as Tolstoy suggests; to assume that Bering Strait was a moat across which Amerinds and Asiatics could not culturally observe and exchange is an absurdity of which no one would care to be accused.

What, then, after these many pages of critical review of Hrdlickan conceptions about the peopling of America, is a supportable alternative? Nothing, perhaps, that the reader has not already deduced; but a clear statement of it is certainly called for.

The physical anthropology of this study is founded on a modest but seminal paper by Charles E. Snow, that same Snow who was a collaborator on the Pickwick Basin studies of some 1200 skeletal individuals and the deducer of the use of head-shaping devices by the Adenans. Out of this background came a paper, delivered at the Viking Fund's 1949 seminar, called "The Sequence of Physical Types in North America," and two of its conclusions are of basic importance to us. Snow believes that: (1) several areas (of America), *and probably all*, were inhabited by very early groups of a type with a long face, high vault and usually—though not always—very narrow and long heads; and (2) many American types may well have developed locally, without the migrations that have often been postulated. It is now logically incumbent to clarify who we believe these early long-heads to have been and to recognize briefly the diversity of local types which a long occupancy of America has given the Amerind race the opportunity to disperse into.

The descriptive similarity of the skeletally gracile Lamokans and Caucasoid Mediterraneans has been called to public attention by Romer. If the primal population of America can be traced with any satisfaction to a root area anywhere on earth, the North African native heath of neo-man would be it; Hooton's polyracist musings amount to essentially this proposition. But it can be gravely doubted that the Lamokans of 5000–6000 B.P. held any heredity of even moderate recency from this geographically remote nativity. The similarity of Lamokans to Mediterraneans we do not doubt, and as Snow depicts it, this is what primal Amerinds looked like; but the Lamokans are, by the chronology, at least 30,000 years removed from their own Amerind ancestors, and the similarity can be accounted for by the extreme conservatism of the culture and the likelihood that population paucity imposed inbreeding upon the stock.

If the dating of Lewisville man at more than 37,000 years gives us the right order of age for the primal population of America, this occurred, as we have been urging all along, during the interglacial stage preceding the Wisconsin, at the very latest. But this "immigration" would hardly have been numerous. Few bands of neo-man would have wandered as far as Siberia; even fewer would have wandered farther, into America; and no band would have been large. When it is considered that the camp sites of these few immigrants, as they were pushed south from Alaska and Canada by the growth of the Wisconsin, were bulldozed out of existence by the ice sheet, it seems miraculous that we have any inkling of the existence of primal Amerinds at all. Certainly we can never expect to find evidence of their existence in Canada unless it be in glacially deposited gravels such as those in which Baggerly located his paleolithic tool series in Michigan.

The spread of population over the immensity of the Western Hemisphere from such paltry seed could only have been incredibly protracted (it is estimated that hunting-gathering populations increase at a rate of ten percent every hundred years), yet it was accomplished and there were Amerinds at the tip of South America at least 8000 years ago. This leads us to the tenable supposition that all or nearly all of the zones in both Americas which have been habitable for 9000 years have in fact been inhabited for this span of time, and this is time enough, as we know from Birdsell's discussion of Mongols, for a race to have phenotypically established itself. But our assumption has been that substantially all Amerinds descended from a mere handful of Adams and Eves who were undoubtedly themselves closely related or of collateral breed. Hence the diversity of Amerinds that was present when America first came within historic knowledge is a multifariousness of strongly adapted local varieties of up to 9000 years in age, hybridized only by migrations of other local varieties. But this was hardly a tight situation, for many local varieties had both the time and the isolation to develop salient adaptive characteristics, with the result that the Amerind race separated into roughly the same kind of climatic-zone peoples found elsewhere in the world—dark, heat-adapted people in tropical areas, lighter, cold-adapted peoples in temperate areas.

"The Indian type," says Nels C. Nelson, ". . . is separable according to some authorities into about ten more or less distinct varieties." Some of the features seen in Amerinds suggest the following to one authority or another:

The Japanese—the Semitic nose of the Mayas suggests this;

Alpine-Europeans—Hooton saw Northwest Coast Indians with some lingering incidence of gray eyes, resembling those of European round-headed sallow whites;

Melanesian-Australoids—this would describe a Negroid, or at least a black-skinned variety;

Egyptians—both Hooton and Roland B. Dixon saw skull series in America which reminded them of early Nilotic skulls;

Pre-Dravidians or Ainus—the "hairy" Ainus, who linger on in Japan in dwindling numbers like the blackfellows in Australia and the bushmen of Africa, are an archaic white race, of the same stock as some of the Asiatic Indian population;

Magdalenian man—the Eskimos, with their Mongoloid faces and most un-Mongoloid long-headedness, have been seen as possible survivors of Magdalenians of 15,000 years ago;

The Pygmy—possibly because of his color and ultraround-headedness and the short stature of some tropical South American tribes;

The Mongol—of course.

When it was thought that America had been entered by migrants *ad lib*, it was not only interesting to try all these similarities on for fit, it was necessary in the pursuit of the truth. We, however, take our text from Snow, who says most Amerind varieties could have evolved locally; we even say they did. Therefore these similarities are pseudo similarities, and are instances of parallelisms: what happened to skulls and skeletal types elsewhere in the world also happened here. Why shouldn't there be Egyptian-looking skulls among the Basket Makers and certain Indians of northern Mexico, as Hooton noticed? Here were the same desert-Egyptian conditions.

Yes, the over-all "Mongolism" of the Amerind is a specious Mongolism and I think we should be no more surprised by it than fooled by it, any more than we should be surprised that when the Amerind race pooled into local varieties it should produce pseudo Egyptians; the human race is not infinitely variable. Kurt Stern in *Principles of Human Genetics* has defined race as "a genetically more or less isolated division of mankind possessing a corporate genetic content which differs from that of all other similar isolates." It would seem to me that by the sanction of this definition we may say we believe in an Amerind race.

The whole argument has to rest squarely on whether American archaeology has ever presented us with evidence of humans of pre-Wisconsin age; it has, and that evidence was found in Denton County, Texas, near Lewisville.

7

Old-fashioned Winters

The birthing of Lewisville man from his gravelly matrix in 1956 was attended by such a jury of archaeological midwives, including Alex Krieger, E. H. Sellards and Jack T. Hughes, that no scientific bar sinister can ever be slashed across his escutcheon. He is, unfortunately, no more a man than the quondam residents of Tule Springs and Santa Rosa. He is a hammer stone, a flake scraper, a chopper, many hearths and the bones that were the garbage of his feasts. From these it appears that he ate both high and low on the hog. He did not disdain turtles, snails, mussels and snakes, but by one dodge or another he was able to come by bison, a wolf, rabbits, deer, a camel's head, a prairie dog and a mammoth leg. What one of these meat-taking dodges was seems plain enough from the evidence at the site, but few are quite willing to believe in it.

It is a single spear point, bifacially worked and of the fluted design called Clovis, and if it were accepted at face value it would be evidence beyond our wildest dreams of the inventiveness of the Amerind. Lewisville man has been accorded an age, as we have several times stated, of more than 37,000 years, but this, Krieger says, is twice the age of any other spear points found anywhere in the world, and these oldest of points elsewhere are unifacial, made on struck flakes, by Neanderthal.

No; this Clovis point is more than we are prepared to embrace. A half-dozen points, plus the industrial debris to prove that they or their like were actually fashioned at Lewisville, and we might listen to a revolution in conceptions of universal archaeology. But the chopper, hammer stone and flake scraper do not pose even a predisposition toward a projectile-point industry. These are the artifacts of a Tule Springs culture in an even more primitive stage, which is fitting enough, considering the age of Lewisville.

Then is the dating wrong? This does not seem likely. There is hardly a C14 date in America with such impeccable credentials. One thing Lewisville does not lack, in its 21 hearths, is all any laboratory would need of datable charcoal. And the two laboratories which ran the C14 tests were those of the Humble Oil Company, which used the latest and best in techniques, or no such date as 37,000 could have been recorded, for the ultimate dates possible by less advanced techniques range from 20,000 to 30,000. The first test was run on charcoal from Lewisville hearth number 1, where the projectile point was found; when it registered its astonishing 37,000-plus, a second test was undertaken on charcoal logs from hearth number 8. The result did not vary—it was still 37,000-plus. How much beyond 37,000 years the Lewisville hearths reach cannot be known until some other method of dating is devised; C14, because its half-life is only about 5500 years (see footnote pages 16–17), will count no higher.

The possibility of fakery by "planting" the Clovis point has been raised, and discussed, by Krieger, who has exonerated the excavators. Probably the most famous paleontological forgery of all time is the Piltdown jaw, which was finally pinned down about the time the Lewisville excavations were in full progress, and some by-stander could have had a mischievous notion set ticking by the news reports. If so he gave up an archaeological valuable in order to have his fun, for Clovis points are not easily come by. The Piltdown forger, it must be admitted, was cleverer; what he did was to treat the jaw of a modern chimpanzee to give it the same patina and other appearances of age as a human skull, to which he attached it. Anatomists never were satisfied with this contradiction of a human skull with a pithecine jaw and dentition, and kept doubting it until they had a means of attacking. The test used, the chlorine-dating method, was that by which the Swanscombe skull was shown to be of the same age as the interglacial fauna found in the gravel bed with it. The chimp was no older than the man who stole his jaw, but now the Piltdown skull is known to be a venerable 50,000 years.

But about the Lewisville hearths there can be no cavil; who

can fake 37,000-year-old charcoal? And so much of it. The 21
hearths range from 4 to 10 feet in diameter, and some of them
are 18 inches deep. There can be no doubt about their culinary
character. The bones of about 50 species of animals, from
snakes and snails and mice to bear, mammoth and camel, have
been identified as the dietary refuse of Lewisville man, with
one very revealing insight being afforded by it: no skeleton of
any large animal is found in entirety. What parts there are give
us to think that Lewisville man was not able to down specimens of big game, but probably had to salvage a leg or so by
driving off other scavengers like himself after the kill had been
made and the killer's share had gone to a more formidable animal.

As mentioned, no human skeletal material was found with
the Lewisville hearths, but by a correlation of geology a very
long-headed skull (cephalic index 60.7) found in 1920 in a
sandpit about 25 miles downstream and called Lagow Sand
Pit man is plausibly related. But this is not all that the geology
has produced. Lagow Sand Pit man and Lewisville man were
found in what is called the Upper Shuler formation, a stratum
which has always been supposed to have appeared during the
latter half of the Wisconsin glacier. But evidence has been accumulating lately that the Wisconsin formed only about 25,000
to 30,000 years ago. If this estimate is accurate, his more than
37,000 years make Lewisville man distinctly pre-Wisconsin.
On the other hand, if the Upper Shuler is only half the Wisconsin story, the duration of Wisconsin glaciation (whose last ice
disappeared a mere 3000–4000 years ago) is suddenly doubled
just at the moment when everybody was beginning to agree
on it.

But in either case, man can still be taken to have been a pre-
Wisconsin migrant and Lewisville man is certainly "ice-age"
man. And we couldn't say very much about "ice-age" man without saying something about the ice.

The term ice age, like cave man, is misunderstood by nearly
everybody, including the *New York Times* and the *National
Geographic*. It can properly be used only as an equivalent for
the geological age called the Pleistocene, which includes the
formation and spread, the recession and disappearance of four

great continental ice sheets and the three long, tropical, iceless periods between.

Ten or fifteen years ago the Pleistocene was thought to have been a neat 1,000,000 years long. Since then one line of reasoning and another have caused this to be cut to 600,000 and this is still very much an estimate. Every branch of science has contributed information on the duration or the cause and cure of glaciers, from cosmic physics to palynology, which is a specialty concerned with gathering pollen from a geologic soil stratum and deducing from this pollen what kinds of plants grew during the constitution of that stratum, hence what kind of climate then prevailed. Within a decade the duration of the Pleistocene may be known more exactly than it is now, because C14 dating, which cannot itself reach very far back into the glacial age, has stimulated experiment with other radiological approaches and the Rosholt or uranium-daughter-products method has lately begun to be used on subjects which, like Lewisville man, are "more than" the C14 result.

But dating of glacial materials is only half the problem. The other half is identifying what is dated; that is, this bone or that peat layer or fossil log was associated with which specific glacial advance or retreat? For not only were there four great glaciers, but the last one, the Wisconsin, left evidence behind of two or three major advances and subsequently two or three minor advances, all separated by retreats, and it is the Wisconsin and its aftermath which contrived the geology that most interests archaeology in this hemisphere, and the landscape that most interests us.

It has been determined that continental icing was worldwide during the Pleistocene. Glaciers occurred simultaneously in North American, Europe and Asia. Slight glaciation also occurred simultaneously in South America, but it is of little concern to American prehistory, though of great concern to those who try to explain glaciation by theories of change in the tilt of the earth's orbital axis, since such a tilt would have deiced the Southern Hemisphere like sun on a frosted windowpane instead of glaciating it.

More or less corresponding to the glacial periods in the lands that were glaciated, were the periods of very heavy rain, the pluvials, in the melt-warm southern climes. Thus while nobody is quite sure what caused the reign of climate that induced glaciers, it is positively known what formed them: There was an enormous amount of precipitation, and where it fell as snow it did not melt; and that is what a glacier basically is, a monstrous snow pile, so vast that it sets up its own system of climate and its own life cycle.

The way the term ice age began to be misused seems to be that when Louis Agassiz first proposed glaciation as the cause of certain observable geologic phenomena he thought there had been only one period of icing. The initial formulation and demonstration of the theory of an ice age made news in the mid-nineteenth century; the subsequent discovery that this ice age had consisted of four separate glacial periods made only the pages of textbooks; this was not news, it was hair splitting, or higher mathematics, or both, and of importance only to eggheads. Newspapers and magazines are not written for eggheads, so the journalists continued to write of ice age and ice-age man, utterly indifferent to the fact that each glacial period was an ice age of its own, was separated from other ice ages by intervals of universal warmth from 60,000 to 160,000 years long, and has different human associations. Nine times out of ten the journalist means by ice age and ice-age man, the last or Wisconsin glacial period (in Europe it is called the Würm) and Wisconsin-age man; the tenth time he uses the terms accurately, but he has already cheapened by misuse the only words by which he can convey his meaning.

The first ice age or glacier period came upon the world about 600,000 years ago, very abruptly. Glaciation is not a regularly recurrent climatic event, happening every ten million years or so, like winter following summer. It is thought to have happened only once before in the 3,000,000,000-year course of the earth's geologic childhood. During most of this unimaginably long period, terrestrial climate had been comparatively mild, seasonally equable and without polar ice. Had it continued so, without the menace to survival of weather mortally changeable, man might very well still be leading the life of a hunter–food collector, in a universe of South Sea Island paradises. Who would have needed Edsels or Sputniks?

In Europe this first glacial period is called the Günz—the four European glaciers are named, in convenient alphabetical

order, Günz, Mindel, Riss and Würm—and in America the Nebraskan, after the state where its drifts or moraines were first
recognized. It lasted about 50,000 years and set the curious
precedent of pendulum-like behavior that seems to mark each
of the four ice ages: the glacier expands steadily to a maximum
coverage, recedes as though it were going to disappear entirely, and then comes crunching back to approximately its original extent—the periods between these climaxes of icing are
called interstadials. The effect on man and beast and vegetation of these reversals of climate, from wet and cold to hot and
dry and back again, was to keep them all constantly on the
move in search of conditions they could live with. Apparently,
during early glacial times most animals did better than man;
man had to keep moving around because he was naked and
ignorant and superstitious, but some animals, like the rhinoc-
eros and the mammoth, grew hair mats to repel the cold, and
lions and bears took to cave dwelling. The latter part of this
first glaciation was the time of Kanam man, who was, you will
remember, an equatorial African.

Why the first glaciation came to an end in 50,000 years
rather than, say, 100,000, is a question without final answers;
suffice to say that it did and even the geologic memory of it was
obliterated by the following interglacial, the Aftonian, a long,
semitropical age of 60,000 to 70,000 years, which eventually fell
victim to the second glaciation, the Kansan. This did not differ
substantially from the Nebraskan, save that it was followed by
the immensely long Yarmouth interglacial, during which the
climatic mechanism that initiates glaciers seems to have failed
to switch on, for the Yarmouth lasted 160,000 to 190,000 years,
from two to three times as long as the other two interglacials.
The Yarmouth was the summer of Swanscombe and Kanjera
man, hand-ax makers, and you have to go back to the crude
pebble tools at the base of the Olduvai series to convince yourself that they have made any progress since their Kanam ancestor.

It would not be at all strange if men of this breed drifted into
America during the Yarmouth. The ecology they then lived by
was as favorable in Canada as in Miss Swanscombe's bejungled
England, and we have already discussed the likelihood of the
road being open. No reasonable scientist can accept it as doctrine that warmth-loving Yarmouth-age man did not scatter

out during this near 200,000-year period to any place his feet
could take him, for a warm climate was nearly universal. The
world was truly then one world. The fact that the bones or
artifacts of any such man have not been found in all places is
not the argument it would like to be. Beyond the fact that
such remains would be scarce in any event (we certainly don't
find more than a billionth of the bones of individual animals
that once existed, nor, perhaps, more than a tenth of the species) is the further circumstance that these remains would have
been under attack by chemical, geological and climatic engines
of destruction for a quarter of a million years.

It is not earnestly important to the prehistory of America
whether Yarmouth-age man lived here or not. If he left progeny they would hardly have been numerous, and when their
numbers were augmented by the immigrants proposed by us
for the next interglacial, the resultant population would still
have been as racially related as Miss Swanscombe and Mrs.
Fontéchevade were, which was quite closely, according to
Coon. But to place the possibility of a Yarmouth American under archaeological interdict only succeeds in preventing us
from a frank and determined search for him in the right places.
One of the right places for a warmth-needing man to have
lived during the Illinoian glacial period that ended the long
Yarmouth holiday is the vast lowland that exists now as the bottom of the Gulf of Mexico. Withdrawal of ocean water for formation of the Illinoian certainly bared much of this vast area
for plant and animal life, and Lewisville is within what was at
least a temperate grasslands region roughly equivalent to the
Kanam-Kanjera environment during pluvial periods.

I am quite sure that, at this moment, I am not up to belief in
a 250,000-year-old Yarmouth American, but he cannot be rejected summarily; the negative evidence is simply not that positive; after all, there is a 250,000-year-old Englishman.

But Lewisville man, or his ancestors—depending on whether
the Wisconsin began nearer 30,000 or 60,000 years ago—gives
us our evidence for an Amerind during the Sangamon interglacial which followed the third, or Illinoian glacier and preceded
the fourth and last, the Wisconsin. During the Illinoian, which
is the Riss in Europe, there lived the first European who seems
to have been able actually to abide an icecap. This was not
Neoanthropus; it was Neanderthal, the first cave man, when it

was very smart and progressive to be a cave man, for neo-man had not yet learned to pull a cave around him for shelter and was still running off to Africa at the first cold snap. He did not come back to Europe until the Sangamon had warmed it up again. This Sangamon European is the Fontéchevade fossil, and as we know, cranially it was nothing in advance of Swanscombe, but its presence tells us this much: Miss Swanscombe had not been just a chance visitor to England; whenever the climate warmed, neo-man spread far and wide with the warmth. By adding the 190,000-year Yarmouth, when the world climate suited Neoanthropus, to the 60,000-year Sangamon, which was equally suitable, we get a total of a quarter of a million years for man to have found the back door of the Bering bridge into America. I think the odds are very much in favor of his having found it.

The crude stone pebble tools Baggerly has reported from the Thumb District of Michigan, and to which we have alluded several times, are found water-washed out of moraines which consist of materials laid down in Canada during an interstadial or interglacial and moved south to Michigan when the Wisconsin swept the Canadian decks. Most early man authorities in America, including Alex Krieger, and some European experts, accept some of Baggerly's collection of tools as man-made, which brings up the question, not yet answered, about which glacial advance pushed the moraine where the tools are found into its present position. Was it the first advance of the Wisconsin, after the Sangamon interglacial, so that the tools themselves were manufactured in Canada during the Sangamon? Because they are the tools of a paleolithic, pre-projectile-point culture, this seems very likely; the makers of such a culture were, as we have seen over and over, warmth-loving folk. But the moraine, and hence the tools, may be explained in another way; the Wisconsin itself, behaving in the way all glaciers seem to, made an initial advance, then withdrew somewhat, readvanced, retreated again, and during these major periods of advance and retreat fluctuated along its front like a gourmand fighting out a diet. One of the readvances may account for the Michigan tool-bearing moraines, with the tools themselves having been made during an interstadial, but if this be true, when and how did the makers get south of the ice?

In Europe the Würm, the Wisconsin's equivalent, is regarded as having had three climaxes, but the American Wisconsin is believed to have had two climaxes, the Iowan and the double-barreled Tazewell-Cary, with the third and last peak of activity divided into a complex of oscillations called the Valders, the Mankato and the Cochrane advances. This makes tough reading for the geologist, but one of the facts about the Wisconsin he is sure he is sure of is the identification of the Upper Shuler stratum, where Lewisville man was found. It has been correlated with the second major or Tazewell-Cary climax —not that the Upper Shuler was formed by the Wisconsin directly, since no glaciation ever invaded Texas, but the pluvial or rainy period that accompanied the Tazewell-Cary's occurrence brought about the laying down of this gravel layer. The lowest Lewisville hearth is at the bottom of the Upper Shuler, near the unconformity that separates it from the Lower Shuler, which was accumulated during the first or Iowan stage of the Wisconsin. When geologists say that one formation rests unconformably on another what they mean is that one or more strata are missing, like pages torn from a book, between the two contiguous strata, erosion being the agent of destruction. This unconformity fills in the picture of the Wisconsin as it affected Texas by accounting for the ice retreat or interstadial between the Iowan and Tazewell-Cary climaxes. Such interstadials are usually warm and dry, and warm, dry periods, which can quickly bring on desert conditions such as now prevail in the southwest, by killing off vegetative ground cover, are notoriously periods of erosion.

Because of what appeared to be a corroborative set of C14 dates on peat and wood and the like, associated with the advances and retreats of the Wisconsin and with the beaches of the several stages of the Great Lakes as the Wisconsin's fluctuations raised and lowered them, authoritative opinion was beginning to nucleate about the idea that the whole Wisconsin period was only about 30,000 years long; this is the "short count." Before C14 dating it was generally thought that the Wisconsin had been much like the previous three glaciers in its growth and dynamics, and hence must have been of the same order of duration, at least 60,000 to 80,000 thousand years—the "long count."

Unless the long-standing interpretation of the Upper and

Lower Shuler formations is forthwith repealed, Lewisville man, dated at more than 37,000 years, confirms this "long count" for the Wisconsin, a disconcerting eventuality for glaciologists and geologists who have been laboring for the last decade on the short count chronology. Obviously the archaeologists are also concerned, when their hypotheses rest on geologically dated events. Until the Upper and Lower Shuler formations are reconciled with other conceptions there can be no peace of mind. But I think I could accept the long count on the evidence of the first three glaciers, that a continental glacier is a self-regulating physical system that must run its course, rather like the common cold which lasts seven days if you go to bed with it, and is over in a week if you don't.

Whenever it began, the Wisconsin, as well as its predecessors, did not form where nearly everybody imagines its incubation to have been—the North Pole. The egg was laid many hundred miles south of there, much nearer to present-day Pittsburgh than the Pole, as a matter of fact, in the plateau east of James Bay, which hangs down, udder-like, from Hudson Bay into Ontario to a latitude of about 52 N, only 10 degrees north of the Bronx. Thence it spread in all directions, north as well as south and west. When it spread north, this arc of the glacial advance, called the Laurentide, met and joined up with an icecap that was simultaneously forming directly west of Hudson Bay, called the Keewatin. There was another ice center in Greenland, which eventually reached the North Pole, but this influenced prehistory very little though it's there yet. These ice sheets were very much like gargantuan boils on the face of the continents, and anybody who has ever suffered through an attack of boils will have no trouble seeing the beginning nuclei as the cores which give rise to the progressive swelling and spread of the excrescence.

Estimates vary, but the depth of ice at these cores was probably no less than 2 miles; some have guessed 5 miles; some as high as 10, or taller than the highest mountains. From these peaks the ice sloped off, at a gradient probably not perceptible by the eye, to the edge of the mass hundreds and hundreds of miles away because the surface was subject to water melting and running downhill. It is interesting to try to imagine what an exposed ice surface—that is, an ice-scape—would look like.

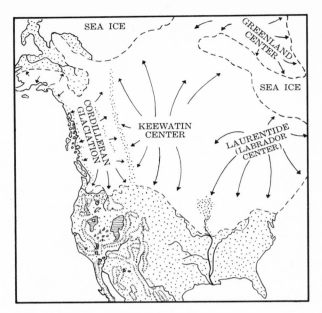

MAXIMUM GLACIATION

Shown here is the putative maximum extent of the
Wisconsin glacier. The Labrador or Laurentide Center
spread somewhat westward but mainly south, and it seems
to have been the one that most affected the United States.
The Keewatin Center spread west, west by south and
west by north, and is mainly Canadian in extent. Until it
met the mountain glaciers creeping out of the Rockies,
there was a corridor along the Rocky Mountain eastern
foothills between unglaciated Alaska and the unglaciated
Great Plains.

On the one hand it is thinkable that here was one vast, ocean-
flat plain, with snowfall after snowfall lying in even layers one
on top of the other, and brief spells of thaw under bright skies
melting the unimpacted snow and water running into the low
spots, filling them brimful, and the wind exercising a leveling
influence over all. Or this may have been a storm-ravaged topography, with melt-stream-ravaged gullies in it, and vast
short-lived lakes forming overnight under occasional summer
conditions, and drifts accumulating into permanent hills. For
the blizzard gales, as soon as some features of irregularity appeared, would begin to aggravate these; that is, where an ero-

sional scoring was effected in the surface, the wind would certainly begin to drift snow behind or in front of the elevation, and once such an obstacle became emplaced it would be subject to both aeolian destruction on its windward side and aeolian aggradation on the leeward side. Wind direction would have kept some flats polished and free of new snow, and wind deflection would have caused the wind-carried snow to be deposited against a near obstruction. The process would have been somewhat like dune making on the desert, except that ice is a more resistant material than sand, though snow is not, and that a most undesert-like factor, running water, would have been seasonally at work.

For there must have been warm-weather streams in this vast ice-scape, linked into real though short-term river systems and emptying into lakes serving transiently as seas. What summer was like on this glacial ice-scape cannot be compared too closely to what explorers note on the great Antarctic icecap, for an instantly comprehensible reason: the great continental glaciers were temperate-zone phenomena. Nor is this a semanticism. The temperate zones are the temperate zones not because they are so called after the fact of present climate but because of the angle at which the sun strikes them—that is, their positions relative to the tropics of Cancer and Capricorn. There had to be seasons of warmth on the continental glaciers as the sun approached and receded from its equinoctial zenith. Polar ice fields are never in receipt of such hot-eyed attention; they get only a curt and sidelong glance of sun for brief summer periods. We are left in no doubt that there was a summer during glacial epochs—a period of positive heat, not just a period of comparatively less cold—because Alaska was not glaciated (not enough precipitation), and Alaska had a growing season that produced well enough to support browsing and grazing animals, their carnivorous dependents, and tag-along man.

It is not too much to expect, then, that the glaciers were subjected to six weeks to two months of above-freezing temperatures, and even a month could produce a prodigious amount of melt water. Along the edges of the ice mass this could pour into overland streams outletting to the nearest sea or could reservoir into lakes, but there were places within the glacial area that were hundreds of miles from outlet. Melt water therefore had to pool on the ice-scape, and while in pool it would have added to what must have been one of the most important estival phenomena—evaporation and its attendant fogs and mists.

Probably the world's greatest authority on solar evaporation, and a rare distinction it is, is Ernst Antevs. He has never, as far as I know, discussed evaporation as it would have operated over a glacier in summer, but his studies of the drying up of the sprawling lakes of the Desert Culture area (one of which, Lake Bonneville, left Great Salt Lake behind like the last dregs in the coffee pot) confront us with the mighty potential of this process that we know best through the drying of the weekly wash. It appears likely that during periods of glacial growth the water vaporized by the sun must have lingered in the atmosphere until the dew point was reached, when it simply fell again as rain or snow on the glacier-scape, in a constantly replenishing cycle.

But change the main wind currents so that a dry, constant sirocco blows across the slush and ponds, sponging up the moisture avidly and carrying it off the ice, then so much bulk of ice might be removed by combined evaporation and run-off in a summer that it could not be replaced by subsequent snowfall; obviously this is the way glaciers died, by long periods not of warmth alone, but of warmth and drought.

We have already noted the similarity of the life cycles of all glaciers; one aspect of this is that they seem to have stopped at approximately the same line of advance—not precisely, of course; bull's-eye accuracy could hardly be expected when the factors being balanced are so titanic. It might be proposed that this was because south is, after all, south, and the farther you go that way the nearer you get to the equator, which is directly under the sun's rays a good part of the time. But this accounts for only one of the components, warmth. The drought factor, the switch from moisture-laden to dry air, must be explained somehow as deriving from the world ocean, which is the only source that could provide the amount of water that goes into a glacier.

Now what was happening to the ocean as the glaciers grew was that it was shrinking. When it had been reduced by the 400 feet that many estimate it lost, it must simply have stopped being the moisture supply for the winds blowing onto the North American continent. This could not have been because the ocean was dry—there was still plenty of water left—but it may have been that by now the continent loomed too high out of the water, especially in the area of the Rockies. For not only had sea level been lowered, but the incalculable weight of the ice mass depressed the land beneath the ice by as much as 1000 feet. The concomitant effect of this was to raise the continental edges at the shore lines, where there was no burden of ice. The Bering bridge would have been thus upthrust. What happened then, at least on the Pacific Ocean side of the continent, was that the winds began to drop all their moisture on the seaward side of the mountains and to sweep across the icescape wrung dry and moisture-avid. This is, of course, the reason for the western deserts of the United States today; they are arid not only because of scant rainfall but because what there is evaporates as soon as it hits the ground.

Why then, when the glacier had melted somewhat, replenishing and raising the sea level, did not the winds begin to blow moist again off the Pacific and fill the air with snow? Apparently they did make one strong and one moderate recovery which resulted in the two main climaxes or oscillations after the first onset. But then the dynamic wore down or the pattern was broken. Why? It is not easy to mint an explanation, but one factor was that even when melting removed the weight of some ice from mid-continent the land did not recover its height, nor did the coast lines lose theirs in immediate redress of balance. Instead, the continental rim and the continental interior seem to have "sprung" back into place, in a relatively short time, only after the glacier had, to all intents and purposes, disappeared.

This explanation of glacial retreat seems to leave in silent refutation of it the many lesser readvances of the Wisconsin's last 12,000 to 15,000 years, after the Tazewell-Cary maxima. Where did the water come from to supply the precipitation for these if the mountains to the west blocked the rain clouds? I strongly suspect it came from the Wisconsin's own melt water, which had collected in huge inland seas like Lake Agassiz, which once covered Minnesota, North Dakota, lower Manitoba and Ontario, and from southern pluvial-created lakes like

Bonneville and Lahontan and Cochise. Actually the available
drainage systems, the Mississippi and the Hudson, do not strike
us as having been able to carry off more than a fraction of the
ice that must have turned to water during a hot summer. Half
of the face of the land must have been water covered, and from
this source the snowfall-glacier cycle was regenerated for short
periods and minor readvances by local conditions of precipitation, until the available drainage system had returned, fraction
by fraction, most of the water to its original owner, the world
ocean.

It may further be objected that while all this may explain
plausibly the American glaciations, it does not explain the corresponding European-Asian ones, since no such barrier as the
Rocky Mountains walls off interior Europe from the North Atlantic. But the difference here, as we see it, is in the oceans.
While the Pacific did not freeze over, the North Atlantic did,
and very little moisture is going to be picked up by cold winds
passing over floe packs. Thus the Atlantic itself was "glaciated"
and its moisture locked in, and as the ice packs pushed farther
and farther south, the moisture-laden winds coming off open
southern waters dropped their precipitation farther and farther
short of continental Europe, starving its glaciation of needed
replenishment. But readvances here may have coincided with
retreats in America, where the dry winds, picking up moisture
off the Canadian ice-scape, carried it intact across the low-
lying Atlantic and did not drop it till they hit the higher European coast.

Very likely there is an optimum size for glaciers, a point at
which no amount of climatically possible rainfall can support
them any longer, or at least can continue them in their growth;
and a glacier cannot hold itself in abeyance. It can easily be
imagined that glaciers are self-perpetuating, inertial engines of
natural forces; once commenced they can propagate the conditions of their own continuance, as a Diesel engine, once its
pistons are heated to the firing point, will run, theoretically,
as long as fuel is fed into them. Thus glaciers seem to run on
until they have reached the size at which they upset so critically the geo-climatic balance that they cut off their own fuel
supply, i.e., precipitation. Once glacial decay has set in, it cannot be halted short of near extinction, because the inertia is in

that direction and melting begets the conditions of melting; the readvances, the temporary successes at stopping the regression, do not indicate that the geo-climatic balance has been shifted back in favor of reglaciation but only that limited, local contraventions are briefly ascendant. It would seem that once the glacier has borrowed to a certain maximum, the world ocean is suddenly reminded to demand full repayment of all that has been taken from it, and though the glacier procrastinates, delivering its melt water onto the land first, and then repossessing what it can, eventually it has to pay the entire bill.

What has been said here seems to de-emphasize the importance of temperature in the formation of glaciers, despite the pollen analysis of soils and the sedimentation records of ocean cores which show the correlation of low-temperature interludes on land and sea with glacial advances. But to say that there is correlation is not to discriminate as to whether the low-temperatured climate is the cause or the result of glacial advance. Too often and incautiously it has been assumed to have been the cause. This is not inevitable, for glaciation as certainly affects climate as an ice cube affects the temperature of a Tom Collins. What must not be forgotten is that while ice is water— and a glacier is, in actuality, a land-going sea which reduces the earth under it to the ineffective status of a sea bottom—it is a different kind of material in its thermal behavior from water and from rock, which its solidity makes it resemble. Its heat- and light-reflecting powers are much greater than water or the usual terrestrial mantle of rock, soil and vegetation, and its heat-absorbent powers much less. To compare the heat loss by reflection from ice with what heat would have been absorbed and retained had it fallen on an equal area of soil and vegetation, is certainly the first calculation that must be made in determining the climatic effect of a glacier in being. And when heat is absorbed by ice and used up in the melting process, the only possible result, as any observant bartender knows, is to cool off the surrounding medium. An ice cube as big as a continental glacier, or two ice cubes, one as big as the North American glacier, another as big as the Eurasian glacier, along with attendant, smaller cubes of glaciation in South America and in the Andes and Himalayas, are more than enough refrig-

eration to account for boreal types of pollen in soils and cold-
water deposits in sea-bottom sedimentation.

A drop below present temperatures does not seem at all
necessary, therefore, to explain the insemination of the glacier
egg. As a matter of fact, one of the most nearly convincing
theories about glacier formation posits a rise in temperature
to produce more precipitation-bearing winds to flow over
Canada, and there is one theory that very little alteration in
current climate patterns is needed to produce glaciers as
quickly as bad economics can produce business recessions.
This theory depends on the operation of Pacific maritime highs,
familiar to anybody who has ever watched a Tex Antoine
weather forecast. During the summertime, when the heat is
on the Pacific, these barometric-high-pressure systems sweep
cross-country from the Pacific to the Atlantic strongly enough
to ward off the push to the south of weather originating over
the Arctic Ocean. But these warm Pacific highs are weaker in
the winter, and frigid Arctic highs shove over or through them
and thrust almost straight south from the polar regions to the
Texas Panhandle, sweeping thence eastward across the country as the earth revolves on its axis; several times during the
winter of 1957–58 such Arctic highs put the blast on the highly
advertised tropicality of Florida, after overcoming Pacific
weather fronts.

Occasionally, however, usually in the late fall or early winter,
an especially strong Pacific high will actually ward off a cold
Arctic high, which will then drift eastward just north of the
Canadian border, and when it does the coldest temperatures
are usually registered at James Bay, that same James Bay in the
vicinity of which the Laurentide ice center was born. This area,
as a glance at the map will show, is a triangle of land two sides
of which are aqueous, with James Bay to the east and Hudson
Bay to the north, a perfect position over which cold winds coming from the west meet warmer, moisture-laden winds coming
in off the water and force the latter to drop their moisture as
snow. Apparently all this system requires to begin operation
now is somewhat warmer winters over the Pacific, which
would impel stronger maritime highs eastward during January,
February and March. And, not incidentally, these same
warmer winters would provide the winds coming off the Pacific into Canada with more moisture, the stuff of glaciation,

since warmer air can, of course, carry a higher moisture content. The mechanics of this theory can be better visualized if we assume for a moment the removal of the Rocky Mountains from their present satisfactory location and their lining up parallel to the Canadian border. Thus placed they would provide a positive year-round barricade against the invasion of the United States by Arctic highs, and climate here would become Mediterranean, to say the least, though probably better watered. And Canada would, in all likelihood, become a perpetual Greenland, or Siberia, depending on the amount of precipitation.

It appears, then, that to accept without question that the cold climate contemporary with glaciation preceded it somewhat, and was a cause of it, is injudicious. Calculations have been made which show, on paper, that a drop of 4 degrees Fahrenheit in the average annual temperature would start a glacial wart forming again in Canada; other calculations make this as high as 11 degrees. But none of the hypotheses about how temperatures can be made to drop, in the absence of a producer of cold like a glacier, have come up with a tenable causation; the temperature of the world through 98 percent of its climatic history has been on the average much higher than at present.

By far the most attractive hypothesis of glacier formation is that of the Pacific maritime high, which places its temperature changes not all over the weather map but in a single locality, and the right locality at that. It gets cold weather to James Bay and it gets some precipitation there. But it does not get precipitation there in really convincing amounts; and it does not illuminate what seems to be the periodicity of glaciation. A theory that Fred Hoyle advances in his *Frontiers of Astronomy* may supply this deficiency.

The fact that during the last 600,000 years we have had four great glacial periods in cyclic rotation of glaciation and complete deglaciation seems oddly at variance with the absence of ice sheets for the 100,000,000 years before then, and most hypotheses, such as the axial-eccentricity theory, which have taken the late periodicity into account, are confounded by the earth's failure to glaciate when the predicated causes had occurred before.

Hoyle's explanation, after he points out that there has not

been any lag on the part of the sun which would cause temperature drops, or any speed-up which would produce heat spells, runs thus: Something unusual must have occurred in the last million years which had not occurred in the 100,000,000 years before that, and this unusual occurrence, he says, was the breakup of comets and the entry into our atmosphere of the tiny fragments of debris, normal size about a thousandth of a centimeter in diameter.

Falling into the highest cloud layer, which is about 20,000 feet above the earth, these particles would probably cause the condensation of the moisture concentrated there into precipitation, a probability familiar to us since the first experiments with cloud seeding to induce rain artificially. But if this moisture were caused to fall as snow or rain it would destroy that protective layer of vapor which prevents radiation from escaping from the earth, and the effect would be as though the earth had taken off its topcoat. Add the Hoyle theory to the Pacific maritime high theory, which depends only on a warmer Pacific —and that can be had by the land-bridge blockade of Bering Strait which we believe existed, to keep the cold Arctic ocean currents out—and the sum is imposing. Now we have an explanation that encompasses glacial periodicity and the unique occurrence of glaciers in the last million years; it provides the necessary additional source of moisture—for the water vapor at 20,000 feet is rarely caused to fall as rain and represents a vast reservoir of water; and finally it provides for the *simultaneous* occurrence of rain and cold. Since all we needed in the beginning was a matched set of conditions which would get a glacier started and on its way, in the belief that it could then take care of itself, the meteorological aspects of glaciation may now be considered threshed out; but then, is any hypothesis ever fated to be utterly and absolutely and eternally right?

Three centers of glaciation, all in the eastern part of North America, have been mentioned up to now; there was a fourth one in the west, the Cordilleran, so called because it formed in the cordillera or mountain range of the Canadian Rockies. It was not, strictly speaking, either a glacial center or a continental glacier at all, but a flowing together of all the piedmont and valley glaciers of the coastal massif. Its direction of expansion was eastward, so that in time it met up with Keewatin ice expanding westward, and Canada was ice-bound from coast to coast. But this seam did not weld the two masses together into one ice sheet. When melting began in earnest, both the Cordilleran and the Keewatin masses withdrew from their own margins toward their centers, and the split between the two ice masses occurred on the leveled plain east of the Rocky Mountains, leaving an ice-free corridor, swampy but passable, roughly the route of the present Alaskan Highway, which leads from Alaska to Montana. This is probably the most arresting and suggestive feature of the Wisconsin glacier and the effect it has had on theories about American prehistory must be immediately apparent.

An ice sheet did not lie in insurmountable blockade across Canada from coast to coast, interdicting communication between ice-free Alaska and the regions south of the ice front through all the glacial period. It was penetrated during most of that time by two parallel routes which made migration theoretically possible until the last minute before glacial climaxes and immediately afterwards. Besides the eastern route beyond the mountains there runs the length of the Rockies, and within them, a geosyncline, a series of connected valleys called the Rocky Mountain trench, down which winds what has been called the oldest aboriginal trail in the world. Ice-free late and early like the corridor, its narrowness would have made it conducive to travel, not to lingering.

The corridor was closed for the last time during the Tazewell-Cary glacial maximum at about 12,000 B.P., and when it opened after that, Asians were free to parade into Montana at will. The actual trail along the trench ends at Flathead Lake, Montana, but if you take the right turns you can detour into the Great Basin, that enormous area between the Rockies and the West Coast ranges. With the Folsom hunters dated at 10,000 B.P. in Colorado and a Clovis fluted point recovered from the MacHaffie site in Montana; with materials from Fort Rock Cave, Oregon, dated at 11,000 B.P. and Danger Cave, Utah, dated contemporaneously—it is hardly any wonder that prehistorians have been seduced into the delusion that the Clovis-Folsom hunters and the Desert Culture people of Danger and Fort Rock caves were pilgrims come south along these ways. When, going cross-country, you strike a path and following it

you find habitations at the end, you feel justified in assuming
that path and inhabitants have a use relation. But you must
make sure of one detail: which way the traffic goes. These
primitive Alaskan Highways were not one-way streets, they
could be north-to-south routes, or south-to-north routes, and
you cannot say which until you have taken observations.

It would seem that in the orderly course of narration the effects of the Wisconsin on the cultural prehistory of America
should wait until that glacial period has been defined, described and calibrated with the ecology or living conditions it
imposed on the habitable portions of the hemisphere. There
were men in America during this ice age, so how did they
live and develop as a result of living under glacial or subglacial
circumstances? That is our narrative line. But what must also
be dealt with, apart from this effect of the Wisconsin ice age, is
its role as a determinant of initial settlement. And in order to
present this role properly and test it, we must scout somewhat
ahead of our story.

The fact is that there is nothing notable among the Amerinds
after 15,000 B.P. that should cause the prehistorians to look in-
quiringly north, up the Rocky Mountain trench, for an explanation. If we accept the short count, of about 30,000 to 35,000
years, for the Wisconsin, we perceive that Lewisville–Tule
Springs–Santa Rosa man had no need of the corridor; he was
already south of the Wisconsin before it formed. And if we accept the long count, of 60,000 to 80,000 years, these primitive
Amerinds must have been forced south by its advance; they
would not have sought a corridor through it, for they were not
a cold-climate people.

Now it is an opinion later to be expanded that Lewisville
man was the forebear not only of the Desert Culture people,
but of the makers of the Clovis-Folsom fluted-tradition and
less celebrated types of projectile points used by the herd hunters of mammoth and other now extinct kinds of big game.
Whether the reader is prepared to accede to such a view at this
time or not, the likelihood that Clovis man was south of the
ice by 12,000 B.P. seems beyond question.

Eliminating the Clovis point found at Lewisville from the
argument, for reasons already given, we must admit that no
satisfactory prime or earliest dating for a Clovis point has yet

been rendered, but Clovis fluteds have several times been found at sites *beneath* Folsom points which have been satisfactorily dated at 10,000 B.P. The dating for early Clovis is accepted by Krieger at 12,000 B.P. at a minimum, and 18,000 B.P. maximum. We do find both types of points in Alaska, but when we find them there, they are not only scarce, they are in context with a sharply different culture, of an appreciably later date. It can hardly be held, then, that the makers of the later fluted points found in Alaska were the originators of this unique type and lost the Alaskan specimens on the way south to Colorado or New Mexico. The Rocky Mountain trench-corridor was used for route marching, it is safe enough to say, but the users were fluted-point makers wending north.

Since this "sharply differing" Alaskan culture of a later date has been introduced, it had better be described, not only to emphasize its differences from that of the fluted-point makers and the Desert Culture people, but to establish what kind of culture was in Alaska during the corridor days and might have come by the corridor, *but didn't;* or at least not until so much later that the corridor had widened out into a milieu. The date of the type site of this culture—called the Denbigh Flint Complex because it was found at Cape Denbigh, a hundred miles or so up the coast from where the Bering bridge must have collapsed—is about 8500 B.P., by geological reasoning, and J. L. Giddings, the excavator of Cape Denbigh, has, in the *Scientific American* for June, 1954, described its lithic technology as the most "sophisticated" in the world at this time, and for some time thereafter.

"Sophisticated" seems an odd modifier to apply to a lithic technology, but it is here not without its aptness. In the first place, the tools produced by the Denbighites are fine to the degree of being dainty; they are diminutive and precise; they have been made by hands long skilled in work of exact touch; and since there must be, if "sophisticated" is to be nicely used, a hint of artifice bordering on artificiality, a description of the technique of production will prove the warrant for it.

Stones of the type of flint, jasper, obsidian, etc., are said by petrologists to fracture conchoidally; that is, when a nodule is struck casually, both the flake nicked off and the depression left in the nodule are clamshell-shaped and look like clamshells even to the tiny concentric striations that clamshells show. But the Denbigh Flint artisans knew how to do it differently. They trimmed off the bulbous end of a pebble or nodule until it was flat on top, to prepare what is called a striking platform; this platform was then beveled around the edges at an appropriate angle. (Several peoples in the history of the world have worked flint this way, and what this angle was seems to differ, but each user of the technique seemed to have a favorite angle, which was always kept to. One point does appear to be obvious: Since the objective of this beveling was to prepare the exact spot where the knapper struck his blow to knock off the flake he wanted, the angle of incidence was the angle of bevel plus or minus the angle at which the blow fell. A great deal of masonic nonsense about this technique, called blade making, appears in sober literature on the paleolithic.) Having thus prepared his work, the Denbigh knapper then struck the prepared nodule on the bevel with what has been described as a sharp but weak, or delicately controlled, blow. The result was not a scab- or conchoid-shaped flake but a long, narrow, parallel-sided flake shaped like the blade of a table knife. Where the blow falls there will appear on the flake a pimplelike extrusion called the positive bulb of percussion. On the stone core whence this positive bulb came will appear a little indentation called the negative bulb of percussion—and where these bulbs of percussion are in evidence, cores and flakes are accepted, in the paleolithic as well as the neolithic, as the unquestionable evidence of human workmanship. It is in these bulbs of percussion that the trade secret—and the sophistication of making flint break against its natural disposition—of the Denbigh Flint masters is revealed.

Where the Denbigh craftsmen are, perhaps, matchless is in the delicacy of their work. In most other places in the world where the blade-striking technique is used, the blade product will be large, ranging from three or four inches to as much as twelve. Few blades in the Denbigh material—and in other cultures in America in which this technique appears—are over two inches long, and there are blades that can only be called tiny. As a matter of fact, the Denbigh products are called micro-blades, as distinguished from the macro-blades of other blade producers. They are also called lamellar blades, in one of those unfortunate accidents in nomenclature to which American archaeology seems particularly prone. "Lamellar" is the anglicized adjectival form of *lamelle*, French for little blade, which among its several meanings includes blade of grass, and in the original it seems a felicitous choice of appellation since not only are the struck blades rather like broad blades of grass in shape, they are also gracefully curved like a half-bent finger; this arc becomes more and more pronounced on blades struck off nearer and nearer the center of the core. But if you look up "lamellar" in an English dictionary you find that it is the adjectival form of "lamella," which means "a thin plate,

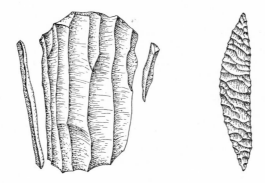

STRIP-BLADE CORE AND RETOUCHED TOOL

When a Denbighite craftsman skilled in the strip-blade or lamellar-flake technique went to work on a sound stone core, there was very little waste of material. The long, blade-shaped flakes, double-edged and sharp, were themselves tools as soon as they were struck off. But these could also be retouched into more finished tools like the delicate "side" blade at right.

scale . . . of bone, tissue . . ." and this gives it an equivalence to the conchoidal or scablike or squamate flake, which is exactly what the Denbigh bladelets are not. My own solution to the problem is to call them strip blades; unless modified, the word "blade" in American archaeology connotes a biface— worked-on-both-sides—blade; to use the word "strip" gets us around that difficulty and not only says what the blade is shaped like—a strip—but how it is produced—by stripping a core.

The subject of the Denbigh strip blade has been lengthily dealt with here so that the Sunday archaeologist, happening on such strip blades and cores, will realize that he has encountered not casual flakes but actual tools, as intentional as arrowheads or axes, and of a significance no less than potsherds. Their incidence is one of the most useful lines of investigation in American prehistory, for when they begin to appear in regions south of the icecap we can begin to suspect real intra-American cultural diffusion and to discern the broad pattern of it.

This diffusion had not taken place, we insist, at the time of the habitation at Cape Denbigh except as noted, with the herd hunters coming up the corridor in random hunting bands. What these makers of fluted points made contact with was not, however, a culture of newcomers. Giddings' observation on the sophistication of Denbigh technology is accompanied by the natural conclusion that this technique was old and had been evolved to produce a kit of tools adapted very specifically to a sharply defined living environment. This environment, Giddings says, was undoubtedly the taiga-tundra zone, the taiga being the northern limit of tree growth, which consists of coniferous species, and the tundra being the treeless plains beyond. This borderland afforded advantages of two habitat areas; the taiga supplied fuel and poles for tents or other shelter, and such game as moose and bear; on the tundra beyond were the herds of caribou, one of the better all-purpose animals. Giddings regards these taiga-tundra-adapted folk as representative of a circumpolar people who inhabited the top of the world and had less than a passing interest in the rest of it.

The achievement by these folk of security and comfort in an environment that would be murderous to the ill-adjusted can only be supposed to have been gradual. Somewhere their ancestors evolved a culture to meet advancing Arctic conditions at the same rate that those conditions evolved. These taigans did not mind being "trapped" in Alaska, then, when the Rocky Mountain corridor was closed, because it was their home anyway—as the Desert Culturists did not mind or even notice the closing because the Arctic was not their home. Hence the old question poses itself: Where did the taigans originate?

Migrationist-minded archaeologists take the usual way out and summon them rather recently from Asia. Since it has been decided that this cold-adapted culture must have developed gradually in response to glacial conditions, the putative migrations have to be supposed to have occurred after the Würm-Wisconsin began to retreat, and the taigans, following this retreat, spread along the ice front more or less laterally from a center in the Russian plains, and before that in the Aurignacian of France. This is a very attractive and persuasive theory, and was unassailable until lately. For it depends on the dating of the Alaskan taigans. The Denbighites, at 8500 B.P., are of just the right order of age and cultural sophistication to have been immigrants from France via a millennially long trek over the Russian steppes and the Siberian tundra. But the vision now arises that the Alaskan taigans had ancestors *in situ,* and these ancestors push their origin back to a time when working northeastward along the retreating ice front was not feasible. This vision arises, phoenix-like, from the excavations by Richard S. MacNeish out of a site at a literal end of the earth, in Yukon Territory, Canada, near where the Firth River enters the Beaufort sea arm of the Arctic Ocean. It is something of an archaeologist's dream, this incredibly placed habitation site, since it has nine distinct cultural levels. The top, or latest, three levels are of Eskimo-related cultures; the three middle levels are non-Eskimo but pottery-bearing, and the lowest three are preceramic and typologically ancient.

At the bottom of this stack is what MacNeish has called the British Mountain Complex, of lanceolate projectile points, flakes struck from prepared *discoidal* cores *and* bifacial choppers. Next above is the Flint Creek Complex, said to be a quite different flint-working industry, with Plainview and Angostura (herd-hunter) points, and both micro- and macroblades.

The third-oldest level contains a Denbigh-like inventory.

We have no right, while we await MacNeish's interpretation of these materials, to say that this sequence is developmental at this site, particularly since it is stressed that the second-level material is quite different from the material at the bottom. Yet we cannot help remarking that the prepared-core-flake theme runs through these three levels and continues upward through the next two. The cultural relationship of the three lowest levels, figured as it is on other sorts of tools and suggested habits, may not be that of ancestor-descendant, but the prepared-core-flake technology, being a fundamental way of arriving at tools and tool stock, is not culturally specific and can be adapted—and it was—to cultures as widely separated in time and geography as the Cape Denbigh taigans of 8500 B.P. and the Ohio Hopewell Mound Builders of 2500 B.P.

In the very first issue of information about the Firth River site, it was mentioned that below even the British Mountain Complex, in the sands that overlay the bedrock and were separated from the above-mentioned nine layers by a thick layer of clay, there was found a collection of ten artifacts, which included choppers, large crude end scrapers and side scrapers. What could this be, descriptively, but a manifestation of some very old friends of ours, the Tule Springers and the Lewisvillians? And what could such a manifestation mean but that a basic Amerind population developed differentially, according to regional variations?

What set us off in the first place on this disquisitional meander into Alaska was the fling we were taking against the Rocky Mountain corridor and its presumed function as a sort of funnel through which a population trickled into the empty barrel of America. It now appears that this cannot have been so. What was south of the glacier could not have seeped down from what was north of it; the strip-blade tradition is neither the herd-hunter nor the Desert Culture tradition. The Wisconsin glacier did not have any role in the peopling of America. What it did, we see now, was to divide North America in two, simultaneously dividing the basic population in two, and each population fragment then coped with the milieu the glacier allowed it with different and locally suitable cultural equipment.

As the glacier diminished, giving the land back to the Indians, the northern and southern Amerinds began to meet with each other and to affect each other culturally and physically, which is a later chapter of our story.

We may take it without further arguing that these early clans and tribes and cultures were not opportunistic; they were not looking for new lands and more exploitable environments;

thoroughly conservative, they wanted only to continue to pursue the kind of life they had developed for themselves in the kind of environment it was adapted to and they felt at home in. Taigans were not going to become Great Plains big-game hunters as long as there was an extensive taiga; big-game hunters were not going to become Desert Culturists as long as there were mammoths and great bison to hunt. None of these had the special knowledge and skills required to survive in the other's bailiwick. But these bailiwicks were not static territories; their boundaries changed from century to century, even from year to year, with the inconstancy of the glacially dominated climate.

The fact that the last 12,000 to 15,000 years must have been a time of constant meteorological change is self-evident. After a period of 60,000 years, by the long count, or 30,000 by the short count, when the climate is such as to maintain a major glacier at or near its maximum, that climate switches tack and within the next 7000 to 8000 years has, to all intents and purposes, destroyed the massive edifice of ice it erected. But this destruction, as we have noted, was not without its vacillations, its reversals of trend when glaciation resurged in the minor advances called the Mankato, the Valders and the Cochrane. Obviously, nobody ever got old enough to notice any such thing, no change being perceptible in a lifetime.

It is all too easy to overdramatize postglacial climate and its accompanying topographical changes as though they were violent upheavals, instantaneous and searing blights, and paradisiacal interludes. Even when you read the low-keyed résumés of postglacial events in the bare, scientific styles of George I. Quimby and Wesley I. Hurt, Jr., each of whom has chronicled them, you have the feeling that somewhere in the empyrean an adolescent godling is practicing away at his powers of control of natural phenomena and not doing too well in a monstrous way. I have a disagreeable recollection of a piece of rock-and-roll prose I read once in which the stylist coined the phrase "The horror of the glaciers." He happened, as I remember, to be talking about the west of the American cowboy, where there was no glaciation except in the mountains. Despite its implacability, no word less befits a glacier than horrible; you would as quickly call a splendid mountain horrible. A glacier moves, yes, but like a turgid avalanche; the weight of ice is so great that the ice which is in contact with the earth melts and freezes, melts and freezes, so that the glacier never fuses with the earth but keeps slowly gliding-sliding-flowing over it. This may gain a glacier an advance of maybe a few hundred yards a year, or a mile, or maybe two; but it is not capable of visiting horror upon man as, say, an erupting volcano can, or a tidal wave. The temptation to read a glacial advance as one of these catastrophes is understandable, but should not be yielded to. For glaciers, the Wisconsin in particular, were in effect teachers of mankind, and because of them man learned to invent the instruments of livelihood and adaptation to change.

No, the glaciers were not horrible, as the Swiss, who live with them, can well attest. When an Alpine glacier begins to spread itself, after a hearty winter, too far down the valleys and onto the tillable fields, the Swiss back their carts and wagons up to it, dig up the encroachment and haul it off to the local glacier dump. A continental glacier is something else again, of course. But mankind lived just as familiarly with the Wisconsin, never aware of what it was doing to the land and to the human race because it did nothing personal to any man to mark it in his memory. Yet all the while he was its pupil and his culture its lessons.

Both Hurt and Quimby use the 30,000-year short count for their synopses of the postglacial story, but even should the long count prove to be correct, the succession of events they present is too well documented in the field by Antevs, the late, highly respected Kirk Bryan, the comprehensive Richard F. Flint and many others to be greatly amended in these particulars.

Quimby begins his chronology of the epoch thus: "Radio-carbon-dated events suggest that the Mankato ice advanced about 12,000 or 11,000 B.C. [14,000 or 13,000 B.P.] and had retreated before the Valders advance about 9000 B.C. [11,000 B.P.]"

It requires not much power of insight to see this 2000-to-3000-year period as crucial to the Amerind. Climatic changes came with relative rapidity—two glacial advances and retreats within a period not much longer than the Christian era. We can only mark that this time of relatively rapid fluctuation coin-

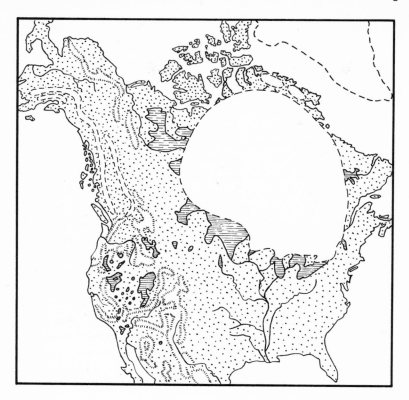

GLACIAL STAGE, 10,000 B.P.

This is Quimby's estimate of the extent of the Wisconsin glaciation at, roughly, 10,000 B.P., at the time of the Great Extinction of the larger Pleistocene beasts. There are huge fresh-water inland seas all over the landscape, even in the now arid Great Basin area. Notice that the Mississippi is the principal drainage system for glacial melt lakes. This is the time of the early occupations of Danger Cave and Modoc Rock Shelter.

cides with what seems to be, by the archaeology, a time of cultural advance among our Amerind population of the Western Plains and the Great Basin province, who appear to have been content with the scavenging kind of existence we have imagined for Lewisville–Tule Springs man during the advance and climactic phases of the Wisconsin. In the face of instability there were two adjustments such a man could make: he

GLACIAL STAGE, 7000 B.P.

By about 7000 B.P., according to Quimby, the Wisconsin looked like this, smaller but still vast, as the climate
continued to warm toward the climax of the Altithermal.
The Great Lakes have begun to emerge as we know them
today. Quimby is using the "short count" for the duration
of the Wisconsin. The Old Copper culture of Wisconsin-
Michigan dates from as early as this.

could hold his wonted ground in the vicinity of his trusted land-
marks and learn to subsist on what the meteorological fates
sent him; or he could pick a known source of food and follow
it wherever on the landscape the moody climate shifted it. The
stick-it-out type became the Desert Culture; the wanderer is
by definition the herd hunter of mammoth and bison. So we
conclude that the bifurcation of the basic Amerind culture
probably took place at about 15,000 B.P. The herd hunter never

GLACIAL STAGE, 3500 B.P.
During the late, slight ice readvance called the
Cochrane, the expiring Wisconsin glaciation looked like
this, in Quimby's reconstruction. The Great Lakes are
much as we know them now but are still receiving water
flow from glacial melt lakes, and Lake Michigan drains
into the Mississippi. Note that the Ohio enters the Mississippi in what is now the state of Mississippi.

changed his ways; but the Desert Culturist's food-getting vir-
tuosity, on display at Danger Cave, which dates from this period, must have been acquired during it, when every third or
fourth generation must have been faced with some new problem of commissary.

The period following the Valders is called by Antevs the
Anathermal, or period of return of heat, though tests of ocean
sediment show a relative cold—relative, that is, to present

temperature norms. During these bracketed millennia, from
9000 years ago to 6500 years ago, the climate was such as to
cause the entirety of the continent north of Mexico to be, according to Quimby, one huge natural area; that is, anybody
could travel anywhere within it with some expectation of finding something to make a meal on. The Great Basin still supported lakes, pine forests were advancing northward as the ice
retreated, deciduous, nut-bearing trees encroached on Arizona,
and the Great Plains grew a fattening pasturage for the bison
herds. These must have been halcyon days, when every century was climatically more agreeable than the last; but its
very prodigality of only good things must have relieved the
Amerinds of any necessity for cultural change. And the archaeology seems to show this.

But climate did not stand still; it trended warmly on into an
age between 6500 B.P. and 4000 B.P. which Antevs calls the
Altithermal, or period of high heat, when the climate was,
probably, during climax periods, warmer than it is now by as
much as 5 degrees Fahrenheit. Quimby says, "The high plains,
formerly a rich grassland, became probably a desert and certainly a marginal area. The grasslands, like the people, moved
eastward or westward or disappeared. At this time grass
reached its maximum in the northwest and prairies extended
across the state of Ohio. In the eastern woodland areas the
deciduous forests made their northernmost advance. In the
Great Basin the lakes dried up and what had once been a rich
area became relatively marginal, although the plateau area to
the north seems to have been fairly well off. The southwest,
too, became arid and marginal. . . . The eastern woodlands
were somewhat different in Altithermal times. The coniferous
forest zone was farther north and probably formed a segment
of the circumboreal zone extending northwestward through
Alaska and across Siberia, Russia, Finland, Sweden and Norway. The deciduous forests had also spread northward. In the
northern part of the eastern prairie and forest zones there were
tremendous glacial and non-glacial lakes."

After this thoroughgoing summary, with its clear depiction
of a formerly integral continent being sectored off into habitable and uninhabitable, or barely inhabitable, zones, can there
be any doubt that vicissitudes were wrought upon the Amer-

inds? With each decade, with each year, even the versatile Desert Culture people must have found themselves more and more a surplus population on the lands where they had been born, and there was nothing for it but to scatter wherever the grass seemed greener, to the south, to the west, perhaps to the north, and surely to the east; for here the desiccation was not so severe and the forests, perpetually dank and gloomy during pluvials, became pleasant and probably, for the first time, salubrious.

It seems well founded to say that this Altithermal period caused more displacement and intracontinental migration than any natural condition the Amerinds had ever suffered before. In the first place there were by this time more of them, and in the second place the regions where man seems to have lived longest, the Great Basin and its adjuncts, had to be virtually evacuated. The eastward migration of the Laurentian people occurred at this time, and climatic shifts may have caused it. But it certainly cannot have been unique. And just as the Laurentians found the Lamokans there ahead of them, so must other migrants have encountered earlier comers, so that the total effect of the Altithermal must have been to uproot locally fixed cultures and scatter them abroad, to mix with whatever was extant.

It has been stated earlier that there is nothing in the cultures of American Indians at any time in the last 12,000 years that cannot be taken as a consequence of strictly hemispheric events, and we call attention to this thesis again; the latter part of the Anathermal and its climax in the Altithermal were sufficient stimulus both to all the population movement that has heretofore been taken to be Asiatic immigration, and to all the appearances at this site or that of new traits and new cranial types. It was a time of admixture and permutation of cultures and population, and when it ended in the glacial readvance called the Cochrane there was a whole new distribution of peoples in America, peoples who had long since forgotten whence they came and whose forefathers had been longer in one locale than ours will have been in the year 5000 A.D.

This Cochrane period of return to a colder and wetter climate, Antevs has called the Medithermal, or medium-heat period, and we are probably still in it, but in a dryer phase than

marked the beginning, and minus the vestiges of the Wisconsin
ice mass. As Hurt says, "Without doubt, several fluctuations occurred during this period." Fluctuations of moisture and arid-
ity, that is—and similar fluctuations are noted up to the present, very well noted, by those who hark back to the good old
days.

There seems to be no tidy way to summarize the Wisconsin-
Würm glacier except to wonder what the course of prehistory
and history would have been had it hung around another
10,000 years, a mere tick of the watch as geology keeps time.
It is easy to believe that very little would have been different
except the locales of history. It must be remembered that the
brains we own are not of our own devising but are the direct
biological heritage of men who learned their object lessons in a
glaciated world.

8

The Gone Generations

The foregoing hasty review of the majestic decease of the Wisconsin has had to slight a good deal of the spectacular —the way the ice mass shoved the Great Lakes around, throttled rivers in their beds and made main streams out of side creeks, sheered off mountain tops, left the St. Lawrence Valley in such a depressed state that the Atlantic reached Ohio, and filled up valleys with drift like city dumps. But that is geology, and no matter what the glacier did to the landscape, we still have one, and a very satisfactory one at that. What has disappeared forever is the Pleistocene fauna, the like of which we will never see again, unless there is a comparable one on Venus when we get there. After the Second World War a zoo keeper in Berlin was able, by selective breeding of modern strains of cattle, to devolute an aurochs, that fierce bovine ancestor which dwelt in ancient European forests, but this is about as far as we are ever likely to see into the zoological past. Perhaps, if there were enough of them, our current model bison (scientifically, *Bison bison*) might be also bred retrogressively to the huge *Bison antiquus* that Folsom man hunted, or even to the more gigantic *Bison latifrons*, with horns measuring six feet from tip to tip, as against *Bison bison's* quite noticeable incurved variety, like the handles on a teapot. But what could be bred back to a saber-toothed tiger?

Hollywood, when it feels the urge to do something prehistoric, which is mercifully not often, always fills in the bestial background for its cave men with dinosaurs, one of the most preposterous anachronisms conceivable. Man and the dinosaurs are a whole geologic epoch, the Cenozoic, apart; and this epoch was 70,000,000 years long. The few mammal contemporaries of tyrannosaurus and brontosaurus were midges beside them, beasts about the size of a terrier and only half as intelligent, and a hundred thousand species away from the biped descendant that would some day know enough to credit them with initiating his warm-blooded breed.

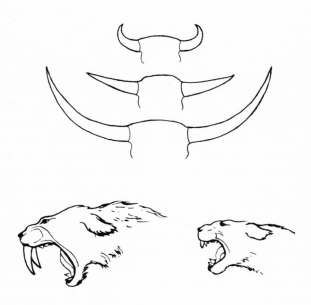

BISON AND SMILODON

At top is a head-on view of the schematized skull and horns of *Bison bison*, the buffalo that gave Buffalo Bill his name. Next below is *Bison taylori*, hunted by Portales man; within the rib cage of one such was found the first recognized Folsom fluted point. Below is *Bison latifrons*, with his incredible six-foot spread of horns. Obviously, the shorter the horns became, the more closely bison could mass together for mutual protection. Crooking of horns helped even more. *Bison taylori* and *Bison latifrons* are both extinct. At the bottom is a view of smilodon rampant compared with a modern tiger, a much better biter and chewer, but distinctly smaller.

But Hollywood's dilemma is understandable. Since dinosaurs were cumbersome, slow-moving beasts, you can fake them plausibly by building effigies and giving these dummies a mechanical animation. Or you can blow up, with a simple trick of photography, specimens of the sail lizard or monitors or iguanas into reptilian monsters. But you can't fake with robots the fierce and fluid muscularity of the saber-tooth, nor, with an artful use of perspective, blow up a house cat into an Alaskan lion. The wonders of Pleistocene fauna are well beyond Hollywood's ingenuity, and the epic of early man is well left undone by the Goldwyns and De Milles.

The bones of every important American Pleistocene beast now extinct have been found at one site or another of early Amerind occupation, with the exception, I believe, of the short-faced bear, against whom the best defense was probably non-association. Even *Felis atrox,* the Alaskan lion, and smilodon, the saber-tooth, are represented. Most plentiful, or course, are skeletal odds and ends of the meat animals—mammoth and mastodon, camel and sloth, the American horse, giant beaver, giant bison, tapir and the dire wolf; yes, even an extinct vulture. Least plentiful—in fact, entirely absent—are the bones of that unextinct Pleistocene form, Homo sapiens, presumably the slayer and certainly the consumer of the flesh from the joints we find at his caves and campfires. The best we can make of this situation is that the early Amerind was not a cannibal, but he was no great respecter of the dead either, and, Pleistocene carnivore that he was, having eaten meat all his life he expected in the end to be eaten, and laid him down to fang and claw without ceremony.

Least known to us of this gaudy zoology, but probably best known to the paleo-Indian, was the dire wolf, larger than any modern wolf but with a dentition that marks him as being hyena-like in habit, a bone gnawer and crusher, very much the type to compete with man for the remains of a lion-slain mammoth. His remains are very plentiful in the La Brea tar pits, now within the city limits (and what isn't?) of Los Angeles, that asphalt swamp that trapped thousands of Pleistocene animals as fly paper traps flies. He was a slim-legged courser with a heavy skull and a small brain and he had not the canniness of the later timber wolf and the prairie wolf—that is, the coyote—or he would have been as nearly absent as they from that viscous cemetery. In some spots at La Brea the number of saber-tooth and dire-wolf skulls averages 20 per cubic yard of excavation. There can be little doubt that the dire wolf's brainless ferocity was close to being a suicidal instinct, but his close companionship even in death with the maniacal saber-tooth, smilodon, prompts the thought that he had to die out when smilodon did because smilodon did the killing for him.

Not any brighter, then, but indubitably larger and fiercer was smilodon (a ghastly pun of a name), a breed which, contrary to a popular pseudoscientific canard, did not become extinct because of the overspecialized, or nonadaptative, trend of its nine-inch-long, dagger-like canines. This is a widely disseminated notion and George G. Simpson has laughed it to scorn in his *The Meaning of Evolution* by observing that the earliest saber-tooth, eusmilus, had fangs as long, relative to his size, as smilodon and that eusmilus was doing very well for himself 40,000,000 years ago. The question is whether the species Homo, with his overspecialized acquisitiveness, will survive 40,000 years.

I have always thought that the saber-tooth, which is no more a tiger than it is a lion or a leopard, has been at least partially misunderstood, not as to his character, which was incontestably horrid, but as to the function of his most prominent feature, his two big front teeth. He was no biter, as the weakness of his lower jaw attests, and not much of a chewer either, his back teeth generally being not well suited to mastication. It is suspected, therefore, from mouth and palate formation, that he took much of his nourishment vampire fashion, by blood sucking. Sizing him up further, we find that his legs were short and heavy and his powerful forelegs were considerably larger than the hind pair—no miler, he—and he had a massive back and loin region and a very short tail. Taking all this together, along with the only way he could have used his great fangs— which is by striking down with them, like a snake—we arrive at a deduction about his attack that has never, as far as I know, been proposed before—that his fang teeth were used as grappling hooks. Which must be explained.

Since smilodon couldn't run worth a lick by comparison with most cats—a lion, for instance, can outrun a gazelle for twenty or thirty yards—he must have leaped on his prey from ambush. If he made this strike good, with his nine-inch fangs sunk firmly in flesh, he was then securely grappled to his prey, which he could thereafter claw, with those frightfully armed and enormously powerful forepaws, to death if he found the jugular, or into a crippled inability to continue running if he severed shoulder muscles. Perhaps the punctures of the grapple-hook teeth brought blood spurting into his mouth and he was able to feed on the run, like a mosquito. Everything about smilodon's structure contributes something to this theory. The powerful back and loins would have been necessary to control and maneuver smilodon's hindquarters, while he hung by his teeth, both to curl them out of harm's way and to help the hind feet claw for purchase; and a short tail would have been a necessity, since a long tail dragging the ground while the prey raced on could easily be stepped on in such a way as to dislodge him. There is, I am sure, a great deal more to the function of these saber teeth than that of simple fangs, the insufficiency of the saber or ripping theory of the use of these teeth being that, as long as they are, they are not long enough to inflict a mortal stab on a beast as large as a sloth or a mammoth, and smilodon would not have had a second chance to strike the same prey. I am thoroughly convinced that smilodon's teeth, efficient enough as rippers when he needed them for that purpose—they had tiny serrations or saw teeth (yes, his teeth had teeth) along the blade edges—were nevertheless used in the attack on large prey like the mammoth and bison to fasten himself to these animals on the gallop while he dismembered them with his forepaws.

But if saber-tooth was no tiger, *Felis atrox* was a proper lion and he looked like one, except that he was a quarter bigger than the current king of beasts. His bones are abundant at La Brea and in the muck beds of Alaska beneath the perma-frost. A latecomer to America, he probably followed the bison herds, also Pleistocene immigrants, and though he was the faunal analogue, in North America, of the European cave lion, he was habituated to plains hunting, not cave haunting. Bigger-brained than smilodon, he appears at La Brea in a ratio to smilodon of 1 to 30. His bones, like smilodon's, have so far been found but once in man's company. This was at Ventana

Cave, Arizona. Smilodon appears at Friesenhahn Cavern, Texas. And this is about the ratio in which they were likely to have been sought by man.

The North American opposite number of the cave bear, with which Neanderthal disputed for leases on available cliff overhangs and rock shelters in Europe and Africa, was the short-faced bear, so called because he had a flat-muzzled face like a bulldog, topping an eight-foot frame when he chose to stand erect, as he probably did; or at least the only surviving bear that can match him in size, the Kodiak, uses his size this way to spy out his food. Paleontologists say the short-faced bear's teeth show him to have been carnivorous, which makes him easily the imperial carnivore, the *Tyrannosaurus rex,* of the Pleistocene. It is not likely that early man was a bear hunter. One twelve-foot specimen of a short-faced bear from Nebraska has been reported but this is too terrible to think about. Even as there are no bones of the short-faced bear in the excavated offal of the feasts of early man, so there are no bones of man among the scraps of bear dinners; the distaste of each for the other seems equally marked on the record.

Jaguar and puma, lynx and gray wolf, the grizzly and the wolverine, and all that we think of as animal life today, were, in the menagerie of the Pleistocene, but modest feral figures. But this is no reason to believe that they were less numerous then than after *Felis atrox* and smilodon and *Canis dirus* vanished into paleontology, for there was meat enough for the great and the small. The game that the Great Plains must have supported while the pluvials kept them watered and green as a Dutch polder might well have outnumbered the entire mammalian population of our world of 1958, for that was the climax of mammalian prosperity and since then we have had to be content with, according to Alfred Wallace, "a zoologically impoverished world."

Of all the animals that roamed the land, none could have carried more meat, individually and by numbers and distribution, than the cropping and browsing mammoths. The imperial mammoth, which bears the magnificent title of *Archidiskodon imperator,* stood about 14 feet high; *Archidiskodon maibeni* was bigger. The eastern variety of mammoth, *Parelephas jeffersoni* (named after Thomas Jefferson, a president who was interested in science) was eleven feet tall; he could barely have walked under the basket on a basketball court, and maybe, in prime condition, he couldn't have done that, for the mammoths appear to have stored fat in a lump on the top of their heads steatophageously, to carry them through the lean days. Three genera and seven varieties of these Pleistocene elephants, each adapted to a specific habitat and/or climate— so that some varieties were woolly and some not—found a region on this continent to their liking, from Central America to Alaska.

The biggest thing on four legs, the mammoth was not the biggest on two; more ponderous than an elephant, and able to rear up 20 feet in the air when he sat on his massive tail, was megatherium, a ground sloth, slow moving, a diner off the tender top tips of tree leaves but probably nothing for even a saber-tooth to get careless with, being armed with formidable claws on short, powerful legs, the fore pair of which he could have used manually to pick an attacker off him as with ice tongs. Grudgingly we will have to admit that megatherium was the biggest thing, bulk wise, on four legs, too; but as a quadruped he must have been a groveling peasant compared with the monumental nobility of *Archidiskodon imperator;* from the front he had the look of a sawed-off, wildly bowlegged Eng-

ELEPHANTS

At left is the slump-shouldered mastodon, and in the center the imperial mammoth. At right, for size comparison, is a modern elephant, which is not a descendant of either mastodon or mammoth, though related to both.

lish pug dog, except that his head was distinctly tubular, being, apparently, little more than a nozzle through which he sucked food into his tank-truck body. Mylodon was another variety of sloth, and not much different from megatherium, but

nothrotherium was considerably smaller and his dung, hair and
bones have been found in Gypsum Cave, Nevada, with evidence that man ate him and burned his dried dung to roast
him with.

Transiting rapidly from the grotesque to the familiar, we
find that an astonishing ten species of horses foraged the
Pleistocene landscape, from the little Shetland-pony-sized
Equus tau of Mexico to *Equus giganteus* of (wouldn't you
know it) Texas, bigger than a Clydesdale or a Percheron. The
eastern forests had a nice riding-size horse, *Equus pectinatus*,
and on the plains roamed a cow-pony-like species, *Equus
complicatus*. There was a horse with the proportions of a zebra,
and one with the build of an ass.

But unfortunately the early Amerind looked upon all this
horseflesh not with the eye of a Vanderbilt or a Whitney, but
with the eye of a sausage maker. He never saw them as riding animals, or draft animals or dairy animals—he was too self-
reliant, maybe—and he ate them without ever grasping the
simple mathematics of their four legs' being twice as good as
his two. Few of the might-have-beens of prehistory seem sad-
der than this, now that we know how the Indian and the horse
took to each other once they were made properly acquainted.
Had this introduction taken place early enough the American
horse would never have become extinct, and the cultural
achievements of such peoples as the Mayas and the Hopewells
might have been caravaned the length and breadth of the continent in bulk and quantity to the envy and hence the advancement of the backward. But we must say "might have," for when
the Indian did acquire the horse as mount instead of meat, it
became an inducement to slip back from a village-horticultural
mode of living into the old free, wandering, wonderful life of a
big-game hunter, and to hell with civilization. It is hard to believe, but the equestrian Sioux who rode over Custer had, not
300 years before, been pedestrian agrarians.

As this feeling of opportunity missed applies to the horse, so
it also applies to the camel. The Incas used the cameloid llamas
and alpacas and vicuñas and guanacos as beasts of burden, but
they were small, relatively, and could not carry as much as a
man as fast or as far; they spelled man, but they only spelled
him as a beast of burden and they were only pack, and not

draft or riding animals. But the cameloid whose bones were found with Tule Springs man was another matter entirely; he was camelops, a big and powerful beast, seven feet at the shoulder and bigger than the Bactrians and dromedaries that have been bearing the desert-adapted cultures of North Africa and the Middle East on their humped backs for all these long-suffering centuries. Judging from his pictures, camelops would have been easier riding and easier loading than either of the Old World varieties, and he had a wide climatic range, from Florida to Alaska. It is interesting to guess what might have happened in the Great Basin and its northern sector, the High Plains, during arid Altithermal had the camel been a household appliance at that time, and perhaps it might have been done; he was conceivably still extant up to Altithermal times, for a solitary camelops skeleton has been discovered in a cave in Utah with some hide and hair still attached.

If the horse and camelops were ignored, it is pointless to ask why the fearsome mammoths, true elephants and probably as smart, or the mastodons, smaller (about 9 feet at the shoulder, which was higher than the head) and less smart, or the bison, which were the nearest thing to cattle or oxen in the hemisphere, were never domesticated. It is not likely that any race of people was ever better fitted to be handlers of animals than the Amerinds; they had lived with and observed for hundreds of generations the habits and dispositions of the herds they trailed and fed on; they certainly did not fear them with the shunning fear of the unknown; and they must have approached an intuitive identity with the animals that were their neighbors. Perhaps this notion should be further examined, for herein must lie the answer to the riddle why the Amerind never thought of making animals his servitors.

J. Eric Thompson, in his beautiful *The Rise and Fall of Maya Civilization*, places a Mayan peasant in a situation in which he must go hunting, his family being hungry and the day propitious. Before setting out, the hunter, in Thompson's words, behaves thus:

"He prayed to the sun, the morning star and Ah Ceh, god of the chase, that his hunting would be successful, *excusing his wish to destroy life* by explaining his need and his poverty, and *promising not to kill more than he needed*." (Italics mine.)

A deer having been killed, the hunter, before dressing it, builds a fire. "As the black smoke, with its sweet scent strangely blended with a certain acridity, billowed up, he began to address the deer, and through it the god of hunting, *begging the deer's pardon for having killed it,* and explaining that, as the crops had not been too good that year, his family needed food." (Italics mine.)

There is something more in this touchingly natural piety than superstition and idolatry; there is a mystic sense of the equivalence of man and animal that would make it almost impossible to muster the arrogance to conceive of enslaving a free-living beast by rope or corral. It is reminiscent of the master word of the jungle taught to Mowgli by old Baloo, the bear —a hiss for snakes, a call for birds, a growl for beasts, followed by the most proud yet humble of words: "We be of one blood, thou and I."

This is charming nonsense, of course, and has no place outside of *The Jungle Book,* but deodorized of its Rousseauism, it does make a point. The Indian did not expect to bamboozle a bear into doing him no hurt with a reminder about their brotherhood, because he knew perfectly good and well that each had to be ready to defend himself at all times against the hunger and need of the other. But the Indian knew that he and the bear were, thus, of one nature, and he would no more have knifed the bear unless he felt the need, or in defense against the bear's need, than he would have killed his own brother. The Indian was never a "sportsman," a wanton slayer, a trophy seeker, and this was the expression of his respect for animals who were but himself furred and clawed, that he assumed them to be as native to the world, as endowed with prerogatives within it, as he was. Not at all sentimental about animals, as too many of our pet-fond are, whose doting is a fixation rather than affection, the Indian was not squeamish about killing because of the pain inflicted. What he recognized was the transgression against, by the obliteration of, the individual personality. No Indian in a hunting stage of cultural development was likely to have known of the qualitative difference of self-consciousness that made his personality essentially unlike that of an individual animal's; man and animal had eyes, ears, nose, mouth, senses and appetites and breeding instincts, alike

—hence the difference was one of form only, and of master soul. This would have been the lesson not only of every day of a man's life, but of every day of the life of the entire human race, during most of which time man had little reason to consider himself either superior to many of the swarming species with whom he lived, or singularly blessed by heaven among them. For he was neither the biggest nor most numerous nor instinctively the canniest of the animal population.

It is possible to carry a discussion of this relation of the Amerind—of any people in a state of savagery—vis-à-vis his animal compeers, to the place where it seems to become mere politesse, which is ridiculous. The savage deals with animals respectfully and honestly because of what he believes about them—that if he violates the right of an individual animal, the group soul of the breed will see that meet punishment is visited on him. The power of this group soul to see justice done was a matter both of lore and of personal experience, and every instance of mischance that befell a violator, whether the injury he had inflicted was deliberate or not, confirmed its operation as a benign protector of its own. And the savage had to believe in this group soul—that is, he had to believe in some supernal power that could be dealt with by propitiation and cajolery—or he had not the slightest control over his meat and sustenance.

The savage had to assume that this group soul or master spirit clearly understood the facts of life, that all the individuals of a breed would die and it was inevitable that many of them would die and disappear down the gullet of a predator; but equally he may have assumed that the confinement of an animal and his impressment into the forced service of man would constitute a violation of the breed's inherent nature to roam. This is not as sophisticated as it sounds, after it is rephrased thus: You may take an animal's life, if you need the flesh to feed yourself; it is the purpose of flesh to be eaten; but you may not take his freedom, because it is his nature to be wild.

There are many theories about how man came to domesticate animals, but the one that seems to me most probable is that they domesticated themselves; cut off, with man, in some oasis, some circumscribed environmental isle, they grew accustomed to man's company, and he, in turn, following the code of killing only what he needed and knowing that what he did not kill could not escape him, had a chance to learn the first lesson of animal husbandry—don't kill off the cows, whence will come tomorrow's meat. Symbiosis is nothing rare in nature, except among animals of approximately the same size, and I doubt that man, the weakling partner, would have thought of taming animals until they showed some faint talent for being tamed.

Apparently none of the horses or camels or elephants or mastodons or bison in America ever got caught in so tight a corner with man that they had to consider compromise with him. Or perhaps the Amerind's obtuseness let him kill off when he should have spared. But the domestication of animals didn't really happen in America; the Indians even ate their dogs.

I have often wondered why no enterprising meat grower has ever tried to raise American bison for the table, at least as a change from turkey on Thanksgiving. The tales the mountain men told about the delicacy of buffalo-hump ribs must never have reached the ears of the Meat Institute of America; nor the other tales about the gourmet palatability of panther loin and beaver tail. But the plentifulness of bison, when they were to be had at all, was certainly reason enough for Indians never to have bothered to domesticate them, especially since they are reputed not to have a tractable bone in their bodies. Add, then, the fact that America was never crowded enough, never so Mother-Hubbard-cupboard-bare of food, to the fact that it was against religion and you have the full explanation of why, amongst the most wonderful assemblage of animals the world has ever seen together in such numbers at the same time, the Amerind found not one, save the llama family, that he could get along with. True, the dog was made a beast of burden in some places, dragging sleds or the travois and being put under pack, but he was an imported animal; Mexican and Pueblo Indians kept turkeys; bees were hived for honey in Middle or Meso-America (southern Mexico and Central America); the parrot was apparently semidomesticated, for the same odd purpose it serves now; the guinea pig was here and there raised for food; none of these instances invalidates the generality, or the reasons for it. And while the mind of the Amerind lay oblivious in the shadow of its religio-traditional block, and indolent before the sight of meat in plenty, the boon disappeared and there was whisked from the face of the earth like a gift from the gaze of the ingrate all the magnificence of the Pleistocene animal kingdom.

In 1950, when MacGowan's *Early Man in the New World* appeared on the publisher's lists, this disappearance, called the "Great Extinction," of the characteristically Pleistocene fauna was a central problem in the controversy over the earliness of man in America; the discovery of projectile points with mammoth or sloth was argued by some to mean that man had to have been ancient to have hunted this long-gone game. But many, of Hrdlickan persuasion, saw it the other way around: projectile points meant that these beasts had endured perhaps to the days of Columbus. Legitimate as this latter position was, as argument it was a flouting of consistency; when stone tools were found with the bones of Pleistocene beasts in Eurasia it was always assumed that the association meant antiquity for the man who had made them. But the Hrdlickans had no fear of inconsistency as long as it kept the doors barred against early man in America, and they cohabited with it cheerfully for as long as it served them.

This service ended with the C14 date for Folsom man, at 10,-000 B.P., and the Hrdlickans were wrong again. In 1952, E. H. Sellards published his *Early Man in America,* wherein he made some highly significant observations. The Folsom hunters had killed only bison—*Bison taylori*—never mammoth. The makers of Plainview, Long-Angostura, Scottsbluff, Milnesand and other such points which covered the 2000 or 3000 years subsequent to Folsom—these hunters had killed only bison, never mammoth. Therefore the mammoth was gone before 10,000 B.P.

How long before? Not too long, it would seem. For the makers of the Clovis fluted point, presumed to be ancestral to the Folsom fluted point, not only killed mammoths, they hunted them with Clovis-fluted-point-tipped spears. The heyday of the Clovis hunters has never been C14 dated (forget Lewisville man), but where their artifacts are found with Folsom artifacts the Clovis point is always below, and therefore is older than, Folsom. It is better than a guess, though less than positive, that

the mammoth died off 11,000 years ago from all of the continent north of Mexico.

But maybe, it can be argued, the Folsom, Scottsbluff and
Long hunters simply lost their nerve, and avoided the mammoth to concentrate on bison, which were not gigantic—only
as big as a truck. Maybe— Except that south of the border, in
the valley of Mexico where the southern herds lasted a little
longer, a Scottsbluff-like point was found with one fossil mammoth at Iztapán and two Long-type points were found in another. The mammoths would have been hunted had they survived past 11,000 B.P., it seems safe to say.

After that date the Great Plains hunters seem to have found
no further horses or camels to kill, either. Man's occupation of
Gypsum Cave was C14 dated at about 10,000 B.P., and that is
the last we find of sloths. Once it was thought that the mastodons, leading a sheltered existence in eastern forests, made a
stand therein at least till the time of Christ. When their bones
are found, rarely with projectile points, the points are always of the stemmed or notched varieties regarded as being of
the so-called Archaic time period, roughly the Altithermal, and
subsequent to the era of the makers of Folsom, Scottsbluff,
Long-Angostura and Yuma points. "Conservative" archaeologists have for years rested their view of late mastodonic persistence on this association, despite the fact that while herd-
hunter points are found thinly scattered throughout the east,
none has ever been found with mastodon. If a conclusion had
to be drawn it should be that the mastodon disappeared early
—before the migration eastward of the herd hunters.

The only C14 tests on mastodon bones—not in a human cultural context—have given dates of about 11,000 years; the
latest test run on mastodon material from New York State, in
forested environs, yielded almost exactly that age. These mastodons, while not necessarily the last survivors, must have been
near the end of the line nevertheless. The Archaic period is
known from hundreds of sites east of the Mississippi, but at no
site of this period has mastodon turned up in the garbage
dumps. Nor do either of the two oldest, long-time-span sites
east of the Mississippi show any sign of the cohabitation of
any of their residents with this demielephant. The lowest cultural level at Modoc Rock Shelter, in Illinois, dates at 10,000

B.P.; the lowest level at Russell Cave, Alabama, at 9000 B.P. But these two caves produce something more than negative evidence; the projectile points recovered are of Archaic pattern. Hence the occurrence of only Archaic-pattern points with mastodon remains proves nothing about the late survival of mastodon because Archaic-type points are not necessarily Archaic-Altithermal in age; they may be 3000 to 4000 years older either in the east or, as Danger Cave shows, in the west.

To be cautious, then, we will put it this way: There is no reason to believe that the mastodons lasted any longer than 10,000 B.P., either.

This was the time of the Great Extinction, then.

But why?

What was so deadly about the thousand years between 11,-000 and 10,000 B.P.? Allowing for the fact that we are treating a millennium as though it were a decade, and that the mammoth may have disappeared from one part of the continent a thousand years before he disappeared from all parts, and that he may have disappeared altogether a thousand years before, say, the mastodon disappeared altogether, still there is no distortion in seeing 10,500 B.P. as the crisis year in extinction. Any of the great Pleistocene fauna which was then surviving we now, in hindsight, know to have been doomed.

But why?

It could not have been a lethal change in climate, for smaller beasts would surely have been as hard-hit as larger ones. Some species of Equus were outsize, but some were no larger than a deer, and deer survived. Nor was this Great Extinction solely an American affliction, though it struck here absolutely, whereas camels, elephants and horses did hang on elsewhere as species; but these, according to Simpson, are smaller, and different varieties from the macro-strains which were Pleistocene; they are not merely diminished descendants. Whatever explains the Great Extinction in America, then, must also explain it in Europe and Asia, yet climate is the only simultaneous turnabout which these two land masses suffered in common.

We have already been over this ground. Ten thousand B.P. was, perhaps, the time of the Mankato ice readvance, not a very severe reglaciation, compared with some; or it may have been the interstadial between the Mankato and Valders readvances. So there is no clue here to the fatal weapon or malady, for the great Pleistocene fauna had seen vaster ice sheets and longer hot periods than any of these relatively minor climatic whims. Some strange new bubonic plague, then? Or was it man, finally come into his own as a hunter, and roving over the landscape killing animals in herds by means of fire drives and mass slaughter?

But not all the animals that man hunted died out, and others became extinct which could not in any serious way have been affected by him. Herds of *Bison bison* came through, while the short-faced bear, the dire wolf, the saber-tooth and the Alaskan lion passed from the earth. But they did not pass because of what they were, predators who had eaten themselves out of hoof and horn, because the grizzly lived on, and the timber wolf, and the cougar. Somebody has said that it was only the large, exotic species that failed; but these species would not now seem so exotic were they not now extinct, and not all of them were large. MacGowan, who is always thorough, points out that certain mollusks, a variety of toad, a subfamily of rabbits and three varieties of antelope also drop from the record. It does not seem possible to assign the demise of all these to a single cause.

But ecology is a matter of curious interrelations. Since we know nothing about the feeding habits of the rabbit variety that vanished, we may speculate that perhaps he fed only on grasses immediately fertilized by mammoth dung. Odder ecological adjustments have been known—the koala bear lives on the leaves of not just a eucalyptus tree, but those of only four or five out of a hundred or more species. Perhaps the antelopes herded with the mammoths as a protective device. And who knows about toads? Perhaps there was an increase in the activity of snakes on the prairie after the thundering herds of horses, mammoths and camels thinned out, and these snakes ate the toads all up. Odder things have happened—the kangaroo is becoming scarce in Australia because the English introduced foxes there in order to continue the dear old sport of riding to hounds. Foxes cannot kill grown kangaroo, but when they chase them the baby kangaroos fall out of their mothers' pouches and are crippled and so decimate the next generation. Of such things is natural history made. But one statement can be made with assurance: Once the great beasts had ceased to be, there would be repercussions the length and breadth of the land.

This had happened once before, this sudden and utter collapse of a fauna in the apogee of its dominance—when the dinosaurs, after 200,000,000 years of success, foundered so completely that no single Miocene reptilian species survives today from that period of saurian supremacy. Here again climate is thought, perhaps too facilely, to have been the assassin. World temperatures dropped, it is said, and the cold-blooded reptiles were immobilized; the earth's crust cracked and threw up mountains, changing the course of the free-wandering rain winds, drying up the swamps where the Brontosauri and other herbivorous types had fattened themselves to be consumed by the Tyrannosauri and other carnivorous types. And so an integrated eating society fell apart, with the failure of its basic-diet members. All this seems at once clear and logical, yet completely mysterious. Surely not all favorable environments disappeared; surely there were some varieties of dinosaurs, the adaptations of which to special environments were fantastic, which found themselves in environments as good as if not better than before. But if they did it availed them not. The dinosaurs were under edict, it seems, to go.

It is not without a sense of premonition that a member of the human race reviews the fact of these two great extinctions, of the saurians and the great mammalians. For each of them, the moment of success was the turning point to absolute failure; to flourish supremely was to begin to die. Philosophers have noted the cancerous effects of success on individual personalities and on societies; it would be interesting to discover that such an effect has a genetic or biological basis. But what seems more likely, in human affairs, before the final extinction of all races, is the eventual transcendence of the yellow over the white, then the black over the yellow, unless some sort of harmony is achieved before it is too late, for how man will be eliminated already seems predictable—he will eliminate himself.

Philosophy and the enigmatic processes of genetics aside, we ought to be able to arrive at some sort of cause-and-effect explanation for the disappearance of the Pleistocene's princi-

pal inhabitants. MacGowan writes of one scene of disaster:
"The most puzzling of all the fossils of extinct animals are those
in the deep Alaska muck beds. Their numbers are appalling.
They lie frozen in tangled masses, interspersed with uprooted
trees. They seem to have been torn apart and dismembered
and then consolidated under catastrophic conditions. Yuma
and Plainview spear points and perhaps one generalized Folsom have been found in these chill beds. Skin, ligament, hair,
flesh, can still be seen."

This descriptive note leads memory in two directions: one to
those myths about burial grounds which superannuated elephants sought out to lay themselves down and die; and the
other to the Predmost mammoth hunters of Moravia.

It is not known how the Predmost people killed mammoths,
for it was not with a spear, but they killed them in great numbers and the remains of nearly a thousand have been recovered from their ancient camp site, near a pass through which
the mammoth herds had to travel, going between winter and
summer pasture. It has been reasoned that the Predmost hunters would have concentrated on killing the younger and
weaker beasts, and in doing this scotched the herds at the
roots, since elephants, with a gestation period of two years, are
slow breeders. No thorough excavation of the Alaskan muck
beds has been attempted, which might verify their similarity
to the kill site at Predmost, but the projectile points that
MacGowan mentions suggest that the hand of man hovered
over them.

Yet the mind simply boggles at the idea that the Amerind,
armed only with spears, killed off everything in sight, and outside of Alaska such bone yards of mass slaughter are nowhere
reported. No, the mammoth herds probably did not die in
Armageddons but in single, individual deaths, like most of us.
And the cause may not be far to seek. The mammoth was a
grazing animal, and while he declined another grazing animal
seems to have been doing very well. He was the bison, not of
the *Bison latifrons* variety, or the *Bison crassicornis*—both of
these kinds huge beasts that had lived as neighbors with the
mammoth for tens of thousands of years—but the relatively
smaller type that Folsom man killed. All we have to assume is
that the bison herds began, in this smaller version, to increase

in numbers, so that they encroached on and eventually stole the mammoth's food from under his nose. This wouldn't have been possible when moisture kept the range limitless, but when drought constricted it, competition meant that something had to give. And now we have to assume further that grazing over by bison left grass in a condition unusable by mammoths, as grazing by sheep denudes a pasture as far as cattle are concerned, and we can see the mammoth herds melting away year by year. As they grow scarcer and scarcer the big meat killers, especially the saber-tooth, whose need for warm, living blood must have been insatiable, depended more and more upon horse and camel and sloth until these had likewise gone to destruction. And when this supply was exhausted so were the big carnivores. But why didn't they fall on the bison herds? Perhaps they tried and failed. Bison have a habit of stampeding shoulder to shoulder at the slightest alarm which would make it extremely likely that a saber-tooth, for instance, that struck a bison would never live to eat it.

If the Great Extinction is ever satisfactorily explained it will undoubtedly be by some such chain reaction of events as this. But nothing so pragmatic will ever satisfy the imaginative human ego, which will have noticed that when the great Pleistocene fauna left the stage it was exactly at the time that man was coming on it, no longer an animal himself, but a maker of devices, a turner of events, a setter of purposes, a discoverer of ways and means. The great beasts died out simply because their day was over and man's had come.

9

Man of Parts

Some pages back there was introduced the proposition that 15,000 B.P. was a time of division among the basic Amerind population; the herd hunters became confirmed in their big-game way of life probably because of their achievement of a specialized kind of hunting tool, the stone-tipped spear; and the Desert Culturists had already set their pattern of omnivorous exploitation of all available food sources. It has been suggested by an assemblage of prominent archaeologists that the technological period the end of which we have arbitrarily set at 15,000 B.P. be called the "unspecialized lithic," since no projectile points or manos or other tools any more specific than flake scrapers and choppers were then being made. This is wholly sound and illuminating classification, it seems to us, but, although accurately descriptive, somewhat narrower than our thesis of a basic Amerind population diverging into the cultural variations which follow 15,000 B.P. Our choice of a designation for this pre-15,000-B.P. millennial span is the Period of Primal Population, and it was chosen because it will cover the eventuality, which now seems unlikely, that American primates evolved a distinctly human race, as well as the pre-Wisconsin migrations (whether during the Sangamon or Yarmouth interglacial) now favored as the most likely origin of Amerinds.

Because our thesis is what it is, the era after 15,000 B.P. names itself—the Trifurcate (split three ways) period of population. What these three branches are has been mentioned often enough: the herd hunters; the Desert Culturists, hereafter to be called the usufructians; and the taiga-tundra hunters, to be called simply the taigans. We have called this a period of population, rather than simply a period of habitation or culture, because it seems likely that each of these three Amerind elements, following its own specialized way of life and breeding mainly within its own kind, grew more and more physically distinct during the next 7000 to 8000 years, until the dislocations of the Altithermal scattered them all and caused a commingling of strains.

It has been the custom among Americanists to speak of the people we have named herd hunters as the paleo (old)-Indian, or the paleo-hunter. But this usage carrries the connotation that when the paleo-hunter roamed the west he was its sole inhabitant, a view we know to be inaccurate. It is more helpful to describe him in terms of his way of life—hanging on the flanks of big-game herds and shifting with them—as a herd hunter; the Sioux and Blackfeet and other Plains Indians of history were herd hunters. There was no period which can truly be called the paleo-hunter period for the very good reason that the usufructians were just as contemporary with the herd hunters as neo-man was with paleo-man.

"Usufructian" is an unwieldy word, but it describes the kind of subsistence practiced by the Desert Culturists as no other does; and we cannot go on talking about Desert Culture when this pattern of subsistence is found in the eastern woodlands. The term anthropologists use for this period of hunting, snaring, fishing, scavenging, gleaning, grubbing, scrapping and scrounging is characteristically restrained; they called it food gathering or collecting, or hunting-gathering. The American College Dictionary defines "usufruct" thus: "*Roman and Civil Law*. The right of enjoying all the advantages derivable from the use of something which belongs to another, so far as is compatible with the substance of the thing not being destroyed or injured." Derivation: *usus*, use, and *fructus*, fruit. This exactly defines the subsistence pattern of the food gatherers—they availed themselves of all the fruits of the land without the slightest concept of ownership of it, and they enjoyed its fruits without damage to it of any kind, neither clearing it nor breaking it for cultivation nor wasting it in any way.

The origin of the designation "taigans" is obvious; it recognizes both the habitation of a restricted taiga-tundra zone and the boreal location of that zone. The taigans were hunters, but rather less intent on the pursuit of a single kind of big game, if Giddings' conclusion about them is correct, and they were not entirely American in that the bicontinental province they occupied embraced Alaska and eastern Siberia. As we shall see, however, they participated in one postglacial cultural development of North America as equal partners with the usufructians and the herd hunters, receiving as well as giving.

There is nothing dogmatic about setting the time of cultural trifurcation at 15,000 B.P.; it merely happens to be a round number and, as a multiple of five, more convenient. Krieger has given his opinion that the Clovis fluted point may be of this age (but no older than 18,000 years), and a distinctive type of point, with a single shoulder, has been discovered beneath Folsom points in a cave in the Sandia Mountains of New Mexico and guess-dated at 15,000 B.P. Antevs has given his opinion that the Clovis points found with a mammoth at Naco, Arizona, are about 12,000 years old. With this kind of information to deduce from, it is pointless to try to be exact. Even when an indisputable Clovis site is, as one some day must be, C14 dated, it will be difficult to say whether it is early or late in the fluted-point sequence; not only was the culture of these herd hunters minimal, it was so conservative that nothing about it changed for thousands of years; the only guideposts in the long span of the tradition were set up when the mammoth became extinct, and Clovis points ceased to be made and the related Folsoms began to be, and were used against *Bison taylori*. At the MacHaffie site in Montana a stray Clovis point was found in a wash, possibly from a nearby location which had 8000-year-old Scottsbluff points at the bottom and late types near the surface; but in all the time here encompassed, perhaps 10,000 years, the point type was all that had changed; the rest of the artifact inventory was the same; the technology had not even improved.

The date 15,000 B.P. will have to stand, then. What we need more than an exact date is some clue that will indicate to us that Clovis points were "invented" in America. Since the unique fluting feature is found on points nowhere else in the world, we can approach the search for a clue with some confidence that it is there.

We have already suggested two courses by which the stone-tipped spear came into being: the evolution from a poke stick applies to the usufructians; the fending-stick, hafted-knife explanation comes immediately to mind when you take a look at the 15,000-year-old Sandia point mentioned above. Even unhafted it looks like a knife; it is a stemmed point with but one shoulder, instead of the two found in the typical, bilaterally symmetrical, stemmed point. In general form it is like a table knife and it has the two different linear edges that it is my impression most Amerinds favored in their knives—one straight edge and one excurvate edge.

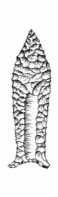

FINE FLINTSMITHING

At left is a Clovis fluted point, in the center a Folsom. Not all Folsoms were as finely done as this. The evolution from Clovis form to Folsom form seems fairly obvious. What links the European Solutrean blade at right to Clovis-Folsom is the startlingly meticulous retouch so early on the technological scale. After the Solutreans no such precise work was done in Eurasia and Africa for thousands of years, and in America it seems to have petered out after about 7000 B.P.

But the flute in the Clovis point suggests that this type had its own origin. It has been the tendency of American archaeologists to think that because the Clovis is a point which is lanceolate in form, and has a flute in it, the lanceolate form comes first and the fluting was a feature added later, as a sort of refinement. The reasoning by which this notion was arrived at is opaque. If we accepted it, the origin of the Clovis point would only be put off, not solved, and we do not have to put it off, by reason of either archaeology or technology. The posited pre-Clovis lanceolate has never been found in America and we can safely predict that it will not be. The unfluted lanceolate form, of which the Plainview is the best example, occurs in American archaeology *after,* long after, the Clovis point ceased to be made, for the very good reason that only by this time had technology changed to the place where the flute was not needed.

A short review of this change seems to be called for and it has to begin with the explanation that while there are short Clovis points and long ones, well-made and carelessly made ones, they are typically long, narrow, rather digital in outline and comparatively thick. In order to make a neat jointure where the base of the point slips into the split end of the spear shaft, this base had to be thinned somewhat. The flute, which is really not very pronounced in most Clovis specimens—it lives up to the term only in the Folsom—consists of one, two or three longish flakes struck off lengthwise of the blade from the base. As often as not, this fluting is found on one side only in the Clovis, though Folsoms usually are bifacially fluted. When it occurred to some herd hunter to thin the whole point, fluting was dropped, but not from the Clovis lanceolate; it was dropped from the Folsom, for the Plainview is Folsom, not Clovis, in outline and has been called the unfluted Folsom.

We will have to consider the Clovis fluted, it seems, as unique, so that it has to suggest its own origin. We might therefore be baffled by it except for the fact that Krieger has pointed out that at the Clovis type site there are evidences of a pre-Clovis occupation during which no stone points at all were made and weapon tips were of bevel-base pointed bone. This recalls to us that splintered bones, which may have been used as tools, were found at Tule Springs, and the fact that a bone splinter would be one of the most easily obtained of pointed, penetrating devices. We must now assume that the Clovis people began attaching bone splinters to their fending sticks as a way of protecting or stiffening the point, which perhaps they did not know how to fire-harden. This can be done simply, for a wooden shaft will fit into the marrow channel of a bone of the right size very snugly. But bone is not a strong material, compared to stone, and where its use for spear or harpoon points is most highly developed, as among the Eskimos and the Aurignacians, the customary game is thin-skinned, such as seal or deer. Against the tougher hides of mammoth and bison, bone was probably little better than wood, except that its use could suggest the idea of an attachable point, made of a more durable material. I think it safe to assume that the Clovis people knew enough about the properties of stone by this time to think of substituting it for bone in projectile points. And when they did, they did the most natural thing in the world; they imitated the shape of a bone point in stone. But bone is hollow and stone is solid, and when the problem of jointure of the point to the shaft came up it was also solved by imitation—by inlaying a slight "marrow channel" in the stone.

This stone-pointed spear must have been all the Clovis hunters hoped it would be, because they went on making it for at least 5000 years and perhaps 8000. And it must have satisfied them utterly because, after the burst of inventiveness that produced it, they seem to have invented nothing further of significance. It was undoubtedly the efficiency of the Clovis fluted point that committed its makers to their herd hunting, and such was its attraction for them that they wanted no other way of life.

This attractiveness of the big-meat, plains-wandering life must be the explanation for the most notable aspect of the herd-hunting cultural tradition, the number of strongly differentiated projectile-point types. When, after the mammoth disappears, bison herds take over their pasturage, it is not only the Clovis-like Folsom that is made; now appear the Long-Angostura, the Plainview, the Plainview-like Milnesand, the Scottsbluff, the Nebo Hill, the Gypsum Cave, the Abilene (which may be the prototype of the Long), the Lake Lahontan, the Yuma-technique lanceolates, the Lerma and many others. The tendency has been to think of all these as variations on or evolutions from the two established earliest types, Clovis and Sandia. This is undoubtedly a valid line of thought, but to it must be added the likelihood that groups of Desert Culture peoples abandoned their usufructian ways and, going all out for herd hunting, adapted their traditional point types to their

new trade. There is, of course, a distinct possibility that there
were more tribes of mammoth hunters than the Clovis and the
rare Sandia; that there were tribes which have not yet appeared in the archaeology. We would expect this. If, as we
have been supposing, the earliest Amerind was a coyote kind
of herd follower, the evolution of many bands of men into
herd hunters is the likeliest eventuality in the cultural world.
As an eater of the leavings of killer beasts, this coyote man had
to learn to fight off coyote animals and other carnivorous rivals,
and he learned his lessons well.

10

 *Troglodytes?*

Those who did not learn their lessons well, or were too skittish about big game to hunt it, or were unlucky and could not find enough of it to support them, became the usufructian Desert Culture. But this was a scrounging tradition, too, on the land in general instead of on herd beasts, and as such was as natural a development out of the basic Amerind as hunting specialization. It was the more successful tradition of the two: herd hunting, on the archaeological evidence, had to be abandoned during the Altithermal that blighted the Great Plains pastures, but the usufructians were adaptable to any situation or habitat that could provide foodstuffs.

To place the time when they began to shape a culture to this scrounging economy at 15,000 B.P. is merely to project the argument backwards from Danger Cave's 11,000-year level. There are no other dates at present to go by. If the Danger Cave usufructians, at 11,000 B.P., were living in cave or overhang shelters; having a care for their own comfort by making beds of bark and grass; shoeing themselves with fiber sandals; parching seeds, or grinding them into flour and making mush and gruel; cooking stews in watertight baskets or containers of skin by the hot-rock method—if they were doing and making all this by 11,000 to 9000 B.P., to allow them 4000 to 6000 years to learn how does not seem unreasonable.

Jennings, the excavator of Danger and the other two Wendover caves, evaluates this culture as accretional, not developmental. New tool items and new methods were added to the cultural inventory without really changing it or, in a sense, complicating its pattern toward the complexities of higher types of society. What is meant here is best illustrated by the fact that as early as 15,000 B.P., European paleolithic man was a painter and sculptor "whose artistic accomplishments," according to Ashley Montagu, "could not be bettered by any artist who has lived since." And these accomplishments were but threads of a fabric of intellectual and social progress that included rudimentary ideas in religion, philosophy, social organization or government, and science.

Hence, to arrive at the basic, unspecialized-lithic, generalized-scavenger Tule Springs type at 15,000 B.P., we merely have to subtract traits. For one by one these traits had been experimented with, tested, adapted. These usufructians had to be as conservative as snails; to abandon one habit in favor of another, to modify the rote—this might be no better than a beggar's gamble, the safe crusts against a fatal nothing. But nature is not conservative, as we have just permitted the glaciers to teach us, and it tried the Desert Culturists sorely. Every time a staple was withdrawn from their diet a substitute had to be found, and often this required the invention of a new tool or method of acquisition, or of a new process of rendering it edible. True, the Desert Culturists outwitted nature at every turn. Anybody who has ever worked in a steel mill or in any place where the dust is noisome and noxious knows that a tobacco cud is not only not unsanitary, but is a necessity of oral hygiene, as well as a practical substitute for a dipper of water every five minutes. Living in an atmosphere not too different from that of a steel mill—hot, dry, full of alkaline dust—the Desert Culturists did not chew tobacco, but they chewed quids of what they had—bulrush and other such fibers. Fiber quids have been discovered in Danger Cave. Undoubtedly there was some food value in this primitive equivalent of chewing gum—which, incidentally, Amerinds in Meso-America discovered eventually, probably as a consequence of such quid chewing. And just such an inspiration as this is the milling of seeds into flour and the preparation of this into mush, as a food stretcher; mush and hoecakes fill bellies better than raw grain, and stew or soup makes a meal out of a cut of meat that would not provide a bite apiece around for the members of a growing family.

Jennings lists the following in the material inventory for early Danger Cave: basketry and cordage; netting and matting; the use of fur cloth made of rabbit hair; tumplines as a carrying device; sandals as early as 9,000 B.P.; the atlatl, or throwing stick, which means the manufacture and use of projectile points; pointed shafts used without stone points; flat milling stone with cobble grinding stone by at least 9,000 B.P.; the digging stick; the fire drill; horn spoons.

This is a considerable aggregate of accomplishment, and archaeology now, after years of underestimating the Amerind, must bow to the irony that, despite the artistic accomplishments of the Aurignacians, at 10,000 B.P. these Desert Culture usufructians, with their accretional economy, were among the most advanced people in the world.

Danger Cave, in which Jennings not only reports at length and in detail (even the fecal matter was analyzed for food use) on the Wendover Caves occupants but establishes the character, age and prehistoric significance of the whole usufructian tradition, has at the moment an importance in American prehistory that will probably never be exceeded, since it establishes a source of illumination deep in the past which casts its beams in both directions—deeper into antiquity and as modernly ahead as our day.

Here, in the Wendover Caves, Jennings has found just that treasury of traits—of basketry, projectile-point forms, manos, footgear, small-grain use, etc.—on which the archaeologist can draw to explain what he finds elsewhere in America. He now knows where to turn—and it is not toward Bering Strait —when he wishes to trace population and cultural relationships; American prehistory explains itself.

It is not difficult to trace this Desert Culture from Fort Rock Cave in Oregon, where sandals were dated at 10,000 B.P., to Ventana Cave in Arizona, as famous archaeologically as Danger Cave and dated in its lowest level at the same 10,000 B.P., and thence to Lake Texcoco, in Mexico. These marginal-land usufructians reached, trick by trick, by trial and error, the ultimate possible adjustment to their environment in millennia long past, and when they reached it they stopped like a man climbing a flagpole: they had got as far as they could go. When archaeologists come upon the occupation areas of this culture, so uniform everywhere throughout the Great Basin, and so like what was practiced into historic times, it would have been

strange if they had suspected an 11,000-year duration for it;
how could they have suspected that these were our American
"cave men"?

The roll of western caves wherein have been found the poor,
priceless artifacts of these durable people is a long one: Danger, Juke Box, Raven, Fort Rock, Ventana, Fishbone, Roaring
Springs, Lovelock, Humboldt, Leonard Rock Shelter, Stick,
Crypt, Gypsum, Etna, Promontory, Black Rock, Tularosa,
Dead Man, Pictograph—and the roll is not here complete nor
likely soon to be ended.

A long life, but a hard one; only toward the end, Jennings
says, did these usufructians make crude clay figurines. They
played games, gambling games probably, but "no great evidence of a concern with art or decorative efforts is noted. . . .
The lack of artistic development and of leisure time for elaborate games seems to re-enforce an earlier interpretation that
there was little leisure and a relatively bleak emotional-
esthetic life."

Most of a certainty these were not the Aurignacians or the
Magdalenians, but were they uninventive, backward, ambi-
tionless, benighted, numbskulled?

No.

But let Jennings tell it, as he does in his final chapter, "Implications" (in archaeological reports the final chapter, usually
labeled "Conclusions" or "Implications," is the important one
and you read it first so that you'll know what the text is all
about), and as he does to the eternal reshaping of American
prehistory. He says:

"For example, at the time of writing, the Danger Cave
twined basketry from level II is among the oldest dated basketry or textile known to archaeology. These pieces, along with
the Oregon sandals, the twining from Leonard Rock shelter
and the twined specimens apparently found on level IV of
Fishbone Cave—all older than 7000 B.C. [9000 B.P.]—permit
a suggestion that simple basketry and probably other weaving
techniques (e.g., the Fishbone Cave matting) were widely
practiced in western North America before textile work was
known in the Eurasiatic neolithic. It is even possible to speculate on evidence from radiocarbon dating that American weaving is antecedent to Old World textile work and *was perhaps
introduced from here to Eurasia.*" (Italics mine.)

"Similarly the harvesting of small grains and the milling of these for food was known over the Desert West—and Middle West—by 8000 B.C. [10,000 B.P.]. The harvesting and milling techniques, and probably gruel cookery, are not reported from the Near East before 6000 B.C., so, for the moment, it is possible to suggest that *this complex also is an American invention which entered Asia from the east.* [There are, of course, milling stones from undated Asiatic sites which are labeled mesolithic; the latter term is a cultural designator rather than an absolute time indicator.] While making no attempt to establish in detail a theory of continuous two-way trans-Pacific contact since Wisconsin's time I am fascinated to note that a very early east-to-west intercontinental exchange can be argued from today's evidence. And it can be argued that the domestication of small grain may have been begun on this continent, to be abandoned only when maize, a crop more easily handled by aboriginal techniques, was developed. In any case, the Basin provides the semi-arid climate regarded by many as prerequisite to the beginnings of plant domestication." (Italics mine.)

Jennings bestows on Luther S. Cressman his accolade for formulating the idea of this ancient usufructian complex in 1940, and of maintaining it stoutly ever since. Jennings says, "He has never wavered from this position and must be credited with having correctly assessed the scanty archaeological, geological and cultural evidence at his command." Further, Jennings says that the complex is certainly pre-Mankato in age, and has been long in place.

There can now be no turning back to that Hrdlicka-Hooton past of tides of culture-bearing immigrants. What could they possibly have brought that the Amerind did not have?

Vindicated now, it would seem, is the autochthonous, or home-grown, origin of Amerind culture. Hooton's opinion of this view has already been quoted in one memorable passage. He repeats this opinion in other passages, one of which we will quote for an extension of our purpose:

"American anthropologists usually deny that Old World cultures have influenced to any great extent the pre-Columbian development of the American Indian. [Pay no attention to this; it is an old theatrical trick, to proclaim that your enemies oppose you in overwhelming numbers and you are a lone hero standing against them; most Americanists were then and still are on Hooton's side.] We have set up for aboriginal America a sort of *ex post facto* Monroe Doctrine and are inclined to regard suggestions of alien influences as acts of aggression. This is probably a scientifically tenable position, although I am afraid it has often been maintained in part by an emotional bias—an 'America for Americans' feeling."

As we have noticed before, Hooton has a genius for composing arguments to refute what is utterly beside the point. But here he touches on the academic atmosphere in which American prehistory has been investigated for three-quarters of a century—the smog of emotional bias—and this is very much to the point of our subject. At no time during the period of study of American prehistory was the evidence in favor of culture-bearing migrants decisive; at no time was it any more than predisposing. The assumption that it was decisive, and the action on this assumption, had to be, therefore, emotional; and castigation of the kind Hooton, Hrdlicka, *et al.*, saw fit to administer to those holding a contrary view was never demanded by a stern and disinterested sense of scientific discipline. It would hence seem urgent to advance some theory or other of a cause for this attitudinizing.

When I was somewhat younger, attending, as was my right, William S. Hart and Tom Mix movies on Saturday and reading the early Zane Grey books after lights-out, the pioneer's hate-fear for Indians still prevailed in literature and public psychology. They were marauders against the innocent, murderers of women and children, and the only good one was a dead one. Helen Hunt Jackson's *Ramona* was a cry in the wilderness; Indians, except Uncas and his father, were villains from the moment they burst from ambush on screen or printed page. But the generation is gone who heard at their grandfather's knee what horror was felt through the nation at the news of Custer's massacre, or the Minnesota uprising of Red Cloud's Sioux during the Civil War, and a humaner, less partisan feeling for American Indians pervades our books and movies and TV programs.

Slowly it is beginning to be clear to us as a nation that our forebears were collectively guilty of a deed for which there was not even a name until the Second World War caused it to be coined; they were guilty of what, if you are among the winners, is justifiable survival of the fittest, but if you are a loser is genocide. I have a suspicion that the emotional bias of American prehistory theory is not unrelated to some awareness of this historic tragedy.

For in retrospect we now see that instead of killing off Indians like species of buffalo there might have been adopted the attitude of John Rolfe when he married Pocahontas—they might have been racially assimilated; with many tribes the color difference from whiteness was so slight that recent physical anthropology insists on the strong Caucasoid or "white" strain in the Amerind; and the comeliness of tribe after tribe, the Crows and Shawnees, the Senecas and Creeks, was attested by contemporary observers. The Indian held no inhibitive prejudice against interbreeding with the white man; but where the quondam Europeans interbred they deliberately debauched, and that gentlest and most humane of all possible ways of conquering a people, by absorbing them into the blood stream, was made to seem a social degradation by a self-styled Christian people.

There was never any government policy on Indians other than extermination; there was never any social attitude toward them of any vogue except the usual businessman's attitude of exploiting them and cheating them until they perished, and then appropriating their lands. The government made contracts to buy Indian lands at the point of a gun and then let its own agents steal the purchase price; it sent dishonorable army officers to deal with Indians, and it sent even more disastrous "honorable" ones, like George Custer. Had the Indians been cattle they would have been better treated, and allowed more pasture to graze on, for cattle can't be fattened on the prairie at more than one head per acre, but the Indians were expected to live on land without "cattle," that is, buffalo. Out of forty-eight states we couldn't give one back to be the sanctuary and training ground and homestead of Indians.

We could not even give them the satisfaction of knowing they were giving way to an admirable people. One looks down the 350-year history of the dealings of "civilized" and "Christianized" white nationalities without finding a single instance

of any large attempt to treat Indians other than as sacrificial
beasts. Here and there a mission was set up by Franciscan or
Moravian, whose influence in a specific area was benign for
a while, but whose ultimate effect was that of a Judas goat,
to lead the tractable to the slaughter pen. White-Indian relations always culminated in a land treaty, and when a land
treaty was written its provisions were always that the Indians
vacate their homelands absolutely; it was never that they keep
this village and that, and these fields and those bottomlands,
by which to support themselves as long as they kept the peace.
The Shawnees of Ohio and Indiana had such villages, of cabins
as snug as any the pioneer battered up, and surrounded by
orchards and cultivated acres of corn and beans and pumpkins.
But, of course, Mad Anthony Wayne, after the battle of Fallen
Timbers, did not say in the treaty of Greenville, "Keep your be-
loved Piqua and Chillicothe and till in amity and prosper and
become good friends to us." The standard form of the epic of
America in which the pioneers thrust westward sweeping aside
forests, ripping up the plains and overstriding mountains is
only half the story of titanic devastation; they pulverized a
race of human beings, too. But it is never quite told this way,
and this presents itself as a reason why the epic of America
has begot only political oratory and Hollywood spectaculars,
few literary gems and no dramatic masterpieces. We shudder
from the truth and mourn only the loss of the big woods and
the sea of grass.

Given such an outline of the case, any cocktail party psy-
chologist could predict accurately the syndrome of exculpatory
pretexts that a guilty society would contrive for the easement
of its conscience.

It would be held that the Amerind was a latecomer (not
earlier than 3000 B.P.) and hence hadn't really secured title
to these lands by length of occupation; and even if some hunters had stopped by here briefly in 10,000 to 12,000 B.P., they
were shiftless vagabonds who left their patrimony untended
and vanished seven or eight thousand years ago. It would be
held that the Amerind was pretty much of a savage, with bar-
barous moral and religious ideas and, while technically a man,
deficient in the qualities of, say, a John Jacob Astor. It would
be held that he was racially backward and ineducable and not

likely to become much even if allowed to live and propagate. It would be held that he had invented nothing, had as a matter of fact borrowed all he possessed, and hence was owed not even an abstract debt of gratitude by humanity for any contribution to its progress. It would be held that he was a member of an alien and hence inferior race (surely there are those reading this who remember the Oriental Exclusion Act of the 1920's), and hence was without claim on any blood loyalties or neighborly sympathies. It would be held that there was nothing about him that need interest us, in our academies of advanced science; he was neither primitive enough nor advanced enough, and when he vanished we had lost nothing we couldn't replace from a more convenient source.

Scientists, of course, like to think themselves not susceptible to this kind of topical mass mood, and when they recognize it they can usually avoid succumbing personally. But what they usually fail to realize is that it is what the populace is disposed to listen to that elects some of their number to eminence and others to obscurity. The industrial revolution made quick ears and approving eyes for Malthusian economics, as the aftermath of the Second World War left the English-speaking public attentive to Toynbee's philosophy of history. Although it would be extravagant to imply that any great number of American citizens ever cared one way or another about whether the Amerind was a late Mongoloid immigrant, that the view was not more critically questioned argues an almost personal acquiescence on the part of those who did care, the origin of which is not nearly as scientific as it will be passionately affirmed to be. Evaluation of evidence comes down, in the end, to a will to believe, and the roots of the will to believe are in the emotions. Hooton was quite right, in all probability, in claiming emotional bias, to the point of chauvinism, in the proponents of all-American Amerinds. But a great deal more might have come of his idea if he had suspected that what he found in others might be equally inherent in him. For who is prepared to advance an idea or defend it as, say, Huxley defended *The Origin of Species* unless he has first intimately embraced it?

It is tempting to take the hand dealt us by Danger Cave and Jennings and play it to the limit; perhaps, with emotional bias,

overplay it. Can't it now be urged, on the evidence, that the
Mongols received their small-grain domestication (they raised
millet) and even their very Mongolism from the Amerind? It
could be, but it will not be, by us, for we are already on record
as quoting with approval Rainey's observation that there are
no signs of migration across the Bering bridge and through
Alaska during the time when neolithic culture bearers were
supposed to have been on the move; such negative evidence
would apply equally whichever way the migration was moving. But we have gone further than this, and supposed an im-
penetrability for Alaska that we cannot now disregard. This
was the region of the taigans, Giddings has suggested, a culture as finely adapted to it as the Desert Culture usufructians
were adapted to their marginal environment. Why would the
usufructians have left the land they knew best to go to Alaska?
How could they have lived during their passage through this
alien territory? By alien we do not mean to imply hostile. They
could have gone up the "corridor" and through Alaska without
interference—except for the climate and the environment,
which would have fought them all the way. The taigans did
not move south, except as the taiga-tundra spread south; nor,
we think, did the usufructians move north to find living space;
it's a big country.

Jennings found at Danger Cave that the Amerind invented
his culture and this is an important "victory," if you will, over
the opposing view; but strangely enough, it is not the one this
study hopes to win. Though our main concern here is American prehistory, and our protagonist is the Amerind, we are
students of all humanity and do not root as partisans for one
race over another as though prehistory were a football game.
The victory hoped for Jennings' Desert Culture is over the
cramped and crusty view that the human race could invent a
method, a trait, a technique, a tool, only once.

Human beings are quite capable of having invented plant
domestication in the Jarmo area of Iraq and the Great Basin
of the United States separately and without the Amerinds
prompting the Jarmoists or vice versa, and the reason they are
capable is that the human brain is a standard and dependable
organism which functions very reliably, and not a sort of Christmas stocking into which Santa Claus has stuffed imagination

and inventiveness for some favorites while leaving empty those of the naughty.

The brain, like any other muscle, makes itself with use; it is all that it has been able to do and has attempted but failed to do; it is both its own emotion-impressed memory of past experience and the sensuous awareness of, as well as engagement in, present experience. Which is to say that there is imposed on every new experience the lingering afterimages of past experience and these modify the new experience in such a way that it is never precisely new, yet never precisely repetitive. The more an experience is repeated, therefore, the more certainly will modifications accumulate, until a kind of conceptual sport takes place and the mind thereafter begins to "have" an experience in an entirely new way.

Because of these modifications, of eons of them, it is probably forever beyond us to think ourselves back to how even the Desert Culture mind "experienced" stone and growing things. We now know too many things about stone that primitive people did not, to guess what values, what memories, what superstitions, what sensations coalesced in the brain of an Amerind of 15,000 B.P. when he happened on a piece of flint. Yet the mind is not so vaporous a thing as we tend to think when we refer to it as mainly a spiritual essence. Its muscle, the brain, is engaged in the constant exercise of holding tight to past experience and tugging it out of the past into the present and, finally, ejaculating it into the future. Obviously the brain, and the mind, are not dealing with a protean substance of an innumerable variousness of forms when they deal with stone, and experiences with stone. The modifications which can take place from repetitive experiences with stone must be, necessarily, limited: the sharpness of stone chips, therefore the sharpening of them; the penetrating pointedness, therefore the sharpening to a point; the heaviness and shortness of stone, therefore the conjoining of its sharp, pointed shortness to the slender, light lengthiness of a wood shaft. But the modification of experience of things has to eventuate in a modification of the things experienced; the modification of experience becomes, in the mind, thought; in the thing, invention.

This modification of experience, were it occurring only within an individual, would be an extraordinarily protracted progress were it not also that the difference in modifications between individuals can be communicated by speech, which itself is an invention. Not only does language convey my experience to you, so that each of us sees the disparity between our experiences, but my telling about it also modifies my experience, for I am summing up what is physically absent and must therefore be experienced by you in an entirely different way than by me, a participant. And I cannot help but make the difference in my experience clear to you, for I may have experienced the sharpness of stone by slicing my finger, while you may have a more vivid experience of stone as heavy by having thrown it and knocked over a sitting rabbit; we may, therefore, have different names for stone sharp and stone cast, and so I induce a modification of your experience of stone and you induce one in mine by disagreeing with mine (O glorious, fruitful spark and light-giving principle that disagreement produces the hybrid new, and agreement produces the reiterative stagnant).

Despite our differences in experience of stone, neither of us is ever likely to believe that stone can fly like a bird, though our word for the cast stone may denote that we have observed a similarity in aerial progression; nor are we likely to conclude that it can cut without a sharp edge. Our experiences with stone must therefore be corrected and directed by the nature of stone itself, in an ineluctable or "logical" pattern. Having experienced stone or growing things for a long time, and in all ways possible to us and to them, we cannot avoid becoming more knowing, more "sophisticated" about them, and this sophistication will not permit us to act as though we did not know while directing us to act in the light of what we do know; and how else can invention be described?

I daresay that when peoples who were once highly inventive, such as the Greeks or the Mayas, reach a state of cultural entropy or become more and more vestigial to the body of human society, the cause has nothing to do with a deterioration of individual or collective minds; the mind cannot be stopped from learning or developing except by itself, by a McCarthyism which is the use of the mind to reject the works of the mind, the use of the fact of being to prevent the coming into being of the uninvented. A society can stifle itself by accepting the often plausible doctrine that modification violates what must remain inviolable by order of the instinct of self-preservation. This radical and unnatural doctrine is strangely enough usually called conservatism and it has, fortunately, not yet prevailed over the entire world at the same time. When it does the human race is on the verge of its great extinction, even as nations and races have atrophied because of it.

It is scarcely to be thought, however, at a time like the present when nearly everything that was believed to be gospel begins to turn apocryphal (and even the law of parity, that fundamental axiom of physics without which no valid conclusions could be reached at all, it was thought, has been whisked from under the universe), that the venerable postulates of American prehistory were any more immutable than the rest; the never really tested hypothesis that the Amerind was an Asiatic transplant had to go, and the Desert Culture has banished it, but the axiom on which it was based, that the human mind could invent the rudiments of human technology and culture only once—that is likewise irreparably damaged. As it had to be. Nothing would seem to be more obvious than that the human animal brain was capable of learning from others only after it had become capable of learning from experience. In the isolation of America the Amerind had nothing but experience to learn from.

11

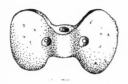 *Eastern, or Late Variety*

Some pages back there was told the list of caves wherein the usufructians of the Great Basin had left relics of their ageless culture. Omitted, for good reason, were Graham, Modoc and Russell. These are to the eastward—Graham in Montgomery County, Missouri; Modoc Rock Shelter in southern Illinois; Russell in northern Alabama—and the migration of the usufructians from what we have assumed, not too positively, to be their heartland in the Great Basin is at these sites corroborated for dates as early as 11,000 B.P.

Much has been made already of the stimulus to population movement that climatic change quite evidently was, but this may not be the whole story. The earliest date on Russell Cave, a good two thousand miles east of Danger Cave, is 9000 B.P. At the tip of South America, six thousand miles from Danger, is Palli Aike Cave, dated at 8500 B.P. This was, on first discovery, identified as the site of a hunting culture; but I think we may overlook this; so might Danger Cave, at that time, have been called a hunters' shelter, by reason of the finds of projectile points. Certainly the Palli Aikeans were not herd hunters. I think we may take them to be our usufructians, and they give us an extension of this tradition from Illinois and Alabama, from Oregon and Utah, all the way to Chile. However immoderate the climate, it would appear that there must have been a strain of usufructians who were just plain peripatetic.

But the usufructian talent for piecing out a livelihood from whatever was edible was equally suited to clinging to a stringent environment or taking to the road. These scroungers were not restricted to a single principal source of all benefaction, like the herd hunters, nor to a complex but special ecology, like the taigans. They ate of whatever was set on the table, and their table was the earth. They left no stone unturned, no tree unclimbed, no field ungleaned, no pool unplumbed; and they would have been as hard to get rid of as fleas.

What we must now note is that the Desert Culture was a distinctive manifestation of usufructians, with tool kits and methods perfected for dealing with particularized living conditions. Because those living conditions were demanding, the Desert Culture early reached the stage of versatility that we have boldly proclaimed the most advanced in the world at the time. The eastern usufructians do not merit the same appraisal. In the east living was fatter, and the eastern usufructians put forth no more effort than was necessary to get it.

Our first instance of the eastern usufructian is at Modoc Rock Shelter, in southwestern Illinois, barely trans-Mississippi and located at the time of habitation in a mixed prairie and woodland milieu. The artifact recoveries from the very lowest zone, C14 dated at about 11,500 B.P., immediately establish the relationship of the Modocans with a Tule Springs–into–Desert Culture tradition. The prompt preliminary report by archaeologists-in-charge Melvin L. Fowler and Howard Winters lists the following for the bottom zone, at 21.5 to 26.5 feet below the surface: 1 generalized grinding stone; 2 projectile points; 2 thick end scrapers and 10 flake scrapers; 1 split bone awl; 1 perforated pebble pendant. Yes, the chopper we have become accustomed to finding in these contexts is missing, but it, with a plenitude of hammer stones, shows up in the next level, which is probably contiguous in time.

There is nothing at all here to discourage us from believing that Modocan ancestors came east, or northeast, or east and then north (Modoc is in the Mississippi alluvial plain and we see these people as striking east to the river and then drifting north up the valley), at some time prior to the full development of the Danger Cave Desert Culture specialization; that is, some time during the Playa Sequence time in the lower Great Basin territory. For almost as we find the Modocans, they have already become something different—and locale adapted. In zone II there appear a celt fragment and an ax. It requires

something close to willful obtuseness to read these as anything
other than woodworking tools, implements for which the Desert Culturists had little need, and for which the Modocans
would have had many, including the making of dugout canoes.

Fowler and Winters make the point that the Modoc artifact
assemblage from the beginning of occupation to the top or
V zone is of one continuous, though improving, cultural tradition, which they call the Archaic (a term not of their coinage, and one which we will modify in a later section). What
is clear from this is that Modoc gives us something to compare
with Danger Cave, and what seems even clearer, by reason of
this comparison, is that the Modocans were not as "advanced"
as their Danger Cave contemporaries and that the reason is
not far to seek—they did not have to be.

They did not have to be, for the simple and basic economic
reason that food was not as hard to come by. Evidence for the
preparation of vegetable food at Modoc is present, but weak;
these usufructians placed their dietary reliance on another
staple, the deer; mainly the white-tail deer, which is, incidentally, not a herding animal. Paul W. Parmalee, in his
analysis of Modoc faunal remains, reports that from 85 to
90 percent of the 23,200 unidentifiable fragments of bone were
of a large animal, probably deer; bones of deer were found
plentifully at all levels and in 85 percent of the excavation
units. If we are looking for an answer as to why the Modocans
settled in this vicinity, here it is, this abundance of deer, and
it must have been the deer that largely shaped their culture,
for such a quantity of deer bones bespeaks not only a quantity of flesh butchered, but a considerable expanse of hide
stripped off. What need, then, for the Modocans to weave
matting and make cloth of rabbit fur and entwine fibers into
cordage, when a deer hide could be cured and cut into mat
and moccasin, line and binding, clothing and containers? One
of the tools in the Modocans' kit when they came into this land
of faunal plenty was the atlatl (a banner stone—that is, an
atlatl weight—was found in zone II), and the Modocans simply specialized in its use, rather than in the use of the mano,
on which they had to rely, probably, only on rare meatless
days. They were, it can be safely said, still usufructians who

specialized toward the exploitation of the best available supply of food and other cultural goods.

Perhaps it is unfair to infer too positively, from the absence of matting, basketry, cordage and other such items of perishable manufacture from the Modoc refuse, that the Modocans never learned to make them, or ceased to make them if they had brought such skills from the west; after all, no buckskin is preserved there either. But usually, where basketry and matting is used, even though it disintegrates, impressions are left behind in the soil—such impressions were taken from both Graham and Danger caves. The preliminary report on the first Modoc excavations uncovered no such clues; it would not be strange if later work did uncover them, but it would be strange if they were uncovered in any profusion. We doubt that the Modocans ceased entirely to be western usufructians in the process of becoming early Illinoisians. The question to be resolved is what they brought with them from the west; did they arrive at Modoc before or after basketry and matting?

That these were usufructians we cannot doubt as we pore over their debris. Parmalee lists about 30 species of shellfish, 10 of fish, 17 of birds, 25 of mammals and 5 of turtles as identifiable in the skeletal material. The rodents and snakes he found he suspects of having been themselves inhabitants of Modoc, but we know enough about the usufructians to be sure they were fully accustomed to dining off mouse and mole and meaty reptile. In his note on turtles, Parmalee flashes us an insight that convinces us we are dealing here with the incurably omnivorous Amerind of Lewisville lineage. He writes: "Both of these species [the pond turtle and the painted turtle] are commonly found together in most river and lake habitats; they often become extremely abundant in sloughs and backwaters and in such localities were captured with probably little difficulty." The usufructian overlooked nothing, not even in the sloughs and backwaters.

It must be immediately apparent, now that we have acquired eastern as well as western usufructians, that our field of speculation has been more than slightly enlarged. The Modocans have wandered far from their hereditary heartland, in what seems to have been simply a roving mood. Yet when they arrived at Modoc they stayed in the vicinity for as many millennia as the Danger Cave inhabitants clung to their seasonal shelter. What can be made of these two apparently contradictory dispositions, toward extreme conservatism about locale, and toward vagrancy?

Jennings points out that the social organization of his Danger Cave people conforms to the conclusions reached by Fred Eggan in a study of Hopi social organization as related to ecology, and these are, mainly, that these usufructians lived in small, expanded-family bands—that is, the extended family of children, parents and grandparents, though it is doubtful that anybody living in such a band was not related by at least two blood lines to every other member, since it was what the anthropologists call "not exogamous," but was instead what we would call incestuous, and the clan did not grow in orderly generations.

The size of these bands was dictated by the amount of food they were able to take, with the means at their command, within the area which it was feasible for them to exploit. Obviously, during a protracted period of a relative abundance of food the membership could increase; an ensuing lean period would necessitate that the band contract its size, and customs or "laws" about how this contraction would take place must have been part of the social tradition. At a guess, it would be the younger, more vigorous members who would be expected to go, though it is also possible that because these were stronger the older and less able were expelled coercively. The former is the preferable guess because by argument from later, analogous societies it would appear that the separate bands assembled in common encampment at certain times of the year, possibly with ceremonial-biological purpose but under duress of the weather, which would have immobolized them anyway in their band shelters. Such congregations make a point for comity amongst territorial populations, rather than for the feuds and animosities that would have arisen from rejection.

We may, in the absence of anything to contradict, suppose that a system of primogeniture was in operation, by which the oldest son was expected to stand by father and mother, and younger sons and daughters were expected to strike out for themselves. If this manner of band division had the sanction of custom and was willingly acquiesced in, what we would expect is that the sibling band would go no farther from its parent band than the nearest suitable food location.

When we apply this kind of social dynamics to the Modocans the question is immediately raised whether they were migrant in any real sense of the word at all, or only a sibling band that had found a homestead only a few miles from their place of birth and rearing. Our interpretation of the character of the usufructians inclines us to accept this explanation of the habitation at Modoc; these folk were not trekkers; they were inchers. They were not going anywhere; they were only trying to stay where they were.

Yet this is the way the Americas were populated from Illinois to the Argentine. If we find this increase-and-divide theory plausible we must accept the fact that by 11,000 B.P. the usufructian-habitable land between Danger Cave and Modoc Rock Shelter was thinly but continuously peopled.

There is another possibility, of course: Lewisville–Tule Springs man may have long since scattered himself over the landscape and each regional culture was a regional development. No sites equivalent to Lewisville have been discovered in the east, which leaves this possibility unsupported; but it would not really change our notions about the usufructians if it should happen to be demonstrated. It would only corroborate that the more of them there were, the more they were the same.

By 9000 B.P., at the latest, this cell-by-cell growth of the Amerind racial body had extended into Russell Cave, in northern Alabama. It is a by now familiar state of affairs that we find here. Carl Miller, leader of the National Geographic Society party which excavated the cavern, found charcoal at a 14-foot level in his first year's dig which C14 dated at about 8000 B.P. In the next year's work, charcoal was found at 16 feet which dated at about 9000 B.P. Perhaps there are still older deposits, and perhaps the earliest date here will mark the beginning of an occupation that was continual till about 1650 A.D., when the white man first began to distribute his gimcracks among the natives.

No study of the archaeology of Russell Cave, either preliminary, like that by Fowler and Winters on Modoc, or defini-

tive, like that by Jennings on Danger Cave, has appeared as
of this writing. But such information as has become available
leaves no doubt that we are here seeing both repetition and
singularity. From near the lowest level came a banner stone;
in all levels there were projectile points, changing styles with
the general changes noted far beyond the premises of this occupation; in the 7-foot level there was a charred basket with
its burden of charred seeds still in it; at the 6-foot level there
was encountered the burial of a forty-five-year-old man, only
5 feet, 2 inches tall, who had died of an advanced case of
pyorrhea, a not surprising malady for a persistent consumer of

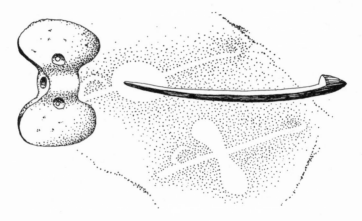

ATLATL AND BANNER STONE

In the background of these depictions of an atlatl
and a banner stone is a pictograph carved in rock, by the
Amerind users themselves, of an atlatl with banner stone
attached. Some banner stones, like the one shown, were
bored through and slipped onto the atlatl. Others were
simply tied on or, possibly, slotted into it. The banner
stone was a weight that added force to the spear cast.

a breakfast-cereal diet; buried with this Russellian was, if he
but knew it, the instrument of his destruction, a stone pestle,
used to reduce grain to meal or flour; in all but the earliest
levels there were fishhooks cut out of deer toes; bone awls
were plentiful; mussel shells were used for spoons, instead of
the horn used in the Desert Culture.

All this is very much in order; we miss the matting and textiles of Danger Cave, but the Russellians themselves probably did not, since they must have substituted hides, as we have surmised for Modoc, for the laborious manufacture of such materials. But the Russellians had a few tricks of their own: what are certainly bone rings, one of which may be a finger ring, turned up; the Russellians had thrown up a hide canopy on poles to protect them against a drip from the cave ceiling; a hinged fishhook of a type regarded as northern and used by recent Eskimos was found in an 8000-year context, and contemporary with it was the foreleg bone of a bear which had been hollowed out, packed with fat and used as a wick lamp, an implement heretofore regarded as Eskimo also. Even more than the Modocans the Russellians had flattered themselves with personal adornment; they painted themselves and hung themselves with beads and pendants, and the women kept their hair out of their faces with trig bone pins.

Russell Cave is probably as fine a reference library on the eastern usufructians as archaeology will ever come upon, and its total excavation may give American prehistory, if not a new sense of direction, at least a re-enforced confidence in the sense of direction given by Danger Cave; and it has already yielded one such re-enforcement—the hinged fishhook and the animal-fat lamp. These two items simply ought not to be (1) where they were found and (2) as old as they are. It has been said that they have a much more northerly and specifically an Eskimo connotation, which means not only sub-Arctic but relatively late. Their occurrence so early at Russell Cave can hardly be construed as cultural borrowing, for taigan and Alabama-usufructian contact at 8000 B.P. does not make archaeological sense. The only supposition that does make sense has been spoken, of the lamp, by Miller: "But by the end of the Archaic culture period—perhaps 5000 B.C. [7000 B.P.]—man had risen to a stage where he could think out such an invention, actually make the device and reap the results of his thought."

I think we may no longer tremble to say such a thing about Amerinds, or to propose that hinged fishhooks and animal-fat lamps may have followed a cultural trail from south to north, not vice versa. There is nothing endemically arctic about either.

Probably because we know the northern Alabama region to

have been during its history richly food productive, the impression left on us by these Russellians is of a people living comfortably, not to say cozily (the cave was naturally air-conditioned and a constant draft through it blew away the smoke of campfires), with few crises, not too many enemies (though one male skeleton was found with a projectile point in the back), and with very little to distract them from the serene enjoyment of what they probably enjoyed most—eating. The male-female situation was Oedipean enough, but there were probably none of the social repressions that incite Oedipean conflicts. To say that life must have been drab is but to compare it fallaciously with our own. No life is unbearably drab when so many generations suffer it unchanged for so long. It all depends on what you're interested in.

As one of life's most recurrent satisfactions, relishable food ought not be overlooked as an advantage of having been an eastern woodlands barbarian; many, perhaps most of us who are citified, will probably go through the rest of our lives without knowing the ineffable delicacy of the cereals known to the Russellians, of vegetable foods sun and wind ripened, of truly stream-fresh fish, of truly fresh-killed meat. The gustatory preferences of Indians may seem bizarre to us, but I very much suspect that the Indian taste buds were accustomed to food eaten raw or cooked in the full maturity of its savor, whereas the problem the American housewife has to deal with is how to induce into the bland comestibles sold as food in the super markets all the sapidity their packaging overenthusiastically claims for them. Food that ranged from frog legs and crawdad claws to the drumsticks of pigeons, from the marrow and brains and *boudins* of the croppers and browsers on sweet grass and tender new hazel leaves, to the fat-marbled steaks of the black bear, from the roots of wild turnips and the tubers called potatoes to the highest-hanging wild fox grapes, from pawpaws and frost-sweetened persimmons to bee honey, from the white meat of rattlesnakes to the white breast of turkey which the pioneers were later to call simply "bread"—this only begins the commissary list of the Amerind. Anybody who has ever drunk sassafras tea sugared with a drop or so of maple sap will wonder why all the pother about the East Indian kind— except, of course, for the element of caffeine. But the Amerinds to the south knew all about caffeine, too; and they were prime producers of it, in maté, and in cacao and lesser-known vegetals.

At the time of the discovery of America, there were something over 100 plants under domestication by Amerinds north and south—maize, white and sweet potatoes, pumpkins, peanuts, tomatoes, tobacco, half a dozen kinds of beans, the pineapple, manioc (tapioca), the strawberry, many plants not important to us now, and some, such as the grain amaranths, used for pot herbs, cereals and dyes, that we have forgotten ever existed. But food bulk was not all that the Amerind was interested in; apparently he subjected everything that grew to the taste test, and the list of his condiments was as long as the spice shelf of any *cordon bleu* graduate, beginning with the potent wild onion and the mints, and including chili and arrowroot and dill and ending with what the soda-fountain industry would collapse without—chocolate and vanilla.

Fats, of course, were to be had for the butchering and rendering, but since the Amerinds were not herdsmen it might be thought that they had nothing that resembled butter. They did; it is called bone grease, and here is the recipe: Let stand to dry for a day the stripped bones of buffalo, deer, elk or any such large animal; by pounding reduce these to chips the size of a fingernail; put these on to cook in a pot of cold water; when the water comes to a boil, reduce it to a simmer by adding cold water (snow, when you can get it); skim the grease off as it forms, with a horn spoon, and store in the bladder of the animal from which the bones were taken (it should still be around some place), and in this container it is guaranteed to keep for two or three years. The yield from the bones of one buffalo should be about five or six pounds; the same operation using, instead of bone chips, the viscera of fish, will produce a similar fat, but tasting very essentially of fish, and it should be used very sparingly, though it is highly recommended as a baby food. Bone grease was, however, good for any use that margarine or butter is good for, and was very likely used in making popcorn balls, among other things. Those who think that popcorn was first invented by M-G-M to fill movie theaters may now begin giving credit where they hadn't thought to give it—to the Amerind. The first maize cultivated

was a popcorn, and many American small grains, especially
varieties of the grain amaranths, exploded when heated, as the
Amerinds must have discovered a good 10,000 years ago, when
they first began seed parching. Whatever notion was knocking
around in their heads—religious, festive or sheer japery—when
they first thought of agglutinating the popped grains together
with a syrup into popcorn balls, insight, not archaeology, will
have to tell us, and I, who had always thought that popcorn
balls had been invented by a Sunday-school teacher as a
Christmas-tree decoration, choose now to believe that they
were a trick to make a handful of grain and a little sap into
a concoction that would take half an hour to eat instead of
half a minute; you cannot make a bigger, showier, tastier, gayer
meal out of next to nothing than by this ingenious technique.
It is almost like the miracle of the loaves and fishes.

Of one thing we may be quite sure: the Russellians knew a
great deal more about food than any but the specialists among
us are ever likely to; if they can be said to have had a profession, they and the Modocans and Dangerians, getting and preparing food was it. It would be quite inaccurate to think that
they spent the round of seasons in the shelter of their cavern;
wherever berries were ripening or nuts falling or a meadow
stood in ripening grain they probably set up their lean-tos and
feasted, beginning with the strawberry season (or earlier) and
drifting thence to the dewberry and huckleberry and blackberry patches (I have heard that one of the surest ways to
find Indian sites is to look in the vicinity of a long-standing
blackberry thicket), then on to the grass meadows and finally
to the nut groves.

In the piedmont of the Carolinas, not so far from Russell
Cave that you couldn't make it in a week or two of foot travel,
J. L. Coe reports on a series of small, almost inscrutable sites
called the Guilford Focus; Jennings has called attention to the
Guilford Focus as probably being related distantly to the Desert Culture people; he bases his opinion on the similarity of
projectile-point forms, and these Guilford point forms certainly
do resemble, at a comparable time level, the Russell Cave
forms. The Guilford sites are small, and are placed on hilltops
or at the ends of ridges near streams, and it is easy to see these
locations as one- or two-week camp sites of groups who fol-

lowed the wild crops through the sequence of their maturing.

It would be very difficult to convince people like this, when, after a normal spring-summer-fall, they had taken up winter quarters in a Russell Cave, and were sitting with their backs to its fire-warmed stone walls, with rabbit stew in the pot and a store of grain and nuts cached away, that they lacked very much of human contentment. Testimony as to the comparative rarity of sickness among the Amerinds of contact times—when not ravaged by some pestilence of the white man's infestation—is strong enough to allow the assumption that endemic immunities had long been operative against exposure debilities, the kind of affliction that would take off the civilized man who had to live under primitive conditions. But the usufructian had discovered a great deal more about the plants of his kingdom than whether they were edible. The pharmacopoeia of almost any historic tribe—and many have been studied by the Bureau of American Ethnology—shows specific remedies (usually accompanied it is true by some mumbo jumbo of homeopathic magic) for use in the presence of rather keenly differentiated symptoms; this pharmacopoeia must be assumed to be an ancient lore, and probably accomplished as many cures or alleviations (the Amerind is the "inventor" of both ipecac and the enema) as any European doctor or apothecary until the detection of the bacterial cause of disease; it was as inclusive and comprehensive as thousands of years of close observation of the failings and wayward behavior of the human body could make it without the assistance of a microscope. Amerinds had even gone so far that, finding it needful to practice abortion and to limit conception, they had discovered the herbs for the inducement of the one and the prevention of the other. The setting of broken bones, the poulticing of wounds, even crude surgery and dentistry (the treatment of cavities by sticking a blazing splinter in the hole strikes me as being altogether heroic), these were undoubtedly no less efficacious than in historic medical practice as late as the middle nineteenth century. What had civilization to offer the Amerind of 2000–1000 B.P. in his cave in the heart of a tranquil, food-various Alabama woodland that he should strive for it?

Social satisfactions? Intellectual stimulation? Entertainment? Knowledge? A keener sense of humanity?

The Amerind did not lack knowledge—he probably had as much information packed away in his head as the average assembly-line-working citizen, partly because he had nowhere else to keep what he and his kind knew—since there were no libraries, few experts and no secretaries to dictate file memos to—but mostly because he had to have everything he knew where he could instantly lay his hands on it. He didn't expect to have time to look something up or seek advice from a professional in those critical or flash situations in which what he knew and how he used it meant the difference between a whole hide and permanent retirement; and in a sense all situations were critical, for the Amerind was paid by production, not by the hour. Paul Mangelsdorf, who has contributed importantly to the study of early man, says, with a very pleasant simplicity, "There is no evidence that ancient man was inherently less intelligent than his modern counterpart," and if one cared to take the time he might even successfully advance the proposition that ancient man, by the enforcement of his way of life, had to be smarter than we are, for it is certainly the brain he developed and bequeathed us that we tend to be so loftily proud of now, as though each of us had personally fashioned his own to his private specifications. If mind is, as Percival Bailey says, "simply a name which we give to the functioning of the cerebral cortex," no one can seriously believe that the cerebral cortex has suddenly been stimulated to function in a way it never did before within the last five thousand years, any more than he can believe that the disappearance of the caudal appendage is a late development. It seems most reasonable to suppose that the cerebral cortex had to attain a certain efficiency of function before man could become what we insist on calling "civilized"; and he did become civilized because the functioning of this cortex made it possible for men to live civilly together and to learn from one another. What we call civilization is a communal construction, not an amassment of the end products of increasingly improved cerebral cortexes. Most of us partake of the goods of civilization without adding to them, except in the same way as an early Amerind added to his culture by "producing" fish from a stream. Most of us live out our span without ever having produced anything but run-of-the-mill ideas, which were not ours to begin with, yet which we repeat with the conviction that the ability to assimilate and repeat is the equivalent of having conceived. From what we have seen of the usufructians we can hardly continue to deprecate them for lack of inventiveness or ingenuity or self-reliance, or for ignorance or backwardness. They knew their jobs, they knew their business. What they had not yet invented, and what they were slow to invent, because they didn't need them, were societal instruments—forms of government for the organization of society for the accomplishment of large projects like the pyramids—or like the Hopewell mounds and Maya ceremonial cities and Inca roads. What seems to me to have been operating against such an invention was a fierce appetite for individual freedom, and a complete satisfaction with the rewards to body and soul of the usufructian way of life.

Just what effect the chance to live such a life can have on a relatively modern man has been tested. After Colonel Henry Bouquet had raised the siege of Pittsburgh during the rebellion of Pontiac he moved his army westward and brought the Shawnees in the Ohio country to their knees by burning their villages; one of the articles of their submission was that they return to civilization all white captives taken during the years of that border conflict, and a day was set for the deliverance of these long-held prisoners at Ligonier, Pennsylvania. In accordance with their given word the Shawnees appeared more or less on time, herding with them the wretches they had forced to live in hardship and heathenism and fear, for a joyous reunion with civilized relatives. That the children did not rush into their parents' arms, but hung back with their adopted Indian foster brothers and fathers and mothers, unwilling to leave, was disappointing but not inexplicable; but when white women, since taken under the blanket as mates by Indian braves, made it plain that they were in no wise pleased to return to legal white husbands, you can hardly fault the one such shamed and rejected husband who beat his stubborn spouse's brains out. The liberation of the civilized from the mortifications of barbarism was a thoroughly disillusioning affair, creating "as much unhappiness and sense of loss as it allayed."

Technically the Shawnees, who had horticulture, were barbarians, according to a terminology adopted in Europe a generation or so ago; the early Russellians and Modocans and Wendovers were savages. But it is not a distinction that need prevent us from suspecting that there is nothing about civilization that is more body-and-soul-satisfying to man than either savagery or barbarism. There are only a few exalted intellects among us now, percentage-wise, who, hounds of heaven, must chase the tail of the origin and meaning of the universe though it take them to the borders of the cosmos 10,000,000,000 or 100,000,000,000 light years away. The rest of us are content with, basically, the same goods and satisfactions as the Russellians: food on the table now and a chance to earn tomorrow's; shelter, as both a place of rest and a sphere of warmth; companionship, and a share of the favorable regard of companions; religion, that is, a renewable reassurance that we have a well-founded right to exist in the world where we find ourselves and to partake of its resources to fulfill our needs. Which of these civilization affords in more abundance and savor than barbarism and savagery it would be hard to say. There is still much want and periodic scarcity even in the United States, where now, in the middle of our current prosperity, many are out of jobs—which, as Calvin Coolidge remarked, always seems to result in unemployment—and at least half the citizens now alive can remember the dreadful depression of the 1930's; and whether a period of exigency is man-maneuvered or nature-imposed, the belly aches just as insistently. It is certainly not a matter of common experience among us that we rest any better under our mortgaged roofs than the Russellians did under their leaky cave ceiling, and most of us *feel* no warmer than they did because they could always pile on the fuel without a quiver of concern about the bill. The matter of companionship and security or position within a tribal confraternity, as opposed to the civilized man's unremitting exposure to personal and group hostilities, need hardly be mentioned, and we need go no further with it than to point to the statistics on mental illness and personality failure.

It were the better part of humility and candor if we admitted that civilization did not happen to us because we willed it, sought it, or needed it. Using the Bailey technique of definition we may say that it is the name given to the compromises, accommodations and conflicts occasioned by the fact that some

4,000,000,000 people now inhabit this earth, and more are coming. What it is, is not an escape or a rising above barbarism, but a product of man's success as a barbarian, as barbarism is a result of the success of savagery and its methods of getting a living for ever increasing numbers of savages. The Russellians were competent and happy savages and not in the least interested in advancement out of their freedom and contentment.

Though Graham Cave, in Missouri, is the least eastern of the three early eastern usufructian sites, and should have been, by logical order, considered first, if we hold that usufructianism spread cellularly from west to east, it has been given last place out of deference to the opinion of its excavator, Wilfred D. Logan (and also of a subsequent excavator, Carl H. Chapman), that its Archaic character (what we call usufructian) was inspired from the east.

In all important particulars Graham Cave resembles Danger, Russell and Modoc to the point of corroboration. Beginning with a C14-dated bottom-level occupation at 9700 B.P., it shows continuous use until well past the beginning of pottery making, and the familiar choppers, manos, pestles, mortars, atlatl weights, axes and adzes in early levels, bone-splinter tools, sandstone abraders or "whetstones," heavy and large flake scrapers, bone pins, twined weaving, and beads, pendants and paint—all this gives us the feeling we have been here before. But Graham Cave, like the other usufructian sites, offers its variances. Stone balls are noted in the inventory, and these have been suggested as parts of the bola, best known for its use by Argentine cowboys and certainly used by some usufructians, as the sling seems to have been used by others; strip-blade knives, though without the cores noted in the Denbigh Complex, appear in the earlier levels; hollow bones have been identified as shamans' sucking tubes, for the sucking out of evil spirits from the ill or afflicted, these tubes being thought by many to be the origin of the smoking pipe; and in the lowest level fluted points, considered the indubitable marker of the herd hunter.

It is the opinion, I believe, of most American archaeologists that the herd-hunter period preceded the Archaic period, identified by the occurrence of the cultural materials we have been

calling usufructian. This misapprehension has been mentioned
before, and we will address ourselves to it more fully in an
appropriate place. We take it up now, briefly, since the fluted
points at the base of the Graham Cave archaeological column
have been regarded as corroboration of this view: that there
was a long period when the herd hunters were the dominant,
if not the only, population in America, and the Archaic period
succeeded this, with the influx of a people who practiced our
usufructianism.

But the weakness of this view is that a point type does not
a culture make. The fluted-point fashioners of Graham Cave
(these points look, subjectively, decadent and verging on ob-
solescence) were living in a usufructian situation, and no bones
of any of the large animals that made the life and livelihood
of the herd hunter were found in that situation. There is no
alternative, it seems to me, but to believe that the Graham
Cave fluted points were those of herd hunters who had abandoned herd hunting for usufructianism, possibly for exactly the
same reason given earlier for the division of the basic Amerind
into hunters and usufructians—the band no longer had the
man power to continue the chase.

It has not been emphasized, but it is true nevertheless, that
no bones of mammoth, bison or mastodon were found at Modoc
or Russell. This seems particularly striking at Modoc, located
in a semiprairie landscape where bison, at least, must have put
in seasonal appearances. Even Russell raises a question because
there was a smaller, woodland-type bison that seems to have
been ubiquitous. Boone shot this type in Pennsylvania and it
was still an occasional, though very rare, animal in Tennessee
as late as 1790. What is deducible, then, is that if the usufructians did not actually avoid the big-game beasts they did not
seek them out and seldom came in contact with them. Hence
the occasional association of Archaic types of points with mastodons in the east does not argue a concern of usufructians
with them, but only for bands of hunters who made an Archaic
type of point.

Logan's assessment of Graham Cave materials as having been
influenced by southeastern Archaic cultural patterns was made
before the analysis of Danger, Modoc and Russell caves and
before the surprisingly early date of its earliest level had been

ascertained. This southeastern influence may be the correct explanation, especially since the lowest-level fluted-point makers soon began to work in standard usufructian point design, but I doubt that the direction from which usufructian influence fell on Graham Cave's occupants is a serious problem; usufructian influence could at this time have come from any direction, and the strip-blade knives almost certainly came from some place north of Missouri. Even so, Graham Cave may have been as much influencing as influenced, standing as it did near the center of the usufructian demesne.

But the truth is that this group of caves, which have afforded us our first wide-angled, three-dimensional apperception of American paleo-history, are immensely more important to us—because they have been found—than to the real course of that Amerind paleo-history, of which they cannot be truly representative for the simple reason that their inhabitants went on living in them, whereas there came a time when the principal populations began to move into villages and to show signs of beginning civilization. Certainly there came a time when the clever, conservative Desert Culture was surpassed and other peoples in America went on to bigger and better things. But up to well into the Altithermal this was probably not true, and Russell, Modoc and Graham will always be fundamental references on the eastern usufructians even if the bulldozers, now tearing up the terrain at the rate of 3000 acres a day, spare us a few more such sites.

The period of usufructian leadership in world culture ended between 8000 and 7500 B.P. The beginnings of agriculture, as we have reported, date from about 8000 B.P., and while the Desert Culture, at least, had the seeds of agriculture, so to speak, in its hands, it did not cultivate them to civilizing advantage. Elsewhere in the world agriculture and animal husbandry became the foundation of village living, which is the basic social unit in the construction of civilization. The changes in the Old World nuclear areas between 8000 B.P. and 5000 B.P. were explosive. While the Amerinds were just beginning to mud-daub pottery vessels the brilliant Minoan civilization of Crete, the twin Indian cities of Mohenjo-Daro and Harappa, the two Egyptian foci of civilization on the Delta and the Upper Nile, and the Sumerian city states had exfoliated almost simultaneously. One has only to become passingly acquainted with the Minoans, the exquisite sense of chic of their women and the masculine massiveness of their architecture, to ask himself what happened to the Amerinds. The answer is easy to suggest, and hard to prove: They had food, and they had freedom.

12

Beside the Point

This entire chapter is an aside on projectile points. It carries the narrative of the Amerind forward not at all and so may be skipped by those who are in pursuit only of the argument, and are not interested in expatiation. But some understanding of projectile points is necessary to the beginning amateur, who will probably feel he has made a beginning only when he has a feeling of knowledge about them, since they are the most numerous kind of artifact he is likely to pick up, and the most bewilderingly multiform.

Stone projectile points have been made in America, if we accept Krieger's authoritative estimate of the earliest Clovis, for about 18,000 years, from the first one chipped out until the last one true-made for service at, say, 1900 A.D. (Fakery in projectile points is a minor industry as this is written.) This lengthy period of manufacture, the extraordinary variety, their extraordinary gross numbers, and the fact that those varieties are without exception bifacially worked, are almost invincible premises for the conclusion that projectile points, ergo the weapons of which they were a part, are Amerind inventions.

Until the invention of pottery, the projectile point, because of its variety of forms, is one of the most important of diagnostic artifacts, especially since it is indestructible and is intrinsically interesting because, for all its apparent simplicity, it rewards careful study with continuing revelations. Although this can be said of almost any class of artifacts, few classes are likely to be represented by so many specimens in a collection.

MacGowan says, "Only Solutrean man [of the late European paleolithic; mark him well] and the American paleolithic made

truly efficient points." It was not until the neolithic that Old
World cultures gave any great attention to good ballistic form,
and the biface point was in America from the beginning,
whereas the earliest Old World forms were unifaces, made on
flakes. Tolstoy, as will be remembered, finds that the earliest
eastern Siberian (Lena Basin) points were unifaces. One of
the most popular of early flint points in Europe would not
even be recognized as a weapon element by Americans, and
it does not seem to have ever been made here; it is a poor
thing to look at, and only the discovery of it in Europe attached
to shafts explains its function. Called by Wilson (of the hand-ax
contretemps) the tranchant transversal, it is no more than a
cornered chip, with the acute serving as the point; it must have
been deadly enough, and simple enough to make, and it was
used by hunters whose mouths it had to feed, but it wholly
lacks flair and design; there is not the true missile look to it
that you see in the most carelessly made American point, and
the whole Eurasian paleolithic leaves the impression that
though these populations were, perforce, killers of game large
and small, they were not the Nimrods even the usufructian
Amerinds were; the Eurasians were fire drivers and pit trap-
pers, clever with snare and springe, but the Amerind was the
real shoot-to-kill marksman. Amerinds used fire drives and
stockade traps and snares, too, but projectile points would not
be the most numerous surviving artifact on almost every American prehistoric site if the Amerind were not much more the
stalker-hunter than the slaughterer-butcher. The European upper paleolithic, it is true, does not lack weapon points, but
these are bone and horn or antler harpoon points. Amerinds
made bone points, and the harpoon was an everyday weapon
with the sub-Arctic hunters both on land and sea, but these are
qualifications for the sake of accuracy; the Amerind was the
hunter of the flint-tipped shaft and he was the hunter non-
pareil.

The plenitude of stone weapon points in America owes something, of course, to the fact that they were used here for 2000
years, more or less, after most of the rest of the world was using
metal, though metal points were made by the Old Copper
hunters of Michigan and Wisconsin as early as 7000 B.P., before
metal was used in the Old World. Yet it was flint and chert,

quartzite and obsidian, jasper, rhyolite, quartz, basalt, even siltstone, that the Amerind preferred to work millennium after millennium, and with good reason: comparative tests have demonstrated that the vitreous rocks penetrate farther into flesh per foot-pound of pull than anything but the finest steel, with which they never had to compete; and, indeed, the Indian bowman, within the range of his weapon, which was about 75 yards, overmatched the white soldier with his musket embarrassingly and often mortally. The musket was a clumsy arm which could only approximate hitting a target, while even an average Indian archer could hit a man-sized mark as far as his arrow would carry accurately; the bow was a rapid-fire weapon, too, for an active bowman could keep three shafts on the fly at the same time. The Indian weapon had not the long-range power of Robin Hood's longbow, the great bow that won Agincourt, but it was a better armament than anything the white man had until the improvement of rifling brought the Pennsylvania, more often called the Kentucky, rifle into the field.

Even then the bow was still a more stealthy weapon, noiseless and quicker to reload. The North American continent was not won by a superiority of weapons, nor by the side which killed greater numbers of the enemy; it was won, as always, by the side that could replace its losses. It was the white man's epidemic maladies, measles, whooping cough and smallpox that decimated the Amerind.

The term projectile point is not a stiff and pedantic usage for what might just as easily be called arrowheads or spearheads or lance heads. It is an avoidance of anything so specific for the very good reason that no archaeologist can be quite sure what kind of weapon was tipped by the points he recovers from his diggings. We cannot even be sure, always, that they are weapon points at all; many of them, on short hafts, could as easily be dagger-like knives; many which seem to be points show use as reamers, others as strike-a-lights, and some, beyond question, were made specifically for the point to be used as a perforator or awl. Exactly what several uses an Indian had in mind when he chipped out a point only a stone-age hunter would know, but they probably were auxiliary and did not negate the primary intent. Yet to say that a point is an arrowhead is to say what cannot be known to be true, unless the point is attached to an arrow, which it almost never is.

The use of the atlatl by the Danger Cave people has been mentioned. Atlatl is an Aztec word for the throwing stick or spear thrower, which is a two- or three-foot length of wood, usually grooved or channeled so that a spear shaft will lie in it, and curved at the end, or fitted with a hook to engage the butt of the shaft. The atlatl is still in use among the Australian aborigines today. In effect it makes the thrower's arm longer and his cast that much harder and farther. Its shaft, which is called a dart, can be either simple or composite. The simple dart is a single, integral shaft of wood or cane, four to six feet long, with a point attached; the composite dart consists of a short foreshaft, about arrow length and diameter, to which the point is attached, and a larger distal or rear shaft with a shallow, tubular orifice in the proximal end in which the stem of the foreshaft fits; when the composite dart is thrown, the foreshaft fixes in the target and the rear shaft falls away. Foreshafts of composite darts have been found at Gypsum Cave that may be as much as 8000 years old.

A later improvement on the atlatl was the attachment of the banner stone (it got this nonrelevant name before William S. Webb had figured out what it was, from his Green River excavations) to give it balance and to add momentum to the thrown shaft, as a heavier bat will drive a ball farther than a lighter one; the weight probably prevented kick-up and thus flattened out the trajectory of the missile, making possible a greater accuracy.

The atlatl is more than a tool, it is a machine, among the first ever invented by man, and its early occurrence at Danger Cave does no harm to the opinion that it was an Amerind invention. If it is an Amerind invention it must have been preceded by the simple, hand-thrown spear or javelin, a logical step in its evolution, and certainly the part that had to be in use before a machine would be thought of to launch it. The necessity for a javelin-throwing period is one of the reasons for setting the Desert Culture phase back as far as 15,000 B.P., but there is no evidence that the phase lasted after the invention of the atlatl, which seems to have spread rapidly over America with the usufructians. The big-game hunters may not have used the atlatl, however; they may have preferred the javelin, which must have its advantages too, since the Kaffirs and other African tribes still use their version, the assagai, with which it is said they can hit a two-inch bull's-eye at fifty yards two out of three times.

Of the other long-shaft weapons using points, the lance is nothing more than a spear carried by a horseman. It was used by the Plains Indians after they acquired mounts, but that would not concern prehistorians overmuch. By the spear is meant, nominally, the so-called short spear, a point on a stout cudgel which, though it can be thrown, is meant for hand-to-hand combat; when a soldier fixes a bayonet to his rifle he is making a short spear of it. Nothing we know about Indians encourages us to think they were spear fighters; the tomahawk and club and knife were their close-in tools of combat. The best-known historic use of the spear in America was by Mexican peons, who used it to kill bison; they emplaced it not by a cast but by direct thrust, like a long-handled knife; there is something about this method of meat killing that suggests a long, long practice at it, and before the Plains Indians took to horse, in addition to stockade drives and cliff stampedes, they may have killed bison by this extraordinarily daring approach.

In the eastern woodlands there was no game nor beast that would, as a matter of habit, be better met by the spear than with a missile weapon. The cornered bear and perhaps some cats were such adversaries, but hunting the bear would have been an occasion rather than a hunting routine; the fact is, however, that the bear appears to have been held in such high and ceremonial esteem (a skinned bear looks so shockingly like a man as to seem to have been a human wizard hiding in a disguise of fur) that special weapons may have been used against him. An archaeologist cannot, therefore, eliminate the possibility that some of the points he finds at a site, especially those that do not fall into the size pattern of that particular site, are spearheads.

The bow, according to Krieger, who asked not to be considered dogmatic about it, was first used in the southwest, about 500 A.D., and at a later date, perhaps 1000 A.D., in the Great Plains region. The date of inauguration is argued from the first appearance of very small points which, ballistically—that is, by size and weight and design—are similar to points we know, historically, to have been used as arrow tips. These tips are attached to shafts of arrow cane (*Phragmites communis*), a very light reed which would obviously be unbalanced by a heavy point. Heavier, woody shafts would require somewhat heavier points, but points twice, or even thrice as heavy as the specimens used with arrow-cane shafts would still not be very big.

If Danger Cave had been excavated before C14 dating, its store of artifacts would have undoubtedly caused it to be labeled an A.D. site, and one of the canons that would have helped to dispose toward this conclusion would have been the undersize of its projectile points. There has long been a rule-of-thumb among archaeologists that the line of division between arrowheads and spear-dart-javelin heads lies at about 45 millimeters, or 1¾ inches, in length, when the breadth and thickness are proportionate; a very heavy, chunky point, though under the maximum length, would not, of course, be considered fit for arrow tipping, weight being the real determinant.

The categoric emphasis has always been on the elimination of oversized points as suitable for arrow, rather than a straight exclusion of the undersized ones from the category of dart or spear points. Nevertheless, a series of small points has usually swung judgment in the direction of arrowheads and recency. But Danger Cave, with its coincidence of small points and atlatl use, has cut the galluses of any such presumption, and a series of tests by Oren F. Evans of the University of Oklahoma has put the old saw about big points being unsuitable for arrows in the same class with the one about toads causing warts.

Evans' tests were conducted with such a simplicity of methodology and purpose that we laymen can well wonder why they had not been conducted long before 1957: he set up a target and shot arrows at it. The essence of the test was that he used unfeathered shafts, on the reasonable assumption that unfeathered shafts would have been used before feathered ones, as unweighted atlatls were certainly used before banner-stone-weighted ones. What he found was that you not only could, but had to, use a heavy point on an unfeathered shaft, and the heavier the point the farther and more accurately the arrow flew, until the parabola of trajectory became exorbitant. The unfeathered shaft needed a more powerful bow, and that was the only gimmick.

Evans writes that points up to 4 or 5 inches long—125 millimeters long and 90 milligrams in weight, about three times as large as the literature now allows—can thus be accurately propelled, since the efficiency of the unfeathered arrow is all a matter of balance between point and shaft, with the best balance achieved when the center of gravity is between two-thirds and three-quarters the length of the shaft, measured from the nock end. It follows, then, and the tests confirm it, that the arrow-cane shaft and its diminutive point, when shot unfeathered, had the accuracy and deadliness of a puffball thrown by a southpaw housewife.

The appearance of little "arrow" points at about 500 A.D. in the southwest need not mark the debut there of the bow, we must now acknowledge, but only of feathered shafts, and the bow's date of appearance (Krieger's estimate was made in 1948, before C14) must be earlier than 500 A.D. because *Phragmites communis* arrow shafts, some with the feather quills still attached, came from level V at Danger Cave, C14 dated at 5000–4000 B.P. But this is beginning to be quite early. According to Coon the bow appears in western Europe, as an import from elsewhere, probably from Africa by way of Spain, during the mesolithic. If C14 dates of circa 10,000 B.P. on the Magdalenian and upper paleolithic culture are correct, then Coon means that the bow is less than 10,000 years old. Add some time to the feathered shafts of Danger Cave for the use of unfeathered shafts and large points, and the Amerind bow begins to look as though it might not have had to originate in Asia either.

Again, there is to be no urging by me that the Amerind invented the bow and gave it to the world; I continue suspicious not only of west-to-east cultural commerce after the Bering bridge fell down but of Alaska-to-Siberia cultural freight. The only claim here is that the Amerind, as probably the greatest of all hunters, is wholly likely to have invented both the atlatl and bow for himself. Whether it was the Amerind's hunting instinct that led him toward experimentation with better and better implements for the chase, or whether the invention of these implements confirmed him in venery, is a chicken-and-egg

question, and only a chicken could answer it. But it would be
obtuse to overlook the Amerind's specialization as a hunter by
weapon, and hence whatever explains it, and whatever it explains.

There was noted by Krieger in his basic *A Suggested General
Sequence in North American Projectile Points*—which, having
appeared in 1948, has suffered some attrition—that there in-
trudes into projectile-point sequences during the Archaic period—6000 to 4000 B.P.—a trait of making quite large stemmed
and notched points. In 1948 these seemed so novel in design
and of such noticeably large dimensions that Krieger guessed
that they signaled the entrance of the atlatl into the American
scene. But we now know three facts not known in 1948: (1) the
atlatl had already been on the scene for some thousands of
years; (2) there is no integral correlation between the atlatl
and large points; (3) there is really nothing new about the
shape of these intrusive points, only about the sudden appearance of these shapes in blown-up sizes.

What new habit or weapon could have prompted this en-
largement? A sudden popularity of short spears, because of an
onset of a warlike disposition among people trying to encroach
on each other? A wave of bears, or of ceremonial consciousness?
It is perhaps not wise to give a flat no to these, but if we return
to Evans' experiments we will see that these large points are
suitable for use on unfeathered arrow shafts; we also know that
with most inventions or innovations the first models are apt to
be the larger and clumsier ones, with the smaller, refined ones
following as the maker-user gains the knack of better making
from the experience of using. Nor should it be overlooked that
the first arrow shafts would probably have been adapted dart
shafts, probably foreshafts, which are not feathered. The first
trials with these would have given most unsatisfactory results,
since the dart points were small; and this would have led to the
discovery of the necessity of the heavy point, which would
have been followed by the comprehension that the principle of
the successful unfeathered arrow is in the weight balance of
shaft and point. Since Siberia does not seem to have been hot
and boiling over with large stemmed and notched points at this
time, and since the forms themselves were already in America,
at least in prototype, it seems that a very patient hearing will

have to be given to the case for the bow having instigated the big-point fashion that Krieger has remarked.

That the archaeologists are not being classroom mealy-mouthed when they speak of projectile points ought by now to have been sufficiently demonstrated. What remains for consideration is the importance and the fascination of projectile points.

They are, in the first place, when made of stone, imperishable, a most necessary quality for prehistoric importance; and, as we have said, they are complex enough artifacts as to be style-variable. It is style variation as much as trait inventory that gives the archaeologist his clues to culture-time relationships. Just as high-button shoes and loafers are indices of different periods of cultural change in America, so are patterns and styles of projectile points useful in separating cultures and cultural change as well as relating them. After pottery came to be made, its changes in patterns of pots, composition of clay, method of manufacture and styles of decoration became more important to the archaeologist, because he has more modifiable characteristics to examine; and pottery is therefore a more sensitive index. Basketry and textiles would be equally helpful for prepottery periods if they were not so fragile that they are preserved only under the most favorable dry-cave conditions. Before pottery was made, then, American archaeology, so richly blessed with projectile points, finds that the most consistent trait present at its sites—for even the poorest sites will yield one or two, except when they are, like Tule Springs, too early—and the one that gives it most to work with, is the projectile point. This is in marked contrast with Old World sites, where stone points are inconsequential until the late Mesolithic.

The fascination of projectile points is something that does not have to be explained to a male American who has ever found one; the response of the primordial in him to its form and purpose is a combination of racial nostalgia and boyhood recollection. It instantly sublimates into the fantasies of youth, when Indians, above all other symbols, could stir us to delicious terror and fill our heads with resolves of heroism, and in the next instant it stabs us with the reminder of how far we have come since we made our living with a trinket like this and defended our lives and all we possessed—how far we have come, yet how near we are to it and how easily we can revert to it if we misstep on this tightrope walk we call civilization.

Other kinds of tools may leave you with a detached admiration for the craftsmanship of the maker, or an impersonal pity for a people who had to labor with the likes of them; to pick up a projectile point is to feel you have just taken it from the hand of its owner; he laid it aside, or lost it, and yours is the next hand to touch it and the millennia between are no more than a night and a day, or the time it took him to lope out of sight. Every flake scar is a sort of pen stroke in an indecipherable language: if we could read it, a man's signature, Red Fox, or Strong-as-a-Bull or Afraid-of-a-Knife. Somebody held an unminted stone once, and while he kept a workman's eye on it, as he placed his punch and struck his deft blows he talked to a friend, was distracted and hit off center, flawed the job, paused a moment of indecision, continued, but more charily, finished it, rubbed it against his bear-greased thigh, held it for an invocation of the god of hunting on it, noticed (or perhaps did not) the rich mottle of the flint—or the coruscations of the icy quartz —tied it with sinew and gum to the shaft and then went out with it, and killed.

Foe and food, this was the blood these points were made to let, and let it they did, so that any point you pick up may have been the one that saved a tribe, by defense or provision. And whenever you pick one up you know it to have been a possession closer to him that made it than anything you own is to you, for we do not make the things we live by in these days, and this was the one *thing* as intimately his as his finger. The Amerind had many artifices for killing what he needed to kill: for game, traps and pits and snares; for fish, weirs and nets and hooks, and the fish poison rotenone; for birds, the bola and the sling of the type that made David bigger than Goliath; but none of these are as explicitly symbolic of those who made this earth ready for us.

The man who decides that he wants to know something about projectile points passes through four stages: In the first all projectile points look alike, except for obvious size variations, and the smaller ones you call arrowheads and the large ones spearheads. In the second stage no projectile point looks like any other, and you become aware that, since each is a separately and distinctly fashioned artifact, handcrafted by imprecise methods out of materials that were not uniformly sized nor of genuinely homogeneous composition, it will be sheer coincidence if you ever find two that are replicas. Follows then the stage when—after you have looked at a thousand or so and have found a hundred or two yourself—to exacerbate your need to know something about them, they begin to group themselves into loose patterns, and you begin to construct a tentative taxonomy based on plane form and proceed to stuff everything you find or see into it, calling the subpatterns varieties, until you begin to see how absurdly many subpatterns there are and that whatever shape Indians were trying to bring out of stone they were not as consistent about it as a neat taxonomy demands.

In the fourth stage, having realized that you cannot file projectile points as though they were letters, you come to the conclusion that what you have first to do is to read the mind and mood of the maker: How good a craftsman was he? What were the faults of the stone he was working on? How big was his hurry? What element of the point did he think was most important? Was he trying to make the best point of which he was capable or only something that would serve him the next day? Then you begin to realize that the knapper sat down to his work in something of the spirit of a free-form artist—to get out of a piece of stone the point that was in it—but that as a practical matter he had to get two things out of it, a point at one end which would pierce the target, and a means at the other end for attachment to the shaft. Further, it may be the custom among a people to put the point of a projectile to some secondary use, perhaps as an awl or perforator; hence the maker would trim the tip to a needle sharpness, leaving the body or blade of the whole point rather thick. Or it may have been the custom to make an auxiliary use of projectile points as knives, which would dictate that they be flat, and that the first consideration in making them be given to the edges of the blade, so that the tip then becomes merely the sharp convergence of two edges. When he came to make the haft end, the maker had to keep in mind the way he was accustomed to unite

point and shaft, whether it was by stem, notches or thinned
base, and to eke out the expedient for a fit; this provision could
be crude, yet adequate, or it could be refined and proportioned
to the symmetry of the whole piece; but the difference between
adequacy and shapeliness in stems and/or notching often
makes for such an overt dissimilarity as to cause two points
within the same manufacturing tradition to seem of diverse
types.

The body of the point between base and tip—that is, the
blade—is determined, like the tip, by possible secondary use,
even when not every point is expected to be put to that use;
or by some observed or supposed mechanical advantage or
"medicine"—that is, magic potency. But this too is subject to
degree of skill, workability of material, trueness of eye and immediate interest, so that the shoulders may vary in width from
one point to another, changing drastically the outline of the
whole; or the hardness of the material may cause a lazy workman to leave the sides convex instead of straight; or some pe-
culiarity of stone or workmanship may suggest the placement
of the notches. Despite all those possible contributors to irregularity, most of the points at a multiform site can be assigned to
distinct varieties with some degree of confidence.

Still, the longer you study projectile points the more convinced you become that they were not made according to any
Platonic master image or prototype concept, but were a sum of
desired characteristics synthesized into standardized forms by
the operation of traditional techniques. The distinction is not
merely verbal; nowhere does the early Amerind show himself
to have been artistic—that is, a worker toward the realization
of concepts. He was pragmatic; he put things that worked together; he was an observer and an opportunist, not an imagist;
he was very much what the present-day American would have
been under like conditions.

A comparison of the Amerind of 10,000 years ago with his
European contemporaries makes this thesis succinctly. Aurignacians could draw brilliantly, and they could model and
carve; it might even be said they could sculpt. In the profound
recesses of caves they drew bison from concept, and modeled
bears in bas-relief, with a magico-religious, not an artistic motivation, and still were artists. But if any community of Amerinds ever had artistic inclinations, before they began to work

plastically with clay in the making of pottery, they have left no record of it. The Amerind directly produced things; he did not reproduce concepts concretely; and when we begin to understand projectile points this way we have entered the fourth and final stage of studying them, and now we are ready to compose a classification system for projectile points because we have at last arrived at the principle of composition. It is inductive, not deductive; we cannot first lay out a taxonomy by plane form—that is, by all the geometric possibilities inherent in point forms—and classify the points by their congruency with these forms, as you arrange folders alphabetically; you must, instead, know substantially all the varieties of projectile points (by variety is meant the sum of desired characteristics already discussed) made by the Amerind, and work upward from there, by prominent similarities, into species and genus.

Now it happens that most people who are at all interested in American archaeology have had that interest originally piqued by artifacts they themselves have discovered or have handled, and it is artifacts, usually arrowheads, that they want to know about first. But hardly anybody's initial interest is sufficiently poignant to force him to undertake an examination of all continental data on projectile points in order to have some knowledge of five or ten or even a hundred, just as we like to know the names, at least, of the birds and plants of common experience without feeling any compulsion to become ornithologists or botanists. It is for these earnest all-American citizens, as well as for the incipient student who does not know quite how to take hold of the subject, that we sketch out our own classification system, and those who find such information so overparticular as to be tedious—like the little boy who, writing an English-class review of a book about penguins, said with damning simplicity, "This book tells me more about penguins than I wanted to know"—may re-examine their contracts and note that they don't have to read it.

While the tip or point is the most important working part of a projectile point, the most important concern in the design and manufacture is the provision for hafting. The variations here give us our primary divisions of projectile points which we will call pattern, and which are herewith presented:

A. Unstemmed, unnotched points. This pattern is, in essence, the naked, unadorned blade, which may be either lanceolate (willow-leaf shaped) or triangular; there are neither extrusive stem nor intrusive notches in it. Clovis points (circa 12,000 B.P.) belong in this class.

B. Mono-shouldered points. This is actually a stemmed point, with but one indentation at the shoulder instead of two, and it seems to be an evolutionary step away from lanceolate points and a step toward stemmed ones. Sandia points (circa 12,000 B.P.) belong in this class.

C. Stemmed points. In this pattern the stem means exactly what it means in a leaf; it is an appendage from the blade and is narrower than the blade. Lamoka points (circa 5500 B.P.) belong in this class.

D. Notched points. Notching may be thought of as a worked intrusion into the blade itself, to constrict it to the width of the shaft so that blade and shaft may be bound securely together. Many New York Laurentian forms (circa 4500 B.P.) belong in this class.

E. Shouldered, yoke-base points. This pattern ought perhaps to be included under either notched or stemmed points, but because of this anomalousness, the special feature of the yoke base, and the strong distribution of this pattern over North America, it deserves an independent position. Pinto points (circa 6000 B.P.), from Pinto Basin, California, belong in this class.

Applying the principle of induction previously arrived at, that is, using the most apparent characteristics, we can subdivide patterns into firm and recognizable styles (1, etc.) and types (a, etc.), as follows:

A. Unstemmed, unnotched points

    1. Lanceolate

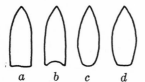

a. With flat base

b. With yoke, or indented base

c. With pointed base

d. With butt base

a   *b*   *c*   *d*

2. Triangular

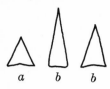

    a. Equilateral

    b. Isosceles

3. Pentagonal

    a. With flat base

    b. With yoke base

B. Mono-shouldered points

    a. With flat base

    b. With rounded base

C. Stemmed points

    1. Standard stem (The stem is not long, short, wide or narrow in proportion to the blade)

    a. With flat base

    b. With rounded base

    2. Wide stem

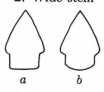

    a. With flat base

    b. With rounded base

    3. Narrow stem

    a. With flat base

    b. With pointed base

4. Short stem

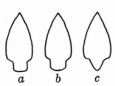

a. With flat base
b. With rounded base
c. With pointed base

5. Long stem

a. With flat base
b. With rounded base

6. Contracting stems

a. With flat base
b. With rounded base

7. Expanding stem (These often grade into notched forms)

a. Pinched stem
b. Waisted stem

D. Notched points

1. Side notched (Notches are parallel to base)

a. Base width less than shoulder width.
b. Base width equal to shoulder width.
c. Base width greater than shoulder width.

2. Corner notched (Notches are at about a 45-degree angle
to base)

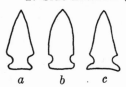

a. Corner invaded
b. Corner removed

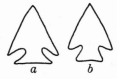

3. Bottom notched (Notches at right angle to base)

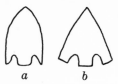

a. With pointed barbs

b. With square barbs

E. Shouldered, yoke-base points

a. Stemmed type

b. Side-notched type

Though I know of only one kind of point in the world, Wilson's tranchant transversal, which cannot be classified according to the foregoing outline, we have not yet reached the point where we actually pick up and hold in our fingers and try to understand that sum of desired (by the maker) and observed (by us) characteristics. For what we hold is a specimen of a variety, a point made within prevailing traditions of a socially related group, or community, of people. There are hundreds of these, and it is the privilege of the finder of a site and the describer of its point variety to name that variety. There is no quicker way to make an original contribution to archaeology and to see that contribution made use of than this. But one warning must be sounded: It is not considered *de rigueur* to name a variety after yourself; it should be named for the site, or the locality. The East Orange or Sheboygan or Tule Springs lanceolate would be soberly recognized in the literature, if it were a valid variety, but the John X. Smith III lanceolate would be circumlocuted at every opportunity.

If you are a Sunday archaeologist and have hunted a site and descried within its collection a series of small, stemmed points of chunky appearance, you may eliminate a great deal of your classification and description chores by referring to the foregoing class index. You find the pattern to be C, the style 1, the type, apparently, b. The first thing you will note, then, is that, all this having been duly and justly credited, you have by no means described the sum of characteristics you have under puzzlement. Your point has rounded, not sharply defined shoulders, a rounded stem, excurvate blade (I am describing an atlatl point discovered in small numbers in the inventories of certain kinds of Lamoka-related sites in the Hudson Valley), and is rounded in cross section. Impressed by the all-over roundness and chunkiness of your variety, so different from the flatness, or flattenedness, of most points, you decide to call it the Croton (you first noticed it on the banks of the Croton River) chunky; dissatisfied by this, because this is your baby and you want to do nothing but the best for it, you search your imagination for a more immediately communicative epithet and, having noticed that it looks more like a bullet than a projectile point, inspired, you hit on the name "slug," so you call it the Croton slug (C1b); but it bothers you that nowhere in this shorthand have you given an inkling of length; you do a quick consultation of your ruler and decide that points under 15 millimeters are diminutive (d), between 15 and 30 are small (s), between 30 and 45 are medium (m) and over 45 are large (l). Proud of yourself, you now write on your file card "Croton slug (C1b)^s" and the job is done.

But not quite. By this time you have expended a great deal of concentration of this (C1b)^s, and while the decision-making part of your mind is satisfied with "Croton slug," the little gray cells in the pondering department are not. They go over the visual data again and again until they have completely transformed it from what you thought you saw, in the light of your classification system, to what it actually is. And then they drive you back for another look, and this time you know what your (C1b)^s is.

Most styles of projectile points have thinned bases, so that they will slot into a median split in the end of the shaft. But it is wholly unthinkable that the pencil-thick stem of your Croton slug could be shaft-conjoined this way. How then? Plainly, by slipping it into the end of a hollowed-out shaft, perhaps a reed such as *Phragmites communis,* like a tenon into a mortise. You have discovered something as important, technologically, as the flute in a Folsom fluted point, and time may show it to be as important culturally. You go to bed knowing in your heart that you have established a new facet to your character; you are an archaeologist. Now you know what your point is. It is the Croton tenon stem (Clb)^s, and nobody is ever likely to dispute you successfully about it.

Chances are that, once you have dogged through such a bout of classification and come up with a win, your commitment to archaeology, and hence prehistory, is out of your hands. You will begin to loathe winter, when freezes armor the subterranean against your spade, and you will watch the snow fall, no matter how angel-feather it looks, with the resentment of being personally persecuted, because it erases the last hope of winter archaeology—surface hunting. You will begin to find that your weekly or semiweekly excursions have become necessary to your physical, mental and emotional health and that your appetite for investigation recurs with the regularity of miss-meal cramps. For archaeology provides the tremens of adventure without physical hazard; it is hunting and bringing home game without the killing; it is intellectual absorption without the dangers of mania because it does not narrow interests, but stretches the mind with the pull of questions from all directions: What kind of stone is my Croton tenon stem made of? Where did it come from? How did it get here? By trade? By travel? What kind of reeds grow hereabouts now that might have served as a shaft? What? Why? How?

You will discover very quickly that archaeology will attend you with such a success as the Croton tenon stem less often than it will confront you with your own ignorance. Your experience with (Clb)^s taught you how to handle projectile points (and projectile points only), not all about them. You might just as easily have discovered a Folsom fluted lanceolate, researched its characteristics (Alb)^m, reached the brilliant conclusion (it must be brilliant because archaeologists were years in coming to it) that the fluting or grooving was meant to lay the split halves of the shaft end in, only to find that someone had beat you to it.

But there are, say, five hundred and fifty-seven varieties of points still beneath the sod and you may think there are five times that many when you sit down to analyze them, for one of the greatest of variables is the shape and proportion of the blade. There is a school of projectile-point students who have posited the blade as the most important component of the point; the result is that they did not classify types of projectile

points, but multiplied them. Blade shape may be of considerable importance in some varieties—careful analysis of the most
desired (by the maker) characteristics will force the knowledge of this importance upon you—and we have used blade
shape as a means of differentiation for nonstemmed points. But
this is easily defended because in the A-pattern points the
blade is the stem. The way to approach the blade is the same
way you look at a girl: admire it if it is shapely but look elsewhere for the real qualities. For the truth is not necessarily in
the curves.

It is tempting to reel off a list of the varieties of better-known
projectile points—Clovis and Folsom, Scottsbluff and Plainview, Pinto and Gypsum Cave—and to trace these varieties by
their styles and types around the continent, but enough
has been said by now to persuade that projectile points are the
place to begin to be serious about American archaeology; and
if you should happen to become an expert on the subject you
will probably be one of the few in the Western Hemisphere.
Here is what the Amerind was, and how, and perhaps why he
continued so long to be what he was, a sort of perennial
juvenile, a fierce and realistic Peter Pan, huntsman, warrior,
roamer, woodsman, adventurer and, above all, free man.

Excavation of the second Iztapán (Mexico) mammoth. It is *Mammuthus (Archidiskodon) imperator leidy*, the largest American species. Two projectile points and a biface knife were found with this herd-hunter kill. Courtesy of Photographic Archives of the Instituto Nacional de Antropologia e Historia (Mexico).

Disinterment of the Naco (Arizona) mammoth, *Mammuthus (Parelephas) columbi falconer*. The excavator in the upper left-hand corner has uncovered two teeth. Courtesy of the Arizona State Museum.

These eight Clovis fluted projectile points were found within the "target" area of the Naco mammoth, near the atlas vertebra, in the neck. The point in the middle, on the right, probably carried the fatal thrust into the mammoth's spinal cord. Courtesy of the Arizona State Museum.

The central tomb of Dickison Mound 478, a Hopewellian burial mound in Illinois, before detailed excavation. The tomb's roof timbers have collapsed into it.

This is a cross-section of Dickison Mound 478. In the foreground is the central tomb, isolated for detailed excavation. To the

Completely excavated, the tomb reveals seven burials. A cache of fine
Hopewellian projectile points was found with the upper left burial.

right is isolated a cast of logs that formed the tomb chamber.
All three photographs, courtesy of the Illinois State Museum.

Hopewellian mother, standing. Her skirt is of red cloth, decorated with shell or river-mussel-pearl beads. Her footgear is of tanned hide. Because of either caste or status as a wife-mother she is not as elaborately bedizened as seems to have been the Hopewellian disposition.

Hopewellian mother, sitting. The two statuettes on this page and the two on the facing page are reproductions in wax done under the supervision of Thorne Deuel from ceramic figurines found in the Knight Mound, Calhoun County, Illinois. All four, courtesy of the Illinois State Museum.

This Hopewellian woman has been interpreted by B. M. Frost, who did the Knight figurine reconstructions, as a ceremonial dancer. Her turkey-feather fans are conjectural, from ceremonial paraphernalia known among the later Sioux.

A painted warrior of the inferred Hope-wellian warrior caste. He is the only male of the five sex-determinable Knight figu-rines. Six were found. They are now in the collection of Dr. P. F. Titterington of St. Louis.

This 20-feet-deep mound of shell and flood deposit is the accumulation of probably two to three thousand years of intermittent Amerind occupation. It is on the Tennessee River, 12 miles west of Muscle Shoals, Alabama, in Pickwick Basin. Courtesy of Mound State Monument, Moundville, Alabama.

13

Strong Right Arms

Projectile points have been used from the time of the Playa Sequence, which we have guessed at 15,000 B.P., by the usufructians and perhaps longer by the big-game herd hunters. With these latter it seems to have been the sole food-getting implement, and their accuracy of eye, daring of spirit and power of arm were what kept them in business for 10,000 years, give or take a millennium. Any people who left so indelible a mark on the American scene over such an eon deserves the memorial of as full a recounting of their exploits as it is possible to construct from the evidence, and we therefore address ourselves to the pleasant task.

It was not the most unexpected sight in the world when laborers, digging an irrigation ditch near the village of Santa Isabel Iztapán, 20 miles or less from Mexico City, in July, 1950, spaded into some enormous tusks; probably someone in the gang even knew what they were, for mammoth remains had been encountered in the course of other earth-moving projects in this area before; at any rate the word got around and came eventually, in 1952, to the newly organized Dirección de Prehistoria of Mexico, which in March sent Luis Aveleyra Arroyo de Anda and Arturo Romano to investigate. Joined later by Manuel Maldonado-Koerdell, they began what looked to be another routine paleontological excavation of a type of Pleistocene beast already well known from this geologic horizon in Mexico, and from skeletons much more complete. But after four days of digging it was no longer paleontology; it was archaeology. When the dirt was whisk-broomed away from a pair of ribs in the left side of a mammoth (*Archidiskodon imperator leidy*), no less a cynosure caught the eye of Aveleyra than the base of a projectile point. Within a matter of three days three other artifacts, all classed as scrapers, were coaxed into view. Work stopped and messages went out to a roster of authorities in Mexico, in France and in the United States.

There were two good reasons for this summoning of international authority to the exhumation, and the first was that in 1947, at Tepexpán, within eyeshot of the Iztapán mammoth site, Helmut de Terra (of the Oreopithecus find) had dug up a fossil human skeleton from the same geologic horizon as the Iztapán burial and had announced to the archaeological world that he had found a Late Pleistocene American. What fell on his ears was not plaudits. Whether de Terra had a bumbling photographer or was himself a bumbling excavator will probably never be known; but it was after examination of the photographs only that a whoop and a holler was raised against de Terra's claim by every archaeologist in the United States who fancied that his position and/or reputation gave him a right to an opinion, and the outcry impugned not only the fossil but de Terra himself. I quote one such voice, saying, "The photographs show an incredibly sloppy excavation," and it then goes on to a contradictory interpretation, from these photographs only, of what de Terra had already reached conclusions about from direct observation. Probably all that de Terra was being arraigned for was bumptiousness, a youthful overeagerness to make a significant find, but what it sounded like was that he was being called a liar or an incompetent or both. Certainly by 1952 this imbroglio of 1947 had not been forgotten.

And the second reason was that Aveleyra and Maldonado-Koerdell knew they had something. It is hard to believe now, only five years after publication of the full Iztapán report, that the question of man's association with the mammoth was distinctly moot, though Hugo Gross had just published, in 1951, a paper on this association at several sites and had concluded that it was highly probable. The Iztapán artifacts nailed it down as positive, even though the variety of point found was of Scottsbluff style (C2a)[1], which, as Sellards had noted, is never found in the United States with mammoth, but only with bison.

Six artifacts in all were found in or about the Iztapán mammoth, the last two being classifiable as strip blades, and the whole assemblage constituted, as Aveleyra mentions, a small industry: a projectile point, a side scraper, an end scraper, a scraper with a spoke-shave concavity in it (for smoothing down shafts), a strip-blade knife, and another blade with a concavity in the end that could have given possible use as a burin or bone-engraving tool. The mammoth was a nearly mature Archidiskodon, of quite imperial dimensions. The skeleton was entirely within a "green muck" (not that it was, at this date, either muck or green) that had been the marshy margin of a Late Pleistocene lake. All the picture needed, to be complete, was the signature of the artist.

Some time between 10,000 and 8000 years ago, while mammoths still hung on in the valley of Mexico, a band of hunters had come upon a lone mammoth (it is difficult to see how they could have cut a hale and hearty individual out of a herd) and had so goaded and confused and misled him by throwing spears and baiting him that he had got himself bogged down in the green muck and couldn't pull free. Stuck there, he had to suffer himself to be beaten and bled to death by stone and spear thrust, and when this mound of steaks and chops fell to earth, the women and children of the band were waiting, ravenous, on the dry beach, and the first meat was probably ripped off the carcass while the mammoth still drew breath. You have no trouble seeing the carcass swarmed over by man, woman and child, each making his little incision in the hide and sucking away at the warm, brothy, nourishing blood. It is highly likely that man could have learned such a practice from his competitor, the saber-tooth, if he had to be taught it at all.

How long would such a stock of provisions last a hunting band? It depends, obviously, on how big the band was. How big was this one? The tools simply do not tell. For whatever purpose the scrapers and knives found with the Iztapán mammoth were primarily manufactured, the conclusion is inescapable that their provenience within the carcass defines them as cutting tools in this instance. Anything that had a cutting edge was used to detach gobbets of flesh, and some of the implements were lost, slipping from greasy fingers or being simply mislaid. Day after day the members of the band waded out to their larder for breakfast and dinner and snacks between, with only a few duties for the nonce—to repair their weapons, make

such use of the hide as they knew how, and save their kill from
the scavengers. Fires along the shore would have to be kept
up; the sentinel probably watching while perched on the mammoth (we might picture him squatted on one of the tusks like a
robin on a bough) would be a boy, or girl, with a stick or stone
tied to a thong, to whirl about and keep the carrion-eating
birds away. But how long would this supply last? There's no
telling whether it was eaten to the last available scrap (that it
had got distinctly high would not have bothered our hunters;
Indians liked it that way, and thorough fire roasting destroys
the poisonous effects of bad meat) or whether the hunters had
to move on, to keep up with a drifting herd, packing what
they could but leaving much, including the mired-in portions,
to be stripped by other teeth.

The optimum number of hunters in such a band would be
about eight to ten, for surely no fewer would dare hunt mammoths in the open; and this would work out to a community of
from 25 to 35 (there would have been no large families under
these conditions). In three or four days all the delicacies of
Archidiskodon would have been devoured, certainly, and much
more of it if other bands in the vicinity, possibly invited by
smoke signal, had, themselves meatless, decided to come to the
feast.

It is not too hard to imagine a way of life for these people.
Because they were committed to staying in the immediate
neighborhood of their Grand Union, they must have had to
give some thought to artificial shelter. We must permit them,
then, some sort of lean-to, or half-tent. The hide of the mammoth would have provided roof material for such a shelter, but
it gives us pause when we think about somebody's having to
lug a whole tent all over the plain, so we can think in terms of a
new one being set up at each kill, the hide being cut from a
mammoth flank in a large rectangle and erected on saplings in
what the G.I.'s called a shelter half, with the hair inside and the
flesh side turned to the weather, which it would certainly be
proof against, since under the hide the mammoth wears a layer
of fat. Beneath this covering the precious hearth coals would
be preserved from the rain and as many people as could get in
would huddle out of a storm.

The rhythm of this life is easily discerned. A period of relaxation, plenty and festivity began with each kill, and the hunters, freed for a time of their fundamental responsibility, could follow their inclinations. What inclinations? They were not artistic, we know, so we have to believe their predilections were social and possibly magico-religious. This was the time for sexual activity, probably, that might have appeared to us, had we witnessed it—ethnographers have reported such post-hunting practices by savage people—as orgiastic. But the human talent for ceremonializing and adding values to what is both habitual and humanly important had probably long since turned these into some sort of meaningful fertility ritual. Not only does nomadism not create the most favorable atmosphere for connubiality, but it seems to have been a universal notion, rooted deep in some ancient human experience or observation (probably that animals are most easily attacked and killed during mating periods), that sexual abstinence must precede a hunting or warring foray or, indeed, any exclusively masculine duty. Released from this obligation by the success of a hunt, male and female would have spent themselves to satiety, as they indulged their hunger or any other appetite, and passed quickly on to the next swell of their life rhythm. (The sexual behavior of the usufructians would probably have seemed much more normal to us.)

For the women during the post-kill period of stability there were the chores of hearth keeping—and talk. For the men there would have been—talk. We can be quick to say that this was sheer indolence and the way of a man in a man's world, but we would be overhasty if we did. Out of this kind of confabbing came the beginnings of all we now regard as purely intellectual—philosophy, ethics, religion, the synthesis of ideas, the conveyance of experience, the recording of new observation. Probably the first business of a council of hunters was a review of the just-completed, successful feat; it would have sounded like male braggadocio to ironic-minded feminists, who would overlook the lessons in right conduct, proper hunting methods, and new data conveyed by the harangues. These accounts were, in effect, lectures or sermons, inspiring and inculcating the attitudes without which the adolescents and tyros listening in could not be instructed in the hunting life. It is no mere matter of acquired skill to drive so monstrous a beast as

Archidiskodon imperator to his doom; the heart must be stout
and steady and neither eye nor arm may be allowed to be jig-
gled by the demons of fear; a craven who deserted his post
when the game was afoot and the drive was on could mean
long days of no rations for a whole band.

It was on sessions like these, probably, that the human race
nourished its passion for narrative and, eventually, for the
novel, which is the recital of the sequential conduct of human
beings participating together in some such crucial event in
their social life as a mammoth kill, in which clear implication of
rightness or wrongness of conduct can be gauged by the consequences of it; the successful kill, with or without casualties,
or the fateful failure. Here is the taproot of ethics—the way
people must discharge their responsibilities toward each other;
of religion—the effect of what is apparently chance, or the inexplicable, in the determination of outcome, and the meaning
of the inexplicable; of science—the observation of how events
are caused to occur by physical forces; of debate and judicial
decision—for in every action in which these huntsmen participated in concert, there must have been more than one point
of view about how it happened and about the part each man
played in it, and these points of view would have sometimes
been contradictory, especially as to rightness or wrongness,
and as to bearing on the outcome; hence there would have
been not only debate but dispute that had to be adjudicated in
some way for the preservation of the band's social serenity and
continued efficiency as a food-making unit. I strongly suspect
that every tactic known to modern conference dialectic, from
the covert bluff to the open appeal to sentiments of home and
mother, were discovered in the rudiment by minds engaged in
the affairs of such councils 10,000 years ago. Man did not become what he is the day before yesterday.

These post-mortems lasted, at a guess, as long as the meat,
and then there was nothing for it but to decamp and head
across the plain again, scrapping together meals of small animals and edible plants until another mammoth or sloth or bison could be done to death. It is equally possible to argue that
these hunters did not roam the plains at large, but stayed close
to the lake shores of Texcoco, Bonneville, Lahontan and such,
waiting for the animals to come there to drink or feed in the

marginal meadows. But this supposition does not gainsay their basic nomadism; their route of travel was from kill to kill, rather than a round of removal from area to food-producing area, like the usufructians. The kill of a mammoth by the usufructians would have been a windfall, and probably would not have been undertaken except under fortuitous conditions; with the hunters it was a sought event—their moves, the rhythm of their life way, depended on it.

These are the hunters, these Iztapánian mammoth killers (a second mammoth kill, with two Long-type points in it, was excavated in 1955 near Iztapán), who are the other cultural tradition in our period of trifurcate population from 15,000 B.P. to 7500 B.P. They lived, if not side by side with the usufructians, at least within hailing distance of them, without being tempted to abandon their free-roaming ways. Probably there was occasional contact; the mortality rate among hunters must have been high and the wombs of the women would have been hard put to keep up with the death rate; we can imagine a hunting band, near extinction, raiding a usufructian camp for female replacements; or perhaps there was trade for them—the tenor of life among the usufructians was certainly better suited to raising children than the ceaseless trekking and daily hazards of the hunting profession. Nor can cannibalistic raids be ruled out. But the fact that neither the usufructians nor the hunters were exterminated by each other can mean only that they were not interested in each other to the point of either extermination or absorption. They went their separate ways. They met sometimes in peace, sometimes in war, but probably not as instinctive enemies, neither envying the other enough to want to supplant him.

Still, we are a little disappointed with the revelations at Iztapán. The Iztapánians killed mammoth, but in somewhat more devious a way than we would like to have seen; they did not go forth with a weapon in their hands and place that weapon so strongly and accurately in the vitals of the victim that he had to die of their marksmanship. They worried him to death like a pack of wolves. True, they used their weapons on him, and this is more than can be said of the mammoth butchers of Predmost, and they must have used them with lethal effect on less formi-

dable game, and to kill a mammoth at all is admiration-inspir-
ing—but could a man with a spear kill a mammoth? Not by
placing it between the ribs, where the Iztapán spearman's projectile point was found. In prime condition a mammoth would
have up to four inches of fat overlarding his ribs, and within
the rib cage the heart lay deeper than a human arm could
drive his stone. A mammoth could be hurt, or even crippled—
African Pygmies kill an elephant by inflicting stomach wounds
and then following him around for days until he dies of perito-
nitis, to make a gruesome-sounding meal—but as fair game it
did not seem likely that he could be killed unless— Unless by
some chance man had learned about the atlas vertebra, at almost the highest point in a mammoth's stature, in the neck
just behind the head, and unless his marksmanship were true
enough to hit it just right and split it. But nothing was more
unlikely.

In September, 1951, young Marc Navarrete walked into the
Arizona State Museum at Phoenix with a pair of projectile
points he had recovered from an excavation, undertaken by
himself and his father, in the bank of an arroyo near their
home at Naco, in Arizona, not far from the Mexican border.
The points had been in association with the bones of a large
animal the skeleton of which had been partly exposed by an
August washout. The points were almost certainly Clovis fluted
lanceolates.

In April of 1952 a party from the Arizona Museum under
Emil W. Haury undertook the completion of what the Navar-
retes had begun, and such a committee on credentials witnessed the unveiling of a mammuthus (*Parelephas columbi*)—
Ernst Antevs, E. B. Sayles, curator of the Arizona Museum,
John Lance, paleontologist of the University of Arizona, and
Haury himself—that the data and conclusions will forever go
unchallenged by photographic second-guessers. It must have
been a busy four days, but hard work could have been no objection—there was something to show for it. One by one six
more Clovis fluted points were probed out of the matrix; with
the two already found, this made eight in all. When they were
plotted as to provenience it was as plain as handwriting that
they had all been aimed at one small target area, the bull's-eye
of which was, to mix a metaphor, that Achilles heel, the atlas
vertebra. And one of them had hit the bull's-eye dead center.

This was no bog-trapped animal, floundering himself to death in a hopeless morass; his bones were found strewn on sand which was dry when he laid himself down there to expire, and they were not water covered until some years later, when the nearby stream, of which it was a shore, ponded and silted with clay. Of the dart point that rested against the atlas vertebra, after noting that *Parelephas columbi* was not mired down, Haury says conservatively, "This spear may have been the disabling one."

But this is what we have been looking for. Here were crouched over their kill the greatest hunters who ever lived, the bold destroyers who hunted the greatest of beasts with a stone tied to a stick; here camped the marksmen who did not have to seduce the mammoth to his own destruction but could down him where he stood. There is all the difference in the world. This Clovis spearman, Sellards' Llano man, did not have to haunt the marshy lake shores or the muck sinkholes waiting for his prey; he could go where he pleased, that is, wherever the herds took him. Now we see not just the periodic pulsations between kill and kill; we see the whole plan of life, if the mammoths held to the same habits as the elephants do now. There is, probably in the late spring or early summer after they have recovered from their winter-poor condition, a great concourse of the small herds from a wide area for the rutting season. And when the mammoths congregated, then would the scattered bands of Llano man have come together for their high season, of taking mates and celebration and super councils of all the hunters of old reputation or lately proven prowess; then the names of the slain would be recalled, perhaps for the last time before being forgotten forever, and the deeds in which they died recited in final tribute. Then would the legends and traditions and mores of a whole people, scant in numbers but close-knit in blood and loyalties, have been retold until they were older than, as they must have seemed as divinely promulgated as, Mosaic Law. This is the occasion, this rendezvous, for which the Llano spearmen lived their fiercely free yet conservatively ordered lives. This must have been the center of the universe and the densest concentration of population they were ever to see; it must have been a time of dressing up and games and humor (probably the grimmest of practical jokes), of the elevation of personalities until they became myths, of cere-

mony and pantomime and the consideration of policy, much of
it scandalously savage and yet much of it executed, I wish to
believe, on an impressive level of decorum, as befitted men of
strength, endurance and courage.

To reassure the reader that the foregoing is not the fancy of
a novelist, we quote Ashley Montagu on the social behavior of
the historic Copper Eskimos:

"Among the Copper Eskimos the dance song takes the place
of the daily newspaper, for in the great Copper House where
the Eskimos daily assemble every important incident is recorded in dance song. Song and dance, poem and story serve
not only to assist in binding the group together, in keeping it
informed and alive by serving as the vehicles for traditional
lore, for myth, ballad and magic formula, but also serve as a
means for reducing personal and interpersonal tensions. For
these purposes many peoples provide opportunities for dramatic experiences, ceremonies and plays in which every member may play a part. That such experiences can have a bene-
ficial effect was discovered by non-literate peoples long before
the development of modern psychology."

It is no great strain to credulity to attribute this kind of group
behavior to the herd hunters. By what other mechanism could
they have kept their culture so integral for 10,000 years?

Llano man would have had these rendezvous go on for
months, no doubt, but sooner or later the mammoth herds, as
the female period of heat and receptivity wanes, break up into
small groups of compeers: a band of old bulls crony off in one
direction; younger bulls—those born the same season—go a
different way; congenial she's and their calves form their parties and, chasing off buttinskys, flounce off to where the grass is
greenest and the herbs sweetest for the nurture of their offspring.

Now the festival must break up, too, and the tribe separates
into its bands, each band choosing a mammoth group, probably
of females and young, to follow. It would be hard to guess how
many mammoths would compose such a group, since it was a
matter of grazing; too few mammoths could not protect themselves against the great carnivores; but too many together
would make for thin eating. We can easily suppose that each
Llano band chose a group to follow not only by count but by

the number of young, easily killed individuals, and the eight spears at Naco provide us with a clue as to the size of a working band. You are free, of course, to interpret the eight projectile points as you please—as all thrown by one master spearman, or each thrown by a different one, or placed by two or three experts—but the probability that one man was able to place more than one spear does not seem high, for the mammoth, though he could not really run, could cover ground at a rate that is in man a good run. But this eight-spear pattern looks rather like a volley cast from ambush and the fact that the darts were left in the target area of the carcass strikes me not as carelessness, but as a very human gesture. The darts were left in the flesh, their shafts pointing upward in stiff pride because they had hit the target area. Those that did not were probably very quickly withdrawn from sight by their abashed owners, as the misses were recovered without much ado. Ten or twelve spearmen would not be an unreasonable estimate of this squad of bushwhackers; counting the two or three men who probably decoyed the prey into the line of fire, this band would have numbered fifteen full-fledged hunters, and, counting a woman and a child per hunter, thirty other persons—a thriving group, for a hunting band, which it may well have been, if its spearmen were always so deadly.

But of one thing we may be sure: These people were never likely, in 5000 years, or 10,000, to become civilized, not as long as there was big game to hunt. There were never enough of them cohering in a social body over a long enough time to create the population compression which sets in motion the kind of nuclear process by which higher and higher cultures combine until civilization is synthesized. They were not progressive in any discoverable material way, and unless the usufructians borrowed traits from them which are now believed to be usufructian traits they left nothing but the streak of their spears across the enthralled vision of memory to remind us that they went out to hunt, weapon against beast. For thousands of years they did nothing but hunt for a living. But that they did surpassingly well.

Nowhere else in the world has there been discovered a technique of grooving a point that resembles the Clovis fluting. We have already insisted that it was invented by Amerinds, of primal population extraction, which is what Lewisville man indicates (without necessarily proving), and that it was derived from a transference of function from bone to stone. In Europe, in an equivalent level of development—that is, the herd-hunting stage—the tradition in projectile-point making (except for that of the Solutreans) was the harpoon of bone or antler. This kind of point is quite sufficient for hunting the supple-hided reindeer, but for the tougher beasts it simply will not do; it breaks much too easily. Our Amerind hunters had either to find something more irrefrangible than bone points or to give up altogether the idea of killing mammoths and big bison by piercing them mortally.

The Amerind uniqueness of Llano man's fluted point has already been stressed, and in all the unearthed world of archaeology there is only one other hunter–point maker who will bear comparison with him at any stage of prehistory, the often-mentioned Solutreans of about 15,000–12,000 B.P., whose "empire" centered, archaeologically, in the Loire Valley in France. Geoffrey Bibby says of these people:

"With the second glacial maximum of the Riss [Illinoian] comes the second great puzzle of the last ice age, the Solutrean culture. To understand the puzzle we must look ahead a little. When the ice is once more retreating we find over the whole range of central and western Europe previously occupied by the Aurignacian harpoon makers (of about 15,000 B.P.) a new culture called the Magdalenian (of about 11,000 B.P. or less). The Magdalenian culture is the true heir of the Aurignacian. Every aspect of the life of the Magdalenians, their flint and bone tools, their art, and their personal adornment, is recognizably related to and derived from that of the Aurignacians. But between the Aurignacian layers and the Magdalenian layers, in the caves of a restricted area covering Spain and southern France, and more sparsely northern France and southern England, is found the occupation debris of a completely different culture called after the site of Solutré in the Loire Valley.

"The men of Solutré were the finest flintsmiths the world had yet seen—and were not to be surpassed for well over ten thousand years. . . . On the other hand the Solutreans had no implements of bone at all, and they had no art.

"How and why they suddenly superseded the Aurignacians in western Europe, and where they came from is unknown. And equally unknown is where they went."

This, as MacGowan observes, presents interesting possibilities.

How and why the Solutreans displaced the Aurignacians may be unknown but it is not inestimable. Their stone-pointed weapons were superior to Aurignacian bone ones; they were more weapon-conscious; and they must have had the combination of fearlessness and steadiness in the face of charging danger that the Aurignacians were not, judging by their habits, trained to. But where could this exotic culture have come from? Not, surely, from continental Europe, where both bone-working artisanship and depictive art in the service of fertility rituals were prevalent, and even rudimentary flint projectile points were not made. Had the Solutreans worked their way out of the east they would more than likely have adopted from the people they encountered, who were, after all, hunters like themselves, not bone points, and perhaps not even working in bone with its distinctive use of the burin or engraving tool, for they did not need these poorer substitutes for what they already had; but there was something the Aurignacians had that, as hunters, the Solutreans should have found most attractive —the rites of increase of game and success in hunting by homeopathic magic, the first principle of which was the drawing, carving or modeling in clay or stone of the fertility and victim figures. Judging from their adeptness as flintsmiths, the Solutreans had the innate craftsmanship to make ritual effigies had they been convinced they should.

This kind of speculation aside, there is nothing in the east of Europe to provoke notions of Solutrean incubation there. The Predmost mammoth hunters do not qualify at all as ancestors or cultural kin, and they seem to represent the kind of mammoth-flesh-based culture that was dug in (literally—they lived in pit houses) throughout the Russian plains; for they did not herd hunt, made no spears, were not nomads, and were carvers of *objets d'art* in bone and ivory, the most significant of which were statuettes of seated women, with the exaggerated sexual attributes of fertility symbols.

But if, having reappraised the Solutrean "empire's" position on the western verges of Europe, we should happen to look farther west for an explanation, that is, to America, we have, in Llano man, the perfect answer to everything except how Llano man got from America to the Loire.

As decisively as the Solutreans differ from the cultural progression they interrupted in Europe, just as decisively do they resemble the Amerind big-game-herd hunters. Here is striking congruity, from obliviousness to art magic, to the kind of weapons used and the way they were used. The challenge is to explain it.

Most of those who have remarked this congruity have assumed, I believe, that if there was a relationship between Llano man and the Solutreans the relationship was not direct and came about from a common ancestry. From a homeland possibly in the Caucasus or thereabouts, two bodies of Solutreans branched off, one herd-trailing westward into maritime Europe, one eastward to America. If any archaeological evidence of this had been produced, there would be no need to speculate about the Solutreans, an exercise in which we are about to engage. For there appears to be left but the one explanation just presented: the Solutrean is a Europeanized Llano man or Llano man is an Americanized Solutrean. If the existence of a land bridge or any other means of passing between Europe and America were ever geologically demonstrated I imagine that most archaeologists would prefer to believe the movement across it was from Europe to America; but our commitment to an Amerind origin of Llano man directs us to the opposite view.

We are not without means to support this view, for it is the Solutreans who are out of place in the western Europe cultural evolution, not Llano man in his American context; it is the Solutreans whose origin remains veiled after a hundred years of European excavation and after the outline of the European paleolithic has been firmly drawn by its archaeologists. Let us begin, then, with a Llano man who is perfectly at home in New Mexico and Arizona and Texas; he has abandoned bone as a material because he does not work it very well (probably because he didn't think up the burin, the tool for mastering bone), and his alternative, the stone-pointed spear, is so dependable a weapon he does not fear to go anywhere with it; so he follows the drift of game eastward—Clovis points have been found in the eastern American woodlands, though never at a datable site—and eventually he happens on the American end of an Atlantic bridge. Still pushing east, probably decade by decade rather than day by day, he becomes European millennia before any European became American. It makes a great deal more sense that the not-so-well-made Clovis lanceolate be ancestral to the finer Solutrean laurel-leaf points than vice versa, since from good to better seems to be the direction of Llano man flintwork even in America. Bibby calls the Solutreans the finest flintsmiths in the world for 10,000 years; he is being too Continental; their work is, indeed, impressively handsome, but the makers of the classic Folsom fluted and the masters of the Yuma technique of parallel and ripple flaking often found on Scottsbluff, Eden and other types of points which follow Clovis in America, surpassed them, and it is not a matter of *de gustibus non est disputandum.*

The Llano man–Solutrean congruity is exactly like those riddles that used to be propounded to us in our youth: Why is a lollipop like a horse? Because the more you lick it, the faster it goes. We feel the congruity is there, if we could only think how to relate the one to the other. The obvious answer is an Atlantic land bridge; even stepping-stone islands are not satisfactory, because we know that Llano man was a herd follower and, though he might have got from island to island, if he were hungry enough, beasts are not boatmen. It would take a notarized photograph of a Clovis spearman paddling an outrigger to convince me that Llano man ever ventured on or into salt water above his kneecaps.

But there is no proposal in all of archaeology of which the Americanist is more intolerant than that of an ancient interchange of European and American populations, especially by a land bridge. It makes him snort like a cuckold bull walrus. The only places the Old World and the New approach each other at all along their Atlantic shores, he will say, are the Arctic and sub-Arctic, which in paleolithic and mesolithic times were blockaded by ice. Sea voyages by dugout or raft in an ocean noted for its bad temper were manifest impossibilities. Recent studies of an enormous crack in the earth's crust have produced scientifically convincing arguments against continental drift, the theory that the Western Hemisphere broke away from the Eurafrican land mass and has been inching westward toward Asia ever since. And how dare anybody throw up a land bridge, anyway, across the pelagic trench of the Atlantic which has always been as permanently under water as the Appalachian Mountains have been permanently above it?

These are the facts to which archaeologists point with a certain asperity when an Atlantic isthmus enters the conversation; they have had their fill, over the years, of pseudo scientists who popularize schemes of Mayan civilization as a product of Egyptian Children of the Sun via the fabled lost Atlantis, or of Meso-American acculturation by contact with the inhabitants of the Pacific counterpart of Atlantis, the lost continent of Mu. Their short temper is very forgivable when you see how such flamboyant fictions invariably draw more attention for a season, and more credence altogether, than the laboring scientist can borrow, beg or steal in a lifetime, by his little monographs of understated, isolate conclusions.

But to bracket Atlantis and Mu as though they were opposite faces of the same coin is uncritical and unscholarly. Mu, a vast Pacific land mass where there developed a civilization so superior to ours that the inhabitants even made flying saucers, but could not avoid the catastrophe that dunked them to the last superman under the briny, is a modern, personal invention of James Churchward's, though a cult has grown up about it. But the fabled lost Atlantis is not the invention of Ignatius Donnelly, who spent a fortune bruiting its attributes to the world, and upsetting archaeology by peopling it with classic Greeks and then theorizing these Greeks into Mexico to Hellenize the Amerinds. And it is not to be disposed of by sweeping Donnelly's Atlantis exposition under the carpet. Atlantis is not exactly a fiction; it is a reference in Plato. Just so was Troy a myth, and the whole Homeric narrative with it, until Heinrich Schliemann, with the simplicity of a believer in fairytales, dug it up, right where Homer said it was. Perhaps Atlantis was, as A. W. Brøgger surmises, America itself, discovered by seafaring traders of the very maritime Bronze Age, and then lost sight of, because the knack of getting there in galleys designed for coastwise travel was buried with the brains of two or three master seamen. Or it may have been something a great deal more substantial and intermediary on the high seas between the Old World and the New. Or it may be no more than that Plato had been conned by an ancient visionary with the Jules Vernean imagination of a Churchward.

What American archaeologists should, in all honesty, say about an Atlantic bridge is this: If there was one, paleolithic man undoubtedly used it, but since our work to date, both in Europe and America, has turned up nothing that requires to be explained by an Atlantic bridge we respectfully request permission to be skeptical about it, and to devote our office hours, meanwhile, to other problems. This would at least provide them with an exit in case a land bridge, an island-hopping route, a lost Atlantis or something else equally mischievous pops up.

One gets the feeling occasionally that it may. There is somewhere or other in the library of the desultory and self-indulgent reader an account of a break in 1924 in the telegraph cable between Capetown, South Africa, and Napoleon's old summer estate, the island of St. Helena. The break, for which there was no apparent cause, was traced out by a repair ship of the Eastern Cable Company, which discovered it some 800 miles north of Capetown. Records showed that at this point the cable had been laid in 1899 in a 3-mile depth of water; it was picked up from water about three-quarters of a mile deep; that's still 600 fathoms, much deeper than it's safe to swim in, but a sea bottom that can heave up 2¼ miles in 25 years out in the Atlantic cannot be denied the power to hoist itself into dry land given 10,000 years to do it in, or subside into the pelagic during the same period.

The mysterious Davis Land, or Davis' Islands, is a case of the reverse of this process; it, or they, apparently sank a couple of miles. Sighted in 1687 by a British vessel, the *Bachelor's Delight,* under the command of a competent master, John Davis, it was not approached for inspection or explored because Captain Davis and his crew, happy in their bachelordom no longer, were in a hurry to make home port, and, after all, the islands— there was thought to be a chain of them—would be there when they got back. Captain Davis reported the position of the archipelago—about 27 degrees south and about 105 degrees west, in the general area of Easter Island—and named it after himself. Captain Davis' reputation being good, it was accordingly entered on the charts. And it was never seen again.

The eyesight of a crew of homesick English sailors may be safely disparaged at an interval of nearly 300 years, but an item that appeared in the *New York Times,* in the Sunday edition of September 22, 1956, on the science page of the News of the Week section, is certainly enough to start an argument with.

The report, taken from the Swedish geographical magazine *Ymer,* was written by a Dr. René Malaise of the Riksmuseum, Stockholm, and recounts the work of Dr. P. W. Kolbe, a colleague, in oceanography. Dr. Kolbe, while taking sediment cores in 12,000 feet of water in the Atlantic, brought up one in which the diatom shells were exclusively of a fresh-water type. The *Times* piece says:

"According to Dr. Malaise these fresh-water diatoms in the ocean bottom can be explained only by assuming there was once a Mid-Atlantic Ridge which crossed the ocean above the surface and that the core taken by the Swedish expedition came from a fresh-water lake bottom once part of the ridge. This ridge acted as a barrier to the Gulf Stream so that the Arctic Ocean was landlocked from Europe to Greenland only 10,000 to 12,000 years ago. When the land barrier sank the Gulf Stream could reach the Arctic Ocean and the Ice Age ended. This conclusion has been confirmed by Russian scientists who did some ocean-bottom exploring in the icebreaker Sadko."

This seems sober and authoritative enough to draw at least a mention from American archaeologists on whose cultural conclusions a mid-Atlantic ridge would—or will if it is further corroborated—have a distinctly destructive effect; yet in the few years since the report appeared I have not talked to an archaeologist who will acknowledge having read it or who can be engaged in conversation on it. It is hardly a cause, however, that needs a press agent. Either it is right, and the data will make the case, or it is wrong and there is another answer to the mystery of the Solutreans. Coon, for instance—and to him we always listen with respect—believes the Solutreans have Neanderthal blood in them, which would make them Europeans or Asian-Europeans. But in another passage he points out that there is not a single skull which is accepted by all physical anthropologists as being Solutrean—and this is one more Solutrean parallel with Llano man, who was equally careless, or it may be secretive, about his mortal remains.

In his *Ymer* piece Malaise makes no mention of transatlantic contacts, perhaps out of politeness, since he is not an archaeologist; but, like many before him, he cannot refrain from bringing up the lost Atlantis, for this is not archaeological private property. Literarily documented, it is in the public domain, and Malaise believes that the breakup of Kolbe's mid-Atlantic ridge started the legend on its way to Greece. If this happened 10,000 years ago, the age is too early for the peak civilization reputed to Atlantean attainment, but island fragments of it might very well have, like Davis Land, lasted much longer and provided the scene for what we now regard as a Platonic romance.

Unless Atlantis survived long enough to inject seminal influences into Meso-America, a proposition that seems likely never to be tested unless its land mass reappears from the sea and can be excavated, and its culture thereby correlated with the Meso-American, it will probably not concern American archaeologists too much. But the mid-Atlantic ridge, if proved, would reorient American archaeology by 180 degrees. The big-flake industry of Tule Springs and many other American sites is regarded as Clactonian, and the Clactonian takes its name from Clacton-on-Sea, in England. The big-blade makers of 11,000 B.P. on Manitoulin Island in Lake Huron—discovered by Thomas E. Lee in two summers of excavating—are less puzzling if their makers drifted in from Europe, and, of course, that would solve the Solutrean mystery, but by what everybody, I am sure, would regard as a backward migration.

Now it happens that there has always been an element of the late European paleolithic in America. There is no evidence that Neanderthal ever trekked here, and Aurignacian man has left no *art mobilier* in Nova Scotia or New York; the Magdalenians and the Azilian-Tardenoisians (who succeeded the Magdalenians), with their geometric microliths, nowhere appear. But no less a skeptic in such matters of European immigration than Hrdlicka once noted the similarity of the boreal hunters, and of Eskimos in particular, to Magdalenian man, who appears in Solutrean territory in Europe after the Solutreans disappear. He, as we have noted from Bibby's quotation, is the true heir and executor of Aurignacian culture. So there is a prima-facie case that both Aurignacian and Magdalenian may have entered this continent in small, adventurous bands via a land bridge from Europe, but before and after, not during Llano man's trail eastward; for Llano man, who summarily dispossessed the Aurignacians of their French-Spanish home-land, can easily be seen as just the type to turn back any Aurignacians going the wrong way on his one-way street.

To say that the mid-Atlantic ridge is proved, and all that we have just outlined in the foregoing necessarily follows, would be flagrant quackery. The mid-Atlantic ridge is now but a suspicion; yet suspicion must invoke investigation, and investigation will establish the corpus delicti, if it is there. Meanwhile it is not premature to cock an ear for the rumors that may prove to be more than that. The pelagic trench may not every-where be as profound as it is now alleged to be, for, let us re-peat it, we do not know what the geography of our world was like four or five millennia ago. The debris of the archaeological ages that we want to find, as Richard J. Russell mentioned a decade ago, may lie a hundred miles out to sea on the con-tinental shelf.

The parallelisms of Llano man and the Solutreans do not cease until their separate disappearances, and the timing of their disappearances is the final coincidence. Bibby has been quoted to the effect that the Solutreans seem to have evapo-rated without residue, as the glacial-period climate began to warm up again, even as they had appeared without explana-tion where there was a resurgence of ice. Now it cannot be that they died of heat, for it did not wax that warm all at once, and they could have hugged the retreating ice sheet, as the Magda-lenian reindeer hunters did, if it were simply that the tepidity devitalized them. The heat was not the cause of their disap-pearance, we may take it, but the cause of the cause, or a necessary condition, and this can mean only one thing: In Eu-rope this period is quite positively taken as the end of the Pleistocene fauna, and when the horse and mammoth herds were depleted, then their solely dependent culture, the Solu-trean, lost all that gave it continuity and character.

And it appears on the record, according to Sellards, that

this is when the Clovis fluted point ceases to be made—when there are no more mammoths, horses or camels to blood it. Among the casualties of the Great Extinction certainly can be listed the flintsmiths of Solutré and, perhaps, the knappers of the Clovis.

The mammoths die off and the Clovis fluted ceases—abruptly, to all appearances—to be made; does this mean that

EARLY HUNTERS' POINTS

At left is a Sandia point, found beneath Folsom points in the excavation of Sandia Cave, New Mexico. In the center is a Clovis fluted point, found beneath Folsoms at Clovis, New Mexico, and other places. At right is a Gypsum Cave point C14 dated at 10,000 B.P., contemporary with the Folsom. It was used against the sloth.

the maker, too, ceased to exist? That the Clovis ceased to be made at just this time, after having served Llano man thousands of years without alteration—surely this bespeaks a lesion of some kind, mortal or not. We can doubt that Llano man felt any need to change his point type simply because his target was no longer mammoth, but had become bison. Both bison and mammoth bones have been found at a Clovis-point kill site at the Lehner Ranch, near Hereford, Arizona, so Llano man knew Clovis points would kill bison as dead as mammoth.

Nevertheless, when there are only bison to be killed, the point
that is used to down them—the *fluted* point, that is—is not the
Clovis, but the Folsom.

But why make such a major thing of this? Is not the Folsom,
by reason of its unique fluting, the true heir and offspring of
the first and only other fluted point in the world, the Clovis?
I can't imagine what reason anybody would give for saying
that it is not. The flute is as hereditary a feature as red hair.
But this family characteristic only serves to emphasize the differences between father and son.

The Clovis is a competent point, with an air of no-nonsense
about it. In outline it is straightforward, with either parallel
edges from base to where it tapers, somewhat bluntly, to its
tip, or else a gentle and quite pleasing excurvate sweep from
base to business end. The grooving is no longer or deeper than
will serve the purpose; the basal third of the blade has both
edges dulled by grinding so as not to cut the lashings; the base
is indented or yoked, and the two prongs or toes left at the
base point straight down and fall within the simplicity of the
overall outline. There is no uniform length; the shortest of
the eight Naco specimens is 58 millimeters, the longest exactly
twice that, 116 millimeters, and the other six fall randomly between.

But the classic Folsom is as tricksy as a piece of costume
jewelry. It continues the fluting, but this is longer, relative to
length, than in the Clovis (most Folsoms fall short of the shortest Naco specimen). It has a better controlled, more sharply
defined groove than the Clovis, and the ridges between the
groove and the blade edge are flattened by minute retouch.
The basal prongs usually flare out; and with the blade narrow-
ing above them, then swelling to its maximum width past the
mid-point, and then cutting acutely, rather prowlike, to the
tip, the silhouette as a whole is decidedly double Mae Westish.

If it were only the Clovis which had undergone this suspected qualitative change, we might pass over without comment the change to Folsom as nothing more than other-times,
other-customs. But the Scottsbluff, the Yuma Eden, the Long-
Angostura, the Plainview, the San Jon, the Browns Valley, the
Nebo Hill—all these at this same time make what seems to
be a fresh and sudden apparition on the big-bison hunting

grounds. Can this be? Did the big bison stimulate hunters to cope with them by experimentation with a whole new inventory of types? Or did several new tribes appear among the bison hunters, each with his own distinguishing brand of projectile point?

Closer inspection eliminates both these possibilities, and we become conscious that what seems to be a proliferation of point types is nothing more than that the same agency has been at work transforming and sprucing up obscure early types contemporary with Clovis that refashioned Clovis into the Folsom. Now rare and somewhat puzzling points such as the Abilene,

CLOVIS, FOLSOM, SOLUTREAN
POINTS

This reiteration of Clovis, Folsom, and Solutrean work serves to exemplify how the broader flaking of the Clovis contrasts with the fine retouch of a Folsom, and how the Folsom compares with the Solutrean at its best.

Lake Mohave, Silver Lake, Lake Lahontan, Gypsum Cave, Sandia and perhaps Desert Culture types fall into precedent place as ancestors of later, better-realized forms. There was no break in the big-game hunting tradition, but there was, I think, ebb as the mammoths faded and then, as the bison herds increased and flourished, renaissance, but a renaissance that derived its vigor, as so often happens, from contact with a new people, who had a fresh technological viewpoint to impart. These teachers? The Denbighites.

Giddings, excavator of the micro-blades (which we have been calling strip blades) of Cape Denbigh, is the first, I believe, to have some inkling of the importance of Alaskan complexes to the Plains hunters. In his Denbigh material there were a broken Folsomoid point and a dozen fragments of blades or points done in what is called the Yuma-oblique fashion of chipping. Thought-provoking, this, for on the Plains Denbigh artifacts are not found mixed in with bison-hunter materials.

It should be mentioned here that once upon a time the Yuma was considered a separate point type because of its uniquely handsome method of parallel flaking, until H. M. Wormington perceived that this characteristic was merely a method and seems to have been used on several types of points. There are two kinds of Yuma techniques, one called the oblique, in which the single flake scars run diagonally all the way across the blade from edge to edge and give an effect of rippling stone; in the other, called the collateral Yuma, the individual scars run only to the center of the blade, with the same ripplelike regularity, from each side, leaving a dorsal ridge from base to tip. It is a matter of taste which is the handsomer, and when Bibby lavished his superlatives on Solutrean lapidarianism it must have been in ignorance of Yuma technique.

It was Giddings' imputation, if I read him aright, that, because of the presence of the Folsomoid and the Yuma-technique fragments at faraway Denbigh, here lay the rootlets of Folsom and Yuma. But he and D. M. Hopkins of the United States Geological Survey date Denbigh by geology (C14 gave unsatisfactory results because of contamination) at 8000 B.P., and this is obviously too late for Denbigh to have fathered the 10,000-B.P. Folsom, which had been fathered by the 12,000-to-15,000-year-old Clovis. But he had this to say of the Denbigh flintworkers:

"The flintwork of the Denbigh Flint Complex, the oldest cultural horizon yet identified in the Bering Strait region, is not only unique but possibly the world's most sophisticated. It shows no signs of having been brought there in toto from elsewhere. The Bering Straight region was already a 'culture center' at the time of deposit of the Denbigh Flint layer. Its emanations were being felt both to the east and west."

And, we believe, to the south. If the fluting in the Folsom point is deeper, better channeled, longer, and the whole point has a more complicated shape, it is because the pre-Denbighites had something to teach the fluted-point makers about their own product. Striking off long, thin flakes to leave the channel or flute in the Folsom is exactly what the Denbigh flintsmiths were best at; but the Clovis knappers were not very good at it at all.

Fluted points, Long-Angosturas, Plainviews and all the herd-hunter types are found in Alaska in the right places and at the right times to give us leave to think that, following the doomed mammoth herds, all the early herd hunters of the Plains went north at one time in the prehistory of America and sat at the feet of the world's most sophisticated lapidarians. And in Alaska, with the Denbighites, they really learned flintsmithing.

We have made the estimate that between 11,000 and 10,000 B.P. the mammoths became extinct, that at this time the Folsom hunters appear, and that during this period the ice, shrinking toward its Labrador and Keewatin centers, widened the Rocky Mountain corridor till it was a great deal more than a mere corridor. Let us mesh this jigsaw together into a picture: The Keewatin icecap recedes, and the mammoths follow as their habitat recedes with it. Eventually this habitat shrinks into Alaska, until it begins to intersect the taiga-tundra zone. Hence the mammoth hunters, following their herds, are drawn into the habitat area of the Denbighites.

Plains hunter of mammoth meets taigan hunter of reindeer and for once Llano man does not try to dispossess, or at least does not succeed in dispossessing the original resident, as the Solutreans had dispossessed the Aurignacians. Perhaps they had not the numbers, or perhaps the taigans were hospitable and friendly, like the present-day Eskimos; but the odds are that these two peoples coexisted with little or no harm done to either, for the very good reason that there was no conflict of interest. By the time the mammoth has ceased to be as a game animal, bison is beginning to flourish and to spread out over the old mammoth domain. The fluted-point hunters did not have to muscle in on the taigans' reindeer, which they probably did not know how to hunt anyway. They, like the bison, so

similar in habit and habitat to the mammoth, go back to the
Plains again. But the contact has been stimulating, at least to
the herd hunters. All the old types of points begin to show
sharper workmanship, firmer form, the technically advanced
Yuma artisanship—and something new appears, the strip
blade.

Now it must be emphasized that strip-blade making was a
skill only partially acquired by the new bison hunters; they did
not adopt the whole classic Denbigh micro-blade industry. A
review of the artifacts found with the first Iztapán mammoth
will show quite clearly that at least two of them are strip blades
—lamellar flakes—and the unretouched one satisfies the six
descriptive standards for lamellar blades set up by W. S.
Laughlin and Gordon Marsh for their guidance at a core-and-
lamellar-blade industry site in the Aleutians, where such an in-

THE ENGRAVER'S TOOL

These three tools are all forms of the burin, used to
cut or engrave bone, or to engrave stone—though stone
engraving was little done in early America, in comparison
with the more "artistic" cultures of the European late
paleolithic. The secret of the burin is its stout, narrow,
chisel-like point. The center specimen illustrates best the
method of re-edging the burin, by striking it on the point
and detaching tiny strip blades, the stubs of which are
here plainly evident. Specialists do not accept as burins
specimens which do not show the stubs of at least three
distinct re-edgings.

dustry was to be separated from other cultural materials. But
this occurrence of strip blades is something different from a

whole industry based on the production of strip blades; the characteristic polyhedral cores are not associated, in any context so far noted, with bison hunters of the Portales Complex of the Great Plains. We can deduce, from what we have grasped up to now about the big-game hunters, that they knew the trick of stripping off blades, but were interested in using it only to strike off an occasional knife or scraper.

But these occasional occurrences satisfy us that (1) Portales man must have seen these blades made, in order to have made them at all, and (2) Portales man was not a taigan hunter who had transferred his attention from caribou to bison. Not only was the Denbighite a thoroughgoing strip-blade maker, he was a notable worker in bone. We know this not from bone artifacts at Denbigh, which had long since been resorbed into earth, but from the occurrence there of burins. These unassuming little tools, which seem not to be tools at all but chips or blades jaggedly broken, are what make successful bone- and especially antler-working possible. The true burin is a little stone chisel point, sharpened in a special way by delicately knocking tiny spalls off the point, and it went undiscovered in America until surprisingly late, when Henry B. Collins descried burins in certain Alaskan collections. Almost any site of the Amerind, early or late, will produce flakes which have evidently been used to score and cut something tubular, probably bone; but the thin, brittle knife edge of a chip will not stand up under this kind of use very long, and bone working with flake edges alone is tedious and awkward. Portales man made no burins.

But we are not surprised that Portales man, the bison hunter, picked up from the taigans what he did, and no more. He had no use for fragile bone points; strip blades served but little better than casual flakes struck from any pebble he picked up; but keener, and therefore more efficient points—ah, this was something he was interested in, this single-minded man who had no thought but to go on living at the wild, free life rhythm of hunt and feast, carnival and roaming that we have imagined for him.

There can be no doubt that the Clovis-Portales herd hunters made it to Alaska in some numbers. Their points are there, like calling cards—the Clovis, the Folsom, the Angostura, the Eden, etc. But even when found (always sparsely) in taigan contexts they do not look at home among the diminutive jewel-like flints of the micro-blade makers. From that day almost to this the Arctic and sub-Arctic hunters have clung to a habit of making what are called, in America, side blades, a somewhat more readable designation than lunates, which is the term derived from their shape and used in African archaeology, where they are also found. They are parts of points, in that they are made to be slotted into the side of a shaft behind an end point, so that an end point and the side blades behind it, one on each side of the shaft, make one large compound projectile

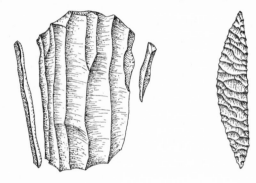

DENBIGH AGAIN

This illustration of strip-blade making is repeated here as a reminder of the kind of lapidary work the herd hunters encountered when they met the Denbighite tai-gans.

point. Why this is preferable to, or even as good as, a single point is obscure to me; it seems to triple the number of things that can go wrong with a point on impact and withdrawal, and thus triple the replacement parts. The big-game hunters must have taken the same view of side blades, for they did not tool up on them; but the compound projectile point must have served some purpose well understood by Arctic hunters, who went on taking the pains to make them, delicate and diminutive and quite at variance in every way with the big-game idea of armament.

All in all the Portales Complex constituents do not seem too difficult to precipitate out of the complex of the Arctic hunters; these two peoples met, had superficial but legible influence on each other—after all, they were in similar but non-competing businesses—and kept on running into each other over the millennia. It shows in the occurrence of scattered Clovis-Portales points and even whole sites in Alaska, and in the workmanship of Portales implements on the Great Plains, but the two were hunters of different game and there was never a mutual embrace.

This, then, is the most psychological of the resemblances of Llano-Portales man to the Solutrean: that each, when he encountered an Aurignacian-like culture, did not fuse with it, but was only stimulated by it to his best efforts as an artisan; as a whole culture these wild, free-roving hunters were never to be reformed. What saved Llano man to become herd-hunting Portales man was that bison herds replaced the mammoths in America; but in Europe nothing replaced them.

It now becomes important for us to give fuller consideration to these circumpolar hunters, these taigans whose lithic artisanship has been touted so highly.

A quick glance at the map will serve to explain their place in prehistory. The basic population of the hemisphere was, as we have been showing, usufructian. Making the wildest sort of guess I would say there were—at, say, 7500 B.P.—upwards of 100,000 of them in bands of 10 to 30 scattered all over that part of habitable North America which was outside herd-animal territory. This herd-animal territory, extending from the valley of Mexico to the Arctic Ocean, is the homeland of the Portales bison hunters, and unless I read them most erroneously there wouldn't have been more than 5000 of them at any one time. There were, and again I guess strictly on my own, rather more of the well-adjusted taigans, but these would have by no means been confined to Alaska.

The taiga-tundra is a botanical zone determined by the position of the icecap. Obviously nothing can grow on the ice; and for a while after its withdrawal, since the ground has been stripped of soil, and since what shallow soil there is will be frozen, nothing can grow in the immediate vicinity of the ice front. In time, however, a low, short-season vegetation will take possession of this ground, which then becomes tundra or cold plains. Trees cannot grow here, for one or both of two reasons

—the cold and the shallowness of the soil. Where, at a sufficient distance from the ice front, it becomes climatically warm
enough and the soil is deep enough, the bush begins, and then
comes the forest stand, of the cold-adapted evergreens.

With the icecap concentrated in the Hudson Bay area this
taiga-tundra zone is determined by it to be a strip running from
Bering Strait (Cape Denbigh area) diagonally across Canada
to the Dakotas, and later, as the icecap melts, to Minnesota
and Michigan; here the glacial front turns east, around the
Great Lakes ice-lobe, and cuts directly across Ohio, New York
and New England to the Atlantic coast, not necessarily in a
straight line, but following along the scalloped edge of the
glacial border.

It is clear from the map that in Alaska or thereabouts, this
taiga-tundra strip intersects the Great Plains, running north
and south just east of the Rocky Mountain cordillera. Here the
Plains big-game hunters were in sporadic contact, as we have
already reiterated, with the taigans. But beginning at the point
where the taiga-tundra strip turns eastward toward the Atlantic (in the Minnesota-Wisconsin area) the taigans, keeping to their natural habitat, are in contact with the eastern
usufructians, who were comfortably in residence here if Modoc
Rock Shelter means anything.

We know that the taigans did come as far south as Wisconsin from Albert Spaulding's report of an antler tool in a collection of Wisconsin Old Copper Complex items which, on analysis, proved to be antler from barren-ground caribou, a tundra
faunal type. With this were the skeletons of a large breed of
dogs almost certainly of "Eskimo" origin. Undoubtedly the
taigans themselves came this far south, but did they go as far
south as Russell Cave, wherein Miller found his bear-leg lamp?
More likely this trait came to them from Russell Cave only
after a long transmittal through other bands of usufructians
who did have contact with taigans.

But the importance of the taigans to American prehistory is
more than that they had contact-influence on both the big-
game hunters and the usufructians. They, if anybody was, were
the culture bearers from Asia. It is evident from the map that
they were the only Americans in a position to receive cultural
influences from Siberian sources. And it is self-evident that

such traits as taigans borrowed would be only those that were useful or attractive to them in their specialized way of life. We will have to think of them as a sort of screen or filter, then, both rejecting and admitting new influences, very selectively. It is the most telling of arguments, for instance, against the Hootonian thesis that Amerind culture was enriched from Asia that it wasn't enriched; where are the bronze swords of the Bronze Age, or the iron weapons of the succeeding age? Copper was used by later taigans, but as a trait, it came from Michigan; iron was eventually smithed by the Eskimo, who got it from Asia but not much before Atlantic coast Indians got it from Europeans. We have said it before, but we must repeat it because it is a cardinal point in American prehistory: The Alaska of this period, as Rainey has supposed, was fit for habitation only by those very finely adjusted to it. Those who were adjusted to it, the taigans, kept strictly to it, not inviting outside influences, nor being challenged or even approached by any—from outside the Arctic.

This point must now be made clear: The taigans were, culturally, not all-Americans—nor were they Asians only or Europeans only; they were all three, for the "continent" they inhabited was Arctica, which appears on no map, but which is, for living purposes, nevertheless a continent. It is all that land which lies in a great circle about the North Pole and it includes the Hyperborean fringes of Europe, Asia and North America; this is the empire of the taigans, who from Norway to Michigan bear a strong cultural resemblance to one another.

Who are they?

The European taigans were Magdalenian reindeer hunters who simply moved north as the glacier receded. And the Asian taigans? Very likely of the same stock and origin. And the American taigans? We have already proposed an origin for them by development out of the basic Amerind population through adaptation to environment. They came by their culture virtually independently, then, and it resembles the circumpolar cultures of Asia and Europe by a combination of parallelism—parallel influences producing similar tools and habits —and trait borrowing. But this borrowing need not have accounted for most of what is American taigan.

It is here relevant to extend Giddings' remarks on the Denbigh culture: "It shows no signs of having been brought there in toto from elsewhere. The Bering Strait region was already a 'culture center' at the time of deposit of the Denbigh Flint layer . . . People at Bering Strait could have passed along ideas received from either direction, but they would also have originated and disseminated ideas of their own."

We are now at that place in our narrative where we have got firmly settled in America in their rightful places the three principal cultural-population elements which commingle to produce the next period of American prehistory: the usufructian inventors of a list of ways and means to exploit the American environment; the big-game hunters, who invented the projectile point, perhaps, but transmitted nothing, yet impress us powerfully with their inimitable exploits; and finally the taigans, who adopt, invent, transmit and absorb.

14

 *Long, Hot Summers*

For two decades or more the period in American prehistory that follows the period of cultural trifurcation—which it is present convention to call the paleo-hunter period—has been known as the Archaic. The name is half of a phrase of Ritchie's coining during a time in the study of New York prehistory when everything aboriginal there was called Algonkin; when the exhumation of his Lamoka Lake site disclosed it to be without pottery, he recognized it as preceramic and designated it as of a very early or "Archaic Algonkin" period.

Webb and DeJarnette, encountering in their Pickwick Basin middens, which had nothing to do with Algonkins, a similar preceramic level, rich in bonework, signified the similarity by calling the manifestation simply the Archaic.

Because it was a sorely needed designation for a whole series of preceramic manifestations throughout the Mississippi Basin and the territory east of it, the term gained general usage. But the more it was used the more it came to mean not only a time span between the paleo-hunter and the appearance of pottery in eastern North America but the types of materials found within that time span: thus the large, broad-bladed, notched and stemmed points that have already been cited as perhaps marking the advent of the bow and the unfletched arrow shaft are regarded as typically Archaic-period points. Undoubtedly they are, temporally, or a good many of them are; but unfortunately American archaeologists have taken this to mean that the patterns of these points—the stemmed and notched types of them—are Archaic, and only Archaic. We now know, from Danger Cave and Modoc Rock Shelter, that this is not true. The Archaic is a time period only, a climatological era within which took place certain Amerind cultural events, and it cannot be properly described in terms of one kind of cultural material alone.

The span of this period is hard to delimit. The terminal date is not convertible into years, since the first appearance of pottery, which ends it and which is so clear a culture marker for the excavator, many have been at 4000 B.P. in one place (in New York a Point Peninsula II grave with pottery has yielded this age) and 2500 B.P. in another. But it is only half true that the Archaic begins with the departure of the big-game hunter, and not true at all when it is used to imply, as many archaeologists do, that the departure of the big-game hunters means their displacement by people of other cultural habits.

What they mean is that the period preceding the Archaic was the time of the big-game follower or paleo-hunter, and nobody else, and he was succeeded by the hunter-gatherers of the Archaic period with a whole new approach to livelihood, a whole new inventory of projectile points and a whole new set of cranial characteristics. They do not say what became of the paleo-hunters in response to climatic changes, or make any serious attempt to explain how, suddenly, all over the continent there are usufructian peoples. They merely say that the curtain is drawn on the paleo-hunter and goes up immediately on a whole new scene full of "Archaic" characters never mentioned in the script before.

This is a very strange error for American archaeologists to have fallen into—this error of succession of cultures like a succession of kings, because European archaeology had already fallen into and recovered from it, and posted friendly warning not to do likewise. Geoffrey Bibby has pointed this out unmistakably. He writes:

"In the last quarter of the nineteenth century, archaeologists were, it can now be seen, somewhat dazzled by the idea of the *succession* of prehistoric cultures. In their reaction against the belief of early nineteenth-century historians in a single homogeneous prehistoric period of short duration, they went far in the other direction. They established a progression of communities, and in their nomenclature of eras, ages and epochs can be clearly seen their unconscious assumption that each step in this progression followed, in time, the one below. It was assumed that at one specific time the whole of Europe could be regarded as in the Old Stone Age, that in another in the New Stone Age and similarly through the Bronze and Iron Age. *Transitions from the one to the other of these ages were assumed to have occurred suddenly, from the outside.* (Russia was the favorite home of these putative invasions.)" The italics are mine, the parenthesis Bibby's.

The reader will have no difficulty in recognizing how American archaeologists have fallen into a similar habit, using Siberia as their European colleagues once used Russia. Any time they needed a new period they brought it in on cue across Bering Strait.

But the disappearance of the big-game hunters does serve, coincidentally, to signal the beginning of the Archaic, only because the approaching Altithermal, which laid waste the pastures of the bison herds on the Great Plains, also caused those changes in the eastern woodlands, changes which advantaged the usufructians, and to which they responded by increase of population. Where it had formerly been feasible for only small, expanded-family groups to work a food territory, now an abundance of shellfish at every river shoal gave an easily harvested subsistence base to all who forgathered on the nearest bank. For an abundance of shellfish was the great gift of the Altithermal's one hand to the eastern woodlands—by warming the waters that had formerly flowed chill with melting snow and ice when they were not themselves frozen over—even as that period of heat took from the western plains with the other.

Probably the best logical order in discussing the Archaic is first to dispose of the affairs of the big-game hunters, not a simple task because they simply disappeared, almost within a generation it seems to us now, like buggy-whip makers. When a previous crisis, the extinction of the mammoth, had come upon him the Clovis spearman, according to our reconstruction of events, had followed the survivor mammoths to Alaska and perhaps had slain the last one with his own thrusts. If we will, with a sharp whack with an open palm, clear our heads again of the notion that the icecap was only in the north and remember that it was also in the east, in the present Canadian provinces of Saskatchewan, Manitoba, Ontario and Quebec, we will

see how Clovis bands would have also pursued the mammoth
herd remnants eastward, for the ice front made elephant
grazing habitat across Illinois, Indiana and Ohio, and well into
New York and New England. Nowadays they are not often
thought of in this way, but the flatlands we know as the Great
Plains and prairie extend without interruption, except by
rivers, from the Rockies to New York, in a single topographical feature, and Ohio could have been as much mammoth park
at 11,000 B.P. as Naco, Arizona. That the Clovis spearmen came
this way is not disputed because fluted points are found
sparsely all over the east; as a matter of fact they have been
found in all of the forty-nine states and in most of the Canadian provinces. What is frustrating about those found outside
the southwest is that they have always been superficial finds,
not datable, and usually they appear to be lost pieces, having
no context of camp site or kill, like the Naco Clovis or the Fol-
som-site Folsoms. (If you know of a site that produces fluted
points, especially if it is east of the Mississippi, you are in possession of more important information than what happened
to the Lost Colony of Roanoke.) As a consequence of their
being here incognito it is always a question whether these
eastern fluted are the earlier Clovis or later Folsom ones, for
few of them are "classic" enough in outline to make classification easy.

Only four sites containing fluted points with accompanying
artifacts are known, as of this writing, beyond the western
plains, and they are all undatable. They are Ritchie's Reagen
site in Vermont; Ben C. McCary's Williamson site in Virginia;
John Witthoft's Shoop site in Pennsylvania; and the Bull Brook
site in Massachusetts, reported by Douglas S. Byers. With the
material from these in mind Ritchie argues that fluted points
are later in the east than in the west; and I believe he is right—
for this material. Placed in a position of having to make a judgment about them, one has to say that they look like Folsoms
gone to seed; they look like the points of a big-game hunting
people who have lost their grip on themselves, who are no
longer in contact with the centers of their own culture, which,
in the case of these hunters, were the annual or semiannual
carnival-councils that we have already described; they look,

in brief, like the points of a driven, outcast people who are about to peter out.

(*The April, 1959, issue of* American Antiquity *carries a note from Byers on the dating of the Bull Brook site. An average of three acceptable C14 dates on charcoal places it at about 9000* B.P., *which average, if it should turn out to mark the beginning date of the site, lends support to the supposition of the immigration of herd hunters from west to east, though it does not prove it; there may be earlier sites. Bull Brook now appears to be 10 to 15 acres in area and may, when fully explored, finally afford adequate information on a paleo-hunter complex in the east.*)

Thus migration must have been forced once on the Clovis hunters of mammoth and once, some thousands of years later, on the bison hunters of the Portales Complex, as Krieger suggested years ago. Looking for the fountainhead of their game herds in the woodlands, as their brethren looked for it in Alaska, they came only upon the end of their day. For they were too specialized a culture to survive long away from their accustomed habitat. Even though a type of bison could be found in some numbers in the woodlands, it did not congregate in the great herds of the plains, and this was exactly the situation the extraordinarily conservative herd hunter required for survival. After the Clovisians and the Portalesians entered the woodlands we catch a few glimpses of their wandering aimlessly about briefly and pathetically and the next evidence of them we find is their point types mingled in slight numbers among usufructian artifacts.

This acculturation of herd hunter and woodsman-gatherer is more than a deduction. There are in fact many sites like Graham Cave, where the last fluted points are commingled with usufructian types, and many of these are, significantly, in the middle west, where the hunters, harried eastward like wrong-way Okies, must have met and joined up with, or settled down and imitated, the usufructians in their Archaic prosperity. The Starved Rock and Faulkner sites in Illinois and the Parrish site in Kentucky show point inventories of hybrid character, and in the upper Ohio Valley William J. Mayer-Oakes has found lanceolate and broad-stemmed points, which he calls Steubenville lanceolate and Steubenville stemmed, which

remind him of the Plainview and Scottsbluff of the Portales
Complex. This, in the end, is what the mightiest hunters of all
time have come to, reminiscent outlines of projectile points
among the slayers of woodland deer—just as the band on a
man's hat is all that remains today of the knightly helm flaunt-
ing the scarf and colors of milady in the Field of the Cloth of
Gold.

The Archaic period, then, is definable as that era of prehistory when the life way of sturdy, grubbing usufructians proved
its worth as against the herd-hunting complexes, and it is
thinkable that, had there been no usufructian culture but only
herd hunters during the Altithermal in America, it would
have been depopulated for a long time—except for the taigans,
and these might not have leaped quickly to the task of regen-
erating the human race in regions that, ironically, seemed to
them not to be livable. The Altithermal hit them, too, it seems
from the record, and the reaction of some of them to it was to
turn to hunting in the richest of all food-producing areas—
the sea—and the first Eskimo, harpooner of walrus and seal
and polar bear, was born.

As a consequence of all this, of hunter-usufructian acculturation, and of taigan-usufructian contacts (to be later gone into),
we must rename this Archaic period the Period of Confluence
of Population and Culture, or simply the Confluent period.

So the Confluent period begins on a note of elegy, for a people whose comings and goings, as we have tried to make clear,
were never more than episodic in the main stream of American
prehistoric narrative. The Altithermal wrought its most important consequence to posterity when it tempted the usufructians from their forest rounds and settled them on the banks of
fecund rivers in at least semipermanent settlements like the
Pickwick Basin shell mounds.

That shellfish beds were not in any sense a discovery of the
Period of Confluence we may take for granted from what we
already know of the usufructians, who left no food source un-
exploited. But during the Altithermal not only did shellfish
increase in the crop-harvest sense but they began to appear in
more and more northerly waters, and everywhere, even as
far up the Ohio as the site of Pittsburgh and up the Delaware

and the Scioto, up the Hudson as far as Poughkeepsie is now, and up the Atlantic coast as far as present-day Maine, the usufructians came out of the woods and stood in line at these natural free-lunch counters.

This must have been the first real leisure the usufructians had ever known, and those whom life in the big woods had made half troglodyte came into a period of sun and space that might well have leavened their whole nature. For the big woods, during the pluvial-glacial centuries, were as dank as cellars, and never quite warm, and as gloomy as windowless rooms. The drying drafts of the Altithermal swept out the musk and sweetened the slow rot of vegetation there; yet this attractiveness could not compare with the miracle of the shoals, where nobody had to go hungry any longer than it took him to wade into the water and scoop his daily mess like picking flowers.

We have been thinking of the usufructians up to now as no more than expanded families—a group of immediate kin, from infants to grandparents, augmented only by the husbands and wives joined to it through mating, and these families following a schedule of seasonal stops at known food-producing patches like a trapper following out his trap lines. They do not give up this schedule—who would want to eat mussels three times a day for a lifetime?—but it has become less onerous; and where once each little band had of necessity to go its own way ceaselessly, now there is a place and a time and the leisure for meeting and for the preoccupations of society—government, religion, personal relations. How close the Confluent-period people still are to their primitive living habits, yet how far they have come from them and in what direction they are moving, is authoritatively described by Ritchie, who, though he is speaking of prehistoric settlement patterns of the northeastern United States, has so synthesized the data that it applies generally to the entire territory east of the Mississippi at one time or another. He says:

"In the light of the total evidence it seems reasonable to suppose that the basic socio-political units of Archaic times comprised small multi-family groups, the members of which were mutually interdependent through co-operative efforts for success in food procurement and that such autonomous groups

existed within a loose and shifting band organization founded
upon kinship and friendship. (Steward, 1936.) We may further
hypothesize, on archaeological grounds, shamanistic attention
to details of hunting magic and the magico-religious observ-
ances attending burial; else how explain the rattles, flutes,
amulets, red ocher, skull burials and other paraphernalia and
mortuary practices discovered at the Frontenac Island site
[Frontenac is C14 dated at about 4500 B.P.]. . . .

"The earliest coastal encampments may now be submerged
as suggested by the Boston fish weirs [large fish traps, C14
dated at about 6000 B.P.], and Grassy and Grannis islands.
The tools for felling and working wood were developed
throughout the period, including at various times and places,
the celt, adze, gouge, grooved ax, chisel and heavy scraper.
Fundamental reliance on the hunting-fishing activity is attested by the wealth of projectile points of many varieties, presumably for the arming of darts and spears; bone fishhooks;
bone points, both fixed and detachable; net and line sinkers;
and possibly bone trap sticks. Food-grinding equipment was
even more standardized among the cultures of this period, em-
bracing an assortment of mullers, flat mealing stones and mortars, and cylindrical pestles, the latter possibly denoting the
use of the shallow wooden mortar. The discovery of carbonized
acorn hulls and nut shells in New York sites of this age and
their associated faunal remains testify to an oak-deer-turkey
biome. . . .

"The general picture emerging from current understanding
of the northeastern Archaic cultures as a whole envisions small
mobile bands of foraging people, following a seasonal cycle of
economic pursuits, resident in temporary settlements of bark-
or mat-covered wigwam dwellings, situated on higher ground
along sizable highways which afforded access to food and
routes of travel by means of dugout canoes."

We recognize these Archaic peoples of Ritchie's digest. They
are the usufructians and they have come out of their caves,
most of them, and they have forgotten nothing and they have
learned a great deal. The beneficence of shellfish is not the
only answer to their triumph during the Confluent period;
these are a ductile people and the lessons are accruing surely
to them in a lore of living that must eventually take them to

the great break-throughs into village-agriculture living and toward civilization.

But we are aware of the painful gradualness of the accrual.
By 4000 B.P., at the time of the Frontenac Island culture, the
kingdom of Harappa, with its twin cities of Harappa and
Mohenjo-Daro (our names, not the inhabitants') had reached
full flower in the Indus valley of Pakistan. Harappa and
Mohenjo-Daro were metropolises of perhaps 20,000 inhabitants
each; they were 400 miles apart, and the territory between
and much else was the nation of their double rule; they were
planned cities, of straight, gridded streets of standard widths,
lined with buildings precisely placed and squared and made
of kiln-baked brick; and each city was citadel-protected. In the
houses were bathrooms with paved floors and there were even
manholes opening into the city-wide sewage system. The inhabitants were literate, for the most part, made cotton cloth,
worked smelted copper and bronze, were artificers of jewelry
of gold and semiprecious stones and used wheeled vehicles for
which the streets were made wide enough that two carts could
pass, and at intersections the corners of buildings were rounded
off for the safety of left and right turners and the integrity of
the brickwork.

To go on is but to widen the contrast between the Indians
and the Amerinds; and Egypt and Babylon were as advanced
at this time as Harappa. Explain? We know a great deal less
about why the Harappans and Babylonians became civilized
than why the Amerinds did not. We have been following the
Amerinds from an almost naked and empty-handed beginning. We have been watching their slow, sure, expected development and it reminds us of tree growth: whatever is
added is added to solid wood that already exists; there is no
spurt, no saltation, no sudden emergence from a chrysalis stage;
it responds to weather exactly like a plant, growing faster in
good years than in bad; it is deep-rooted and can go into
dormancy to conserve itself; it never misses an opportunity,
like the shellfish enrichment of the streams, and it never makes
one. So intimately did these usufructians live with rain and
all weather, and the changes that weather visited upon the
land, that it becomes a necessity for us to wonder what would
have happened had the Altithermal fallen upon North America

a thousand years later. It would have been the Mayas who
were at their cultural apogee when Columbus opened up
America, and neither the Aztecs nor the Incas would have got
around yet to raising their temples and palaces.

But what if the Altithermal had occurred a thousand years
sooner? What civilizations were in the womb of the next millennium in America? We know nothing of the usufructians to
prevent our believing that they would have responded to an
earlier Altithermal exactly as they did to the later one. Lured
to the warmed waters, they did not merely stand on the brink,

POLISHED TOOLS

At left is an adze with a headed or polled end, a
form of surface-ground or polished stone woodworking
tool found in the upper Ohio Valley. At right is a full-
grooved ax. Such tools were usually made of a dense
stone such as basalt or green stone. The grinding-polish-
ing was done with sandstone or, perhaps, loose sand.
Grinding was done very early in America, the edges of
Clovis points at the base being usually dulled by "filing"
with sandstone so that they would not cut the lashings
that bound point to shaft.

they felled trees and made dugouts and began to travel. This
they could have done sooner; up to a thousand years sooner.
They were not the herd hunters; they were educable, to a degree.

Hafted axes, adzes, celts, chisels, gouges, plummets—these
are the new tools of the eastern Confluent, and the adzes and
axes were much earlier, as we know from Modoc, Russell and
Graham, than Ritchie supposed them to be at the time of his
writing. They are woodworking tools and it does not profit a
Desert Culture much to make them. And they are new in more

than form and function, being made by polishing or grinding, sometimes from the nodule, sometimes after a blank has been chipped or pecked into rough form. This technique was one made much of by European scholars in their study of lithic stages there, and polished tools became in the literature the insigne of the neolithic. American prehistorians, influenced, not surprisingly, by European terminology, began to regard the Archaic as a kind of American neolithic, even segregating an early Archaic, as a period before ground stone, from a late Archaic, when it had widespread use.

Even as they still subscribe to the idea of a succession of cultural stages long after it has been abandoned as meaningless in Europe, American archaeologists preserve some degree of superstitious belief in the special importance of the appearance of polishing of stone, regarding it as a sort of industrial advance and, as such, surely an Asiatic importation. It is, of course, neither of these. If it were actually an industrial advance and really produced superior tools all tools would be finished off by polishing. The Laurentians did, in fact, make polished knives and projectile points, but these are of slate, the lensy composition of which makes it more sightly, at least, to abrade or polish than to chip. This example was not widely followed, and everywhere polished or rubbed axes, adzes, etc., lie cheek by jowl with the artifacts of the never slackened knapping technique.

The difference between polishing and chipping in the production of tools lies solely in what the tools were to be used for. Polished tools appeared simultaneously, in America and elsewhere, when there began to be an interest in working wood, not branches alone, but the trunks of trees, and the appearance of polished tools should be interpreted as the infallible sign of such interest. The derivation of polishing, as explained by European archaeologists, is obvious. The first axes for tree felling and the working of hardwoods were chipped. But continuous use in hardwood smoothed and polished them, and it soon became apparent that a polished ax or adze was better for woodworking than a chipped one. Whereupon the ax was ground or polished or rubbed out by hand from the beginning rather than being left to a long breaking-in period of hard usage. No amount of crushing of bone would ever have worn an

ax to a polish, or have made the extra work of polishing worth
the effort. Only its application to hardwoods would do that.

Generally speaking the polished ax in Europe is a farming
tool, used to clear patches for sowing, and few European archaeologists take the neolithic period seriously in the sense that
first caused it to be named, as the period of polished stone tools.
It exists, in present thinking in Europe, as the period of horticulture and incipient agriculture, though polished tools were
also used in boatbuilding by peoples who had no agricultural
ambitions.

In America there is no equation of patch clearing and the
first use of polished tools. They had to have been used for
boat construction and/or shelter construction; and the evidence
for shelter construction is not strong, especially when it is considered that both Graham and Modoc caves, themselves at
least seasonal shelters, produce polished axes and adzes in
levels of about 8000 years. Since this is about the time polished tools appear at Eurasian sites, and since the Denbighites
of the same period do not have them (and they could have
used them even on their taigan softwoods) any transfer of the
polishing trait from the Old World to the New lacks much of
being sustained by argument or evidence. Polishing was an independent Amerind invention and why shouldn't it have been?
The Amerinds had known for thousands of years, from their
seed grinding, about the abrasive effect of stone against stone.

But it was not in the favored east, with its teeming waters
and nut groves and undisturbed fauna, that the usufructian
mettle was tested and found irrefrangible. In Arizona in the
1930's there began to be found along stream beds camp sites of
bands who used grinding stones by the ton, but never bothered
to make a projectile point. For a while archaeologists kept their
minds open to the possibility that these sites signified summer
seed-harvest stations and that the winter hunting sites where
projectile points would be found were elsewhere. By now,
however, the course and development of the grinding-stone
people, called the Cochise, have become too well known to
admit of any such strange and absolute separation of two kinds
of activity. The early Cochise were exactly what they seemed
to be—creek-bottom dwellers who had no acute need for pro-

jectile points in their business. Although there was not enough rain to raise forage on the prairies and hillsides for herd grazing, there must have been enough moisture—perhaps it fell during the winter as snow in the mountains and melted on into the early summer—to keep the stream beds active during the germinative and early growing season. Antevs makes the telling point again and again that it is the lethal evaporation rate that prostrates the southwest; if the precipitation that did fall were not immediately filched away by the thieving atmosphere, a plant cover might root itself and begin the creation of a living environment. If there was any place where plants might have had available a margin of moisture that would have given them a season to grow and mature, it was in creek bottomlands and along stream banks.

Apparently this happened and the Cochise seed grinders, true usufructians, made do with it. Their territories, their homelands, would have been quite longitudinal, then, as they wandered from creek mouth to creek source perhaps two or three times a year. Such an environment would have kept alive a minimal faunal order, adding to the food resources of seeds and berries and roots, and the crayfish and minnows or whatever the waters kept in generation.

The very limitations of this environment give deductions about it a certain inevitability. It is the one advantage of a seed-gathering economy that the seeds are preservable and hence can be set aside and stored for winter, or dead season, use. We have to imagine a sort of tithing system for the Cochise whereby a percentage of the take from each "plot" was rigorously saved and stored. But storage presupposes a permanent cache site. A village existence during the dead season, in a protected cove or canyon, where the winter food supply was centralized and a pool of drinking and cooking water was at hand, is therefore almost unavoidable. We say village, rather than camp, because we imagine these hearth colonies to have been in settlement for perhaps half a year and to consist of some sort of shelter or shelters. I doubt that man, even the descendants of open-sky Tule Springs man, callously exposed himself to the discomforts of harsh weather once he had reason to leave off wandering; even the animals, better protected than man by hide and hair, have their burrows and dens. And if he were a fresh-air fiend there was the preservation of his fire to think of. Granted that the frequenters of such an environment, where combustible material was probably scarce, would have learned how to make fire rather than merely to keep it in order to conserve fuel, the central hearth with its *ignis aeternas* was such a convenience as to be a public utility, even as Consolidated Edison.

To speculate on the kind of hutments the Cochise would have erected is not very profitable. A Cochise-related people lived in Ventana Cave, but Ventana Caves were not, in all likelihood, plentiful enough. You cannot dig pit houses in either rock or sand; you cannot build even bark cabins without trees or felling tools; you cannot make tepees without large animal skins; stone and brick and adobe and *caliche* are as yet undiscovered materials. There seems to be nothing left but reeds and rushes, but these have been contrived into roofs and walls elsewhere in the world and we doubt that any people anywhere were more familiar with the properties of plant fiber than the Cochise.

The Cochise were, obviously, somewhat specialized followers of the Desert Culture pattern, and when the climate took a heated turn for the worse they had the inborn usufructian instinct of opportunism to outwit it. And the hunters, it would seem, came to them even as they came, hungry and driven, to the eastern oases. Traces of lanceolate and other hunter-pattern projectile points glimmer not only among some stages of the persistent Cochise but in most of the Desert Cultures where the sequences are comparatively consecutive. The prodigals have everywhere had to come home, if we see the hunters as having shrugged off the sober frugality of their omnivorous-collecting parents and taken to the flamboyance of herd hunting at circa 15,000 B.P. But can anyone doubt that when agriculture came to America it arrived, not from Asia, but from those creek-bottom winnowers who must have known the size, shape, growth period and yield of every vegetal thing in the southwest?

This is the paradox of the Amerinds—projectile points and atlatls, basketry and textiles, small-plant domestication and hand milling, possibly the bow, and now polished tools—all these they invented as early in the course of human events as any people, yet, either an element or a catalyst being missing, there was no chemism. The Amerind grew cellularly in knowledge, never organically. J. Alden Mason, who is one among many to say the line, writes, "Agriculture is the basis of all civilization." But the Amerind was very close to practicing agriculture for thousands of years—and he was practicing it, at least in some places in the southwest, even before he had pottery (a reversal of the usual order)—and there is one other essential associated with cultures at the beginning point of civilization and the Amerind had it. He had metal first, too.

The metal was copper and it was the working of copper freely and extensively that gave the Old Copper Complex, C14 dated as early as 7500 B.P., its name, one of the few apt and fully connotative ones thought up in American archaeology, which thinkably owes at least part of its popular neglect to the glumness of its nomenclature. Given, like explorers, the tribes, climate and features of a four-dimensional, time and space world to name, the savants of prehistory have forgotten that to name is to describe and have weighted down with obfuscate locutions the peoples and places that might have been brought to imaginative life by *le mot juste*. But "Old Copper" is one of their happier inspirations, because the people so denominated were of considerable age, did use copper in an old-fashioned way—as a stone, not really as a metal—and inhabited the region of the United States known to every schoolboy for its copper production—the Lake Superior region.

To the archaeologist the Old Copper Complex means something very restricted, as of the moment: two cemeteries, at Oconto and Osceola, Wisconsin (and one of these is disputed), and widespread finds of copper implements of certain types over the northern tier of middle-western states, mainly Wisconsin, Michigan and Minnesota, with southern Manitoba and Ontario thrown in. This, remember, is the region where the Keewatin-Laurentide icecap turned the corner from a north-south direction and fronted east-west. We use the phrase "Old Copper" much more generally, to include a more extensive region through a much longer time: a region that includes all of the territory north of the present course of the Ohio, across Indiana and Illinois and into Iowa, where copper tools were

made, not just bartered; and through the time they were made
—from at least 7500 B.P. to perhaps 1000 B.P.

The use of the term does not signify that all the peoples who
inhabited the region through the time period set up were
linguistically or genetically related—though most of them must
have been—for this we cannot know. It means, mainly, that the
people who inhabited this space-time region were sooner or
later acculturated by whatever happened within it, more or
less immediately and directly, by unavoidable contact. The
Adena and Hopewell people of 3000–1000 B.P., the climax culturists of this region, are no less Old Copper folk, in our sense,
than the specific Old Copper Complex from whom we have
borrowed the name.

Now we encounter a phase of Amerind prehistory where
their accretional kind of cultural advancement begins, somewhat desultorily, to amount to something. Here the cultural
and, in a lesser degree, the population confluence for which we
have named this period begin to interact and induce a slow
fermentation.

The Old Copper region folk were the most advanced of all
Amerinds in the Western Hemisphere throughout most of the
Archaic era. They were not quite on the through track to civilization as the struggling Cochise were, because they were not
spending much effort on the development of an agricultural
base for urbanization (they had eventually to borrow this),
but they were being needled by influences from several directions and they were, as we have noted of all usufructians, not
ineducable.

The first worker of copper must have picked up a surface-
occurring lump of it under the impression that it was a workable stone like any other. The first blows must have surprised
him into considerable curiosity. Instead of chipping, it was
malleable, and as soon as he saw this, gone glimmering was
any hope of an Amerind metallurgy; for these lumps were not
ores, brittle and refactory; they were pure copper, as pure as
refinery metal, and as malleable and ductile.

Almost on the spot, it seems, the Old Copper folk learned
the tricks of cold and hot hammering by beating the nuggets
into sheets and rolling them into beads and conical projectile
points and smithing out rings and bracelets and clasps, axes

and pike heads and knives, awls and hooks (perhaps fish-hooks) and gorges and gouges. Once they had learned about copper-stone, they not only chicken-picked it from the surface, they found the sources and actively mined it, from lodes on Isle Royale and the Keweenaw Peninsula, and they went on doing this until the lodes were forgotten, or were played out to the kind of mining operations the Amerind knew.

Obviously the Amerinds never discovered copper as a metal, never stopped making stone tools, and eventually lost contact with copper because it was not a technological or cultural imperative; they could get along without it, and no great loss felt. They prized it when they had it, for they made all sorts of vanity and ceremonial trinkets of it, but when they did not have it they made shift with stone and shell, and were just as proud of themselves and no less ceremonious. But what seems strange about the failure to realize the potential of copper, which initiated men elsewhere into the metallurgic mysteries of nature—about the failure of the American chalcolithic to advance into a bronze age—is that not one but all the three main Amerind traditions were exposed to copper without being educated to it.

By now the reader must be aware of the conjunction of environments at which this Wisconsin-Michigan region stood. To the north and the east was the glacial and/or Great Lakes barrier, and the tree line advanced and retreated with vegetal sensitivity to the climatic moods we have already reported. But this tree-line environment belonged to the taigans, who did come as far south as Wisconsin and who must have picked up the habit of working copper-stone there to take back, as their environment receded northward, to their sub-Arctic provinces, where there were outcrops of copper to keep it alive. It was a *quid pro quo* exchange; what the taigans left behind was a rather stronger tradition of strip-blade making, and a relative of the burin. When, in the protocivilization of the Hopewells of 2500 B.P., we find a firm grasp of the strip-blade-making technique, and flakes and bifaces that have had burin-like use, we do not have to depend on magic-carpet transport of these traits from Siberian meccas; we know that strip blades had been made longer here than any technological trait now in existence among us.

But this region was not only, we have decided, the place where tree line dwindled into tundra; it was, and is, an eastern extension of the Great Plains. This has already given us leave to bring the herd hunters this way, and when they came, that they passed by unobserved or ignored by the local residents is a little more than we are prepared to believe. Man is not so incurious about other men as this, except where there are metropolitan gluts of them, and it is no less than the first consideration of self-defense to investigate who comes among you and why.

But who were the old residenters, the first settlers of this Amerind crossroads? The answer is in the front of the book— the usufructians who had cousins in Modoc Rock Shelter and who, having lived here, by the C14 dating, for at least 3000 years prior to the Old Copper folk, certainly had acquired some sort of squatter's title. Nobody, however, would call the Old Copper folk usufructians any longer, though this be their lineage. Not only are they property-richer, but deliberate burial, that invariable ritualization of man's reluctance to accept his mortality as absolute and of his hope that it can be appealed from or insured against, is practiced, and in no mistakable way. The Old Copper burials of Oconto, Wisconsin, with their C14 date of 7500 years, comprise, on the present record, the oldest known cemetery in America.

We have been thinking of the Archaic, the Confluent, as the period of population convergence into communities, and no better evidence exists than the Old Copper cemetery of Osceola, where an estimated 500 individuals had been interred, not in primary disposal, but in bundle reburial, which is a quite different thing from digging a hole and shoving a body out of sight. Granted that this is an artificial community of the dead and not a site of a living village, the archaeology, according to Warren L. Wittry and Robert E. Ritzenthaler, its excavators, shows that burying went on over a period of time, and was not a mass inhumation attendant on a single ancient holocaust. There had to be, then, a community of the living to have amassed this community of the dead, and such a community as seems socio-politically in advance of the band organization Ritchie has described for the Archaic generally.

There has been some disagreement among archaeologists

about whether Oconto, which has been C14 dated, is actually an Old Copper manifestation. Suzanne W. Miles, in her thorough analysis of what is and is not Old Copper, calls Osceola the only recognized Old Copper manifestation, though her paper was written before the Oconto site was studied and dated. Oconto artifacts, lithic and copper, are not much like the Osceola inventory. But this is a difference more important to archaeologists than to us. The Oconto site places a copper-stone-working people at an early date, and whether the Osceola people were later or earlier or but distantly related contemporaries does not confuse our broader view of the habitation of this western Great Lakes–eastern Great Plains pooling area by a people moving ahead of their Archaic-period contemporaries by reason of two culturally stimulating influences upon them.

The herd-hunter influence may have been only in the blood, for it does not show in the Old Copper artifacts unless the lanceolate blade shape and better-than-fair workmanship of a series of handsome points at Osceola are from them. Yet Byers has reported fluted and unfluted lanceolate points from the Old Copper stamping ground in Wisconsin, and until they are all dated as unquestionably not coeval with usufructians we will assume that hunters and usufructians and taigans all met in this area and that they exchanged what they could use, borrowed, imitated, stole and intermarried in accordance with moods of the moment in that pattern of inconsistency which has everywhere characterized the behavior of mankind.

More positive was the cultural impact of taigan on usufructian and vice versa, however. One of the minor dilemmas of American archaeology for years has been to explain an "Eskimo" element in many northeastern Amerind cultures of the Archaic and after. The first suppositions were of a direct contact with a land-hunting culture called the Dorset, of the eastern Arctic area, supplying out of hand to southern Indians cultural traits such as bone, combs, the semilunar knife or ulu, triangular projectile points, "rubbed" or ground slate points and knives, soapstone vessels and certain bone forms. C14 dates on glacial events which placed an unbroken ice sheet immediately north of such "Eskimo"-influenced Indians—the Laurentians are one of these groups—nullified this conjecture.

The dilemma is stated in the title of one of Ritchie's papers, "Ground Slates: Eskimo or Indian?" and he answers that they were Indian—that is, they had been invented by peoples south of the ice and had moved north into the Dorset Country.

It now seems likely that they were both, the Old Copper home grounds being the alembic in which ingredients of taiga-tundra adapted peoples were fused into a new cultural alloy. What must be emphasized, however, is that taigans did not cease to be, and remained in their own environment a free and content race, not abandoning their life way even unto this age of the DEW Line; nor were the stimulated usufructians diverted from their environment.

The Laurentians, those easy-going, adaptable, sturdy round-heads who ambled eastward to meet the Lamokans and make common genetic cause with them, are the perfect examples of the half-Eskimo, half-usufructian culture that was the product of Old Copper area intermixture. Their Eskimoid semilunar knives and their ground-slate points were accompanied by a very usufructian pattern of chipped-stone points, and their genetic and cultural alliance with the Lamokans is proof enough of a basic similarity in living standards and attitudes. Ritchie found nothing in his Laurentian material to suggest that this was a culture adapted to any such specialized environment as the taigans kept to, and recent investigations of the Laurentian, reported on by Don Dragoo of the Carnegie Museum in Pittsburgh, give testimony that Ritchie's Laurentians are regional northeasterners who are fundamentally like cultures that exist on the same general time level down through the Ohio Valley.

It does not, therefore, seem unduly impertinent to establish the region of the Old Copper tradition as the cultural general store and trading post for eastern North America, with a modest activity on the side where, for instance, southern stone-grinding and rubbing practices were first applied to northern tools, such as the semilunar knife, which can easily be interpreted as an evolution from the old-fashioned chopper.

Why this must be so is no fiat of ours but of the topographic map of North America as Quimby has drawn it, at the time of the Altithermal. Today we equate north with latitude alone;

it is in the north that the cold center lies. But at 8000 to 5000 B.P. it was rather a condition of longitude, with the cold center in the east and north, and the climatic north pole, or center of frigidity, in the middle of Hudson Bay. Alaska was as habitable to the taigans as Florida to the usufructians and was accessible to and from Michigan on a northwest-southeast diagonal across Canada that we, who think of Alaska as being reached by way of Seattle, would never think of using. But this was not a traveled "corridor," as we have explained before, it was a strip of taiga-tundra living environment within which caribou hunters circulated nomadically without the slightest intention of migrating. To the east of this corridor was the ice, to the west the scorched barrenness of the Great Plains; and the effect of the Great Plains barrenness was to divide North America into eastern and western habitable regions. Gone by perhaps 5500 B.P. was that single great natural area which comprised what is now all of continental United States.

Dominating the eastern area was the Old Copper tradition region connected with Alaska; the west, insulated effectively from the east and probably from the north, consisted of the slopes of the Pacific, the Great Basin with its evaporating but still huge lakes, Bonneville and Lahontan, and the desiccated southwest—now Arizona, New Mexico, Nevada, Utah and Colorado—where the Desert Culture survived hardily and began to adapt itself, as always, to circumscribed, spot conditions. Only one people emerged from this hard land with a clear-cut character, and the thread of their tradition has been patiently untwined by half a century of archaeological effort; these people were the Cochise, who attained an agriculture of maize and beans and squash, who were the first southwestern house builders, and who engendered, as Joe Ben Wheat, Haury, Sayles and others have shown, the later cultures of the southwest, the Hohokam, the Mogollon, the Anasazi—out of which evolved the Basket Makers—and finally the Pueblos. The Cochise region, then, was the cultural "center" of the fragmented west, as the Old Copper region was of the east, and this sums up for us what the "Archaic" period was.

Concurrently there grew, in the Ohio-Indiana-Illinois Old Copper region, a native eastern high culture or protocivilization, the Hopewell, which, stricken mysteriously in its flower about 2000–1500 B.P., still had spread its roots over the whole eastern province, so that everywhere, when the white man came, in every corner there were greening shoots of reviving cultural progress—in the eastern Great Lakes and New York the Iroquois Confederacy, with their strong and imperialistic league of nations, which was basically democratic in spirit even to voting power for the women; all across the south, from Florida to Mississippi, held by the so-called Five Civilized Tribes, the Seminoles, Choctaws, Creeks, Cherokees and Chickasaws, with their semifeudal, aristocratic monarchial organization, whom Oliver La Farge calls "well on the road toward civilization"; and in the middle and lower reaches of the Mississippi, the Aztec-like temple-mound culture, with its oddly Midwest pattern, wherein the temple mound and auxiliary structures were a community center, like an Iowa crossroads village, with "farms" scattered throughout the surrounding vicinage—a culture which De Soto and his trekkers apparently nipped in the bud with the contagion of smallpox and other European diseases, receiving in return a thorough syphilization.

In the western province, reduced to the southwest of southern Utah, Nevada and Colorado, and Arizona and New Mexico, but expanded by the addition of all of Mexico and Central America, it would be carrying skepticism too far not to believe that the Cochise heirs of the Desert Culture spread southward, carrying with them their intimate knowledge of edible vegetation, and perhaps even agriculture itself, under the oppression of the Altithermal, and laid the paving for the erection of the whole Meso-American structure of what America can call without equivocation civilization to equal Egypt's and Sumer's.

And even, in time, did the taigan-Eskimo Arctic influence with some help or tormentation from the Athapascans, produce an apogee, the opulent culture of the northwest coast, which extended along the narrow Pacific coast shore-plain from northern California, through British Columbia, into Alaska? Living in the richest natural food-producing area in the world, these people had all the advantages of agriculture without the work; that is, they did not have to plant and till, they only had to reap from forest, stream and sea, and the profit of leisure they turned to effect in producing a rich and heavily sculptural art.

During the Archaic, then, there was decreed by that climatic adversity named by Antevs the Altithermal, the complex of socio-political organisms which confronted the white man when he first took cognizance of this hemisphere, and of which because he destroyed them before he tried to understand, we have now acquired only a pallid and puttering notion.

15

Watched Pots

What Jennings said about the Desert Culture, that it was accretional rather than developmental, is, as we have sensed, true of all usufructian people; they accumulate their culture trait by trait, and when they finally add pottery the Archaic, a term associated with the great eastern province only, comes to an end. But nothing changes about the way the eastern usufructians live; they go on hunting, and seed and nut and shellfish gathering, and doing a circuit, perhaps from a base camp or semi-village, of food-producing localities, clanning more closely together—and being exactly as they were before. Pottery and pottery only marks the turn from the Archaic to the next period in the eastern province, called the Woodland. In the Old World the traits of pottery and agriculture are usually thought of as inseparable twins, but it was not so among the Amerinds. In the eastern province ceramics preceded any traces of agriculture by a distinct epoch and perhaps by five hundred to a thousand years in some places. In the western province generally, and quite distinctly among the Cochise and the Archaic-stage Peruvians, agriculture preceded pottery. This is not unexpected, among these indefatigable seed gatherers, whose baskets served well enough as harvest and storage receptacles. Nor is pottery such a prodigy among the eastern Amerinds, who were making soapstone vessels for some centuries before they took up ceramics.

Archaeologists now say that the Early Woodland period is the Archaic period plus pottery, which is a very much larger statement than it seems. It means the abandonment of any serious belief in the invasion of America in tribal force by a pottery-making folk with a superior, or at least necessarily different, culture. It means that, since pottery was adopted as a single trait, not associated with any discernible complex of other traits such as agriculture, it must have been invented here.

Most archaeologists will deny vehemently that it was, though some will listen to a compromise of adoption, for the Woodland pottery of the eastern province, where there are found both coil-winding and molding techniques, combined with the remote possibility of invention for the western province, centered in the Meso-American area; for northeastern and southwestern pottery are of apparently different traditions, though both knew early, it seems, the coil-winding method.

The coil-winding method is simply explained. Ropes of damp, tempered clay are laid in a single spiral, as a sailor lays a rope coil about a bollard, in the shape and size of the vessel desired. The coils are then compacted together by being beaten with a paddle. In Early Woodland–tradition pottery, there is used a paddle loose-wrapped with twine or cord, and the striations of this cording left on the clay and then baked in give the pottery so "finished" the designation cord-marked. This kind of pottery is found from early to late in the Woodland province, but rather late, it seems, in Nuclear America, which is the name given to the Mexico–Central America region wherein all the high Amerind civilizations evolved. After a while in many Amerind wares the cord markings are smoothed over, in order, apparently, to permit deliberate decoration. Whether those wares which are net- or fiber- or fabric-impressed—that is, show negative impressions of net, fabric or fiber on their surfaces—are so treated for decorative purposes, or whether these impressions are simply evidential of some step in manufacture, like cord marking, cannot be confidently said. The earliest Woodland decoration consists of simple lines, or of a "stamp" which seems to be something toothed, like a comb, pressed point-down into the wet clay. Usually this stamping, called dentate, is done about the neck or upper part of the vessel, which has been wiped clean of cord marking, the rest as often as not being left cord-marked.

There is no puzzle about why the pottery paddle is cord-wrapped—the clay is thus "grained" across the coil lines, to

make them bond. The effect of cord-wrapped paddle mallea-
tion is that of a combination of a solid and a wire potato
masher: the surface of the clay is broken and remixed, and
then recompacted. It is not too uncommon, therefore, to recover sherds of pots which have broken along these coil lines,
in mute accusation against the carelessness of the maker.

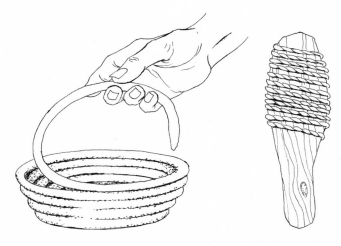

COIL WINDING

Though coil winding appears to be as early a technique of pottery formation as any, it is hard to believe
that lump molding was not equally early, especially if
John Witthoft is right in suggesting that some initial
pottery, at least, was made in imitation of steatite bowls.
These bowls were chiseled out of monolithic chunks of
of material. The "paddles" were very likely not as formalized as the above, but were loosely cord-wrapped
sticks.

Potsherds, very much like projectile points, are likely to set
some strange nerve tickles crawling up the arm of the finder.
Pots had to be so thoroughly handled in the making that wherever you put your hand you put it on top of where another
hand lay, the firm palm and fingers of a young bride making
her first pot for her own household use, or the twiggy digits
of a crone making her last one. Here and there you will find
a sherd with a fingertip imprint in it, and if you want to set up

a psychic current across the ages, stick your own finger in it and tune yourself in.

In the very first pottery made in the Woodland province the practice was to place a cord-wrapped anvil—possibly a chunk of wood—inside the pot against which the seams could be mash-pounded by the paddle. The graining effect was the same, of course, and why it was soon abandoned I have no idea; I even have the impression that these interiorly cord-marked pots have not been cord-marked but scratch-grained, as though the maker was very well aware that as long as the seams showed the pot was subject to heat breakage. But the results of inside-outside graining have impressed me, with my limited experience, since I've seldom seen one that broke because of bad bonding, whereas the breakage of smooth-interior pots—whether these were interiorly cord-marked and later smoothed with a scraper or never marked at all it is not always possible to say—can usually be observed on one sherd or another to be along coil lines. It is plain enough that interior graining would have made it difficult to wash pots clean, especially of food particles, but I have never been aware that Indians were so hygienic as to be fastidious about this.

Pottery was something of a boon to the Woodland usufructians, not because it enabled them to make stews and pottages but because it enabled them to do it with less effort. For thousands of years they had made basketry so tight that, with a little calking, it held water. But basketry cannot be placed in direct contact with a flame. Hence, for nobody can be sure how long, the Amerinds had made their stew by stone boiling—by heating stones and dunking them in the pot till the contents were deemed ready for eating. The labor in this process must have been incessant, for somebody had to be in attendance constantly as fire stoker and stone heater. Pottery eliminated all this, and a pot could be left on the fire all day without a tender and there would still be something to refresh the hunter when he came in from his rounds, even though the women were off nut gathering. Many Early Woodland pots suggest exactly this; about the content of a half-bushel basket, they must have served as communal soup kitchens: one fire, one pot for everybody.

As we would have expected, these Early Woodland usufruc-

tians took up pottery as a strictly practical artifact. It did not
awaken any latent creative instincts in them; it was a long
time before their pots showed any symmetry or attractiveness
of form, or pottery was adapted to uses other than stew cooking, and it is most probable that no more pots were made than
were immediately needed. Since the potters, the women themselves, had to carry the tribal baggage on periodic removals of

DECORATED POTS

The flat basin or bowl and the conoidal-base pots
above are Hopewellian in design. The incising was done
with a pointed stick or stone. The background decoration
of the largest vessel is dentate stamping, done probably
with a toothed tool, such as a comb. Obviously this
vessel would not rest on its bottom and was designed to
be supported by stones set around the base. Poverty
Point tetrapodal "objects" of baked clay are thought to
be such supports, made to keep this kind of pot upright
in the midst of the cook fire. The water bottle is Mississippian.

camp, it may be thought that this paucity answers itself. But
since women have always been willing to hang on to their
household treasures at considerable sacrifice, perhaps what this
tells us is that the Woodland women, true usufructians, had
no housewifely attachment to these utensils. They were, however, frugal about them and they seem to have learned soon
enough the trick of stopping a crack by drilling a hole in the

pot, then plugging the hole, possibly with a wood bung, and continuing to use it.

It needs no further stressing that the advent of pottery among either the Woodlanders or the Nuclear-region Amerinds is without wider cultural implications, and it can almost be said to be of more importance to archaeologists now than to the Amerinds then receiving or inventing it. As a cultural diagnostic it has greater subtlety in change than projectile points, for its material is man-made, as is its form. The composition of the paste, the kind of tempering, degree of firing, surface finish, decoration and vessel form (from which function can usually be deduced) became data as concrete as any whole and separate artifact could be. They tell something about the stability of the Amerind populations making pottery, about their distribution, about their sphere of influence, about their living and ceremonial habits, about their progressiveness. What we would like most to learn from pottery, however, is whether it came to the Amerinds by adoption, or by consequence of their own ingenuity.

There is much about the Woodland pottery tradition that is internally evolutionary, suggesting an orderly and progressive improvement from crude beginnings to better control of fabrication and a more cultivated sense of form. Once it began to be made it follows only from itself; there are no signs of intrusive influence and no sudden sports in its evolution until unmistakable influences, probably from Mexico, seeped into Ohio–Illinois Hopewell territory. Whether pottery was invented somewhere in the northeast—where Ritchie has the earliest date on it at 4000 B.P.—or whether it was dropped there once, like a seed, and grew on its own has to be uncertain on the record now spread before us. At no site so far discovered in the Woodland province do there appear the kinds of experimental objects we would accept as protopottery, but neither do we have from any place in the world any satisfactory precursors of pottery; very likely pottery was not the first ceramic artifact; "images" or cult effigies were probably the origin of man's experience with the fixing by drying and then by baking of the features imparted to clay in a plastic state. But there seems to be, at least in the northeast, where pottery first appears, not even a casual tradition in any sort of ceramics.

Nevertheless, importation does not therefore immediately become the alternative to invention. At Jarmo, that very early agricultural site mentioned earlier, the first pottery is well made, and has been traced, so that it is known to be trade ware. After that the Jarmoans set out manfully to make their own pottery; but until they got the hang of it their efforts were very tyroish. Such an intrusion of trade ware, to show them how it was done, has never been discovered among the Amerinds.

Looking over the situation, we find that pottery might very well have come to the Woodland province by way of the taigans, who had already passed "Eskimo" traits down this way. It surprises us therefore that the oldest pottery is found in New York rather than Michigan or Wisconsin, if pottery came down along the edge of the shrunken glacier, but not all archaeological truth is yet above ground, so, having registered our surprise with the official in charge, we will pass along the taigan path to MacNeish's Firth River site, where there is a long sequence of prepottery and pottery levels.

The first pottery at Firth River is cord-marked, and next above that is dentate-stamped ware. This is the order in which these two types appear in New York and elsewhere. Those who are already disposed to think so will immediately appropriate this evidence for use in their argument that pottery came out of the Siberian cupboard and Firth River was but a stopover on its way to New York. They do this, as usual, recklessly. There is nothing to show which way pottery was traveling when the Firth River folk first set eyes on it. A C14 date for the Firth River pottery associations may decide the issue, or it may only equivocate it, for Firth River is somewhat off the direct route between Alaska and the Woodland province, and may itself lag a little behind the time that pottery was in transit.

(A C14 date on an antler, given in April, 1959, in American Antiquity, *from a level below the cord-marked and dentate pottery, gives a date of 3208 ± 156* B.P. *Plainly, cord marking and dentate stamping are not, at Firth River at least, earlier in Alaska than in New York. Only one C14 run has been made as yet. Froelich Rainey and Elizabeth Ralph report the date,*

obtained by the University of Pennsylvania Department of Physics.)

All the techniques, decorative arrangements and finishes we have sporadically mentioned do appear in Asia, and Paul Tolstoy, in an impressive feat of scholarship, has summed up the data and drawn the parallels between the ceramics of northeast Asia and northeast United States definitively. Having done this, he draws this conclusion:

"In the first place, if we accept the hypothesis that certain pottery techniques diffused in the second millennium B.C. [circa 4000 B.P., and Ritchie has a Point Pensinsula pot dated as this old] from an area where pottery is probably two millennia old, into an area where it seems to be in the process of appearing, the possibility arises that pottery itself, in the Americas, owes its existence to extra-continental influences. It would be futile to maintain *a priori* that pottery can or cannot be invented several times. On the other hand, when chronological data appear to favor diffusion (as they do if one is to accept the evidence of radio-carbon dating) the case for independent invention is weakened."

But Tolstoy's researches have turned up one flaw in the plausibility of diffusion: The first pottery of the Woodland province does not resemble any pottery from Asia. We have thrice and purposively stated that paddle-malleated, cord-marked ware is the very earliest type at Firth River, and in the northeastern sector of the Woodland province. After exampling the resemblances of Asiatic and Amerind pottery till the case of the Asiatic being father to the Amerind seems irrefutable, Tolstoy remarks:

"To postulate the introduction of cord-wrapped-stick impression into the New World from the Old, one has to rely on a hypothetical mainland (Asiatic) distribution for which, at this time, there is not a shred of evidence. The question on the Asiatic side, therefore, remains open."

There is no need for "italics mine" here. To our search for the origins of Woodland pottery only one ware is pertinent— the first. This diffusion idea is one that could very well do with feet of clay, but it has no feet at all and we have no more right to espouse than we have to reject it.

But despite the fact that Early Woodland pottery attempts to seduce us—with glimpses of rudimentary crudeness, developmental vessel shapes and uses, and changes in temper—into believing it original and indigenous, we can't go that far either. For the coil-winding method of building a pot and the paddle-malleated method of consolidating it, with the help of a hand anvil, seems a fairly advanced linkage of artificing habits. How, for instance, would such a technique as coil winding occur to anybody? One would think the first Woodland pottery would be molded, in imitation of the bowl-like, lug-handled steatite vessels that preceded them. The answer to this, of course, is that steatite vessels were probably ceremonial, rather than culinary, and the literal-minded usufructians did not see the connection; but coil winding—how?

We have been at some pains to propose a map of North America for the Archaic which shows the Woodland province separated from the western–Nuclear America province, and it is implicit in this separation that not much cultural intercourse passed between them. With pottery in New York at 4000 B.P. and in Nuclear America about the same time, neither seems, because of the distance-time hiatus, to have been the originator of the other. Nor by any stretch of the imagination or any brief of the available evidence could pottery out of Alaska have got to the valley of Mexico. The pottery of the eastern and western provinces can therefore be reasonably considered as independent in origin, and in the western province to have been of local genesis.

In this western province we find rather more experimentation in plastic mud—the sun-dried clay lumps which seem to be preliminary to the ceramics idea, and later the solid baked-clay figurines that are ceramic without necessarily being precursive of pottery. And it is in Nuclear America that pottery advances early to artistic levels, as though these Amerinds had a long familiarity with plastic modeling which they began to apply to pottery once this utensil use of ceramics was thought of. From these hints and indications it would not be surprising if something that can be taken for protopottery did turn up in the southwest, and it has, although it cannot be said that there is any general archaeological acknowledgment that this is protopottery. Nevertheless, the discovery we are about to introduce not only is technologically the last step before true pottery, it gives us an answer to the puzzle of—how come coil winding?

The discovery, a "bowl," turned up in a cave in Durango, Mexico, and was reported by Agnes McClain Howard of Instituto Interamericano, who says, "The distinctive feature of the bowl is that it is formed of grass which has been thoroughly covered with clay and then wound in the manner of coil-built pottery. After the bowl was formed it was obviously plastered with clay both inside and out and the clay smoothed and worked to form a well-shaped bowl. . . . As this mixture of straw or grass and clay is common building material in Mexico —adobe—we might call these 'adobe bowls.'"

The bowl was not fired—probably it couldn't have been because the content of grass in its "tempering" was too thick and would have burned on baking, leaving the bowl to fall apart —and was apparently useless. But it couldn't be a more fascinating failure. That it fell short of combining its elements of composition into a useful utensil draws our attention to what those elements are and gives us some illuminating answers. Now coil winding begins to explain itself: The maker of the Durango semi-pot was not trying to make pottery; she was trying to make a basket-like container, and she was using grass, the only material available to her that was like the fibrous withes of which basketry is made. But grass is too pliant to hold a shape, and too fragile to withstand use; therefore the "potter" had tried to re-enforce her job by stiffening it with clay, which she knew would harden and retain the form she wanted. But in order to use the grass she had to sheaf it together and wind it, coil-wise, because the usefulness of grass as a construction material is in its length and pliability, and very little else. No, this was not pottery, it was a mud-plastered grass basket; but we couldn't ask for a more likely transition form, a missing link, between basketry and pottery. Not only is the origin of coil winding implicit in it, but we have the clue to why the earliest pottery of the western province and in the southern part of the eastern province is fiber- or vegetal-tempered. Tolstoy says, "*Only* fiber tempering remains as an early southern trait with no plausible northern [that is, out-of-

Asia] antecedents." (Italics mine.) Here again Tolstoy has explained everything but the paramount first thing.

I have heard the Durango vessel deprecated by authoritative archaeologists as a cultural anachronism, the product of a chronologically later, but backward people, or even as a random and archaeologically meaningless fluke. They have every right and probably a duty to do this. Not only is the piece undated, but the cave where it was found has not even been excavated. It is a fact, stripped of all that would make it evidence. But if subsequent excavation and dating of the site should prove it not early enough to have been present at the moment of pottery's birth, it is still only *this* clay basket that is dated and not the practice of making such anomalies, for it is intellectually distasteful to accept that this is the only such example ever coined. It is a "probably complete and finished" bowl, fifteen inches across by six inches deep, and despite its clumsiness and fragility, not broken, which must mean that whoever used it knew of its limitations, and how to handle it without breakage.

Whether it was made by early experimenters or by a people later than the beginning of true pottery ignorantly imitating pottery, it still stands at the transfer point of basketry technique to ceramics technique, and it gives us to think that if it was done by a backward, bumbling people, it could just as easily have been done by an advanced people when they were less advanced, and when it would have been a step in their advance.

It is a utensil very much like this Durango bowl from which that Arizona offshoot of the Cochise derive their name, Basket Makers. They were very late in taking to ceramics and even after they did they continued to make baskets plastered with clay, even increasing their manufacture of this utensil. Because of this it is supposed that the clay re-enforced basket must have had a use apart from pottery, probably for storage, and that there is no technological relation between them, as we have seen there was no technological relation between steatite bowls and pottery.

But we have these facts to consider: Basketry is an old, old trait in the region of the Desert Culture, and when ceramic containers came to be made eventually in this region, and we find a form that is of half-basketry, half-ceramic construction, we must assume that the combination of traits was a deliberate one. Either the makers of plastered baskets got the idea from seeing pottery, or some inventive-minded Amerind got the idea of pottery from seeing plastered baskets. If the makers of the plastered baskets—specifically the Basket Makers—got their inspiration for this utensil from seeing pottery, why did they not, then and there, begin to make pottery, and not, as they did, put off making pottery until 2000 years after their neighbors had it? But if the first pottery maker discovered how to turn a plastered basket into a clay vessel there is nobody to decree that plastered baskets should not go on being made, to serve the purpose they were originally designed for. Pottery can have derived from plaster baskets without having destroyed the egg from which the idea was hatched.

It is the special interest of the Durango vessel to us that it shows how basketry mothered pottery; it is evidence of the necessity that usually gets the credit for invention: the need to stiffen a basket made of grass so that it would be a basket-container at all. But beyond this it fills in the evolutionary progress from basket to pot in another and equally important way.

All across the southern United States, which is at the periphery of the Woodland pottery sphere, the first pottery seems to be tempered with vegetal fiber, i.e., grass. This is in significant contrast with Early Woodland pottery, which is grit-tempered. We may take it that this southern pottery is therefore not of Woodland derivation, but was diffused out of the southwest–Nuclear area, where grass-tempered pottery is the first made.

But how do you explain the use of grass as a tempering material unless it came about as a detail of the process by which basketry became pottery; unless it carries over the traditions we see at their beginning in the Durango vessel?

It seems plausible to think that early potters really had no notion about tempering at all, and came only gradually to understand its importance. The first potters, undoubtedly women, would have learned by observation that some kinds of clays made better pots than others, and examination would have shown them that in texture these were gritty or sandy or mineralogically impure. Simply by following the recipe, by being careful about their ingredients, early potters would have added aplastics to blend clay, totally unaware of why they did it. But grass is an induced ingredient and we can explain its use as a tempering material only as traditional from some former practice.

In order to support this argument with excavated fact, we must go to the remarkable Late Archaic sites of Jaketown, Mississippi, on the lower Mississippi, and Poverty Point, Louisiana, on Bayou Macon. Here we have the riddle of monumental earthworks—at Poverty Point two great mounds about fifty feet high, and a series of concentric ridges about an enclave three-quarters of a mile in diameter—associated with an otherwise Archaic pattern of culture. Archaic cultures are not supposed to have been able to support communities of this size, nor to have had the socio-political organization that could put forth the directed labor and planned effort to erect, basketful by basketful, mounds as voluminous as the pyramids.

But what interests us for the moment is the occurrence at Poverty Point and Jaketown of what are called, somewhat exasperatedly, Poverty Point objects: hand-molded lumps of baked clay in several simple but far from self-explanatory forms. But they have been found by the hundreds and hundreds, so that it is assumed they had a common, everyday use, and it is now the favored view that many of them were substitutes for the boiling stones we have seen in use among most preceramic Amerinds. The necessity for such a substitute is the expected one—stones are very rare in this region of alluvial silt deposit. The "objects" are made of this ubiquitous silt, which is a naturally tempered clay, all ready for firing into ceramics. James A. Ford, Philip Phillips and William G. Haag, the archaeological collaborators on Jaketown, write thus:

"The clays used [in the objects] were consistently of a fine, sandy character. Tests have not been made to determine their origin, but such clays are abundantly available in the alluvial deposits of the locality. There is nothing to suggest that sand was intentionally added as an aplastic, though such a possibility cannot be ruled out."

We have brought up these Poverty Point objects because while they are ceramic objects of wholly orthodox paste, the few sherds of the earliest pottery found are fiber-tempered.

The Poverty Point people had been ceramists long before they were potters, and when they added pottery to their equipment they did not immediately grasp the essential identity of pots and their pot boilers—because fiber tempering was intertwined with the very origin of pottery, and had nothing to do with their clay balls.

The dating for Poverty Point preferred by Ford and Webb is 2800–2600 B.P., rather late for rudimentary pottery when compared with dates for grit-tempered ware in the northeast and even in the Hopewell area, where Ford and Webb are inclined to believe the Poverty Point earthworks complex came from. Gordon Willey, who grants the Hopewellian character of some Poverty Point traits, takes another, and to us more amenable, view—the stimulus for earthworks building, he says with an authority equal to Ford's and Webb's, was projected from Meso-America, which is exactly the point of the compass where we calculate fiber-tempered ware to have come from— down Durango way.

The day of final judgment on the origin of Amerind pottery is not as near as archaeologists once thought it, when an Asiatic origin was taken for granted and all that remained was to corroborate it by excavation. Paul Tolstoy, presently engaged in the most thorough research of Asiatic diffusion of Amerind traits, especially on this Confluent- or Archaic-period level, continues to be convinced of such diffusion; yet he is a conscientious researcher and has plainly pointed out that when he comes to the root of the problem—cord marking and fiber tempering—that root is not Asiatic. We will quote him once more on pottery resemblances of the Old and New Worlds: ". . . with the notable exception of some early Virginia pottery . . . , the actual trait combinations represented in early Woodland pottery have no striking parallels in Eastern Asia."

These discrepancies and several others that Tolstoy has noted, in both pottery and other traits, would present no difficulty at all to him and other American archaeologists if they all simply looked at pottery from a cave in Durango.

Within the purpose of this volume pottery has at least as large a place as we have given it because, while it does not cause any cultural advance or change of theme, it gives us a boundary in prehistoric time after which some Amerinds, in both the eastern and western provinces, cease to be merely accretional and become developmental, advancing from usufructians to something else. In the eastern province this step was taken first by the people called the Hopewells, resident in Ohio and Illinois, known to most of us as *the* Mound Builders.

16

Golden Midwest

With the Hopewells we are now back in the Old Copper culture region, and the Hopewell culture is the climactic achievement of the vitality and progressiveness of the Amerinds of this area, where usufructian met taigan and the big-game hunters crossed the paths of both.

The designation Hopewell comes from the name of a farm near Chillicothe, Ohio, where the first mound attributable to this culture was excavated with archaeological intent, and it is appropriate that it should be known by an Ohio place name. For here in the Scioto-Ohio river drainage (the Scioto flows directly south past Chillicothe into the Ohio) is found evidence of their culture apogee, matched only by a similar apogee among the Hopewells of Illinois. Several Amerind cultures constructed mounds, some larger than the Hopewellian earthworks, and so may be accurately called mound builders, but when Mound Builders are spoken of, without other qualification, they are the Hopewells.

For Hopewellianism was a great deal more than a cultural efflorescence in Ohio and another in Illinois. Its influences extended from Florida to Wisconsin, from New York to Missouri, and it immediately comes to mind that this was a nation, or an empire, that comprised the entire eastern province of the Amerinds. Because travel within this sphere of influence was by canoe, along the Ohio-Mississippi river system, which with its tributaries forms an incomparable transportation network, the temptation is to find this river system the counterpart of imperial Roman roadways and to go on from there to further analogy. But if there is an analogy it is less with the Roman

Empire than the Roman Catholic Church. The unifying force
of Hopewellianism was not military hegemony or police power
or governmental control but a socio-religious ideology and possibly, in implementation of this, an effective hierarchy. Hopewellianism was kept viable by constant internal travel, which
is known to have been for the purpose of trade, but trade in a
kind of goods—ceremonial and religious—that makes it, in effect, cultural rather than economic. It is believed that the
Hopewells of the Ohio and Illinois centers, and probably
those between, were genetically related and linguistically one.
But this could not be true over the whole territory where we
find Hopewellian penetration and the Hopewellian Pax Ro-
mana. Consequently it has been suggested that exchanges in
marriage helped bind the "empire" together by blood and clan
ties into a community that did not need to be upheld by arms
and within which trade intercourse was possibly looked upon
as both welcome and sacrosanct. The Hopewells break the
bonds of parochialism; they thrust themselves so exuberantly
all over the eastern province, they are so startling a departure
from what we have come to consider the character of the Amerind—not only during the Archaic but even at the time of
white contact—that American archaeology has not yet found
its full voice on the subject and only a few enthusiasts have
come to appreciate what they were to American prehistory.

Still, we have been preparing, in the Old Copper area, for
some such upsurge as this, out of the play of cultural stimulation. That the crest of this protocivilization appears in the
southern part of the area is owing, probably, to the fact that
agriculture (more accurately, horticulture, the cultivation of
small garden plots) was more successfully practiced here; not
that the Hopewells chose it this way—rather, the area must
have chosen them, in that those who lived there, in a climate
which today is distinctly southern and mild, prospered and
multiplied on the richer harvests. It pleases our sense of logic
and proportion, then, to find such cultural vivacity here, to see
the exotically appareled Hopewell shamans, in copper breastplates and dyed feather robes, walking the guarded, sacred
precincts of their mounds, while canoes come in laden from
Florida with conch shells and shark teeth, from the Rocky
Mountains with grizzly-bear claws, from Mexico with obsidian

and silver—it pleases rather than surprises us who have had our eye on this region for some time. What does surprise us is to find that there are two cultures, very much alike, both very much superior to anything in the Woodland area, in conjunctive residence of this same Ohio-drainage environment.

This second culture is the Adena, also designated from an Ohio place name, and though the Adenans range rather higher up the Ohio and rather more southerly into Kentucky, their center of highest achievement and most flourishing population is virtually coextensive with the Ohio Hopewell climax area. These Adenans have been mentioned before, as practitioners of cranial deformation, and they were round-heads, whereas the Hopewells were long-heads, though the latter seem to have practiced head deformation too, as a concomitant to a caste system.

The resemblance of these two cultures, which remained mutually exclusive and seemingly irreconcilable for five hundred and perhaps a thousand years, is remarkable. What one had the other had: both constructed earthworks and burial mounds; both were coppersmiths, as befitted residents with roots deep in the region, making adzes and other tools, but forming the metal principally into items of ornament; both were horticulturists, raising the seed or vegetable complex of foodstuffs and, probably, tobacco, since both were makers of pipes and smokers (though there were several score tobacco substitutes among the Amerinds, including the best known— kinnikinnick); both were makers of strip blades, as we would expect in this area of erstwhile taigan influence; and the Adenans, though not as successful at it as the Hopewells, were traders and sojourners in distant places. But everywhere and overall the Adenans produced an inferior product.

Until the release of the first C14 dates, the Adenans, by reason of this distinct inferiority, were slotted into the prehistoric cultural column as the precursors of Hopewellianism and the originators of the cultural complex that the Hopewells nurtured into full bloom. Because of the aforementioned cranial differences nobody ever proposed the Adenans as ancestors of the Hopewells: long-heads do become round-heads, but not vice versa; but James B. Griffin, an authority of long-standing distinction on Adena and Hopewell, interprets, with the help

of Neumann, the physical anthropologist, Adena skeletal material as interbreeding of the Adenans with the Hopewells, or
an actual merging of groups. Ideally this would have meant
that the Hopewells absorbed the round-headed, cranium-deforming Adenans, with long-headed genes remaining dominant.

This violates no principle of logic or biology but it is given
no comfort by the C14 dates.

The 1955 edition of Libby's *Radiocarbon Dating* gives the
following values for Adena: Adena I, Drake Mound, Kentucky
—1168 B.P.; Ohio Adena, Cowan Creek Mound—1509 B.P.; the
Adena-related Tchefuncte culture, Tchefuncte, Louisiana—
1233 B.P.

The Hopewell chronology, viewed with scholarly horror, especially by Griffin, who refuses, I believe, to be reconciled
even to this day, revealed these pitiless figures: Hopewell III,
Hopewell, Ohio, charcoal—1951 B.P.; shell—2285 B.P.; bark—
2044; Hopewell, Havana Mound Group, Illinois—2336.

When the Adenan Toepfner Mound in Ohio was dated at
2780 B.P., appetites were somewhat restored; having regurgitated the Adena-into-Hopewell scheme, archaeologists did not
have to swallow it again, tail-first, that is, Hopewell into Adena.
Consequently the difference in dating between the Drake
Mound and the Toepfner Mound, auditing out at least a 1612-
year longevity for Adena, has not been challenged as discrepant. Let the Adenans live so long. Everybody, with the
possible exception of Griffin, who has earned the right to flout
the trend if he wants to, has been content to live with the new
compromise of Hopewell and Adena as similar cultures, contemporary, cohabiting principally in the Ohio Basin area, for
perhaps a thousand years and interfering with each other's
business no more often than the National and American leagues
turn on each other.

I think we had better accept it, though, that the Adenans
were the region's original inhabitants. Many chapters back it
was given that the Old Copper people of 7500 B.P. were long-
headed, but trending close to round-headedness, and that the
Laurentians who went east out of this region into New York
were decidedly brachycephalic. What we have to explain in
this region, then, are the long-headed Hopewells.

I have recently heard Don W. Dragoo, who works at the headwaters of the Ohio, fair Adena and borderline Hopewell territory, at a meeting of New York State archaeologists, phrase an opinion to the effect that the Hopewells "broke through" into an Adena-occupied holding, and the fact of their intrusive long-headedness supports him and we accept this. To find long-headed invaders we must look to the two possible sources of dolichocephaly—the shell-midden shoreman of Pickwick Basin, in Tennessee and northern Alabama, or the Point Peninsula folk of New York. Since we have to make a choice it will be the New York long-heads, in whom long-headedness was very strong genetically, persisting into historic times—while the Pickwick Basin folk became round-headed *in situ*—and some of whom made projectile points strikingly like some Hopewell forms. It is with no great surprise then, that we learn that Alfred Guthe of the Rochester Museum has recently excavated a preclassic Hopewell mound in western New York—preclassic in that it lacked the classic pottery and other designators such as classic Hopewell points, and because the C14 date is about 2800 B.P., 500 years prior to any established date in the Ohio-Illinois apogee areas.

But Guthe's find, a mounded-over log tomb, is cardinal; it not only looks forward toward developed Hopewell, it looks backward to the cultural beginnings of ceremonial burial, which both Hopewells and Adenans brought to such a state of elaboration that it seems their entire cultural effort was directed toward the moment of a man's death and the aftermath of his interment.

Also in the northeast, and much earlier than this—with a date of about 4400 B.P.—is a less specialized burial complex explored by Ritchie at two sites in upper New York near the St. Lawrence. In burial pits of cremated skeletons sprinkled with powdered hematite were placed as grave goods or funerary gifts—viaticum for the dead—corner-notched projectile points, slate gorgets, copper beads and adzes, bone tubes, a tubular pottery pipe, and other items common enough to both Hopewell and Adena. Also associated was the Woodland province's primary pottery type, the outside-inside cord-marked Vinette I. Ritchie relates this burial complex to the Glacial Kame culture of Ontario, Michigan, Ohio and Indiana and to

the Red Earth focus of Illinois, all of this territory being Old
Copper Complex country and all of these being cultures named
from burial complexes. This widespread burial phase—which
probably *is* the Archaic or Confluent period in much of the
eastern province—culminates, Ritchie suggests, in Adena and
Hopewell, where the entire polity seems, as we have said, to
be constructed as a preliminary to and a preparation for death,
probably the supreme moment of a man's career, since it was
followed by a type of burial that was the ultimate recognition
of his prestige.

Now it is clear to us why the Adenans and Hopewells are
so alike, yet hold, so stiff-necked, to their separateness.

The Adenans are the descendants, culturally and probably
genetically, of the Glacial Kame and Red Earth burial folk of
the very area in which they live out their lives.

But the Hopewells, who practice very much the same burial
rites, yet are a genetically different people, originally established in New York, move westward, and invade Adena-land,
with a result very much as though one Christian sect—say,
Methodists—were to move into the territory of another Christian sect—say, Episcopalians—and both of them were to maintain their sectarian differences despite the common origin of
their basic creed.

Thus it may befall that Griffin, by holding fast to a belief in
the priority of Adena over Hopewell, has grasped at least half
a truth. The Adenans were very probably in the Old Copper
country first, and by reason of their position to the south of the
Ohio were first to receive cultural influences making their way
north out of the southwest; hence they must be the transmitters
to Hopewell of what we found to surprise us at Jaketown—the
building of earthworks and certainly the demimagic of corn-
beans-squash culture, which is the secret of at least Hopewell
prosperity.

The south was much nearer to the Ohio-Scioto country three
thousand years ago than it is now, not because the continent
has since been stretched, but because the Ohio River did not
flow directly west and enter the Mississippi at its present entrance point, at Cairo, Illinois. It turned south much sooner—
just below Louisville—and, using the bed of the present Yazoo
River, entered the Mississippi in the present state of Mississippi

—at the already mentioned Poverty Point culture settlement at Jaketown. The north-south route was thus more direct, shorter and a more natural one to follow, an aqueous *camino real*. This circumstance is what makes Willey's view of diffusion of traits out of Mexico into the Hopewell territory both attractive and convincing. We can easily visualize the earthern-monument-building habit coming cross-country, through the Poverty Point site in Louisiana, to Jaketown, Mississippi, and thence northward; accompanying it would be other traits, and traits which brought still another influence to bear on this Old Copper area which we have already supposed to be a crossroads.

Pottery came this way, too, but southern fiber-tempered pottery stopped at Poverty Point because the Adenans and Hopewells already had a superior ceramics, and passed it on to the Jaketowners, along with the strip-blade technique which found its way to Mexico, though this may have already been in Mexico, an heirloom from the southern hunters who left a strip blade with the mammoth skeleton at Santa Isabel Iztapán. Eventually, it would seem, Woodland pottery got to Mexico along this route, and almost as surely Mexican influences in vessel shapes and decorations returned, to put their impress on classic Hopewell. I doubt very much that either the likelihood or the strength of Mexican influences on Adena and Hopewell can be denied with any vehemence. Neither Hopewell nor Adena communities of a size and socio-political cohesiveness to consummate their earthworks could have existed without a horticulture or an agriculture, and in America this always means maize. Charred corn kernels have been found in both the Turner and Harness Hopewell sites in Ohio and there is only one place on earth for the seed to have come from—Mexico.

Maize—Indian corn—is at once the most sophisticated and cosmopolitan of vegetals used by man, and the most domesticated. About 700 varieties were being grown in America at the time of Columbus' intrusion and these have since multiplied enormously to 8000 varieties, so that corn has become adapted to climes from sea level to 12,000 feet high in the Andes, from belts of almost no rain to belts of 200 inches, from the 90-day summers of Canada to the 365-day summers of the equator, from fields where it must mature between early June and middle August frosts to fields that produce two crops a year. But corn as we know it today cannot live without man because it cannot seed itself.

The ancestry of corn is not, therefore, self-evident, and when botanists looked about for a likely progenitor they began seriously to doubt that there was one. Two wild grasses, tripsacum and teosinte, it was agreed, had contributed to the cultivated form but the main stock eluded the search. At this impasse of frustration some botanists turned to hackneyed Asia, where several kinds of grasses of the same genus as corn grow wild and where a primitive popcorn is cultivated by aptly primitive natives in the Burma hills. But the legitimacy of maize is no longer a vegetable scandal. It is, quite respectably, its own ancestor, and to ascertain this the botanists had only to believe in it, and look in the right places. Fossil pollen of a wild and ancient maize has been discovered in Mexico and it is geologically totted at sixty thousand years of age, for it came from a drill core taken from two hundred feet below Mexico City.

Paul Mangelsdorf, of the Botanical Museum of Harvard, reporting for the team which found and studied the fossil pollen, states the present and probably definitive status of maize as follows:

"(1) Maize is undoubtedly an American plant.

(2) Maize undoubtedly had at least one center of origin in Middle America.

(3) The ancestor of maize is maize.

(4) The ancestor of maize is a form of pod corn, but perhaps not the extreme type of pod corn known today. The ancestor was certainly a popcorn.

(5) Sometime in its history maize hybridized with tripsacum or teosinte or both to produce radically new types which comprise the majority of modern maize varieties of North America."

But nobody within the circulation range of the *Des Moines Register* would recognize this ancestor as corn. A reconstruction of it from the most primitive kind found in association with human habitation makes it a plant with "a short, slender stalk," to quote Mangelsdorf, "not more than a few feet in height bearing a few kernels at the base of the tassel and a miniature ear immediately below the tassel." The husks enclosing the ears spread open at maturity, to let the seed drop, and thus make natural propagation possible. The cobs were the size of a strawberry.

Archaeologically corn has been found under scientifically acceptable conditions at two principal sites: La Perra Cave in the state of Tamaulipas in Mexico, where the C14 date is 4445 B.P.; and Bat Cave, New Mexico, in the roving grounds of the Cochise, where it C14 dates 5605 years old. Mangelsdorf says that the American Indian domesticated maize wherever he found it. It is thought that there are even earlier varieties than those found and that 6000 years is a fair estimate of the span of its cultivation. The rumors about it and the speculations founded on these rumors may now be laid in the same grave. Maize was "invented" somewhere in the western province— by either the Cochise or somebody with as much nose-to-the-grindstone interest in whatever grew into edibility as the Cochise—and in a very early form it is found in our southwest, and he who believes that it spread from there to all parts of the eastern province without other cultural traits and interchange of traits is looking at the matter through his own buttonhole.

Despite sporadic finds of corn under Hopewellian archaeological circumstances there still remains some doubt among archaeologists that the Hopewells had it, and curiously enough they doubt it most strongly who are most convinced of the almost immediate Asiatic origin of Hopewell culture if not the population, long-headed though that may be. The dilemma is painfully clear. To admit that corn arrived from the southwest—and probably beans and squash, for these three are ancient partners in America—is to have to swallow a great deal more. Such major gifts do not come alone, but in complexes of supporting traits, accompanied by ceremonial practices and mythologies, by a whole fabric of magico-religious beliefs. That the earthworks-building trait of the Hopewells, for instance, came out of Nuclear America linked with corn is a great deal more plausible than that it came out of Asia linked with nothing. A barbaric people might be persuaded to build earthworks—the Hopewell earthworks are not mere dirt heaps, but earthen walls built in designs and thought by specialists to have enclosed sacred precincts—if they believed them to be material to the liturgy of invoking the gods of subsistence. What we have learned of the usufructians up to now directs us to accept that they were not accustomed to being managed and we feel they would submit to it only when the gravest principle of livelihood was involved. We submit to management for reasons of livelihood as a matter of course today, but this was the first time the usufructians had ever done it north of Mexico and they did not do it often thereafter.

It is true, to be sure, that both the Hopewellians and Adenans were a death-oriented people, like the Egyptians, and much of their mound building was tomb construction; hence their labor might have been expended in the service of a cult superstition; but such death orientation did not cause the Egyptians to be any less concerned with the fertility of and consequently appropriate rites for the Nile; and the Hopewells may have been just as concerned about an almost similar situation; for they dwelt in river valleys where the spring inundations of river bottoms bear the burden of annual re-enrichment of the soil. But the fact is that death-oriented people are never death-wishers; on the contrary they refuse to accept the finality of death and they build tomb homes in the belief that death is but a birth into a new and longer life in which there can be enjoyed all that was found enjoyable in this life, enhanced by unimaginable new keenness of faculty. Since there are two kinds of construction among the Hopewells, the designed earthworks and the tombs, it would seem quite likely that there were ritual places for the living, for the preservation and increase of the population and the divine principles that sustained it, as well as tomb houses for the dead.

Corn among the Hopewells, with all it means, must therefore be accepted as an intra-American-diffused trait—and where else could it have been diffused from but the southwest?—or it must be accepted as a Hopewell or Adenan "invention." There is certainly no way to explain how a centralized labor force, and the religio-governmental organization which made use of it, could exist without some such basic food economy as corn culture. No usufructian people, getting their food by constant foraging, ever built the Hopewell earthworks, or supported the shamanate hierarchy that made use of them.

It is a glittering temptation to do a fancy job and a job of fancy on the Adenans and Hopewells. Most of the nonburial earthworks were indubitably ceremonial, open-sky temples, but the Hopewells built these in the valleys and threw up on suitably open hilltops embankments that you would have to try hard not to believe were forts. So it is not necessary to believe they are not forts—but forts against whose attacks? It could only have been the Adenans, yet everything we know about the Hopewells points to their predominance in the jointly occupied areas, with vigor enough and to spare to spread over the eastern half of the United States.

But when the Hopewells first infiltrated lands the Adenans may have thought belonged to them, and were comparatively few, then we may suppose they would certainly have needed a place of refuge and defense. A casual observation of Richard Morgan's, in a study of Ohio prehistory, supplies the hint of conflict we need to dramatize this situation. Though the Adenans, he says, were a sedentary folk, raising the corn-beans-squash trinity and perhaps even tobacco—hunting and gathering were probably of more importance than agriculture. Now this reminds us of the warlike Shawnees, who inhabited the Ohio Hopewell region when the white man first coveted it, the people to whom the irreconcilable Tecumseh belonged, the people who harassed the westering whites from the time of Washington at Fort Necessity until the War of 1812, and from the Allegheny Mountains to the Canadian Thames.

So a plot forms, in the brain cells given over to the alchemy of such stuff, of the Adenans in the role of the Shawnees, hitting the war trail when their wrongs have become too much to bear, against the Hopewell settlements—which seem to have been of a farmstead kind—and the Hopewells rushing together into their forts like the grim Kentuckians into the Boonesborough stockade. The irony of Indian outbreaks against Indians, in attacks the whites have always considered themselves the peculiar victims of, would lend a special verve to a fiction which, if it had no other message, would prove that there is nothing without its precedent under the sun.

Or vary the locale, if you will. Picture the Hopewells as the haughty Norman trespassers on Saxon England, lording it within their castle keeps, protected by their men-at-arms—yes, the Hopewells had a military caste—and the Adenans are the freeborn countrymen assembling stealthily for periodic ambushes under an Amerind Robin Hood. Fit enough it would be, to make him a hero of the bow or javelin, though he could not be clad in Lincoln green but needs must go about in a rather explicit breechclout, and white-painted face. And his Maid Marian would be a doll-faced brunette in ankle-sock moccasins, a batik, wrap-around skirt and nothing else. Perhaps it couldn't be done. Not in the movies.

Perhaps these lines of plot are not exotic enough for a situation which, if we are going to deal with it exotically, should get the full treatment. Among the famous Knight figurines, from the Knight Mound, in Illinois, which detail to us much of what we know about Hopewell dress and appearance, since they were made by the Hopewells themselves, there is a woman dancer carrying a turkey wing, and she is in movement to some rhythm inner or outer. She appears not to be a young woman and perhaps she is a medicine dancer, but our fancy leaps to old Russia and to us she is a Gypsy performing for the half-bored Hopewell military, as Cossacks, sitting around the campfire. There is hate in her heart, for the swaggering spearmen have deflowered her only daughter, who she had hoped would become an houri for the head shaman, and while she tries to rivet their attention on her fading charms the Adenans are stealing upon them. She knows that she, too, will die in the onslaught but what must be avenged will have been. Top-ticket musicals have been founded on less—when the music is good.

Archaeologists will frown ascetically on any such fictional treatments, and at the idea of seeing the Hopewells and Adenans as feuding Scottish clans, as Montagues and Capulets or Balkan bickerers; and undoubtedly archaeologists should. Somebody has to compile the facts, just as somebody has to do bookkeeping. But who ever believed that a bookkeeper's statistics recorded the issues for which and by which men live? It has always been a kind of badge of the professional in American prehistory never to suggest that Amerind cultures and situations might have had the color and depth of those in other parts of the world, as though the Amerind were truly estranged from mankind, a breed of Cains exiled, and only quasi-human in that none of the essentially human dramas of struggles for power and ordeals of love ever took place among them. Some day a humanist-anthropologist will be able to break through this significant inhibition and interpret Amerinds as though they, too, had produced an Oedipus and a Ulysses. The notion that Indians were subhuman because they were savages was very useful as a pretext for killing them off as though they were a plague of tigers, but when we enter Hopewell time-space we can relax; it was not they who opposed our land-grabbing. They don't have to be denigrated, and if we look for Oedipus and Ulysses among the Hopewells we might just be able to descry them there with a little insight from analogy.

American archaeology does not verify any internecine war-fare between Adenans and Hopewells; it does not even mention the possibility. When you consider the fact that they seem to have coexisted for perhaps a thousand years, if the C14 dates have given us a reliable picture, you see the reason for this prudence. Yet if they coexisted, separate and distinct, for five times the length-in-service of the American Republic, something kept them apart, and it does not seem to have been that the Hopewells were retiring introverts. Where is there a more intriguing human situation than this?

I think we must assume that there was conflict between these peoples, but that it was seasonal and short-lived warfare, being a sort of deadly sport, as with the Scots Highlanders against the Border Country Lowlanders. Nothing seems more likely than harvesttime raids by the Adenans on the Hopewell gran-aries—possibly under the guise of crusades against unbelievers, for when have human beings not been able to delude them-selves that to steal from or war on the heathen is a form of worship?—with the hope of filling their own winter lockers; and the opulence of the Hopewells must have been a flaunted temptation to Adenan tribesmen, whose cultural remains have been found in earthwork-centered communities, yes, but also in villages of two communal houses, and in caves and rock shelters. And nothing is more likely than that the Hopewells protected their stores behind forted walls and companies of

guardsmen. Would there have been this discernible distinction
between them for so long, if there had not been hostility?

But in the end there was a resolution. Archaeologists are
inclined to interpret the eventual occurrence of Hopewell traits
and motifs in Adena as a late phase of Adena, and since the
C14 dating gives Adena a career of up to circa 1000 A.D., it
would seem that Adena received the last of the declining
Hopewells into their kinship, by marriage if the physical anthropology means anything. But thereafter they both declined;
they ceased their mound building and became usufructians
again in outlook, if not entirely in the social unity of the religious, economic and political organization. The hold maize
and tobacco had on them would not let them slip back all
the way to usufructianism. But it was a cultural stage nearer to
usufructian than to civilization that the encroaching white man
found in the Ohio country when he laid lubricious eyes on it.

But in its period of ascendancy, which may have lasted for
500 to 1000 years—archaeology is not yet sure—Hopewell dyed
the cultures of the eastern province indelibly. Understood
within the proper limits, the Hopewells were rather like the
Greeks in that their sparkle and exuberance was sprayed far
from its fountainhead, as when a geyser shoots high into the
air and a strong wind sows its outburst in laden droplets over
the surrounding landscape.

There must have been something powerfully attractive about
Hopewellianism, more than the glitter of its art, more than the
pageantry in which it undoubtedly had robed the somber essence of its mortuary dogma, more than the self-confidence of
its priesthood and the swagger of its warriors; somehow the
Hopewellians must have convinced all who came to know them
that there was something better and richer about the Hopewellian way than had ever yet been given to the Amerind
world to know. For there was no central Hopewellian authority; in this too the Hopewells were like the Greeks with
their city states. Political allegiance being local, and cultural
adherence being no sign of integration into a state or nation,
whoever was "converted" to the Hopewellian way had to be
attracted and then inclined.

What was the attraction? More, I want to believe, than the

food security of the corn-beans-squash horticultural complex, though, after thousands of years of living on the pendulum swing from want to plenty and back, the usufructians would certainly have welcomed that benefaction. But the beauty that awed must have been in the whole edifice, of life made soul-satisfying by the horticultural complex and all the ceremony with which it was interwoven, and of death made acceptable by the pageantry with which demise was surrounded and immortality guaranteed. When the way man makes his living and feeds his body becomes the means by which his emotions are satisfied, his fear lulled, his joys enhanced and his spiritual hungers appeased—there you have the most culturally potent force in the universe. Even as the mighty cathedral of Notre Dame was the physical realization of medieval philosophy, of man's confidence in his place in a divinely ordained world and the importance of everything he did in bringing that world into being, so must Hopewellianism have felt all that it was, fields and shamans, soldiers and art, subsumed in the temples we call earthworks.

Griffin writes of these constructions:

"It can certainly be said that the development of the earthwork pattern is along ceremonial lines devoted to the religious concepts and beliefs of the group and that this was probably dominated by male shamans who were promulgating the interpretation of the relationship of man to the universe for the population as a whole. This suggests the development of a specialized priesthood."

The earthworks themselves were embankments up to twenty feet, at the original, uneroded height, laid out in geometric forms: circles, rectangles, octagons and combinations of these forms, which are often connected by passageways also bank-walled. Gateways have been left in the embankments so openly as to preclude thinking of these works as defensive positions, and the proximity of burial mounds to them leaves little doubt that the proximity means a ceremonial association. Within the confines of some earthworks habitation debris has been found, not in such quantity as to indicate the maintenance of a village there, but as though a special group, probably the priesthood, kept this as their abode, even as the priesthoods of the Middle East dwelt in their temples. There can

be no doubt that here was both the heart and the head of the
community in a single organ; this was the center of civil and
ceremonial and ideological attention. These earthworks, enclosing from ten to a hundred acres, consumers of a great part
of the labor of the community, keeping place of sacred fires
and sacramentals, were all—for there are no Hopewell villages.

No debris of anything like the size community that Hopewell achievements must represent has ever been discovered,
and it is assumed that the Hopewells lived in scattered farmsteads, like the Mayas, and that any habitation near the sacred
precincts must have been caste-restricted.

As a native of Portsmouth, Ohio, once a great Hopewell center at the confluence of the Scioto and Ohio rivers, I had but
to look out a car window to see why and how this arrangement
would have worked out. The mounds are, or were, on the high
banks on the hills, well out of the flood districts. But the best
corn lands, which would never have needed to be fertilized
because of the silt deposits of winter and spring floods—sometimes as many as six or eight a year—are in the thousands of
acres of flood plain, the Scioto bottoms, where the most magnificent corn in the world is grown. I conceive of the Hopewell
corn tiller–laborer caste as living near their bottomland fields
in hutments not too difficult to rebuild when especially high
water, something that will happen once every few years,
washed them out. Nor would these farmsteads have been able
to remain too long in one spot, for the mouth of the Scioto
wandered from one side of its valley to the other like a sleeper
uneasy in his bed, and it undoubtedly changed course abruptly
more than once by as much as a mile. If this conception of mine
be true, there isn't a chance in ten thousand that Hopewellian
settlement patterns will ever be authenticated for this region.
Too many thousand floods have ravaged the valley since then.

But this dispersal of the Hopewell populace and its very
probable dedication to labor, taken together with the apart-
ness and sacredness of the earthwork temples, suggests the
necessity of another specialized group—a warrior caste of temple guards. Supposing the shamans to have held civil as well
as religious power, we must see this caste as serving both as
defense troops and police power, as messengers from priest-

hood to the peasantry and reminders that spiritual authority had its physical arm. Even an incipient navy can be imagined. For if the Hopewellian traders used the waterways system as we believe they did it seems that prudence would counsel an armed escort for them. Among the Knight figurines is a warrior who seems to wear his paint and hair as though they were caste marks, and certainly the Hopewellian organization had need of professional warriors, if we are right about the Adenans, and of police in any event. Wherever there is theocracy, and sins against civil polity are also crimes against orthodoxy, the smelling out and hunting down of malefactors is a double duty, and when has any subservience of which human beings are capable been sufficient to satisfy one who is both priest and magistrate?

And there seems to have been yet a fourth caste, the artisans. Morgan says, "The Hopewell people, on the whole, produced the best-made tools, weapons and ornaments of any group in the eastern United States. A study of their artifacts indicates that they had specialized craftsmen, for some objects required skills which could only be acquired by long practice. They worked not only in stone, bone and shell but extensively in wood, hides, feathers and other perishable substances. When certain materials or natural objects were scarce they would imitate them in other substances."

Not mentioned in Morgan's summary is the craftsmanship of metals, copper, silver, even a little gold, and meteoric iron. To list all the kinds of things these craftsmen produced would commit us to much more detailed treatment of Hopewell than can be allowed here. The Hopewells achieved enough to be worthy of a full-volume study of their own. But we cannot omit some indicative items, such as copper breastplates; what seem to be buttons with wooden or baked-clay cores covered with copper; ear spools; copper noses (on faces of the dead); Panpipes of bone, reed or wood covered with copper or silver; necklaces and embroidery of hundreds of mussel pearls, or copper or shell beads; copper head plates for the attachment of elaborate headdresses; dyed-feather robes; designs of animals, birds, man, fish, geometric forms, scrolls and swastikas; gorgets of stone; bone, metal and shell; and gruesome pendants of wolf jaws, bear canines and hawk skulls, and of human parietal bones cut into geometric forms; and finally the carved-effigy

platform pipes which are popularly the trademark of all
Mound Builders. The reader may make what he likes of this
miscellany (which does not include, of course, the conventional
tools of metal and stone and such household appurtenances as
pottery, mats, baskets, etc.) in his own reconstruction of Hopewell society. The abundance of items of personal decoration
corroborates the case for a caste system and a heavily ceremonial order of living already afforded us by the Knight and
other groups of statuettes, themselves *objets d'art*.

These ceramic statuettes and the flamboyant ceremonial pottery which is in very small ratio to other types, might also have
been turned out by specialists, with the ware of household usage being undoubtedly homemade. Griffin here is speaking of
Hopewell craftsmanship as a whole, but what he has to say
seems to be particularly applicable to pottery: "We can also, I
think, see in the art forms that in many cases they represent a
very unified art style made by relatively few craftsmen."

Even so, though the artisans may have constituted a closed
guild, not all skills or art feeling inhered in them. The weaving
craft, which was probably practiced by the women, was well
developed. Thread was made of plant fibers and rabbit hair,
which the reader will remember from Danger Cave, and buffalo hair, and the weaving may have been done on a simple
loom. The cloth is "painted" or resist-dyed in batik designs,
with red and black apparently popular or perhaps socially ordained colors, but with many others seemingly present. This
cloth went into women's skirts, male breechclouts, and shirts
and arm bands that were probably official or ceremonial. And
it is very likely that the women, indiscriminately, did the sew-
ing on of the beads and pearls with which cloth and deerskin
garments were studded, though this is not to say that there
might not have been a sacred society of seamstresses.

Whatever their religious practices were, the temperament
of the Hopewells must have been materialistic, but in the creative, rather than the acquisitive sense. It has already been
noted that they often simulated one material in another, and
whatever the objectives of their travel they seem never to have
missed a chance to pick up something exotic. It is at least as far,
by the routes the Ohio Hopewells had to follow, from Florida
to the Scioto as from the Levant to Denmark, yet shells of the

marine Cassis from the Atlantic coast of Florida are almost diagnostic of the Hopewells; these, and marine Busycon shells
and the teeth of recently expired (not fossil) sharks, and mica
from North Carolina. A religious significance was probably
willed into these objects, but there must have been a reason for
directing attention to them in the first place.

Griffin says, of the Hopewell as traders, "These extensive
trade relations are sometime spoken of as though they were
conducted on a rather drab economic level, whereas it would
appear that the primary purpose for the acquisition of these
materials was for their ceremonial utilization by the living people, and then placement with the honored dead in their large
and complicated burial tumuli."

What this description cries out for is the motive that impelled the Hopewells to acquire these materials, and I can
bring myself to believe that it was the delight of the living people in tactile and visual reality, in things for the sake of form
and substance apart from utility, in art for the only sake that
art ever existed, to pose luminously to the man the endless sub-
tleties of the nature that he himself is an expression of, but only
one of the myriads of expressions. Art teaches man about himself and how to be himself. Those who maintain that art does
not teach, or should not teach, simply do not understand it.
What art does that pedagogy does not is to impel the lesson
home through the apprehending senses and the emotional flesh
into the pith of mind. If only the flesh is scored, the effect is
only pleasure-pain, and transient; if the lesson passes through
the flesh like light, it is but learning. Art has to be both experience and lesson, in the usual order and in the reverse, a discipline in the flesh and a sensualizing of the mind. The well-
developed, unstultified personality requires the lessons of art as
constantly as a healthy digestive engine requires carbohydrates
and will find it either in the concepts nature has already framed
in reality—shells and shark teeth, sunrises and willow leaves—
or in his own reproductions of the essence of these realities.

The Hopewells left no objects behind that were art in the
formal sense, no pictures, no monumental sculpture, no genuine
architecture, yet they were artists apperceptively and they had
their ways of converting their appreciation of reality into records of its mold and grain. Thus, we believe, it came about that

the Hopewells traveled in all directions, not in just the easiest ones, with more than a single, missionary motive. They went not only to proselytize and not only to acquire; they went to perceive, and no other Amerind people even begin to be so itinerant. Griffin says, "It has been suggested many times that these trade connections seem to indicate trips of individuals into the far southeast, or into the Plains, or into the northern Mississippi valley and the Lake Superior area, and that they were on regular, definite missions to obtain these raw materials." Had these materials signified merely the amassment of wealth, we would have to rate the Hopewells culturally lower than we do.

Accepting these expeditions makes it easy for us to believe that there was a sixth caste or class, the traders, men who knew the waterways, the materials they wanted, and the alien tongues in which they would have to chaffer. Men who went out to return with things, yes, but with sights seen and accounts of alligator and grizzly bear and the Everglades and the Rockies.

Using them as foreground figures we can now conjecture a Hopewellian scene of some comprehensiveness: A flotilla of canoes is being launched from a gravel bar on the Scioto and in the first craft shoved into the stream kneel warriors, topknotted and paint-pated, swelling their muscles into proud adornment as they hold their spears stafflike before them, the oil-black flint tips spurting flashes of light into the air; the paddlers, of laborer caste, course their dugouts into the current and hold them there with paddles adrag, waiting.

This is a full expedition, the annual Ohio-Mississippi run, and in three canoes following is the cargo of gifts and trade goods, and, perhaps, votive pieces for distribution to those allied in the faith; and on these is invoked the unseen power, in whose honor and glory the Hopewells serve, by a feather-robed shaman wearing a headdress of deer antlers on a copper plate. There are shamans of greater and lesser degree in his entourage and these are engaged in duties prescribed, some allaying demons, some interceding with the genii of fair weather and good fate, some reading the auspices for the right moment. This is a solemn enterprise this community is engaged in: a sending forth of a sort of inquiry whether the known universe is still serene and favorable, and a hope for an answer of prosperity and good will. Wherefore, after the cargo of goods, there are pushed off the canoes the maidens who will be exchanged in friendly towns for other maidens that all the Hopewell land may be of one blood. There is no weeping at their departure, for this is an honor and means marriage with or service to men of power and prestige. Though they are more afraid of the water than the unknown ahead—for one Hopewell society is much like another—they walk proudly, the coil-coiffures of their young heads as bright-black with oil as a looped blacksnake and their slick young skins as softly yellow as gold leaf.

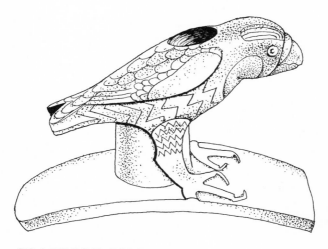

PLATFORM PIPE

This Hopewellian-type platform pipe with bird effigy bowl is probably the most famous and best known prehistoric Amerind artifact.

They wear their necklaces of a hundred mussel pearls, but they will put them off as soon as the leavetaking is over, for these necklaces are not their personal possessions but ceremonial embellishments which designate what they are. Into the next-to-last canoe to leave, the best and lightest craft but the most weathered, steps the trader, who is guide and commander of the flotilla, economic plenipotentiary, interpreter and diplomat; he is bare to the breechclout, like the warriors, and topknotted, because he has come up from the warrior caste, but he wears a bear-claw necklace, has a long, beautiful flint blade in his belt and carries a copper ax. Having taken one last puff from a handsomely carved bird-effigy pipe with the head shaman, he orders his canoe under way. Almost immediately in his wake follows a young shaman who will personally represent, as a legate, the head shaman in discussions and practice of the rituals that must be kept intact and exact throughout the land, or what was brotherhood in belief will became acrimonious schism.

As the expedition drifts with the current into the Ohio, the peasants call their good-bys from their huts, but there are only women and children in the crowd. The men are out hunting, for it is spring and the water is too high for fishing or mussel gathering, the corn, beans and squash rations are at subsistence portions, and the game is wary and gaunt. Yet this expedition is sent on its way with gladness; in a real sense it is the first sowing of the year; what it returns with in the fall adds to the joy or dismay of the harvest of the fields. On what it brings back in goods and news and reports will the Hopewells live through the winter, as much as on their stores of corn and beans.

To pretend that we know the Hopewells lived thus would not be honest. Nobody knows what habits, what relations, what superstitions, what rude loyalties, what traditions, what sentiments suffused the Hopewells, and so we can never re-create them with authority. But if we read about the Hopewells and look at what they left and think about them, and then squeeze out our minds, like sponges, something like the foregoing may emerge. What archaeology knows about the Hopewells is disproportionately thorough in funeral practices and sketchy to nonexistent in living habits, and this is no fairer than if most of our present-day culture were to vanish except for our cemeteries and mausoleums and sarcophagi and monuments to public figures. But it is very difficult to become acquainted with them and not to come to feel as strongly about them as Thorne Deuel, who writes:

"In conclusion, it should be said that the size and variety of Hopewellian earthworks and monuments and the extensive territory over which they spread, imply the existence of a strong political organization, a complex society, and a formalized religion binding together a sizeable population through widespread trade, common cultural ideals and sympathies. It seems indubitable that the Hopewellians were a more advanced people than any met by our colonizing forefathers in the sixteenth and seventeenth centuries. Perhaps the measure of the differences existing between the Hopewellians and historic tribes of the United States might correspond roughly to that between the Roman Republic at the height of its power and the political units of southern and western Europe over a thousand years later."

It is now easy to see why it is fitting to rename the Archaic the Confluent period. Obviously Hopewell and Adena are its products and, taken together, Hopewell-Adena is a culture phase of multiplex derivation: its strip-blade-and-core complex points north; its familiar use of copper falls naturally into the endemic tradition of a copper-producing region; its horticulture and earth-moving complex arrived from the southwest; its pottery is, before ideas from the southwest changed it, that of a Woodland people; and likewise its complex of burial practices is the elaboration of practices that had a long precedence in the Woodland province. As distinct as Hopewell and Adena are one from the other, together they constitute, we repeat, a culture phase, and that phase is best described as what happened when southwest met and married northeast; that is, what happened when the late stage of pottery-making usufructianism called Woodland, whose peoples had for some time been concerned about the enigma of death and had ritualized it with burial, met and married the community-sustaining invention of horticulture; of this marriage and sociological procreation came the labor and leisure to devote to the fabrication of a culture which was philosophical and religious in character, as ours is industrial and commercial.

It is not at all difficult to find similar instances on the anthropological record of this priest-governed, tomb-building-cum-agriculture (or horticulture) phase of cultural evolution; as a matter of fact it seems to be a phase which, like puberty in individuals, most societies that are inherently creative, rather than acquisitive by military conquest, seem to pass through. The example that comes most quickly to hand is the grain-cum-pyramid society of the Egyptians, though neither Hopewell nor Adena ever attained the political cohesion to support a monarch; or at least no such figure has emerged from the archaeology.

In Hopewell-Adena, then, we have a cultural phase which conforms to some natural course of societal growth. The phase itself is thoroughly precedented in world history, and the circumstances which produced it elsewhere were present in America, to produce it here. What we are arguing against, not surprisingly, is the necessity that archaeology has been laboring under, of dragging the Hopewell-Adena phase in from Asia, despite the fact that three other Amerind areas—the Toltec in Mexico, the Maya in Central America and the Inca in Peru— experienced, schematically, the same phase. I seriously doubt that many voices will be raised, after the Danger Cave revelations, in adherence to Asiatic importation of Amerind horticulture. But the other effective element of the phase under discussion, the burial-complex idea, is a matter that must be dealt with separately.

From its beginning among the Neanderthals, ancient burial practice seems to have followed very much the same formula, apparently dictated by the same idea—that death is also rebirth, or a period prior to rebirth. The corpse is usually laid out, where possible, in a fetal position; the body is painted or sprinkled with red ocher or hematite or a pigment of some kind, to rouge away the lividness of death; the deceased is supplied with food and drink, and with the weapons and implements and adornments of rank and honors won during his mortal existence; very often these are "killed," that is, broken. Such inhumations, differing mainly in the wealth that their cultures could afford, were practiced by peoples from Neanderthal to Egyptian to Hopewell, who were preceded in America by a whole list of late-usufructian manifestations whose names were accorded descriptively from their burials—the Red Paint culture of Maine, the Glacial Kame culture of Ohio, the Red Earth focus of Illinois. Hopewell burials attained, it seems, even that final extension of the rebirth-after-death concept whereby a man of rank was buried not only with insignia and viaticum, but with his women and servitors, since they likewise belonged to him and he was not himself without them. This was not done and could not have been done, in terms of wealth or population, among the Hopewells on the horrifying scale discovered by Sir Leonard Woolley at Ur of the Chaldees where in one tomb sixty-eight women, probably concubines, along with wagons and their drivers, had lain down without a struggle beside their dead master and allowed themselves to be buried alive.

The earlier, barbaric notion of life after death seems to have been thus almost universally: The deceased was translated from this mortal to an immortal existence without loss of rank or prerogatives, or appetites or needs.

V. Gordon Childe, greatest of all translators of prehistory into history, of archaeological fact into anthropological narrative, makes one of his most astute observations about these concepts. When Neanderthal man, he says, first sprinkled a corpse with red ocher to give it the hue of life again, and buried it beneath his own hearth fires to restore warmth to gelid flesh, he was a scientist; he was experimenting with a process of life restoration that might, for all he had any reason to know, achieve that effect. But when he had, after thorough testing of this process, discovered that it was futile, yet persisted in repeating it, he ceased to be a scientist and was practicing magic; he took the path to thaumaturgy, to symbolism and to ritual and, where death and its implications are concerned, has remained on it ever since; yet with the processes of living he depends every day more on the liturgy of the laboratory.

Nothing could more keenly expose man's dualism than this concise analysis of Childe's: Living demands that man be a scientist, if he is to survive; death makes of him a mystic. And nowhere is this clearer than in the Ten Commandments. Seven of them are prescriptions and proscriptions for living; they were written by a sociological genius with the intent of establishing public order and private contentment and they have nothing to do with religion; it matters not at all whether you believe in a god or immortality: these laws are the results of a social scientist's observations on how people must live in order to live together and flourish. It is only on the other three—I am the Lord, thy God, thou shalt have no other gods before me; thou shalt not take the name of the Lord thy God in vain; remember the Sabbath Day, to keep it holy—that all the synagogues and Christian churches rest, and in them creed and priesthood find their sanction.

It is scarcely cause for bemusement, considering the resemblances in form and content to universal tradition, that archaeologists looked for extra-American sources for the proto-Hopewell and Hopewell-Adena burial complex. Arises now the trite issue: Do resemblances indisputably establish causal connection between the bearers of resemblance, however removed in space they are from one another? We have been arguing strongly that coincidental resemblance is not decisive, that resemblances must be shown to have evidential interrelationship, and that cultural parallelisms can have happened because shared humanity is resemblance enough to account for similar phases in societal and emotional development, where similar circumstances have set the stage. The archaeological evidence that burial-complex ideas streamed into America from Asia is simply not substantial. It argues only for what the beholder wishes it to argue for, and the resemblances noted are not nearly as arresting as the resemblances of the Hopewellian earthworks complex to causewayed camps and barrows of the English Windmill Hill folk of around 4500 B.P., a parallelism that would shock most American archaeologists if anything were made of it.

But, invigorated by the revelations of Danger Cave, we will not forsake our dogged contention that the Amerinds are a race which, sooner or later, until its virtual extinction, passed through all the cultural evolutionary phases that are generally applicable to humanity up to the industrial age. Most of the societies of men seem to have arrived in time at that development of self-consciousness in which each man realized that death was not something that happened always to others, and always by accident or through the mysterious demons of disease, but that it was inevitable and would happen to him and that the accident that killed him would be no accident, but man's fate. When man comprehended the import of this death sentence, then it was that he discovered that he had a soul. It is heart-breakingly human, how man dealt with this terrible knowledge: he refused to accept it; in defiance of the facts of the science he even then knew, he insisted he would not die; perhaps his body would but there was a part of him that was immortal. This is the path our ancestors set us on and we have not strayed from it, despite a curious ambivalence: insisting that our souls are immortal and that we cannot, in essence, ever be obliterated, we nevertheless fight off the visitation of death with every puny weapon we can command. This is the dualism of being human. We cannot change it (and I would not), and wherever we encounter it in archaeology, in the Egyptians or Neanderthals or Hopewells, we know that we have uncovered flesh of our flesh, mind, soul and heart like our own. Here were not only brains like ours; here is our consciousness, and to say that this is not universally human is to deny conscious humanity per se.

Deliberate burial began, as we have said, sometime during the late Confluent period. I am sure it was not sanitation that prompted this, even amongst the shell-midden folk. The best way to get rid of a body if you live on a river bank is to chute it down a steep bank on the current side. And why sanitation, suddenly, while they lived in as noisome a spot, on a mass of decaying shell, as existed anywhere? Physical sanitation had nothing to do with it; it was the mind that was made queasy by stone-dead human eyes and a suppurating human body. If we confess now to reverence and shame, there must have been a first time that human beings expressed these sentiments toward the dead. When it first occurred to the burgeoning psyche of man to bury the body of a fellow man whose bravery or nobility he mourned, he buried him. It was shame, it was awe, it was admiration, it was self-recognition and a hope that the like would be done him. And so satisfied with the expression of his nature accomplished by this act did man become, that he began to build ever higher the little monument of the earth humped up by the body's intrusion into it until it became a tumulus, and then a pyramid.

All this is, of course, argument from the nature of man, not from the discovered evidence of archaeology, and archaeologists do not indulge in such arguments. What the excavated evidence now says is that Amerinds practiced burial rituals, which reached a Woodland-province climax of elaboration in Hopewell-Adena, and which are very similar to those practiced elsewhere in the world. But we do have a theory from archaeological authority on how the mound-building aspect of this burial could have originated from American roots. Ritchie, noticing that the earliest burials occur in natural hummocks, suggests that the idea of raising artificial tumuli over the grave of an important personage as a memorial to him and a reminder of his period of influence, which may have coincided with a period of prosperity, may have arisen by natural analogy. The Glacial Kame people of Ohio have acquired their designation from the discovery of their graves in glacial kames, gravel mounds heaped up by glacial melt streams. And it also should be pointed out that many mounds are not single graves, but grave-upon-grave, with more fill being added for each new burial, so that what may have begun as a modest heap of dirt became a mound by becoming a cemetery.

But the initial burial? We doubt that this is a trait that was adopted just for the novelty of it; the Amerind did not bother to bury his dead until his mind had become conscious of the meaning of death, when burial becomes the most obviously human thing to do about it.

We have, from time to time, adverted to the cardinal problem of what co-ordination of forces impelled men into civilization; and we have decided that there must be a coagulation of band-wandering men into communities, a means of supporting these communities in a stabilized place and environment, and some constraint on the community, usually from the climate, which poses itself as an adversity to be overcome; of course, this adversity must not be invincible; there must be some means to outwit it by community action rather than by individual escape, and when this means has been discovered it must lead to a long period of confidence, stability and, most of all, prosperity. It is prosperity which puts the pragmatic seal of approval on all human ventures, even though, too long wallowed in, it produces infectious bedsores that may prove incurable.

But this is all within the frame of reference of a sort of sociological physics. Besides this there are two other factors which are even more difficult to bracket in a word except that by now devisucrated term, philosophy. Before they can become civilized, human beings must have achieved that apperception of and attitude toward reality that we now rather hopelessly call art; and they must have achieved that feeling for hyperreality that we call religion.

The Aurignacian cave painters had attached to, it seems, both of these concepts, but they had not the social and physical conditions; they were ahead of their time; and many a smug, agriculturally prosperous people have not bothered with any other reality than their fields and tools. But wherever there has been an efflorescence of civilization, the twin roots of artistic feeling and that obsessive concern for an afterworld that is objectified in great tombs are exhumed by the archaeological shovel.

Why, then, did not the Hopewells become civilized? The answers will be as different as the archaeologists the question is asked of. But the best answer is the most concise.

Civilization is measured by, more than anything else, the trait of writing.

Out of his experience with the earliest inscribing civilizations of the Near East, Ephraim Speiser, the archaeologist and Semitic scholar, has said of writing that it is "the incidental by-product of a strong sense of private property."

The Hopewells were not private-property conscious. They never became commercial. They never quite got over being usufructians.

17

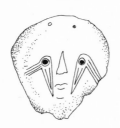

Death Intestate

The Hopewells ought to be but the beginning of succession of Woodland-province cultural advances, but the sad fact is that they begin and end it. Their terminal date is not surely established but it must have been some centuries and perhaps a millennium before the 1500 of the first firm contact by Europeans, and the 1541 of De Soto's pestilential prowl across the south. Some might put it at 2000 B.P., some at 1000 B.P., and some, because Hopewell evidences are found above dated Adena at Tchefuncte, Louisiana, at as late as 800 B.P. But Thorne Deuel has already said it. After the Hopewells came the Dark Ages for half a millennium, in much of the great eastern Woodland province, and Woodland culture fragmented among a hundred tribes who regarded themselves as unrelated peoples. North of the Ohio, from the Atlantic to the Rockies, and down the Atlantic coast to Florida, and all across the Great Plains, there was either a reversion to semiusufructianism or stagnation.

The corn-beans-squash-tobacco complex most of the Woodlanders kept, except on the plains, where there was a drift, if not actually a rush, back to herd hunting, of all things, and an actual later abandonment of horticulture with the white man's Trojan gift of the horse. After Hopewell-Adena there was no distinctly Woodland advance. The old gods, whatever they were, returned with a vengeance, and no ethnologist has ever been able to pick up a clue as to who reigned as the new gods of the Hopewells. The very area where the Hopewells built most extensively, the lower Scioto at its intersection with the Ohio, was not even inhabited when the French explored the

Ohio. It was wooded with a jungle density by oaks and walnuts and beeches and sycamores, all ligatured together by grape-vines and Virginia creeper and ivy into a vegetative mass that was passable only by the waterways and by paths like the tunnels of moles. The native Shawnees did not even, as a matter of choice, hunt there, and its only good to anybody was to get lost in, if you needed to get lost. The Iroquois are said to have defeated the resident Shawnees and to have forbidden them the right to live along the Ohio; be that as it may, the "Ohio country" was a Temperate Zone jungle.

Griffin has a theory that the Hopewells simply exhausted themselves culturally and Hopewellianism shriveled in the heart. Nobody will deny that societies can grow superannuated and expire of complications of senility; it has happened too often and Hopewellianism did live to a ripe old age. But anyone who has ever lived in the Scioto-Ohio Valley cannot help but wonder whether the Hopewells may not have physically declined to the place where they could no longer put forth the effort to sustain a culture grown so rigid and formal it had to collapse suddenly like the one-hoss shay.

In my youth there were still oldsters alive who remembered what their grandfathers had told them about the early settlement of the lands around Portsmouth, at the confluence of the Scioto and Ohio rivers. The first attempt was made in 1798, on ground near the exceedingly fertile flood plain of the Scioto; it was called Alexandria, after Alexander Hamilton, and it lasted three years. The ill and weakened survivors of the original company moved onto higher ground in the nearby hills to escape recurring attacks of what was said to be malaria. Whether it was or not, the tradition still lingered on, to be told to me as a boy, that the night mists off the Ohio-Scioto bottoms were pestilential. That something malaria-like did attack at least the white men who first moved into the dank atmosphere of the big woods and the river valley is confirmed in Conrad Richter's *The Trees,* a fictionalized but accurate account of early Ohio days. The fever and ague fits he describes his Luckett family as suffering are malaria-seeming seizures. It is all too easy to imagine the far-wandering Hopewell emissaries as bringing home from the south malarial infestation and the whole people being periodically ravaged by it, until, like the

Alexandrians, they abandoned the environs they thought accursed and fled their culture centers.

Deuel said, "The Hopewellian influence exerted on subject groups and on neighbors was great and lasted long after their cultural systems had disappeared . . ." and the evidence supports him, but the traits we might have expected to persist even if in a half-hearted and decadent way—burial-mound and earthwork building—ceased abruptly north of Kentucky, and, as Ritchie has pointed out, Indian concern with funerary ritualism in the northeast was merely perfunctory through the last several hundred years of prehistory. This suggests a third possible cause for the crumbling of Hopewellianism—the shaman rulers had made the practice of mound building and elaborate obsequies so onerous as to be hateful and there had been a terrible rebellion against it, accompanied by a decimation of the castes to whom the secrets and skills of the culture had been restricted; followed thereupon a flight to the wilder, freer ways of the woods, made mandatory because the organizing and leadership caste had been so utterly wiped out that the ignorant peonage brought a famine upon themselves.

I have always hoped that some day the carnage of this rebellion will be uncovered because I enjoy seeing the Hopewell shamans as ruthless druidical wizards officiating at midnight black masses in the darkling forest in worship of a thirsty viperine Moloch—an image that was undoubtedly inspired in me by the fact that I first saw the Great Serpent Mound in Adams County in the twilight of a gloomy fall Sunday—and an impression that is undoubtedly romantic flapdoodle, even as the shuddery gossip about the Druids is flapdoodle. But I believe that such an insurrection is as thinkable as cultural senescence or a plague, for it was the ideological force of Hopewellism that disappeared, and true believers do not let inbred doctrine die so easily.

The old-fashioned notion was that the Iroquois had come ripping and tearing up the Ohio from some spawning grounds in the south, had devastated the classic Hopewell centers and then had passed over the conquered territory, as pleasant a land as there is anywhere in the world, for the colder environs of central New York. It was never a very good guess. The Iroquois would have to have been a much more numerous and powerful people than they appear in the record to have stamped out Hopewell centers as far apart as upper Illinois and southern Ohio. The facts seem to be quite to the contrary. Marian White of the Buffalo Museum is presently piecing together a site-documented brief for a main-line Iroquois genesis out of Owasco, an earlier New York occupation, itself at least collaterally connected with Point Peninsulans, who were the long-heads we have proposed as the Hopewellian invaders of Ohio. At any rate, the Iroquois appear on the record at least a thousand years too late.

But it may well be that the Iroquois are the only heirs of anything Hopewellian known to history. Their Confederacy, of five tribes united for maintaining peace by being too powerful to attack and by attacking any people strong enough to threaten attack, bears an outline resemblance to what Hopewellianism may have been like as a political entity. We are free to suppose that high-caste refugees from collapsing Hopewellia, escaping to New York, kept alive by verbal tradition the story of the Hopewellian "empire," and that this tradition was the seed from which the Iroquois Confederacy grew. It is not too far-fetched a supposition. Iroquois traditions about the founding of their federation do not support it, but there is little reason to believe they would if it were true; the Iroquois would not have seen these things from the same temporal and conceptual perspectives that we do and it is this difference in perspectives which causes Indian oral tradition generally to be opaque to the archaeologists.

If the confederacy idea does not make the bridge from the Hopewellian past to Iroquois recency, then there is no fossil of Hopewellianism that can be traced through time. Some sound reasons exist for the theory that the historic Sioux are the descendants of the Hopewells. If this is true the Hopewells retrogressed to the status of herd hunters.

18

Flat-topped Mounds

For what follows Hopewell, picking up Amerind cultural effort again, we must go into the Mississippi Valley, where an Adena phase called Tchefuncte is followed by the Hopewellian phase called Marksville, according to the determinations of Phillips, Ford and Griffin in their encyclopedic *Archaeological Survey in the Lower Mississippi Alluvial Plain.* If the C14 dates of about 2000 B.P. for classic, northern Hopewell are correct, the 1500–1200 B.P. date estimated for Marksville by this formidable trio of experts places the Marskville as a sort of last outpost of lingering Hopewellianism. After it was seduced from the old faith by novelties from Mexico and Mexican influences become predominant, there begins in the lower and middle Mississippi Valley that cultural phase called the Mississippian, which De Soto found this region undergoing on his *entrada.* He promptly brought it to an end.

It is one of the most chilling phenomena of American prehistory how immediately was blighted by the touch of the white man each and all of the higher cultural phases of the Amerind —the Aztecan, the Incan and the Mississippian. The ruder ones were tougher and stuck it out for decades, but the better organized a community was, the more quickly it collapsed on contact with the nemesis white man. Superstition, which rendered Indians militarily unwise, caused the first defeats in all three principal instances, but the white man's diseases turned these defeats into disasters. Most Mississippian specialists think that Mississippian had already begun to decline and De Soto gave it a final kick. If this is true, then the prehistory of the eastern province had come to an end not even within sight of civilization, for it is all too plain that the Mississippian had not even reached Hopewellian levels.

There are those who can develop as heady an enthusiasm for classic Mississippian as for Hopewell, on the visual evidence. Here is a culture of fortified villages, planned layouts of community sites, a mastery of flintwork that expresses itself in many new and apparently fanciful forms, effigy pottery and pipes, a panoply of Hopewellian-like objects of adornment, and, above all, the multitudinous and often immense flat-topped pyramid mounds, those solid piles of earth surmounted by wooden temples, which are to the Mississippians what the earthwork open-air temples were to the Hopewells.

Because much of this that was new, especially the temple mounds and the ceremonies and ideology that required them, came out of Mexico, Mississippian can be called, without intent to disparage, minor-league or farm-club Meso-American. When Hopewell centers ceased to radiate their vitality into the area that was to become Mississippian, what made it Mississippian was that Mexican influences caught on there—immediately, as the archaeological record is read—as though these Amerinds, having tasted the values Hopewellianism had added to life, needed something to rejuvenate them. Ford's pottery seriation studies show a smooth and uneventful replacement of Hopewell-trait wares by southwestern-Mexican ceramic ideas from Marksville to the next phase, called Troyville, which is full-blown middle Mississippian with an increasing emphasis on temple-mound building.

From a distance these rectangular flat-topped temple mounds would not have appeared too different from Babylonian ziggurats, and they undoubtedly were raised to a solar deity; the practice was, as in Mexico with similar structures, to destroy periodically by fire the wooden temples that surmounted them, cover the ruins over with a new height of earth, and rebuild the temple for the next ecclesiastical era. The ascent was by a ramp, or by steps, and the reader will already have noted the difference between this exaltation of the place of worship to an eminence from which it could be seen from afar and the Hopewellian practice of enclosing the sacred precincts within earthen walls, possibly a way of hiding the deeper mysteries from the public eye.

But the Mississippian is a more complex culture than an adoption of pre-Aztecan ideologies undilute, for temple mounds, fortified villages and certain pottery traits do not enter the Mississippian as one complex, at the same time. With the temple mounds already commanding the countryside, two distinct currents of cult notions began to flow toward the Mississippian culture area. The complex of traits called by authorities the Southern Cult, which is familiar mostly through design and symbolism, is the more spectacular, and definable. It includes cabalistic motifs, "weeping-eye" and "eye-in-hand" designs, composite human beings and animals and other representations thought to be of cosmological-mythological origin. Beast-gods, or mythological figures which are part human and part bird or beast or serpent, are common occurrences, of course, in all of the world's "pagan" religions and mythologies, and the only thing specifically Amerind about these examples is the beast—which is quite often the American eagle. Apparently this beast-god concept is a stage in the evolution of religion from animism to anthropomorphism in the human understanding of the godhead. This cult idea stemmed from the southeast, that is, from the Alabama-Georgia region where it can easily be supposed that a Hopewellianly influenced people, too vigorous to falter into desuetude when the Hopewell center collapsed, struck out somewhat on their own into an independent sectarianism. But the Southern Cult designs, if they are expressions of cosmological ideas and not the devices of a secret or semisecret society, a sort of Amerind freemasonry, appear too suddenly full blown; whatever prompted them must have been rather firmly formulated elsewhere, and this elsewhere is presumed to be Mexico, where many tribal cults seem to have been flourishing at this time. When the Southern Cult reached the Mississippian centers it was, then, a hybrid of something quasi-Hopewellian and something Mexican, and the fact that it was not too warmly embraced there may have been due to the fact that it was resisted by other cosmological ideas which were just similar enough in origin to be rival ideas in a sectarian sense. Just so do sects in the Christian religion differ stringently over such matters as how baptism is to be administered and, professing the same Bible as their cosmology, differ over the meaning of what is there written.

Almost certainly the orthodoxy of socio-religious ideas that reached the centers of the Mississippian first and pervaded it from upriver, came from the region of the Cahokia Mound, the most imposing Indian earthwork construction in America, near East St. Louis. This is, or was, Hopewell territory, and, as in the southeast, some sort of organized and effective community life had continued here after the Hopewell debacle and/or expiration. This culture center produced nothing as distinctive as the Southern Cult, but the size of the Cahokia Mound attests to the prosperity and socio-political health of its builders over a matter of centuries. Nothing is more likely, then, than this health and prosperity and the socio-religious ideas integral to it should have radiated far and wide and especially in the direction of the lower Mississippi, whence the very river current must have literally carried it. The Cahokians, then, are the most direct bridge between Hopewell and what comes after in southern mid-United States, even as the southeastern area held a somewhat less Hopewellian bridge from that day of past glory.

What was present in the Mississippi culture centers to receive these gifts and stimulations from the north, the southeast and the southwest was a kind of relapsed Hopewellianism, which had been overlaid in the first place on an extremely interesting late-Confluent- or Archaic-period cultural base. The earthworks at Poverty Point have already been alluded to, in the discussion of pottery, and they are older than the oldest developed Hopewell—which is not surprising since we have surmised that earthworks came out of Mexico. Ford, one of the excavators of Poverty Point, gives it a date of 2800 B.P. through cross-reference with the culturally related Jaketown site and channel shifts of the Mississippi and the Ohio, which at the time entered the Mississippi where Natchez, Mississippi, is now.

The figures Ford gives on the Poverty Point earthworks, which he calls a community layout, are astounding. Basketful by basketful the Poverty Pointers moved 530,000 cubic yards of earth, thirty-five times the volume of the pyramid of Cheops, into these 11.2 miles of embankment. Of the larger of two mounds associated with the earthworks, Ford says that "it is easily the most spectacular of the accomplishments of these people. It measures 700 by 800 feet at the base and rises to 70 feet above the surrounding plain . . . it can be estimated that the finished mound required something over three million man-hours of labor."

It is impossible to imagine this kind of massive accomplishment by a people of usufructian economy, and whether or not the evidence for the cultivation of maize here is archaeologically sufficient, the argument from reason is. By what is probably no coincidence, corn reached Peru at about 3000–2800 B.P. also, and we may suppose that it traveled both north and south from a locus approximately midway between Peru and Poverty Point; assuming an approximately equal rate of travel we can estimate this locus within the Maya area, where there has always been a strongly maize-oriented religion presided over by maize deities. But Poverty Point earthworks closely resemble nothing on either American continent except the Hopewellian earthworks, to which they were not similar in usage if Ford is right about their being a city layout and if Hopewellian authorities are right about the Hopewellian earthworks being temples. What we have to presume for the moment, then, is that when corn arrived in the Poverty Point area—where the fertile river bottoms made its cultivation exceedingly simple— the Poverty Pointers, having no stone to raise up temples to the exaltation of the maize deities who accompanied the maize complex, raised up the two earthen mounds in lieu of the Mayas' limestone pyramid-temples. But this does not account for the earthworks and it may be that there is no accounting for them except as structures independently inspired to serve a local purpose, or as free translations from something in Meso-America not yet recognized as a prototype. There is nothing uncertain or haphazard about their planning; there are the 11.2 miles of embankments, five to ten feet high and arranged in six concentric octagonal figures. The whole design is so enormous that it can be recognized for what it is only from a coign of vantage in an airplane. Considering the circumstances, the designation of Poverty Point as a sacred ceremonial city which drew adherents from a vast surrounding territory cannot be far wrong. Nothing that could be taken for a house plan was discovered by Ford in his excavations, and the ashes of habitations marked the tops of the embankments as the sites where the Poverty Pointers camped. When all its mysteries are unveiled, Poverty Point will undoubtedly be listed with Folsom,

Danger and Russell caves as among the most seminal sites in American prehistory.

For a while the Poverty Point maize-and-earthworks complex went north, up both the Mississippi and Ohio rivers, as we have seen, until the conjugation of it with the Woodland burial complex produced the exuberant Hopewell-Adena phase. For half a millennium thereafter the currents of cultural convection flowed outward from the Hopewell heartland, and the Poverty Pointers were on the receiving end. It and the subsequent period, following Hopewell cessation, were in the lower Mississippi periods of compliance with whatever was dominant and extrovert at the time. When the Mississippian culture did begin to shape into a firm culture phase, what it was, was the effect of cultural confluence from Mexico, Cahokia and the Southern Cult area, plus what Ford and his colleagues call the X factor; that is, the element of local initiative—the reality of which we are fully prepared to accept because the ancestors of these people were the labor and engineers of the Poverty Point earthworks, and the people whose socio-religio-economic ideas made these monuments worth the effort.

They are quite capable of exciting wonder, these Mississippians, and the place where their best seems to have been concentrated most richly is at the Spiro Mound in Oklahoma. This fantastically furnished burial tumulus was, like so many of us, a victim of the depression. In 1933 some gentlemen of the county formed a company and purchased the rights to excavate in the Spiro Mound group for a period of two years. The commercial objective, of course, was to recover salable material, and any effort spent in recording what was found and where would not have pleased the time-study man. It is said that these captains of industry very nearly missed the central tomb and it is one of the tragedies of American archaeology that they were not unluckier. The contents of this unique museum were hauled out in wheelbarrows and sold on the premises, like apples at a roadside stand, to whoever wanted to haggle for them. The strictly business and no-nonsense fervor of the merchandisers shows very creditably in such entries in the accounts as "Shell beads—1200 lbs." and "Pearl beads—2 gallons." It seems rather in keeping with the spirit of the whole operation that when the leasehold was up and could not be renewed, one

of the corporation officers set a charge of black powder in the
tomb and shot up shop.

It can only be said of the efficiency of the operation that it
succeeded in doing what naked efficiency usually does; it
overproduced and broke the market, which in 1933–35 was
weak for archaeological items, as for apples. What was recovered and/or recorded for science from the Spiro Mound was

SOUTHERN CULT MOTIFS

At upper left is a "weeping eye" design incised in a
shell perforated to be worn as a gorget or breast ornament.
At upper right is an "eye in hand" design. At lower left is
an eagle warrior, at lower right a figure with a "speech
symbol" issuing from his mouth. These are found at Spiro
Mound.

the result of long, devoted labor by Mr. and Mrs. Henry W. Hamilton of Marshall, Missouri, amateur archaeologists (professional archaeologists are quick to point out that amateurs often do this kind of thing very well) who spent some sixteen years gathering information on the commercial operations and tracing the scattered items all over America. When they were reassembled it was discovered that, as usual, success had tempted some weak mortals here and there to fraud, selling items as Spiro material that were authentically Indian but not Spiro, and others to the near-art of counterfeit so that museums and collectors had been taken in; but the residue of the genuine, culled by experts such as Griffin, vindicated the claim that here had been the most opulent and informative site of prehistory north of Mexico. A complex and advanced culture very nearly rose to life from the ashes, from the artifacts, and the vivid engravings and inscriptions done in a maturely conventionalized style by artists of merit.

The cosmic mythology of these people may have been nearly as comprehensive as, say, that of the Egyptians or the Greeks. An origin myth, in which an eagle and a woman seem to have mated to give birth to a race of eagle-men, is deduced from a series of sculptured pipes; undoubtedly the Spiroans considered themselves to be the descendants of these, with eagle hearts in human skeletons. In the gallery of demigods must have been the plumed serpent, the horned or antlered rattlesnakes very Aztecan in character, along with the eagles, the owl, the pileated woodpecker and the raccoon. The approximate meaning of composite animals, composite human beings and animals, weeping-eyes, sun and world symbols, animals with speech symbols issuing from their mouths (like balloons from the mouths of cartoon characters), fragments of human anatomy, human figures with symbols on their heads like the Martian beanies the kids used to wear—all this may some day be worked out to reconstruct for our enlightenment the system it must have composed; but there can never be recomposed the true, if verbal, literature that it was, the fabric of narrative and parable which drew into one cloth the relations of man, divinity and the universe. There were probably Homers enough to recite these, but not a single Homer to write them down.

It is disheartening to have to stand in intellectual helplessness before these untranslatable artifacts of a mythology-cosmology that is the summary of thirty or forty thousand years of Amerind experience. Here, in symbolic palimpsest, is what and how usufructians thought and felt; here represented is the Amerind bible and the Amerind decalogue, Amerind epics and Amerind science-magic. Here is all that would enable us to understand and enrich ourselves from our true precursors on this land we now call ours. Here is our chance to be amazed and excited, and perhaps instructed by them, as we have been excited and instructed by the Greeks and Egyptians and Sumerians.

How long, for instance, has there been in America the ethical tradition that is expressed by the Golden Rule of the Shawnees, which they phrase thus:

"Do not kill or injure your neighbor, for it is not he that you injure; you injure yourself. But do good to him, therefore add to his days of happiness as you add to your own.

"Do not wrong or hate your neighbor, for it is not he that you wrong; you wrong yourself. But love him, for Manitou loves him also as he loves you."

To all intents and purposes the Amerind is not represented in the culture of the present-day American. We think of Indians in terms of personality, of Pontiac and Powhatan, of Tecumseh and Osceola and Sitting Bull and Crazy Horse and Dull Knife and Cochise and Geronimo, all leaders of resistance against us. What the Amerind was like when, as an individual and social human being, he was not resisting us finds expression only in Longfellow's "Hiawatha," which never performed the task of bringing the Indian into our cultural heritage that Longfellow had hoped it would. In consequence the impression has now hardened indestructibly that the Amerind is as barbarically unassimilable into our literature and sentiments as he seemed to be intractable when alive. Printed indelibly on our minds is the figure of a painted savage grunting gutturally, "Me heap big chief, ugh"—and we extend this to mean that the language Indians spoke was an ungrammatical English capable of projecting no idea more advanced than this rude self-identification. As a matter of fact the Iroquois language, according to the testimony of the seventeenth-century Jesuit missionary Father Jean Pierron, was as grammar-formal as the Greek, with which Father Pierron favorably compared it. Just how delicately Indians, even the not-too-ambitious Papagos of the southwest, express themselves is well illustrated by the Papago "Song to Pull Down the Clouds":

> *At the edge of the world*
> *It is growing light,*
> *Up rears the light.*
> *Just yonder the day dawns,*
> *Spreading over the night.*

Obviously we bear some measure of blame for the obtuseness and unrepentant historical bias which prevents us from seating the Amerind at our cultural firesides, but the Amerinds, at least those who lived north of Mexico, could have helped us a great deal more than they did by leaving us a literature.

The Mississippian phase must be judged by what it did not do, and it did not invent a legible means of recording what it thought and did. Had it advanced as far beyond its Hopewellian beginnings as Hopewell advanced beyond Woodland usufructianism, it would have done just that and we would have something more Mississippian to beguile us than rows of fascinating but enigmatic artifacts. The point is not lightly made. The Hopewells had kept developmental pace with Amerind progress in Meso-America, and at 2000 B.P. showed as much promise of prompting an eventual civilization as proto-Mayas or pre-Toltecs. Now the Hopewells were struck down, it would seem, by catastrophe, by some eventuality with which they were not able to deal, either natural or internal. But if the Mississippian had passed its cultural zenith before the De Soto *entrada*, and his contribution was merely to insure that it would never regenerate by thinning out the inhabitants epidemically, then the failure of this final cultural push toward civilization may lie, it is suggested by Phillips, Ford and Griffin, not in adversity, but prosperity. The land was too rich, the climate too unchallenging, the life too easy:

"Here again is demonstrated, in micro-cosmic fashion, the lesson that history never tires of vainly repeating, that the land can be too good to the people who dwell upon it, that a reasonable amount of adversity may be a condition to survival."

For survival read progress.

Even the fact that the lower Mississippi gets much of its summer rain from thunderstorms was a blessing, they say. Thunderstorms are sunshine-rain; that is, they form quickly, deliver a great deal of moisture in one short throe and then dissipate, leaving clear skies; wherefore they máke for a maximum of rain and a maximum of sunshine. Growing corn demands just this, the impossible, and gets it in the Mississippi Valley, where the winters are but the season for the earth gods to replenish the soil with the prodigality of floods.

Here and thus does prehistory, as the course of human events tending toward civilization and history, come to a full stop in the eastern province, after a division of it, following the Hopewell collapse, into a nonprogressive Woodland northeast and a progressive but not progressive enough Mississippian south-southwest. The eastern usufructians didn't make it. Like their flat-top mounds, the Mississippians never quite reached their peak.

19

By the Beautiful Sea

In almost any attempt at a synthesis, at an interpretation of cultural progression so that a pattern of relations is discernible in them, there will be that one awkward element
which refuses to be synthesized and clashes stubbornly with
the logic of the design. At first glance this would seem to be the
role of the Amerinds of the northwest coast, the region which
comprises the seaward slopes of the Rocky Mountain cordillera
and the Pacific littoral between the state of Washington and
the Alaska Peninsula. This is a region of relatively mild climate,
considering the latitude, and the rainfall is heavier here than
anywhere else in the Temperate Zone. As a consequence, between the sea and the lushly vegetated and topographically
varied landscape, it is fabulously endowed with natural food
resources. There is a saying about the region that "when the
tide goes out, the table is set." And if you were an Indian who
didn't like sea food, there was not only a lengthy menu of fresh-
water fish, but an epicurean choice of fowl and game.

These Northwest Coast Indians are universally known from
their habit of cutting down telephone-pole-sized trees and
carving their fancied lineages upon them, to make the grotesque pylons we have come to know as totem poles. For those
who pursue this subject further, into the display rooms and
cases of museums, there is an inventory of art and artifact
awaiting so impressive that we are immediately convinced that
these people were the cultural peers of any Amerind society,
have been unaccountably slighted, and are badly in need of a
public-relations counselor. This understandable enthusiasm
will be well founded on the Northwest Coast Indians' achieve-

ment of gabled houses made of planking; enormous seagoing
(if only coastal) and handsomely wrought dugout boats;
wooden chests and dishes and spoons better done than those
used by our colonial forebears; wooden armor, as effective in
their combat as the forged armor of chivalry; raincoats made of
bark and rain hats of basketry; napkins of cedar bark; spoon
and bowls of carved horn as exquisite as heirloom silver; woven
fabrics of mountain-goat and dog hair (the dogs being raised
for this purpose even as we raise sheep) in patterns perhaps
too striking for us; beautifully carved rattles, whistles, tobacco
pipes, combs, dice, necklaces of puffin beaks; patterned baskets, tambourine drums, tattooing, labrets, portrait masks. This
is a partial list of what these Amerinds produced out of the ingredient of time their beneficent environment provided for
them, for time is as much a material as stone or metal or clay;
and there is hardly an item of their manufacture on which
there has not been engraved (they were probably the greatest
carvers, and in this sense sculptors in the Americas) or decorated or patterned the direct transference of what they were,
what they believed, how they felt.

It has no doubt been noticed that there were two very significant omissions from the foregoing list, omissions which
directly give us pause for a new perspective on these Northwest Coast Amerinds: pottery was not mentioned, nor any horticultural or agricultural product. These livers off the natural fat
of the land were innocent of both; they raised only tobacco, the
sole want they had that nature didn't have on display here.
But this is all the clue we need; these are not controllers of environment; they depend on their environmental food supply;
the food supply does not depend on them for sowing, cultivation and harvesting. This is usufructianism—specialized, it is
true, for gathering from the sea as well as the land—but usufructianism nevertheless in so favorable an environment that
it simulates a phase of cultural development considerably in
advance of what it is. By reason of a singular set of circumstances these Northwest Coast Indians have pushed usufructianism as far as it will go, and they are the zenith phase of
savagery, and at the pinnacle of a dead end. Now, instead of
mottling our pattern, the Northwest Coast culture blends into
it. This could have been predicted, that one clan or another of

usufructians would, upon possessing themselves of such a treasure of habitat, have formed their culture to just such a full exploitation and enjoyment of it without attempting to change it or themselves very much.

The Desert Culture is how the usufructians dealt with an environment that wavered dangerously between marginal and uninhabitable; the Northwest Coast culture is how they dealt with a Garden of Eden. With these two manifestations of it as premises we can now be sure that usufructianism is the major theme of Amerind prehistory. The Indians of the eastern province were usufructians until maize was bestowed on them, and after the Hopewell effort had expended itself they returned to usufructianism, with horticulture simply as an added trait. In the Mississippi culture area the Hopewellian faith was not quite lost, and it was fired anew by inspirations from Mexico, but even twice-repeated southwestern cultural infusions did not spur the Mississippians past that fatal euphoria Ford and his colleagues deplored, a euphoria that was exactly like that inspired by the paradise of the Northwest Coast Indians.

There are Desert Culturists today; there are Northwest Coast culturists today; and we cannot but believe that so deep is the psychology of usufructianism in the nature of Indians that most of them would prefer to adhere to it forever, given the choice.

It is the art alone of the Northwest Coast peoples that commands our admiration; here they did best what was best in them to do; every utensil, every object however common, was done with a sense of design and decoration and in a style that was more than craftsmanship. Societally they seem to me to have been quite impossible. Oliver La Farge says of them, "They seem to have been a rather disagreeable, invidious, touchy people," and this is hardly a harsh judgment on a people capable of the infamous potlatch. As nearly everybody knows this is a contest in property destruction. Choosing an opponent whom he wants to ruin socially and politically, a man destroys great quantities of his own property, daring the opponent to match this destruction with the destruction of as much or more goods and chattels to display his prodigality. It is a device for gaining pre-eminence not likely to attract many imitators nowadays, but it does not differ, in principle, from running for political office in the United States as much as one might think. There is one horrifying way in which it does differ, however. Among the Northwest Coast Indians addicted to potlatching, slavery was also a custom. Being property, slaves also went up in these holocausts, knocked in the head for no better reason than that this would compel another man to beat the brains out of an equal number of his slaves in order to save his face. It seems very clear that such a people had nothing to offer to the political, ethical or philosophical advancement of mankind.

They were a polyglot people and, it seems very likely, of many origins. If there were beachcombers along the California shore 30,000 years ago there seems no reason to believe that they would have passed up these coastal tidelands, especially if they came south along them. Certain Desert Culture traits such as basketry and haircloth point to another population element. Undoubtedly taigan bands filtered into the area, because the wooded environment was not too unfamiliar to them. Certainly the people who settled the Aleutian Islands were adapted to the geography of the northwest coast, where islands are as numerous as in the Aleutian chain, and they would have felt completely at home here. And where else would they have got their equipment for and habit of hunting maritime big game than from the Eskimo, who invented both? But treasure that these Northwest Coast Indians are to the cultural anthropologist, who finds among them wealth of trait and property for a lifetime's study, they give testimony in our prehistory to little we do not already know about. What they have done for us is simple but essential—they have assured us that there was such a thing as usufructianism, not merely as a way of livelihood imposed by ignorance of any other way of livelihood, but as a way of looking at living and wanting to live.

20

Out of the Maize

The spell of usufructianism was broken somewhere in the western province, which must be extended southward now to include Mexico, the Central America of the Mayas and the South America of the Peruvians. It was broken, as we know, by maize and its companion crops beans and squash, and probably only when these three products united into a horticultural complex, complete not only with methods and tools of cultivation but with the fertility rites thought necessary to successful cultivation and the socio-religio-political system a dedication to corn imposed. Once a band of Amerinds had made their compact with maize they had sold their souls to the fields in which they invested their labor in order to draw their rations. Now there was property to which the place of abode was fixed; now there was a round of duties, equally fixative, and when the male of the family began to work his fields, though he fished and hunted when he could, he had left usufructianism and the paleolithic behind.

Drawing the line under all this, and adding up, what we get is a quote from J. Alden Mason, historian of the Incas: "It is coming to be realized that, with only minor deviations, practically all of the great ancient civilizations of the world developed along more or less the same lines. A fortunately situated people, on a hunting-and-gathering plane of economy, developed or adopted agriculture. With the increased and assured food supply that this brought, they became more sedentary and multiplied greatly. While the food supply was ample the leisure time between harvest and sowing permitted the development of arts and crafts, social and religious institutions and other concomitants of culture, which culminated in a relatively peaceful 'Golden Age.' "

But this is where prehistory ends. The old quibble that no true civilization ever flowered on American soil because no Amerind people ever wrote their language has now been settled. Several did. In the January, 1958, issue of *American Antiquity,* Y. V. Knorozov, translated by Sophie D. Coe, writes, "Up to the present time, some specialists have held to the view that on the American continent before the European colonization, there was no writing in the true sense of the word. The various systems of writing used by the Indians were regarded as pictographic or ideographic. However, it is now known with certainty that the civilized peoples of ancient America— the Maya, Zapotec, Olmec, and also the Quechua and Aymara —had hieroglyphic writing [which transmits the sounds of speech] of the same type as that of the Old World, of China, Egypt, Sumeria and so forth."

We must, perforce, stop now, short of attempting to summarize these civilizations. Each of them is a volume in itself and these volumes have been written; they belong to American history as surely as any document in that section of the library and ought to be on the required reading list of every American: George C. Vaillant's brilliant *The Aztecs of Mexico* and J. Alden Mason's equally brilliant *The Ancient Civilizations of Peru;* J. Eric Thompson's humanly understanding *The Rise and Fall of Maya Civilization,* which ought to be called "My Life Among the Ancient Mayas," and Victor W. von Hagen's solidly informative, sharp and amusing *Realm of the Incas.*

To attempt to summarize these, which are themselves condensations of their respective subjects, would be a sort of quadraplegic amputation, as it would be, to change the figure, a theft of the egg of pleasure before it could hatch and grow into a full-fledged bird.

How can anyone, for instance, do justice in a chapter to a people like the Incas, who had mysteriously developed a rite almost exactly duplicating Catholic auricular confession though with lesser priests listening, usually beside streams, to lesser sins, and higher-ranking priests being resorted to for greater ones; who held to a belief in a God, human in form, whose name was too sacred, as amongst the Hebrews, to be spoken

and therefore was unknown; who supported cloistered nuns
—the Chosen Women, the Virgins of the Sun, whom Pizarro's
soldiery naturally raped en masse because this is the crime
the conquistador strain of Spaniards most like to accuse others of; who mined gold to the amount of more than seven million ounces annually; who were able to muster, in order to ran-
som the High-Inca, almost twenty million dollars' worth of it,
and who could cast it well enough to make the statue of a full-
sized woman; who built the only road system—about ten thousand miles of it, without a wheel to ride on—to compare with
the Romans'; who developed an empire in which there was no
want, no depressions, and yet some of the most magnificent
architecture of the preindustrial world?

Or to the Aztecs, whose mastery of mass and height gives to
their cities a majesty beside which ours are squalid desecra-
tions of plain and slope; whose classic art catches the sublime
in the real with an effect that makes the Greek often seem
epicene and sentimental; who went to war not to kill their
enemies but to capture them so that they could bring them
home and enjoy killing them at their leisure; who had a ceremonial whereby they chose the handsomest young man of the
race, gave him everything he wanted for a year (they even
watched his weight to keep him handsome) and treated him
as a god whose every wish was a command, and then sacrificed
him at the end of the year, the High Priest ripping him open
and tearing out his heart with bare hands?

Or to the mystic Mayas, whose preoccupation with time un-
derlay their whole cosmology and gave them a sense of its flow
from a primordial beginning to a fantastically remote future
that modern astrophysics is only now bringing us to compre-
hend; whose astronomers, by celestial observation and calculation, worked out a calendar in which the error was one day in
six thousand years; who invented rubber balls and rubber-
soled shoes and rubber rain capes; who invented the corbeled
arch, and a ball game somewhat like basketball played on
formal courts; who confined their prisoners for sacrifice in
wooden cages at night and let them roam at will during the
day, and drugged them before the ritual murder?

These things are not to be summarized; their bearing on us,
their lessons to us, their fascination for us is in their richness

and detail. There is no such thing as knowing a little about
Meso-American civilizations. You know a great deal, or you
know nothing.

The deep prehistoric roots from which these high civilizations grew are not as well known from site records as Amerind
prehistory north of the Rio Grande, and it was long thought, by
reason of the lack of excavated data, that waves of immigrants
moved into the areas where the Mayan and Mexican civilizations burgeoned on an already advanced neolithic, pottery-
making, grain-growing level, and they simply adapted themselves facilely to regional products and conditions. This was
Hooton's view and he admitted these invaders on an open-
immigration quota, directly from Asia. This is not now standard doctrine. Mason sums up what has now come to be understood as sound and defensible thus: "The major part of the high
culture was developed *in situ* from primitive original elements."

And Vaillant writes that "the existing evidence gives no valid
reason for assuming any source for the high civilization of
Middle America except the inventiveness of the local population."

These authoritative opinions were based on the archaeological fact that in the lowest level of whatever site was being excavated the materials there were not those of newcomers, but
derived unmistakably from earlier peoples and cultures long
native to the country.

Hooton's view was founded, then, on negative evidence; and
the fact was not that no such evidence existed, but that it had
not been seriously looked for. When grants for archaeological
work in Central and South America were being handed out by
museums and foundations they were given for excavations of
the much richer Mexican or Mayan or Incan sites with their
possibility of finding treasures of gold and gems, and nobody
had any money to spare for the discovery of the unassuming
artifacts of their progenitors. And no wonder, for the grantors
were being told by the prehistorians that there were no such
predecessors.

Within the last few years South Americans and Mexicans,

with some help from Stateside archaeologists who realized the importance of pre-Inca, pre-Maya and pre-Aztec cultures, have begun to explore this period of prehistory, and Gordon Willey has very lately—April, 1958—summed up Amerind manifestations in South America in such terms that we have no difficulty in perceiving there very much the same picture of big-game hunter and usufructian that previous chapters on North America have familiarized us with, and possibly the same changes due to climatic reversals.

In end-of-the-line Patagonia is the Oliviense cultural manifestation, older than a very early projectile culture in that area; it is geologically guess-dated at 11,000 B.P. plus and is described as a flake-and-scraper complex, which is the unspecialized-lithic category of Tule Springs–Lewisville man. A pebble-and-core culture with pebble choppers, flake scrapers and knives, undated but designated early, has been noted near Monte Caseros in Argentina. Thought to be antecedent to this by the finder, O.F.A. Menghín, is a complex from Misiones, Argentina, that consists of percussion-chipped hand axes, picks and scrapers. That people living in the scavenging tradition of Tule Springs–Lewisville man had traveled the length of two continents is beyond doubt; the only uncertainty is about the date of their earliest arrival. In the 12,000 to 15,000 years included in the "more than" 23,000 years of Tule Springs man, simple-stone-tool-making human beings had more than enough transit time to reach Patagonia and still be as ancient there as Tule Springs' minimum date. But whether the man who reached Patagonia was carrying a contemporary culture or one enormously old-fashioned and backward is the question.

The earliest C14-dated cultures at the Patagonian extremity, at about 8000 B.P., are projectile-point-making ones, and some of them are almost certainly cultures of big-game hunters, apparently hunters of sloth. The presence of hunters of mammoth in the valley of Mexico in 12,000–10,000 B.P. has already been noted in references to the two Iztapán mammoths. The projectile points associated with the second Iztapán kill have now been related to a lithic complex brought to light in Venezuela by José Cruxent, who further relates them to the long, digital lanceolate points found at the Ayampitín site in

Argentina. Willey finds other resemblances to Ayampitín, and
Cruxent finds still further resemblances to Menghín's Proto-
Tehuelchense of northern Patagonia.

In short, the prehistory of the entire Western Hemisphere
has exactly the uniformity we would expect, we who have said
that it was a long one, that it was unintervened upon by culture-bearing migrants, and that the founding and possessing
occupants were of similar stock and outlook. American prehistory, north and south, is a single plant growing from a single
root system.

Of some concern in the prehistory of the western province—
by reason of this uniformity—is the scarcity of sites not so
much on the time level of the Confluent-Archaic of the eastern
province, but of that mature, preceramic usufructian character.
In the eastern province, Confluent period sites are so plentiful
as to give an impression that the land supported more ancestors
than it did descendants. This is delusion, of course; the semi-
nomadic usufructians left camp sites like the prints of wandering feet over the length and breadth of that territory, but
usufructianism plus horticulture supported more people in
fewer settlements. That the pre-Woodland Confluent does not
appear more positively in the southern section of the western
province may be nothing more than the fortunes of excavation;
but we have come to know our usufructians too well by this
time to leave it at that. There cannot be an Archaic period
in the southwest because what has been called Archaic is the
cultural adjustment of the usufructians to the eastern woodlands. Usufructians did not impose themselves on an environment; they reflected it; they became what it was. The phases
of toads which live in forests are not the same as the phases
which live in semidesert places and yet both phases are de-
monstrably toads. So we must say that the Archaic is an eastern
woodland phase of usufructianism and expect to find something quite different in other milieus.

But when we examine the western province we find that it
is nothing like as homogeneous as the eastern province, which
was heavily forested and differed from north to south mainly
as to temperatures and hardly at all, from Labrador to Florida,
in food resources. Likewise in the western province there was
an unbroken domain of mountain forest and jungle from the

valley of Mexico to the montane heights of Peru, but from northern Mexico to the Canadian border the pulverizing hand of the late Anathermal and Altithermal droughts fragmented the region into a hundred different living environments, each isolated from the other by zones of the uninhabitable. In consequence the prehistory of this region is a tangled skein of tribal interrelationships, of forced movements that resulted in acculturations, cultural sports and even loss of identity. The advent of pottery is not a helpful horizon marker of any kind because some peoples, the Anasazi, for instance, who were to become the Basket Makers, did not have pottery until 500 years after some of their neighbors, and agriculture until 2000 years after. The Cochise had agriculture before pottery; other peoples, like the Anasazi, had pottery before agriculture.

Emphasis was placed, in our discussion of the eastern usufructians, on the appearance of an abundance of shellfish with the warming of the land and waters toward the end of the Anathermal. This provides an inexact but rather overt marker, shellfish middens, for the Archaic or Confluent period there. There is no such marker in the northern half of the western province because the climate was obviously taking food resources away, not adding them. But there is a shell-midden period in the southern half, along the rivers of Central America and coastwise in western South America. It continues from preceramic into ceramic time, as do the shell middens of Pickwick Basin, and a midden at Cerro Mangote, Panama, excavated by Charles R. McGimsey, has yielded a C14 date of 6800 years from what is probably not its oldest level. This is contemporary with the date of the early appearance of shell middens in the southern, warmer woodland regions of North America. Such synchroneity gives us reason enough to suspect the outlines of an Archaic or Confluent period in the southern part of the western province.

Our reading of the Archaic was that it was a period, in North America, of confluence of population and cultures, brought about by the climatic agitations of the Ana-Altithermal. Just as these climatic influences coaxed the eastern usufructians out of the woods, it brought southern continental usufructians to the banks of rivers and the sea, but under apparently different circumstances. We would not expect these cultures to resemble

the pre-Woodland Archaic, and they do not. The Cerro Mangote people did not have stone projectile points and their stone
technology is not much in advance of Tule Springs man. Probably they used wooden darts and spear poke sticks. Ceramics do
not immediately change this situation but they seem to herald
or be the vanguard of cultural change, which was an effect of
severe climatic disturbances elsewhere; just so, under similar
conditions, did pottery appear intrusively in the eastern woodland shell middens, as a marker of the flow of confluence.

What we have to consider seriously, then, is that, as the
desiccation of the Great Basin and Plains areas of North America drove peoples and cultural influences eastward they also
drove them southward, and a Confluent period there does
precede the later advances that climaxed in locally invented
civilizations. Among the cultural gifts from the north scattered
among the Mexicans and Meso-Americans during the Confluent period was maize-corn.

Since there are no convenient shell middens in the northern
half of the western province to guide us in understanding the
population events of the Ana-Altithermal, we must look for
some other clue. Here was the epicenter of the whole disturbance that set the cultural, population and ecological forces
of the Confluent period in motion in all directions. Doubtless
geologists or archaeologists will some day furnish us with a
boundary marker—something to do, no doubt, with the level
of the great western lakes of Bonneville, Lahontan, Texcoco
and Cochise—to designate the crisis period in the Basin-Plains.
But for now we will have to be content with what we have,
and this is the population-culture split of the Cochise into eastern and western traditions.

The Cochise have been briefly described before as that
specialized branch of western usufructians which lived in
creek bottoms and did not, in the beginning, have stone projectile points. The absence of this trait distinguishes them from
the Desert Culture until the influence of that culture prevailed
upon them; they took up the trait, and thereafter became dis-
tinguishable but not essentially different from the Desert Culture. Their basic non-stone-projectile-point phase certainly
shows them to have had a common technological tradition

with the Panama shell-midden people. This tradition is descended directly from Lewisville man without much increment; and without projectile points the Cochise specialized vegetatively, a specialization to which the civilizations of America owe their character, if not their very existence.

Antevs has given us a brief outline of the plague of drought that beset the American west during the time of its cultural and population fragmentation. He sets the first onset as beginning with the height of the Altithermal at 7500 B.P., which is called, very aptly, the Long Drought, because it did not end until about 4000 B.P. At 2500 B.P. there was a drought called the Fairbanks; at 330 A.D. there was the White Water Drought, named with some sense of irony; from 1276 to 1299 there was the Great Drought, which stopped the progressing southwest almost literally dead in its tracks. Altogether, Antevs says, the climate in the desert west has not been appreciably moister than it is now at any time in the last 9000 years; and now the evaporation potential exceeds the annual rainfall by from two to eight feet.

The separation of the Cochise–Desert Culture phase into an Anasazi–Basket Maker–Pueblo line on the one hand, and the Hohokam and Mogollon lines on the other, and the later contacts of these lines are a matter of concern to southwestern specialists who have spent upwards of seventy-five years tracing them out. For our purposes it is sufficient to point out that it is now generally accepted that the stone-projectile-point stage of the late Cochise, which has been C14 dated at 4500–4000 B.P., had maize-corn. Bat Cave, in central New Mexico, a major archaeological site excavated by Herbert W. Dick, produced an association of Chiricahua Cochise projectile-point forms and other indicative traits in association with an early form of maize, which gave evidence of a constant rate of improvement in size of cob and production of bulk grain from early to late throughout the site. The effects of deliberate cultivation, that is, agriculture, show clearly in this evolution. Since agriculture, or horticulture, is thought now by most archaeologists to have had a more southerly origin, we must presume that sometime before 5000 B.P. corn began to be raised by incipient farmers in some places it did not normally grow. But agriculture as a system of economics may be quite a different

matter from the initial knowledge of the food resource that
sparks it into being. The first maize, and its companions,
tripsacum and teosinte, are grasses of the pampas and savan-
nahs, not jungle plants, and we cannot avoid the near certain
likelihood that corn was long known to the original, vegetative-
subsisting Cochise, who roamed the grassy plains of northern
Mexico and Arizona–New Mexico–Texas. When the Altithermal droughts pushed some of them south they took this knowledge with them and there either made it available to people
more alert to its potentiality or became aware of it themselves.
For it should be emphasized that the deliberate cultivation of
it probably was begun by a people familiar with it who had
come to live where it did not normally grow.

It is not really necessary to believe that corn culture began
as far south as the valley of Mexico, since we find maize grain in
an early botanical stage being cultivated at Bat Cave in what
we now think of as the Cochise area, for Jennings has pointed
out that "small-grain domestication" is perhaps a 7000- or 8000-
year-old trait in the Desert Culture, north of the Cochise area
of habitat. But it is certain that the corn-beans-squash trio did
combine into a genuine horticultural complex in the south.

So we are now prepared to reduce the prehistory of America, from scavenging Lewisville man to Montezuma, to the
simplest possible terms. The line is straight between the Lewisville preusufructian to the Cochise specialized usufructian
whose close attention to all possible vegetative food sources
caused him to discover maize-corn. This discovery began to
mean something when the droughts of the Altithermal scattered maize-seed bearers into places where the seed they bore
was transformed into agriculture; when agriculture advanced
beyond being an economy and became a religion, it considerably more than doubled its appeal and its power to tempt people out of usufructianism. And it was the Altithermal which
disturbed usufructians enough to place them in situations
where agriculture could reach them and make its appeal.

The prehistory of America is, in few words, that usufructians
found maize, and the Altithermal made them use it. In the end
the efficiency of usufructianism in exploiting its environment
was so thorough that it did not overlook the seed of its own
destruction.

21

Buried Future

Though it is but fair to the high civilizations of America to treat of them not at all, since we cannot treat them in the grand style, this prehistory would hardly have fulfilled itself without saying that all that we have written here does not quite explain them.

Up to now we have unceasingly enunciated the single thesis that American prehistory is a chronicle of Amerinds unincorporated—unincorporated with any other significant racial or cultural element, that is. But over the solid Amerind achievement of civilization in Meso- and South America there hovers, as tenuous as a rainbow, the hue of something not Amerind—something peregrine and exotic, something cryptically oriental. But this is not a pallid coloration from the wan and barren wastes of Siberia; if it came from Asia at all (and we believe it initially did) the origin was southern Asia and we are inclined to welcome this cosmopolitanism both subjectively and objectively as quite fitting for peoples who had come culturally so far. They should have been encountered by the Old World; the adventitious factor always astir in human affairs must have got around to such an incident. After all, Leif the Lucky found his Vinland; had it been a land of Aztecan temples the consequences would not have been so negligible.

Archaeologists will not hear of any of the Meso-American civilizations engaging in any transpacific commerce. None of these civilizations was maritime, and the only American culture that was, the Northwest Coast Indians, took to the water only in coastwise canoe trips. Drucker remarks that even these were most uncomfortable out of the sight of land. About the sea there is little lore among Mayas or Aztecs or Incas and not even a faintly naval vocabulary. The oceanic verge was the end of the world. It is not astonishing, then, that the Aztecs looked upon the ship-borne Cortez as divine, and anybody coming upon them from the sea from the Pacific side would very likely have received treatment no less worshipful. If this Pacific mariner had not come like Cortez, to conquer and destroy, and instead had liked the climate, the looks of the girls and the imperial hospitality, he might easily have stayed, to impart the mores and tastes and ideology of the place whence he came to the population, and what he imparted would have had the effect of divine edict; if this transpacific Cortez had arrived with a company of gifted shipmates, the consequences could have been like a dash of dye in clear water in any of the Meso-American cultures—where only the high priests had to be awed and convinced in order for new modes to be distributed among the populace. This is one of the oldest plots in the world—the arrival of a startlingly alien castaway or explorer or lost traveler (usually he is white) among natives who see his coming as having been foretold by legend or augury, and his accession to supreme power. And it happened, in both Mexico and Peru, to their fearful destruction.

The evidence for influences from afar in Meso-America has been presented by Gordon Ekholm for both popular and scholarly consideration. He does not argue for transpacific contacts but he presents the coincidences of artifacts and art motifs and complexes of these as provocatively as though these coincidences did.

The provocative similarities posed by Ekholm begin with a remarkable resemblance between a temple in Cambodia and a Mayan one, and by no means end with the correspondence of the Aztec game called *patolli* with pachisi, known to us all, and originating in India. He shows likenesses in fishhooks, simple and composite, stone maces and nose flutes (flutes blown by breath expelled through one nostril instead of the mouth), Panpipes and bookmaking, which are rather more interesting as parallelisms than arresting as emulations.

Likewise, it seems to me, the habit of betel-nut chewing in southwest Asia and coca chewing in South America, with lime used in both instances to release the alkaloid so that it attains

drugging potency, is of no more than passing interest. Mangelsdorf has put this coincidence in its place by pointing out that
preliterate man had discovered all the caffeine-yielding plants
in existence, in nine different species and six different plant
families. Wherin is the similarity, then? That the alkaloid caffeine is present in all these plants is a discovery of twentieth-
century biochemistry. This trait no more argues for an adoption by Amerinds of a disagreeable Asian habit than does the
making of soup. Nor are the analogous weaving apparatus and
implements mentioned by Ekholm worthy of more than mild
comment. Now that Danger Cave materials have been dated
we are not persuaded that Amerinds had to borrow anybody's
weaving ideas.

But we have to cock an eye when Ekholm points to wheeled
animal toys from Mexico and from India. The wheel had no
other use in America, and its mechanical potentiality was not
even recognized after the introduction of it as a feature of toys,
or else it was spurned. The pottery toy is not unusual among
Amerinds—if it was a toy and not a figurine—but the wheels
are almost inexplicable except as an imitative feature.

But more compelling is the abrupt appearance of a phallic
cult in a restricted time-space context among the Mayas. Nowhere else in America do Amerinds seem to have developed
much interest in male or female genitalia as fertility symbols.
If the animal effigies made of twigs and left in caves in the
Great Basin area and elsewhere are fertility figures they certainly do not emphasize sexual characteristics. The occurrences
of phalli at Amerind sites are scattered, to say the least, and
suggest random scatological representations, not objects of ceremony or veneration. Ritchie reports from New York the find of
what may be female pudenda scored on a pebble, but this is certainly not the Venus cult of Europe, which produced statuettes of pregnant women with huge breasts and pubic exag-
gerations, nor is it a use of these Venuses such as in the flint
mine in England where, when the vein ran out, the miners
put a fertility figure in a position where she could look upon a
phallus until the mine could be induced to become productive
again. It hadn't, by the twentieth century.

This Maya cult is an incongruous apparition and Ekholm
describes similarly prepuce-bared phalli from India, where

they are common images in Hindu art. The art treatment of genitalia among the Meso-Americans is realistic, and in many cases genitals are ignored. One of the few examples of modeled female fertility figurines occurs at Basket Maker sites, where they are blobs, mere potatolike lumps of clay, with pealike breasts; some of these wear menstrual pads, an odd touch for a fertility image.

These phalli are, as we understand things now, restricted in Meso-America; much less flagrant, and much more to the point, are art and architectural similarities, with Mayan and Aztecan mythology and religion rendered according to conventional Asian modes, postures and arrangements. Ekholm writes, "The serpent columns and balustrades which appear as new and important elements at Mexican Period Chichén Itzá and also at Tula in central Mexico are in my opinion among the most significant parallels to things Asiatic." But the list is much longer than these serpent columns, which nearly everybody who has seen any pictures of Aztecan edifices will remember as open-jawed monsters almost too dragonlike not to cause one to wonder about the childhood traumas suffered by their creators—or the adult guilt complexes labored under. It ranges from the placement of figures in assembly scenes in bas-relief lintel friezes, to details of similar treatment of lotus and lotuslike plants, and to plants growing out of shells; and it includes trefoil arches, tiger thrones, sacred trees or crosses, lotus staves, Atlantean figures (that is, figures like Atlas, sup-porting great weights on their shoulders, steadying them with their hands), doorways which are the open mouths of mon-sters, seated tiger-lions, sun discs and Vishnu figures.

An inculcated art element is both subjectively and objec-tively evident, and just as evident is the fact that however it got into Meso-American art, it did not get there directly and immediately. Stylistically some art of Meso-America is Asian, but at a great remove and only after a long process of trans-position from one mytho-religious system to fit another. That the posture and detail of an Aztecan reclining figure resembles a reclining Buddha is manifest enough, but these similarities cannot obscure the fact that one is the god Chac-Mool, in Aztecan style of figure and dress, and the other is Buddha. What is missing is the record of gradations by which Buddha was forgotten, but some significance, attaching to his posture and to other meaningful details, such as his navel, was retained. The transference is very much like, in my view, the way in which the Roman Saturnalia became the Christian Christmas.

Ekholm writes, in explanation of the contacts by which southeastern Asiatic motifs were got to America: "It is necessary to state my belief in the probability that actual ship navigation across the Pacific was responsible. There is certain evidence indicating the probability that ships and navigation were sufficiently advanced by the eighth century to allow transpacific voyages . . ."

This seems reasonable enough, and we have already said something about how the advent of maritime voyagers and their cargoes of goods, influences and ideas would be received. But these direct donations are exactly what we do not seem to find in Meso-America. That they would be few and we would be lucky to find them is admitted, without committing us to the admission that there were any. What concerns us is similarities in expression that palpably do not indicate any similarity in substance and meaning. It has never been suggested by any testimony of responsible archaeologists that I have heard of, that Buddhist missionaries ever implanted even an idea in Amerind heads. I do not see how navigation accounts for the southern Asiatic influences that reached Meso-America in the attenuated and transmuted form in which they appear there. Between southern Asia and Mexico there is a hiatus of time, of place, of contact. Beyond the present verge of the Western Hemisphere there must have once been a farther west.

It is very much this kind of hypothetical transfer point that Churchward placed on the map when he invented his mid-Pacific lost continent of Mu. But Churchward would, I am sure, be mortally offended to hear Mu called a transfer point, because on it lived the earliest and highest of civilizations, according to his scripture; and he would not brook hearing Mu called an invention. He has proved its existence again and again by a tracery of symbolism, cabalistic traits and mysticism to an apparently large congregation of initiates. But there are no archaeologists of standing among his flock, and anthropologists have generally taken the position that since Mu is mythical anything else proposed for the same location must be. They have not speculated about such incidents as the disappearance of Davis Land and have averted their eyes somewhat from Thor Heyerdahl's attempts to call attention to the importance of the mid-Pacific by drawing a certain amount of attention to himself.

But there was something out there, under that maddening Pacific vastness, and what is left of it is forlorn islands like Easter, Pitcairn and the Galápagos, flotsam from the wreck of what was once a known sea route from southwest Asia, even India, to the Western Hemisphere. To do everybody justice, it was not possible for the scientist to harbor such thoughts until quite recently, but it is now possible for at least the romantics among them to nurse visions of a new archaeology.

What is out there is a discovery of one of the programs of the International Geophysical Year, conducted by the Scripps Institution of Oceanography, which dispatched two ships on a submarine mapping project through that part of the Pacific off Western Hemisphere shores.

There were two principal finds. The first was a range of mountain ridges extending 600 miles southwest from Peru to Easter Island, which looks on the map to be halfway across the Pacific, and in the sense that it is the eastern tag end of a group of islands scattered out from southeast Asia, it is farther than that.

This mountain range rises 10,000 feet above the ocean floor and some of its peaks are even now within 700 feet of the surface of the water, and those who remember that the Davis Land archipelago was sighted in the vicinity of Easter Island have their answer to what those islands were and where they went. They were ridges of this range, now named the Nasca, and dredge hauls have brought up reef coral from some of them; coral does not grow in water under about 70 degrees Fahrenheit, and oceanic depths are not that warm by many degrees. Perhaps these were only stepping-stone islands and the steps were too far apart, but when the Nasca Range is completely mapped and the amount of its subsidence calculated we may find that it was once possible to cross the Pacific by small boat this way.

But more momentous than this is the Scripps Institution's

second discovery, the Easter Island Rise. It too begins in the vicinity of Easter Island and sweeps northward, taking in the Galápagos Islands and fanning out, where it joins the South and Central American continental coast, into a broad, far-reaching coastal shelf, from Ecuador to Mexico. It is about 200 miles wide and 3500 miles long, and its slopes are gradual, which is characteristic of older, eroded mountains. Considering that the disappearance of Davis Land indicates a period of land subsidence in this part of the Pacific only recently passed, if it has entirely passed, we can now make a guess about how man got to Santa Rosa—it was dry-shod, before this subsidence took place.

What was out there? Probably nothing, within the time of the rise of American civilizations, as dramatic as a continent, or a wholly exposed peninsula. Nothing but series of Davis Land-type islands, but islands numerous enough to have made navigation across the Pacific not only safe but attractive for steady trade. Somewhere under Pacific waves there may be an island or a group of islands where oriental influences were received, became attenuated and were transmitted to South and Central America and there garbled in the attempt to imitate or execute them. The legends about Quetzalcoatl, as a culture hero, coming among the Aztecs from the sea and leaving by the sea were so strongly believed that Cortez walked in on Montezuma right out of Aztecan mythology.

Of one thing we can be sure. The kind of Asiatic contact that left on Meso-American high cultures the kind of stamp Ekholm notes was not made across Bering Strait; it had to be made across the Pacific, therefore by sea, and it was not direct or it never would have stopped. It must have carried on over a long period, for the traits that were transported and the goods that were imitated and the ideas that were absorbed were too many to have been in the cargo of a single vessel blown off its course.

Something was out there in the Pacific, and when it is found again it will explain Easter Island and Ponape and Aztecan reclining Buddhas with significant navels. And if it was a part of the Easter Island Rise, it may be found sooner than we expect, that is, soon enough for our great-great-grandchildren to enjoy it. For the indications from the Scripps Institution's observa-

tions are that the Easter Island Rise is on the rise again and
may be in the process of coming back into the world of light.

What seems to have been the exclusive object of our study
in this volume is the prehistory of the Amerind; yet it has been
no more this than the social dynamics—that is, how we came to
be what we are—of mankind; and this in turn frames for us
what has been our real concern throughout these pages; as
usual, it is ourselves. Regardless of what they say in the market
place, there is no study more practical. The proper, the most
needful study of mankind is still, is more than ever, man.

From it we must learn how to continue being a success as a
biological and social species and how to avoid the penalty of
egregious blundering, which is extinction. If our researches
herein have shown us nothing else, they should have shown
us this: that savages are but successful naked anthropoid animals; that barbarians are but successful savages; that we, the
literate, are but successful barbarians. To what success, then,
do we aspire?

It had better be full civilization, with the universal political
peace and interracial amity without which there can be no social health, no wholesome growth. With the weapons at hand
that we, as successful barbarians, have evolved from the savage's first stone-tipped stave, we are now capable of bringing
about what no glacier, no deadly change of climate, no inundation, no epidemic, no massacre, has been able to bring about
up to now—our extermination. If the barbarian in us prevails
we will certainly use these weapons against each other, and
those who survive the holocaust will know themselves to be under genetic interdict to depart the earth, like the Ainus and
the Neanderthals, like the saber-tooth and tyrannosaurus.

It is only by the most liberal extension of the term that we
may call the period in which we now live civilization. True, we
are increasingly *cives*, that is, residents of cities, and of the nations into which these cities are organized. But the working
principles of civility, the first of which is certainly the removal
of the chief causes of human conflict by a reasonable social and
political egalitarianism, have nowhere been satisfactorily em-
bodied in a practical system, either between nations or within
them. To say of ourselves that we are "civilized," that is, suc-

cessful at living in communities of less or greater size, is only intermittently true. There has been no year of the twentieth century without its war, civil or international. Perhaps we ought, realistically, to stop flattering ourselves by our misappropriation to ourselves of the adjective *civilized*. As prehistory is divided into the two stages of early savagery and later barbarism, so might history be separated into an early period of literacy and a later one of industrialism. It would then follow that if we ever become civilized it will be as the result of having been successful industrials. For nothing is plainer than that it has been industrialization that has brought us up hard against the choice whether to become civilized or to close out our racial career forever.

Two dangers that we, as a species, are prone to in crises like this are otiosity and despair. To the otiose, the complacent, the comfortable, there appears no need for self-correction; we are so successful that we are now instinct with success. To the despairing there is no possibility of correcting ourselves; either we are incorrigible, or we have already made our fatal mistakes. It is hard to visualize these attitudes as having biological consequences, but we are still Pleistocene fauna, and if we fail it will be said in some classroom of the year 200,000 A.D., when another kind of intelligent being takes us under study, that we failed as a species of Pleistocene fauna, and in the same geological era as the mammoth. That the mammoth failed because of ecological maladjustment and we from a paralysis of otiosity or pessimism may appear, in that remote future, aspects of the same cause.

But the proper converses of otiosity and despair are not each other; the true converse of both, which are extremes, is equanimity, which is sanguine sobriety. It can derive from but one source, knowledge; not the cocksure knowledge of acquired information, but the kind which is absorbed into the understanding as food is absorbed into the blood stream, to build a sound organ of rationality and to supply the energy that will make that organ function. Thus we engage in archaeology, which is the recovery of the artifacts of past worlds within something like their proper context, and pore over, among other things, prehistory, which is the interpretation of archaeology, because we cannot know ourselves otherwise; we are products and it is prehistory that describes the processes that we are products of. American prehistory, as we are now coming to know it, illustrates these processes in action at their most direct, their purest and simplest: here, plainly, is man at work making himself, without guide or model except an image of himself that was of his own conceiving in the first place.

And so this volume of American prehistory ends, with the near-certainty that the study of American prehistory is only at the beginning.

Suggested Reading

For the nonspecialist who is interested in American prehistory and who reads it half out of intellectual bent and half for instruction, without any of the compulsion of the professional, earning his living and his reputation by keeping abreast of the latest and newest, whether it be orthodox or heterodox, a bibliography here seems unnecessary. Internal textual references have been cited for those who wish to pursue the argument to its sources, and in order to give appropriate credit, though this obligation can never be satisfactorily discharged; the author, not being a primary researcher except in a very small area of a very restricted environment along the Hudson River, must acknowledge that nearly every line written herein is owing to the investigations and inspirations of others, in archaeology and in half a dozen contiguous sciences. Probably fewer than half of those who have contributed in some way to this synthesis of American prehistory have received the mention due them. Quotes that help advance our point of view have often been selected from among many that make the same point, even while it is the consensus of the many which persuaded us to accept the point of view in the first place.

In the observance of these amenities, about which the author wishes he could be more scrupulous, the nonspecialist usually has but a passing interest. What it is presumed he would like, if he turns to a section of bibliography, is a labeled reading list that will extend his pleasure and instruction without directing him into the byways of specialization.

It is on this presumption that the following list, mainly of books easy and inexpensive to acquire, and usually nonspecialist in tone, is compiled.

Introductory

Early Man in the New World, Kenneth MacGowan; The Macmillan Co., New York. MacGowan may have considered himself unlucky in that he had done the research and invested his labor in writing this book only to have it published on the eve of the release of the first C14 dates, which had to have an unavoidably deteriorating effect on its timeliness, but the general reader could not have been more fortunate. So judiciously and incisively has MacGowan shaped up the body of knowledge of early American prehistory at that turning point in its formulation, so economically has he adduced every relevant fact and significant reference, that it is not necessary for even the profoundly interested to read in the antecedent literature. But it is necessary to read MacGowan in order to know with what problems, none of them yet fully resolved, American archaeology entered the age of C14 dating. What is out of date in the book is easily recognized and there is residual value even in that. *Early Man in the New World* sticks precisely to its subject and stops short of the "Archaic," then a much disputed concept, and what follows. This is its self-imposed and only limitation.

Current

American Antiquity. This quarterly is published by and is the official journal of the Society for American Archaeology. It is printed by the University of Utah Press, Salt Lake City. At frequent intervals the regular issues are accompanied by numbers in the Memoir Series, of which *Danger Cave,* mentioned prominently in this book, is one. Material published in *American Antiquity* ranges from monographs which will be almost opaque to the nonspecialist to news notes on archaeological work in progress, effective reviews of all kinds of archaeology-related publications, entertaining and helpful site reports and new theory and synthesis. Most pieces are illustrated, mapped, charted, plated and graphed where they need to be for the enlightenment of the general reader, who will discover that the more he reads *American Antiquity* the more of it he is able to read. For those with a continuing interest in American prehistory it is indispensable.

Early Man in the Western Hemisphere

Ancient Man in North America, 4th edition, revised, H. M. Wormington; Denver Museum of Natural History. Now that E. H. Sellards' *Early Man in America,* with its especially fine treatment of extinct animals, is out of print, this work is the latest and fullest compilation of early-man information extant. Of great interest to us is Wormington's advancement of a concept of a paleo-northern complex, an assumption made in this volume in dealing with the taigans.

Early Man Elsewhere

In order to place the Amerinds in universal context it is necessary to know something about early man on the Euro-Afro-Asiatic land mass. This information is scattered throughout several volumes of regional archaeology, where it usually makes up the beginning chapters, in which the earliest chronology of a region is treated. A series of soft-cover Pelican Books issued by Penguin Books, Baltimore, Maryland, includes many titles in regional archaeology. In the order of their interest to a reader mainly interested in American prehistory they are:

The Prehistory of East Africa, Sonia Cole.
Prehistoric India, Stuart Piggott.
Prehistoric Britain, Christopher and Jacquetta Hawkes.
The Archaeology of Palestine, W. F. Albright.

We might add to this list another soft-cover book—in the Mentor (New York) Ancient Civilization series—*The Origins of Oriental Civilization,* by Walter A. Fairservis, Jr. See especially Chapter 7, on the Mongol race.

Of equal value and readability are these hard-cover books for the general market:

The Testimony of the Spade, Geoffrey Bibby; Alfred Knopf, New York. He is fascinating on many subjects, including the life of European reindeer hunters (like our taigans), shell-midden folk (like our "Archaic"-age people), barrow builders (suggesting our Mound Builders) and transatlantic contacts with America of prehistoric Europeans.

The Story of Man, Carleton S. Coon; Alfred Knopf, New York. The approach to the interpretation of prehistory which led Coon to reconstruct the features of early-man types like

Neanderthal, with emphasis on their humanity rather than their animality, is everywhere evident in this book. A physical anthropologist as well as a digging archaeologist, Coon speaks out for progressive views of early man with peculiar authority.

In Search of Adam, Herbert Wendt; Houghton Mifflin, Boston. In reverse of the usual order, it is the last 200 pages of this 526-page translation from the German which will interest the general reader, because of the information it offers on primitive human and humanoid types. But Wendt's approval of a notion that the Maya used unextinct mastodons to help them with their mighty constructions in stone will be greeted with some amusement by those researchers who have spent decades ascertaining that they were built like the Egyptian pyramids with the inclined plane, the lever and sheer manpower.

Hopewellian and Mississippian Cultures

Archeology of Eastern United States, edited by James Griffin, University of Chicago Press. This is an enormous, unwieldly, expensive volume, containing much out-of-date material, but its text and illustrations arranged by cultural units will orient the interested amateur as nothing else will and its several descriptions of Hopewellian culture constitute a definitive, as of now, treatment of that protocivilization. What is Mississippian is better illustrated than explained, and this volume illustrates it well, along with cultural aspects and foci from Montana eastward.

Sun Circles and Human Hands. The Southeastern Indians: Art and Industry, edited by Emma Lila Fundaburk and Mary Douglass Foreman; Emma Lila Fundaburk, publisher, Luverne, Alabama. This is a picture book, for the most part, with a sufficiency of archaeology-prehistory to annotate the plates. As such it is a museum in a handbook. Taken together with *Archeology of Eastern United States,* it will provide the amateur with comparative material for and some understanding of almost anything he finds.

Lithic Technology

A Manual for Neanderthals, H. Mewhinney; University of Texas Press, Austin. This volume has very little to do with

Neanderthals; it is probably the most practical how-to book on the manufacture of stone tools generally available. Mewhinney has little patience with the hieratic school of experts who speak of some of the techniques of flintsmithing as though they were temple mysteries, and this secular attitude is very encouraging to an amateur. He does, however, confirm an experience of mine that a couple of cut fingers is the price of any finished stone artifact; without workmen's compensation you shouldn't try it.

Digging: How and Why

Archaeology from the Earth, R. E. M. Wheeler; Oxford University Press, Oxford, England. Sir Mortimer Wheeler has distinguished himself as an archaeologist from England to India, and in the light of this experience his preoccupations could not be with the prehistory or the methodology of the New World; but his book affords at once the most serious and most comprehensive instruction in how to dig, no matter where you are digging, and the most humanistic rationale for those who want to dig but are half fearful that the wanting is, to put it in current jargon, neurotic. There are several good simplified pamphlets on regional American excavation problems, but they should be regarded as auxiliary to Wheeler's classic. He begins with pithy frankness, "There is no right way of digging but there are many wrong ways," and continuously deplores the professional trend toward rigidifying archaeology into a discipline, with the result that he cultivates the true humanistic spirit while inculcating the necessary scientific method.

Interpretation

Man Makes Himself, V. Gordon Childe; Mentor Books, New American Library, New York; *What Happened in History*, V. Gordon Childe; Penguin Books, Baltimore, Maryland. What can be done by profound scholarship and a clear, intuitive mind in the transformation of excavation and artifact into the substance of social prehistory has no better examples than these two unique treatises on how history came to proceed out of prehistory.

Man: His First Million Years, Ashley Montagu; Mentor

Books, New American Library, New York. This survey of man, biological, racial and social, is, perhaps, *the* primer for the amateur in anthropology.

Mirror for Man, by Clyde Kluckhohn; Premier Books, Fawcett Publications, New York. If Montagu's book is a primer, Kluckhohn's is the one that should follow it.

Race and Evolution

Man and the Vertebrates, Vol. II, A. S. Romer; a Pelican Book, Penguin Books, Baltimore, Maryland. There is hardly a book in this reading list which does not have something to say about race, but Romer's volume is especially comprehensible on the descriptions and placement of races while quietly reminding us that for all the external differences the body we call human is for all races the same.

The Meaning of Evolution, George Gaylord Simpson; Mentor Books, New American Library, New York. This is an abridgment of the original, published by Yale University Press. It is a study of the mechanism by which life has continuously manifested itself in newer, more complex forms, one of which is man. Without some grasp of the mechanism, one can imagine archaeology only hazily, and Simpson's elucidation of its operation as we now know it has the force of canon.

Sites

The Stratigraphy and Archaeology of Ventana Cave, Emil W. Haury and collaborators; the University of Arizona Press, Tucson, and the University of New Mexico Press, Albuquerque. Just how thoroughly a site can be dug, recorded and presented by American archaeology, when the money can be scraped together, is best illustrated by this expensive, exhaustive, impressive volume, in which every observation and artifact is noted, correlated and illustrated.

Glaciers

Glacial and Pleistocene Geology, Richard Foster Flint; Wiley, New York. Like the Ventana Cave report, this is expensive and exhaustive, but there is hardly any need for pursuing the subject of glaciers and their geologic results beyond the standard popular references unless it is to make contact with the latest of the best authority, which Flint and this book comprise.

Literature

A Land, Jacquetta Hawkes; Random House, New York. This study of the geology of England, with some overtones of archaeology, becomes literature because of the way Hawkes has infused her knowledge of the physical England with the lyrical particularism of her love for it. This kind of science-poetry to America is still unwritten.

INDEX

To index every appearance of the major themes and subjects in this book would be to set the researcher off in all directions rather than to help him in the right one. The policy has been followed, therefore, of noting for reference only those appearances of a major subject in which it is (1) defined, (2) redefined or further argued, (3) placed in new relationships, or (4) factually enriched. All subjects, such as the Amerind race, Tule Springs man, the herd hunters, usufructianism, etc., which are important to the structure of the book, have been indexed according to this principle. The needs of researchers being as various as they are, this arrangement may not at all times prove satisfactory, but the objective has been to provide a succession of references which will lead along the main lines of discussion.

LOUIS A. BRENNAN

has been a writer since the publication, in the Edward J. O'Brien annual collection *The Best Short Stories of 1932,* of a story written when he was nineteen, and a novelist since 1953, when Random House published his first book, *These Items of Desire.*

At about midway between these two dates he acquired his avocational interest in archaeology and that view of American prehistory which, with the announcement of highly significant and corroborative finds and excavations of the past few years, makes the theme of *No Stone Unturned.*

A graduate of the University of Notre Dame in 1932—that unfortunate vintage year for college graduates and hopeful authors —he ran the full unemployment-employment steeplechase of the depressed thirties: from steel-mill hand to private tutor, from gas station grease pit to the window display department of a department store, from road laborer to assistant area director of a federal agency, to construction superintendent for a firm of architects and engineers. In the early days of World War II, he joined the navy and, with the rank of lieutenant, commanded a gunboat in the Pacific theater. He was decorated for "gallantry and intrepidity."

Since moving to Ossining, Westchester County, New York, he has edited the national-prize-winning weekly newspaper *The New Castle News,* of Chappaqua—now defunct—and presently spends two days a week as associate editor of the weekly *Croton-Cortlandt News,* of Croton-on-Hudson.

He is a member of the Society for American Archaeology and is New York State's archaeological representative to the Eastern States Archaeological Federation.

DATE DUE

FE 20 '69			
AP 12 '76			
AP 27 '76			
DEC 2 9 1990 New Card			
MAY 0 1 2004			
MAY 0 2 2005			
AUG 0 8 2007 APR 0 3 2005			
			PRINTED IN U.S.A.